"Traditionally companies have just sought sha leading business schools worldwide. Millennial holistic approach to consumption, and demand and services that serve a greater purpose, rathe. ...an simply shareholder value. In this fascinating book, Tsolkas shows how crises can foment innovation that create shareholder values in purposeful ways that are more than just lip service."

JONATHAN LEVAV, Professor of Marketing at Stanford Graduate School of Business, Palo Alto, California, USA

"This is an eye opener, how companies today can differentiate and grow while helping the world to become a better place. A recommended read from cover to cover."

DR. NICOLAS DURAND, CEO Abionic, Lausanne, Switzerland

"'Christos is a genuine believer in his theory 'purpose rising from crisis' which is carved from firsthand experience. He presents his mantra in an honest manner and each reader is certain to extract their own personal gem from this treasure trove."

NAAVA MASHIAH, Author, Private Equity/Wealth Management expert, Geneva, Switzerland

"Sometimes, crises come into our lives. They are troubling, unwanted, take us out of our comfort zone. We typically find ourselves wanting desperately to get back to comfort, out of the unknown. Though there is no going back but, usually, that is where the opportunity lies. Ultimately, the question is whether we choose to freeze in panic or embrace this opportunity. *The Gift of Crisis* is a brilliant real story with insights and practical instruments to use in order to ride the waves of change and turn it into opportunity. Highly recommend to leaders who are looking for their 'blue oceans'."

ANNA DEREVYANKO, Executive Director European Business Association, Kyiv, Ukraine

"Christos donates a transcendental view on crises and their relationship to us. His book provides a much-needed philosophical system for contextualizing the significance of the perpetuity of adverse events and the confluence of crises. He has taken the time to diligently study the 'new norm' of persistent volatility and draft an aspirational manual for us all."

THOMAS ANTONIADIS, Managing Director Critical Publics, London UK

"Having seen Christos deal with multiple crises as an international executive, I was very pleased to see that he decided to share his learnings and insights with the world and write this book. I know his book will be of great help to all those seeking to take their leadership skills to a new level of conceptualization."

GREG KRASNOV, Serial Entrepreneur, Founder and CEO Forum Capital, Singapore

"Christos Tsolkas has written a must-read primer for those that MIGHT go through a crisis. After reading this book you will have a roadmap and the confidence to sail through it with Purpose."

TRINI AMADOR, Author, Managing Director, Global Brand Marketer, BHC Consulting, San Francisco, CA

"A practical framework backed by rich stories on *how* to prepare yourself to seize the next inevitable crises to galvanize your teams to high performance through meaning and purpose."

FRED MOUAWAD, Founder, Chairman & CEO Synergia One Group of Companies, Singapore

"Humble and witty at the same time, Christos shows how purpose is not just a buzzword, but it can trigger fundamental changes in everyone, and thus change the world."

GIANPAOLO TURRI , President Adamant Namiki, Tokyo Japan

"This is an excellent read in which the author, Christos Tsolkas has developed a very systematic approach to defining "purpose" for an individual or an organization. Christos bases his findings on his own experience in which he succeeded to manage, with good will, a real crisis scenario. I was able to immediately relate to his experience to another similar experience that I personally had. The book is very non-academic and I highly recommend any daring entrepreneur to read it."

AYMAN HIJJAWI, Chairman The Hijjawi Foundation, Nablus Palestine

"Christos Tsolkas and his experiences around the world, at the highest levels of management and within the throws of crisis, give a clear and poignant view of not only surviving turbulent times, but utilizing the energy and uncertainty of crisis to refine and hone one's purpose. When purpose of the individual compliments purpose of the organization, the results create a strength and momentum which is greater than the sum of its parts. A very timely read for all organizational levels and job types, *The Gift of Crisis*, explores a methodology for self-exploration and the tools needed to make real, positive change. A change that benefits the individual, the company and the society in which they live."

Andy Papathanassiou, Professional Motorsports – Director of Human Performance, North Carolina

"In todays fast changing world the ability to manage teams through a crisis is an absolute "must-have" skill for any manager. The best ones turn such events into fires which forge the biggest competitive advantage any company can have: a purpose. Having an insight into Christos's experiences and views on how to not only survive, but strive in rapidly changing environments is absolutely priceless. An absolute goldmine of knowledge for any manager, especially those working on emerging markets, where crisis situations of various types come pretty much every year …"

Andrew Olejnik, Entrepreneur, Founder Homsters, Istanbul

"Christos Tsolkas uses brilliant storytelling coupled with a pragmatic guide and methodology to show how organizations can rediscover themselves, modernize their purpose in 'tech-novative' ways, and aim for success while helping the planet. You can have it all and Tsolkas shows you how."

Charlene Li, bestselling author of *The Disruption Mindset* and Founder & Senior Fellow at Altimeter, a Prophet company

"At many points during our lifetime, answers to our most exigent queries pass by without us paying the slightest of attention as they are not necessitated - even if so subconsciously. There are times however, when in some otherworldly way, what we need the most falls right in-front of us and paves the way. The latter is what Christos' book reflects for some of us, a gift from up above, at the right time."

George Korres, Chairman of the board at Korres Natural Products, Nicosia, Cyprus

THE GIFT
OF CRISIS

THE GIFT
OF CRISIS

How Leaders Use Purpose to Renew their Lives,
Change their Organizations, and Save the World

CHRISTOS TSOLKAS

BEFORE READING THIS BOOK

In advance of diving into this book, take a moment to answer the following questions and check off all that apply:

- ☐ Have you ever faced a personal, family or business crisis?
- ☐ Do you ever wonder how to deal with a potential new crisis before it knocks on your door?
- ☐ Do you believe in the power of teams to solve problems individuals can't manage alone?
- ☐ Do you worry about the enormity and number of global problems that threaten our collective future?
- ☐ Do you think that governments and nonprofit institutions alone are unable to make the world a better place?
- ☐ Do you see a new kind of leadership on the rise?
- ☐ Are you impressed by the technological revolution of our times, and do you hope that technology can help serve a broader cause rather than create more problems?
- ☐ Are you seeking new ways to re-invigorate your life, your team or your company?

If these questions intrigue you, turn the page …

CONTENTS

FOREWORD

In over four decades of work as a coach and advisor to senior executives and leaders around the world, I have encountered many fascinating business leaders who are quietly making their teams, organizations and the people around them better. I learn from each and every one of them.

My friend, Christos Tsolkas, taught me something unique: How a sense of purpose, born in response to crisis, can accelerate team and leadership growth.

I first met Christos in Palm Desert in 2010, where he was attending the Global Institute for Leadership Development, an annual gathering I founded and co-chaired for twenty years. He struck me as another young, curious executive whose ambition and energy for the job was matched by his interest in self-development.

We didn't talk much at first. Then, I noticed him again during some exclusive small-group sessions with the great leadership teachers Warren Bennis and Jim Collins. Christos was one of the more engaged and curious participants. In his questions, he revealed a hungry mind, willing to challenge existing paradigms and the status quo. I took note of him as someone who might turn out to be a "mover and shaker" in his global organization.

A couple months later, I received a call from Christos. He seemed hesitant or even timid about reaching out, but he soon got to the point. Christos told me he needed help in his own leadership development journey, and he wondered whether I would be available to provide him with some one-on-one coaching. He worried, however, that he might not be significant enough in position to warrant my attention. It was a very false assumption. We got started the next week.

Our work started on a very personal level. We focused not just on Christos the executive but also on Christos the person. I won't go into much detail except to say that he had, like a lot of people in their forties, come to question his purpose and path in life. He wanted to be a more effective business leader, but this was tied to a craving for more meaning and fulfillment, too.

In a sense, he had encountered a personal crisis. We enjoyed monthly phone calls and a number of long walks over the next two and a half years. I saw Christos turn his uncertainty and personal chaos around, in a very authentic way, by developing a more profound and energizing sense of purpose. His personal development was very fast. It was a sign of things to come.

Around this period, Christos was leading a sizable and important organization in Greece. As the old blessing and curse goes, "May you live in interesting times." I watched from a distance as Greece descended into social and political turmoil with a devastating economic collapse. And I watched how Christos weathered his own doubts and confusion to lead his organization into stability and eventually a return to growth.

It was a bravura performance, and I knew how Christos pulled it off. He'd applied what he knew about personal purpose to his own team, and he coached and encouraged them through a very difficult time to achieve great results and great satisfaction.

Christos was rewarded with a well-deserved posting, a bigger territory based in Kiev, Ukraine. This time, he didn't want to wait for a crisis to develop his team, so enlisted me to use proven team performance improvement tools to get that process started. We began by assessing the team's current level of performance. Christos made some personnel moves accordingly. Then we got going on the work.

The team started as a Level 3—about in the middle of the bell curve based on SYMLOG research. The goal, as always, is to strive for Level 5 status, which describes a high-performance team that is basically self-sufficient, and in which the senior leadership team is leading with the objective of being the team of teams, i.e., that is committed to developing high performing teams throughout the organization.

Under ideal circumstances, with the right resources, focus and continuity, this can take up to three years on average. Christos' team accomplished this in just one year.

How did he manage the transformation so quickly? The difference was leading from a common purpose and then the crisis.

A few months into our work together, Ukraine spiraled into disruptive turmoil that made Greece look like a day in the park. I had nightmares imagining what Christos and his people were going through. During these dark days, we frequently Skyped to discuss the situation and how to guide and hold his people together. Christos did not see the crisis as a reason to abandon our work on team building, rather as a reason to work even harder. He believed, very simply, that his organization and people would only survive if his team came together at a higher level around a new purpose that all could share.

He was right. Crisis did not throw his team's leadership development process off track, it accelerated it. When we measured the team's performance level a year later, it had achieved Category One status, i.e., they were inextricably woven around mutual accountability for staying on course.

Offered Christos one additional and unusual piece of advice during this period of crisis. Suggested that he take good notes. I wanted him to write everything down in the moment—not only the technical challenges, and the events, but also the experiences and the feelings. In this way, he could record what it was like to lead during a crisis and how that could help others later.

That was the genesis of this book The Gift of Crisis. It is a fascinating personal story and an adventure that combines insights, research, experiences and personal advice from someone who lived and breathed what he writes about.

It reflects an evolution in Christos's thinking and my own. Any crisis—personal, organizational or geopolitical—can be turned into an opportunity, a new beginning of rediscovery and reinvention, one that connects purpose and meaning with development and growth.

Am also proud that in producing this work, Christos took the ideas even further. He believes deeply in what he writes about and has built the business case for purpose as an organizing principle for driving the kind of innovation that tackles the world's biggest problems.

At a time when crisis is everywhere, and it is so easy to get off track or to fall into cynicism and helplessness, Christos's book is a gift to us all.

Dr. Phil Harkins

Author of *Powerful Conversations, Everybody Wins, In Search of Leadership, Skin in the Game, The Art and Practice of Leadership Coaching, Best Practices for Succession Planning, Best Practices in Leading the Global Workforce,* and *Best Practices in Knowledge Management and Organizational Learning Handbook.*

January 15, 2020

INTRODUCTION

My Pitch to You

This is a book about purpose and the role it can play in improving our lives, our work, our organizations and our world.

I call purpose "The Gift of Crisis" because for me it was an unexpected (and, frankly, unwelcome) surprise that led to major, positive changes in my personal life, my career and the way I practice leadership and support others.

At the time I was working as an executive for a global company, heading up territories headquartered in Athens, Greece and then Kiev, Ukraine. As you'll read in Chapter One, I had the strange experience of going from one geopolitical hotspot to another in very quick succession. In both scenarios, our business plans got flipped over like a card table. In Kiev, even our lives were in danger. But our teams came together in ways that showed me the power of fighting for something bigger than business and even bigger than ourselves.

Later, inspired by the insights I'd gained in the field, I explored the power of purpose in other scenarios, experiencing it firsthand in startup environments and studying it through the work of others. My early thinking on the relationship between purpose, crisis and innovation was published in the *Harvard Business Review*. Out of that great honor, I gained opportunities to speak before audiences all over the world, and I started to help companies and leaders engage with their most urgent challenges in new ways that spurred cultural transformation, innovation and explosive growth.

This book is about that story, those insights and the practical ideas and tools that others can use to catalyze their own growth and the growth of their teams and organizations. It starts with crisis—something we all try to avoid—but crisis can be a gift. And if there's one thing I've learned over the past decade, it's that there's always another crisis around the next corner.

The Practice of Purpose

I started working on this book in 2015, which is four years ago now as I write this introduction. My ideas have evolved and grown over that period. Many things have happened in politics, the economy, the environment, internationally and through technology to affirm and prove my theories. I've honed and updated my views in the face of things I've seen and learned firsthand and through the experiences of others.

I'm still just as excited about those ideas and their power to produce real business results as I was when I first encountered them. When I started, the word "purpose" was not used as extensively as it is today. However, even though it is a more common term now, and there has been an increasing amount of research and publications about it, I still believe that practical understanding and use of purpose is off the mark. When I talk to audiences of leaders or to executive teams, I need to explain at the outset that "purpose" and "business" are not operating in different universes, but mutually supportive; that purpose is not about philanthropy, corporate social responsibility (CSR), public relations activities or spirituality, but about business, competition and growth; that it's not just for individuals in their personal growth, but hugely significant for leaders, teams and organizations; that it's not about being a good corporate citizen, but a competitive, innovative organization; that it's not only about doing what's right for customers, but also about finding urgent problems, developing transformative solutions and driving exponential business growth.

In that sense, purpose, crisis, leadership, innovation and growth come together in a single formula which I will explain and illustrate in the pages to come. I believe it's a formula that can potentially change the way your organization succeeds. In the chapters that follow, I will talk about how crisis can give birth to purpose, how that changes our understanding of leadership, and how it leads to innovation, market success and global impact.

We will look at:

- How talented people and teams can flourish in the face of crisis by adopting a galvanizing sense of meaning; (Chapter Two)

- How leadership can and must evolve to meet the new ways people demand to be led; (Chapter Three)

- How business models can incorporate purpose to meet urgent challenges and even global problems; (Chapter Four)

- How that mode of doing business can help an organization flourish in a very new societal and economic environment that is revealing its rules to us so quickly many corporations will soon become lost and outdated; (Chapter Five)

- How the combination of purpose and crisis leads to transformative innovation that can steer a company into profitable "Blue Ocean" territory; (Chapter Six)

- How significant global problems (I call them Level One problems) can be embraced to catalyze exponential corporate growth; (Chapter Seven)

- How technology has never been more available to facilitate and achieve our biggest, most ambitious business plans; (Chapter Eight)

- How you can craft a blueprint for driving innovation and growth through purpose. (Chapter Nine)

It is not my intention or hope to sell millions of books. I know I won't. Although I have been a "salesman" my whole career, I have a different ambition in mind now. My goal is to help people (a few or many) think differently about meaning and work. In the process, I want to give them the capacity to shift their team and even their organization toward a new direction by putting these ideas into practice. The ideas are not all mine. I've been very influenced by the stories and insights of others. But I believe I have brought them together in a new way.

I'm a very ordinary leader with an ordinary career. But I have found purpose to be of great use to me personally and professionally. I'm a happier, more engaged and more successful person as a result. More importantly, I've seen how purpose can engage and energize the people around me and direct their talents and capabilities to accomplish something bigger together. We live in a time when groups—and businesses in particular—have the power to do great and amazing things.

This book is a road map for any organization of any size or stage of development to follow. It will help such organizations stand out from their competition, differentiate themselves to customers, disruptively innovate, expand into new markets and grow exponentially.

It's time we get serious about why we're in business and learn how to make our work matter. In the process, I believe we will uplift our lives, energize our careers and save this precious planet we call home.

CHAPTER ONE

A Test Every Leader Will Face

Every crisis is its own story.

For my team, our crisis started quietly on November 21, 2013, when the Ukrainian President, Viktor Yanukovych, decided to suspend plans for developing closer ties with the European Union. I had moved to Ukraine a few months before to serve as a managing director for my company. Like any international executive working in Eastern Europe, I knew the political situation in Ukraine was volatile. But I had no idea how suddenly and dramatically the country was about to descend into chaos.

Yanukovych had close ties with Russia. Everyone knew that. Russian President Vladimir Putin wanted more control over Ukraine because it had been a major territory within the Soviet Union until its independence in 1991. That was common knowledge too, although few imagined how far he would go. Many Ukrainian people, especially students, were angry and upset by Yanukovych's decision to move Ukraine "back" toward Russia rather than "forward" toward Europe. They felt their future was on the line. So, they gathered in Kiev's Independence Square to protest. Those demonstrations became known by their Twitter hashtag as the "Euromaidan" movement.

For the first few weeks, the protests felt relatively calm and peaceful, even hopeful. The students chanted and sang and demanded an end to Yanukovych's government and called for investigations into corruption. Optimists wondered whether this was Eastern Europe's version of the Arab

Spring of 2010, a movement that had combined protests, demonstrations and social media activism to bring more democracy and transparency to the Middle East. My work colleagues and I were less naïve, but I wasn't too worried yet, even though I definitely had concerns about where the political showdown was headed.

By the end of the month, we began to see how bad things could get. The Yanukovych government became more defensive. Clashes between the police and the demonstrators grew violent. In December, we canceled our annual Christmas party. This was a disappointment, but we were worried that if employees came to Kiev for the party, many would want to join the protestors in Maidan Square. We wouldn't be able to guarantee their safety if they did so, but we didn't want to deny them the right to express their political beliefs, either. As a compromise, we decided to ask everyone to stay home instead.

By January, hundreds of buses were arriving in central Kiev every day as the regime brought in thousands of counter-protesters. The clashes between pro-government and anti-government groups became more tense. On January 22, 2014, the violence finally exploded. Three protestors were shot that day by snipers hiding on the rooftops around Maidan Square. A fourth was kidnapped and found tortured and dead in the woods. That was the first day we met as a team to figure out how to handle a situation that seemed like it could quickly spiral out of our control.

Knowing the crisis had reached a grave new level, we began to exercise more caution in our daily lives and took concrete steps to reduce risks to our employees. We started instituting nightly head counts. Every manager sent in a report every night that all their employees had made it home safely that day. We canceled an annual commercial conference that eight hundred employees were expected to attend from all over the country. Any movement was risky, so we deferred non-essential travel and increased the level of daily communication from my management team to the field force. We prepared a countrywide relocation plan just in case. Even so, we got frequent reminders that the situation could turn quickly in unexpected directions. One night, for instance, one of our company cars was destroyed in an arson attack. We suspected the perpetrators were pro-Russian groups targeting vehicles with out-of-town license plates.

On the morning of February 20, 2014, my driver, Fedir, drove me to the office, as he did every day. We took the riverside route because the roads leading into the center of Kiev were still barricaded. I was tired that morning, having stayed up late the night before watching live streaming and international news about what was happening in my "adopted" country. The past two days had been particularly bad. The police, by all accounts, had begun shooting live ammunition instead of rubber bullets, and there were more reports of sniper fire from rooftops. A dozen or so people were dead. Despite that chaos, the traffic was much lighter than usual that day, a calm that only gave me a strange feeling in my stomach. I asked Fedir what was going on, but he didn't know any more than me. The closer we got to downtown, the emptier the streets became. By the time we reached the office, we could both smell fire.

I rushed inside. Many of our employees were already at the office, but they were all sitting wide-eyed in front of their laptops or standing in front of the big television screens at the coffee corner watching live streams from Independence Square. A few blocks away, the police had opened fire on

the protestors again. Bullets whizzed through the air as the snipers shot everyone in sight. They aimed for the neck because that was the unprotected area between helmets and flak jackets. Before the day was over, sixty-seven protestors had been shot dead, bringing the three-day count to one hundred. Kiev—that beautiful, hopeful, vibrant city—was bleeding.

For my organization, this was the end of any sense that the crisis outside our walls could be managed or contained. We had no idea how we would get by or what was in store for us. Fortunately, we figured out how to work together in a very new way.

Crisis and Its Outcomes

We live in a time of crisis. At any moment, order and normalcy can be overturned by unexpected developments.

From my perspective, this sense of constant crisis has been growing since 9/11. Before then, of course, the world was no stranger to crisis. The '90s saw the dot-com crash. The '80s witnessed the spread of AIDS, the breakup of the Soviet Union and the first Iraq War. The '70s had the oil crisis, stagflation, terrorism, conflict in the Middle East, and the Vietnam War. The '60s had the hippy movements, the rise of rock and roll and anti-war protests in the U.S., Europe and Japan. The '50s seemed peaceful but only because the world had just finished a half century of global war and economic depression.

Still, since 9/11, crises have come fast and furious. The U.S. invaded Afghanistan and then Iraq. Terrorism spread as Al Qaeda and then ISIS inspired attacks around the world. Faith in business was shaken by the Enron scandal, then faith in our entire economic system was rocked by the financial crisis of 2008 which generated the worst global recession since the Great Depression. Many companies went bankrupt, the economies of some European countries nearly collapsed, millions of people in America lost their jobs, savings and homes. A sense of deep uncertainty set in, and feelings of resentment and distrust of the establishment began to grow as the wars and slow economic growth continued year after year.

The populist revolutions in the Middle East and later in Central European countries like Hungary and Ukraine appeared to be positive signs at first, signaling the possibility that waves of change could make the world a better place. Social media seemed a force for good, creating more political transparency and helping to support people who'd been powerless before. Authoritarian dictators got overthrown. Democracy spread.

But then the tide turned. Protests turned into revolutions and then civil war. Millions of refugees flooded into Europe. Authoritarian governments cracked down on democratic freedoms. Social media got used increasingly to spread hate, fear and fake news. In America, the rising stock market seemed to make the rich richer while leaving the middle class poorer and giving millions the belief that the system is rigged. Meanwhile, the opioid epidemic spread across rural America and small towns, killing more people every day than AIDS did at the height of that epidemic. During this same period, austerity measures in Europe led to more unrest and prolonged the economic stagnation and joblessness.

In the wake of all this turmoil, it shouldn't be surprising that we are now witnessing the the rise of nationalist movements and populist authoritarian leaders everywhere. Britain stumbled through Brexit. In France, Austria, Germany, Italy, Hungary and Poland right-wing extremist political parties are on the rise. In America, the election of Donald Trump turned the political establishment on its head. Every tweet creates a new firestorm. Every day is a new surprise. No one, and certainly no company, is immune to crisis anymore.

If you are a business leader managing an organization or a team when crisis comes, you may easily feel overwhelmed by circumstances that are too complex, confusing or fast-moving to control. Maybe the crisis is the result of new competition, a financial scandal, a data breach, political instability, an environmental disaster, a sharp economic downturn or a terrorist attack. Suddenly, your carefully developed plans, strategies or processes can seem pointless. The support you've always relied on—clear communication channels, sufficient organizational resources, a team of people trained to do specific jobs, stable regulations—may not be available to you. The organization itself might feel threatened and vulnerable. As the ground shifts and the rules change, you will have to figure out, in real time, how to survive and navigate a new reality.

Is crisis a curse or a gift? We're hardwired to avoid crisis, if at all possible. Nobody wants to see the world get tipped over or lives and livelihoods get disrupted or become endangered. But leadership is also about facing tough moments and doing what can be done to make things better in the short and long run. A crisis can tear apart a team or an organization, but it can also bring people closer together. A crisis can destroy plans, but it can also lead to better ideas or innovations. A crisis can cause great distress and anxiety, but it can also make people feel more alive and empowered than they ever have before. A crisis can cloud thinking and create confusion, but it can also sharpen your sense of right and wrong and generate great clarity around what to do next and what a better future could look like.

Despite all of the turmoil, distress and damage that can come from a crisis, the leader who faces one is also lucky. Because crisis is where purpose is born. And it is through purpose, more than any other force, that people gain a sense of meaning, and organizations come together and grow.

Standing at the Front

Here's a story that will help illustrate what I mean.

In 1999, before Enron and the dot-com crash, one of the oldest companies in America, a little-known pharmaceutical distributor called McKesson, experienced a financial crisis that nearly destroyed it.

McKesson had been a sleepy company for many decades, selling pharmaceuticals mostly to independent pharmacies around the country. In the 1990s, it began to grow through acquisitions and new market strategies. McKesson was headquartered in San Francisco, the heart of the dot-com sector. As the tech boom took off, McKesson was not immune to the excitement of rising stock prices. Every McKesson office had a video monitor tracking that day's market movements. Then, like other "brick and mortar" companies looking to get into the tech scene, McKesson decided to buy a dynamic healthcare information technology business called HBOC for $14.5 billion. Almost overnight, McKesson became a Wall Street darling with one of the best-performing share prices in healthcare.

John Hammergren was an executive vice president reporting to the COO, who'd been with the company for a few years at that point. Still a young man in his early forties, he'd worked his whole career in healthcare. He'd grown up in central Minnesota in a close family and spent summers traveling with his father who was a hospital supply salesman. Hammergren was only sixteen when his father died suddenly. That tragedy changed his life. He no longer had any financial safety net, and realized it would be up to him to provide for himself and his mother and pay his own way through college. He needed to make a decision about the type of person he would become, and he turned to his family values (trust, honesty, accountability) for guidance. He grew up very fast.

At a number of different healthcare companies he proved himself to be a diligent worker and a good decision-maker who was not afraid to take risks because he believed that's where the best opportunities could be found. He rose quickly through the ranks. At McKesson, he was positioned near the top of the leadership team but outside the inner circle where the key strategic decisions got made. His career looked promising.

McKesson formally acquired HBOC in January 1999. At the end of April, the company held a board retreat which coincided with a special dinner with the senior HBOC team. Hammergren wasn't part of the board retreat, but he went ahead to the dinner. The McKesson and HBOC executives waited at the restaurant for hours for the senior executives and board directors to show up. When the top group finally did arrive, much later than planned, their mood seemed dark and anxious, but they offered no explanation for their delay. Nobody outside the senior group could tell what was wrong.

The next morning, leaving the hotel and about to get into a taxi, Hammergren was handed a press release by a colleague. In the car, he read an announcement. McKesson would need to restate its earnings for the previous year in light of certain accounting irregularities at HBOC. He knew this was bad news, but he didn't know how bad. Eventually, it would be discovered that the leadership at HBOC had inflated its own earnings prior to its acquisition by McKesson by concocting nonexistent deals and backdating sales contracts. This fraud would earn several executives prison time.

That morning, however, Hammergren didn't grasp the gravity of the situation until he saw what happened to the company's share price when the market opened. The $150 million dollar restatement immediately destroyed $9 billion in McKesson's value. The stock price was in free fall, and Hammergren's own personal net worth had been wiped out overnight. He felt shell-shocked.

In the midst of this turmoil, Hammergren got a call from the CEO. He expected some insight into the company's troubles, but instead the CEO asked him to fly to Hawaii in his place. The HBOC sales team was already there on their annual award trip. Someone from McKesson needed to help them absorb the news. Hammergren had nothing to do with HBOC, but he understood why the CEO needed to stay behind in San Francisco, so he agreed to go as the McKesson representative.

Arriving in Hawaii, Hammergren found the HBOC sales group devastated. One minute they'd been celebrating a record year with their spouses and colleagues, the next minute their world had come to an end. Even worse, they felt responsible for the catastrophe since it was HBOC's accounting troubles that had caused McKesson's crisis. People were frightened and looking for answers. Hammergren called a general meeting. Once everyone had gathered in the room, he stood at the front with the senior HBOC team and expected them to say a few words. To his surprise, they were unable or unwilling to address the group. It was as though they wanted or needed someone else to do the talking.

Seeing the dejection in the room, Hammergren tried to raise the spirits of the sales team. He told them, as confidently as he could manage, that they and the organization would get through this. He believed in the quality of the HBOC people and in the quality of their customer base. Together, they'd find a way. His speech was all he could offer them in the moment, but it seemed to help.

Unfortunately, the news didn't get any better over the next few months. The accounting irregularities were just as serious as they'd appeared. The CEO and CFO of McKesson soon resigned. Other top executives were fired. In a turn of events unimaginable a year before, Hammergren found himself one of the last executives left standing. The board asked him to serve as the new co-CEO.

It was not an easy assignment. The company was adrift. McKesson's share price continued to plunge, even as the dot-com boom roared on. Employee morale was terrible and customers were angry. On top of everything else, Hammergren wasn't sure what to do about HBOC. Did its problems go deeper than just accounting errors? He decided to visit the HBOC headquarters in Atlanta and examine the business closely. While there, he went to a major customer meeting to say a few words. The room was packed with about 250 customers, all angry and looking for someone to blame. Hammergren and a colleague figured they would take the stage for fifteen or twenty minutes and answer questions. The Q&A went on for a brutal three hours. It was like a scene from the *Blues Brothers* where Belushi and Akroyd perform behind chicken wire while dodging beer bottles and vegetables thrown at them by the hostile crowd. The anger was much more intense and the problems deeper and more severe than Hammergren could have guessed. Still, the experience helped clarify what needed to be done. He told the room that McKesson would make good on its promises and invest in the future, rather than off-load its problems or cast anyone—customer or employee—aside.

Privately, he wondered how to turn things around. Even though normal business operations continued, the company was in disarray and the people were walking zombies. But he believed that beneath the rubble a great company still had a chance to rise again if he could only inspire hearts and minds. To that end, he developed a set of shared principles for the enterprise, called ICARE, which encouraged people going forward to act with complete integrity and do the right thing on behalf of the customer, no matter what. These values gave everyone something to rally around. Hammergren earned credibility by acting with accountability and talking straight. He backed up all the rhetoric with a formal scorecard for the business in which the measures of success were no longer tied to Wall Street. Instead, the company would evaluate its progress based on customer and employee satisfaction, operational success and financial success that went well beyond stock price.

Finally, he helped employees understand that McKesson was a company that could make a real difference in healthcare and in people's lives. Though McKesson's businesses didn't touch patients directly, the McKesson people made sure that patients and caregivers received critical support in terms of medicine, supplies and information. The way Hammergren described it, employees could see a parallel between the experiences of McKesson and the healthcare system as a whole. The U.S. healthcare industry was on the brink of its own disaster. Companies like McKesson needed to step in to meet those enormous challenges. This perspective helped employees develop a shared sense of purpose, and gave them the hope and resiliency they needed to re-engage with their work and turn the company around.

Eighteen years later, Hammergren was still CEO of McKesson until he finally retired. The once-sleepy pharmaceutical distributor grew dramatically over that time, on all fronts, from number of employees, to global footprint and huge revenues. Today, McKesson is one of the most valuable companies in the world and sits in the top ten on the Fortune 500. That dramatic growth would not have been possible without the crisis that nearly destroyed the company.

The Power of Purpose

In the early 2000s, financial crises like the one McKesson faced were relatively common. Enron, Arthur Anderson, WorldCom, Tyco, Swissair, Parmalat, HIH, Barclays, Barings, and Lehman Brothers were among a host of acclaimed organizations around the world that also got caught up in financial scandals and were either destroyed or only exist today in a diminished state.

Other companies, like McKesson, have met crises, faced potential catastrophe and discovered or rediscovered the sense of purpose needed to turn things around. Johnson & Johnson, IBM, Ford, etc., have made it through different challenges and emerged stronger and more focused than ever.

Then there are the countless stories we never hear about. A crisis does not have to be so large that it threatens an entire organization or industry sector. A small family-owned business or a sales or product development team can face a crisis that is just as serious in terms of its threat. The best way to turn a bad situation into an opportunity for renewal and growth is to sharpen focus on a clear sense of purpose. A crisis helps us think about and understand what really matters to people.

There's an old saying in the military, "There are no atheists in foxholes." It means that people who are in great stress or danger will always turn to God, even if they aren't normally true believers. When problems are too big to handle, only God can help.

I've developed a slightly different view. I think that when human beings find themselves in difficult situations, the support they really need comes from a sense of purpose. For some people this is God. For others, it's a national flag, a family to protect, a major goal, something that matters personally.

All of these things—God, flag, family, goal—come down to meaning. That's what purpose is: a sense of meaning. Viktor Frankl, the Austrian psychiatrist, determined that a sense of meaning or purpose can help a human being survive the most horrible experiences. As a Jew during World War II, Frankl was forced into a Nazi ghetto where he worked as a physician because of his training as a psychiatrist. Later, he was given the task of monitoring the mental health of inmates and helping new people overcome their shock and grief. Then, he and his wife were transferred to Auschwitz where Frankl worked as a slave laborer. In those horrifying, dehumanizing and brutal conditions, Frankl observed that many people simply gave up and died. The ones who had a sense of higher purpose seemed better equipped to survive. As Frankl put it, "Those who have a 'why' to live, can bear with almost any 'how.'"

Crisis/Krisis

I can't fully know how a concentration camp survivor or even the CEO of a company uses a sense of purpose to get through a crisis. Instead, I can tell you about my experience and break that down.

In reality, my crisis story started in Greece, not Ukraine. In 2009, I had just been appointed managing director and was stationed in Athens. It was my first position as the head of a large corporate territory, and I was incredibly proud and excited. I'd grown up in Athens and worked there earlier in my career. Returning as a managing director made me feel like a conquering hero.

Things were a little rocky economically when I started my new position. The global financial crisis had hit the year before, and Greece, like most countries, had just entered a serious recession. Still, I felt pretty confident and saw the downturn as a chance to make up some ground on the competition. I knew the Greek market like the back of my hand and had personal connections with many of the people who would now be my suppliers and partners. I focused immediately on developing the quality of my team and building a culture in which we all felt inspired and energized. We launched our first new factory in over eighty years—a proud moment for me—and I felt like I was setting our company up for strong future growth.

You can imagine how sick I felt in late 2009 when Greece's debt crisis suddenly exploded and the economy collapsed almost overnight.

The downturn was so much bigger than anything I'd ever experienced before. All the confidence we'd felt, and even the general prosperity of the country, suddenly seemed like an illusion. It wasn't just businesses that got clobbered, Greek society fell apart. Jobs evaporated. Political leaders seemed completely lost. Greeks woke up from their dream of good economic times, realized that it had all been built on government debt they couldn't pay off, and reacted with panic and anger. Massive protests ensued. People flooded the streets in scenes reminiscent of the Great Depression. The government responded with severe austerity measures, and businesses started to lay people off. Not surprisingly, workers got angry and launched national strikes, making a terrible situation even worse. Violent riots erupted next. People broke shop windows, burned cars and fought like gangs in the streets. I couldn't believe the chaos and anger. It was incredibly distressing to watch my homeland fall apart before my eyes.

For our business, the collapse was just as brutal. To counter the economic strain, the government implemented a series of heavy austerity measures. Suddenly, no one had any disposable income. The loss of market demand decimated our profitability overnight by more than three quarters. I could think of no way to stop the slide.

I remember actually looking out my window, desperate for answers. That's when I realized that I was facing the Salamina sea pretty much from the same spot where, 2,500 years earlier, King Xerxes had watched his fleet destroyed by the Greek navy in one of the most famous battles of Ancient Greece. I laughed at the comparison, but I was also distraught. The stress was affecting me physically, emotionally and mentally. For months, I had ice-cold hands, a sick stomach and no appetite. I developed a slipped disc in my back, had difficulty sleeping and my thoughts were often muddled. I had a short temper and I felt frustrated all the time.

It helped to talk with some very understanding bosses back in Switzerland. They told me that they didn't hold me responsible for the steep decline in profitability because the financial, political and social turmoil was obviously not my fault. Instead, they would measure my performance and growth as a leader by how I dealt with the crisis. In other words, the crisis wasn't personal, and it was not necessary or even helpful for me to feel responsible for events that were clearly beyond my control. But it was my responsibility to manage it as best as possible for the sake of my team and the company. While that might seem self-evident to someone outside the chaos, I think it's a lesson that every young leader must learn and absorb.

That advice really helped me to focus on what I could do, not what I couldn't, and what my team needed from me to weather the storm. Soon, the crisis became a catalyst for a sharpened sense of purpose. I knew people didn't care as much about brand or market share when the world was falling apart. So we put aside all the many different things that we'd been worried about before—and focused on what was truly critical and mattered to everyone. We all needed jobs. We wanted Greek society and the Greek economy to get better. We knew our company could help. We had eight hundred employees, and we didn't want to cut our workforce in half to keep our margins up. We also didn't want to cheapen our brands to secure easier revenue. We wanted long-term success. So we decided that our new purpose would be to do whatever we could to put our business in a position to survive the turmoil and emerge stronger when it was over.

We called that approach "We never stop," and it became a rallying cry that helped us all work harder, stay resilient and come up with creative solutions for many different complicated problems.

In the end, we did survive and we kept our eight hundred employees and our brand position. Many businesses in Greece didn't make it, and the economy is still struggling more than ten years later. I don't think that Greek society has recovered its sense of purpose and vision for a better future even today.

When I reflected later on the difference that leadership can make during a crisis, I thought of something interesting that perhaps only a native Greek or a classically trained scholar would know. The word crisis is Greek in

origin, but the Greek word "krisis" has a second meaning that goes beyond the English usage. As in English, a *krisis* is a time of chaos and confusion. But the Greek word also means to apply judgment and discernment, or to separate the components of a problem. In other words, to extricate ourselves from a crisis, we must also exercise *krisis*.

That was the mindset I learned to incorporate to weather our problems in Greece. Leaders feel responsible by nature, but that sense of accountability must be balanced by some emotional detachment and sound judgment. They must be able to separate themselves from the turmoil and see the many confusing facts in a clear-eyed and objective way in order to make good, prompt decisions and take appropriate actions.

While I don't think previous crisis experience is essential for a leader, my experience in Greece helped me immeasurably in reacting more quickly and confidently to the confusion I encountered in Ukraine.

Preparing for Black Swans

When I came on board as the new managing director in Ukraine, I was excited to experience life in a new country and to take over an even bigger territory. I had a new apartment, a new gym and a new team of talented international managers. I was looking forward to the challenges of leading a business division with a large market and lots of opportunity. These are the normal things that business people get excited about at the midpoint of their careers.

I hit the ground running and ran into some roadblocks right away.

I think it's a common experience for a leader to take on a new position in a department or organization that seems to be functioning well, turn over a few rocks, and find unexpected problems. Early on, I discovered that our organization was in some trouble. We were losing market share. Our people had no motivation. Most importantly, my management team didn't have a winning attitude or a sense of urgency and was missing some critical leadership traits. I realized I'd need to shake things up to help us reach a higher level of performance.

So I got to work doing the normal kinds of things that any leader in that situation would do. Within six months, we established a shared vision and set of values organized around a campaign called "We Better." We wanted to grow and get better as an organization and as individuals. Things started to click. We stopped losing ground and turned our apathetic attitude around. Our business began to pick up substantially and the numbers jumped. The organization felt revitalized, and it was suddenly exciting to be part of our group. We were on the move.

The crisis, it turned out, would accelerate that progress dramatically.

I can't see the future, and I had no idea what was about to happen to Ukraine, but I'd learned a lesson from Greece that a serious emergency can overturn everything. So I asked an experienced American coach I knew to help us develop a crisis management plan just in case. Nasim Taleb calls unpredictable high-impact crises "Black Swan" events. Our coach helped us think through what we'd need to do in a number of different scenarios that might affect our communication channels, our ability to work from headquarters and how we would delegate decision-making if anything went wrong.

We scheduled a training day for the end of the year to test out that plan and practice implementing it. Ironically, by then, the Black Swan had already arrived.

The Fog Fear

The protests and riots, the unpredictable police violence, the mysterious kidnappings and horrible assassinations, the alarming military activity by Russia … as the crisis worsened, almost everyone became frightened, me included. I remember one ordinary night, waking every half hour to check my phone for updates, when the sudden sound of explosions made me break out into a cold sweat. Was the Russian military attacking Kiev? For the next long minute, I debated whether I should initiate our evacuation plan. Then I looked out of the window and started laughing. The sound of exploding bombs was just fireworks from a nearby wedding ceremony.

In my best moments, I tried to be detached and objective—to exercise *krisis*. But the panic and confusion that we all felt was very real, and I knew that I needed to acknowledge those feelings and allow people to express them so they could learn to manage themselves productively. This was a balancing act at times, but it was particularly tough during the early stages of the crisis before we got used to the "new normal." Later, we came to expect that confusion and fear could escalate rapidly with any sudden trigger.

We had over 1,400 employees. Those of us in Kiev were at the epicenter of the demonstrations and clashes. But eight hundred of our employees worked in a factory very close to the area where Ukrainian troops and Russian-backed rebels were fighting, and many of our field offices were near this hot zone. What would happen if the conflict expanded and Russian troops occupied the area? Our employees were afraid for their physical safety and the safety of their immediate families and relatives. They worried about the future of Ukraine politically, about the ability of the economy to continue to function, and about doing their jobs and managing their responsibilities under extraordinary stress.

Experiencing that level of unrest is truly a helpless feeling. There are so many things we take for granted under normal circumstances in a developed country. The rule of law. Justice. The availability of groceries. A stable currency. Reasonable political leadership. Personal safety.

You feel very small when that goes away, and increasingly vulnerable, as if you have little control over your life; and the violence and insanity of larger events can sweep over you in a minute and wipe everything away. You also become closer with your friends and family and can even feel close to strangers very quickly. People support each other—and help each other out. That part really makes you feel good about humanity.

How can a business leader help the people in an organization manage that much unpredictability and abnormality? Even though we had made plans before the conflict began to hold a simulation exercise on crisis management, the reality of what we actually did experience and how it overturned our world reinforced the notion that it's extremely difficult to plan for chaos. Geopolitical conflicts, pandemics, or natural disasters are events that go well beyond the operational and strategic scope of a business and the normal responsibilities of a management team. I soon realized that the way we responded as a senior team to the daily barrage of unpredictable events would be the real difference maker.

I was very aware that how I appeared to others mattered a great deal. People take their cues from the leader even in normal times, and often model their own attitudes and behavior accordingly. The leader is watched especially closely during a crisis when panic and confusion can rule. I wanted to be the calm and decisive captain who was also visible, hands-on and active. I also needed to be "present" for others. Some leaders hide their emotions and try to appear heroic, all-knowing and supremely confident. Others reveal everything about what they are thinking or feeling and share their vulnerability. I felt that a middle path was appropriate, admitting that I had concerns and worries while being strong for others. Sometimes I had people come into my office and close the door to discuss their fears and even cry on my shoulder. I comforted them with understanding and an ability to help them see options and positive possibilities.

I tried to lessen their burdens as much as possible. I wanted every employee to know that we were looking out for them, and that their most important responsibility was to be safe. This was a challenge, of course. Foreign employees knew that they and their families would be evacuated from the country at the first sign of collapse. We had a plan for that. But the safety of domestic employees became even more difficult to ensure as the conflict went on and some of our people got conscripted into the military.

I also wanted our place of work to feel like a refuge or escape from the harsh reality outside. Mimicking offices I had visited in Silicon Valley, I put in some games like billiards and minifootball to give people a laugh and a way to expend some physical energy, especially when the hours became long. I believed it was important for us to have a good time together.

In Greece, we had turned to the well-known story of Shackleton, the polar explorer, to reflect on the fortitude, resilience, and adaptability needed by a team to overcome daunting odds. In Ukraine, we had recently heard a motivational speech by a modern Antarctic adventurer, Sean Chapple, who introduced us to the concept of "Tent Time." According to Chapple, his exploration team bonded because they spent time together in a tent at the end of every day, sharing stories, memories, and worries in casual conversation. Similarly, the more time we spent together in Ukraine, and the more we were able to share with each other, the calmer and closer we became as a team.

Email sent to our Crimea employees one day before the Referendum which led to the Russian Annexation on March 14, 2014:

Dear colleagues,

I want to let you know that you are not alone in the tough situation you are facing in your homeland at this moment. I also want to assure you we are thinking of you at every moment and will provide you with all relevant support when needed.

Please remember 2 things:

*First, **take care of your safety** and stay away from the areas where large groups are gathering should you decide to take part in the upcoming referendum. I do understand how hard it is to remain* *calm and stay away when these political matters concern you, your families and the future of your country, but I ask you once again, remember that your safety comes first.*

*Second, I am well aware of and share your concerns regarding your future as it might be impacted by the outcome of the referendum. I would like to assure you that whatever scenario comes into play, we have plans for all of them. **As a company we are ready to do our best** to help you get through these challenging times.*

I want to repeat: we are with you in our thoughts and our hearts.

My warmest personal regards to you and your families,

Christos

* * *

We needed to adopt a new way to run the business. People have a tendency during a crisis to dwell on the extremes of negativity or, conversely, to believe that they've finally hit bottom and things can't possibly get any worse. As lightheartedly and humorously as possible, I tried to urge them to avoid despair and false optimism. I assured them that we would survive no matter what, but that they could not know yet how deep and dark the tunnel might turn out to be.

My own brain never stopped processing new information, playing out "What if" scenarios, calculating risk factors, and running through checklists. I tried to infuse my team with this automatic "What if" thinking and attitude, too. We worked hard at imagining possible situations. With each new event or development, we learned to assess what it meant by asking, "What is it that we have in front of us, and what are the consequences of this change?" Out of that thought process, it became easier to imagine the options that were available to us and the actions we should take.

But we knew that in a living, breathing crisis, even those plans could quickly become pointless. So we practiced asking "What if" about those scenarios too, imagining everything that could possibly happen next. We crafted contingency plans for nearly every area of our business, and we identified trigger points that would indicate or predict a new escalation and propel us into action. So, for example, we knew what we would do if our factory, in close proximity to the fighting, was shut down. We knew what we would do if our phones were cut or our email service went out. We knew what we would do if we needed to evacuate our headquarters. And we kept these contingency plans as simple as possible. A page or a series of bullet points gave us more than enough information. That "What if" thinking became the new normal.

It was also important to make decisions quickly, move on them immediately and not become stuck worrying about perfection. Whenever possible, I gave my people the power to make their own decisions. I also assured them that as leader I was fully and totally responsible for the consequences when we failed, even as I gave them all the praise and credit when we scored a win. This helped reduce the pressure to make the "right" decision and kept us moving.

It would have been easy for us to make those decisions in secret, huddled up in our war room, safe from questions and demands. But even though we needed time to absorb new information, assess priorities, have candid conversations, and make big decisions, it was just as important for us to be out with the troops, experiencing the same reality as everyone else, and "leading from the front."

Instead of secrecy, we tried to communicate far more than normal. People were less confused and prone to panic, and more apt to make decisions in line with expectations when they understood clearly what was happening and how we felt about it. We didn't want anyone to think we were hoarding information or keeping bad news from them. It was important to be truthful about what was going on. It would have been easy to sugarcoat reality, sound too optimistic about the chances for success, or take the corporate line. If anything, I felt it helped to downplay expectations and assert our independence from the corporation, so people felt they were getting straight talk.

Put Purpose First

But the most important thing we did was to rely on a shared sense of purpose to steady us, motivate us, bind us together and keep us moving forward.

Our purpose in Ukraine was formed out of necessity. I'm not sure we had any choice. But we articulated it clearly and forcefully as a team and rallied around it. We decided that we needed to:

1. Keep our people as safe as possible despite the danger

2. Figure out how to continue business as usual, despite all the unpredictable disruptions and extraordinary barriers

3. Grow stronger as a team

Why those three things?

Well, the first is self-explanatory. There's nothing worse for a manager to lose a colleague or a report. We did not want to put anyone in harm's way for any reason. As I said, we took every possible measure to remove our people and their families from danger, especially those who were in the worst areas or who might have been targets.

Our second purpose felt important, too. During times of chaos, people—both our customers and our employees—get enormous reassurance from little signs of normalcy. Making sure that people could get the products they favored and that our employees had work to go to and paychecks to rely on seemed like things worth fighting for.

Finally, it was important to grow closer as a team. We needed to believe that we could rely on each other, that the hard work would pay off, and that together, through resilience, fortitude, creativity and luck, we could somehow survive and succeed.

It worked. Because of our shared sense of purpose, we never felt more alive during those months of geopolitical uncertainty and confusion. We were engaged at a deep level by our work and the problems before us. We didn't get tired, even when we barely slept for days on end. We were often afraid, but we didn't lose our ability to reason and make decisions. We were confronted by frustrating challenges and unexpected setbacks all the time, but we stayed resilient and creative and always found ways to make things work. We couldn't plan but we could improvise. Goals changed constantly. Success was measured by getting things done. We developed our professional capabilities as managers at an accelerated pace, learned how to delegate better, make decisions in the moment, act quickly and plan smart. We also grew as human beings. I felt that about myself—that I was really coming into my own—and I saw my colleagues rise above the responsibilities of their roles, and sort of take off their masks to show real empathy and understanding for others and to display insight and even wisdom on many occasions. We became closer as a team—we coordinated faster, collaborated easier, seemed to understand what each other were thinking without a lot of messing around. We formed real friendships across all the traditional barriers of age, level of experience, nationality, native language, and even political beliefs.

It could have been a disaster. We could have fallen apart as an organization, failed to meet our responsibilities, cowered in fear, become selfish and mean-spirited, and blamed each other for failures beyond our control. Instead, we survived and thrived. We somehow managed to keep everyone in our division safe. We achieved exceptional business and organizational results at a time when many companies had decided to "write off" Ukraine. We strengthened our focus, instead, and became more lean in our operations while maintaining our market and customer base.

We also served as a beacon of stability to our customers and the people of Ukraine during a difficult time. Anyone who has ever lived through a prolonged crisis or a war will appreciate how meaningful it is to be able to go to a nearby store and find a favorite product. It reinforces the value of ordinary life and provides reassurances that calm will one day return.

Because of the crisis, we discovered ourselves and became something bigger.

That's the power of purpose.

Every company can develop a vision, a mission, a strategic plan. But there's something missing without purpose. We were "lucky" enough to discover that need through a crisis no one would have wished to experience.

But because of that crisis we saw how purpose could motivate and inspire our people. We also saw how that sense of shared meaning and camaraderie sharpened our focus, resilience and stamina in a way that improved our organizational performance. We knew we were doing something bigger than just selling units and making money. A sense of purpose made everything seem possible.

I left Ukraine knowing I wanted to understand purpose better and figure out how to leverage it more deliberately and consciously in the future—with or without a crisis.

CHAPTER ONE RECAP

- Keep on your toes. We live in a time of constant crisis occurring in unexpected ways. You can't control it. You can't predict the future. You can develop plans for it, but that's not the real remedy.

- Organizations, teams and individuals are better equipped to survive a crisis when they develop or exist according to a higher purpose.

- During a crisis, the team navigates better with transparency, accountability, togetherness, agile decision-making and a common purpose.

- As a leader, if you have already experienced a crisis, you are lucky. Treat it as a gift. It has given you more skills, agility and courage. And for your team it is a reason to find meaning, purpose and wisdom to grow further.

Tools & Resources

My Crisis Management Checklist

This is what we did during the Ukraine crisis. When it happens to you, come back and check it out.

- Determine the role of the crisis team as a whole and each member.

- Determine routines and protocols for communication and briefings.

- Develop a mechanism for monitoring all events chronologically, such as a Log, Whiteboard, Digital Record, etc.

- Establish and equip a War Room—a place where the crisis team will meet.

- Engage in "What if" scenario planning to develop awareness, vigilance and agile thinking.

- Develop Signals & Triggers Map, a list of signals you're receiving from the field that assesses each event or trigger point by their likelihood to escalate.

- Determine who will be your Receivers & Doers—who will actively gather information and who will act upon new events or incidents.

- Establish a Master Book both digitally and on paper (this will include your assets, escape routes, meeting points, telephone lists, etc.). This is useful for all times, actually. The process of developing such a book can be beneficial on its own.

- Obtain Satellite Communications Hardware (satellite phones should cell phone reception fail), or if there is no physical threat in the immediate future, this might read as develop alternative channels of communications beyond the standard ones, just for the rainy days.

- Get your Go-Bags Ready—Emergency bags for the team and team members in case of evacuation, etc. As mentioned before, selecting what you keep with you in any severe crisis can put you in a position to really assess what is absolutely vital for the organization and your team.

Signals & Triggers Mapping

To monitor the events that would lead us toward specific actions helped us to better monitor the evolution of the crisis in Ukraine. We used the below template.

LEVELS OF ALERT APPLIED FOR THE SPECIFIC CRISIS HANDLING

ALERT LEVEL 1 (DESCRIPTION)

ALERT LEVEL 2 (DESCRIPTION)

ALERT LEVEL 3 (DESCRIPTION)

ALERT LEVELS	DESCRIPTION OF LEVELS	INDICATORS/TRIGGERS TO ACTIVATE EACH LEVEL (POSSIBLE EVENTS)	DECISION MAKER NAME(S)

ACTION PLAN FOR EACH ALERT LEVEL			
ALERT LEVELS	ACTIONS (DESCRIPTIONS)	RESPONSIBLE NAME(S)	ACCOUNTABLE NAME(S)
LEVEL 1			
1			
2			
LEVEL 2			
1			
2			
LEVEL 3			
1			
2			

If you want to see a real-life example, visit my site www.christostsolkas.com

The House of Crisis

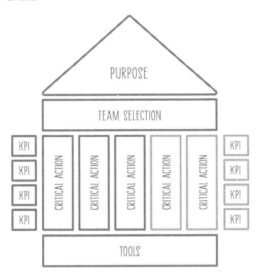

THE CRISIS HOUSE

- When a crisis starts, form and assemble your crisis team. Team selection is critical and depends on the crisis at hand.

- Define your purpose.

- Determine the critical actions required to deal with your situation and achieve your purpose.

- Build, assemble, or collect the skills needed to manage the situation effectively.

- Determine which tools (technological, systems, etc.) will help or are necessary.

- Decide on the Key Performance Indicators (KPIs) (one or two figures) by every critical action.

More info and guidelines on how to construct your Crisis House, you will find on my site www.christostsolkas.com

CHAPTER TWO

This Team Rocks

It was a beautiful summer evening on the beach in Panama City, Florida, in July 2017. Some people walked along the sand, others sunbathed, swam or body-surfed the waves. Then, a few people noticed that something was wrong.

Derek Simmons was picnicking with his family when he saw a crowd gathered at the edge of the water pointing out to sea. He walked over to find out what was going on, wondering if there had been a shark attack. What he discovered was just as horrible. An entire family was caught in a riptide. No one could rescue them. They were too far from shore, and the current was too strong to swim through. It was the most helpless feeling in the world.

Then Simmons got an idea. He turned to those next to him and said, "Let's try to get as many people as we can to form a human chain." He was thinking about ants and how they can come together during precarious situations.

At first people were reluctant. Probably they were afraid and worried about the distance. It wasn't their job to help rescue anyone, though the lifeguards were off-duty. Simmons' urgency shook off that passivity, and soon the group on the beach began hollering to others to join and help. New people ran over, immediately understood what was going on, and waded into the powerful current to take their place at the front of the growing line as it stretched out to sea, closer and closer to the stranded swimmers. A team formed one person at a time.

It took eighty strangers in the end. As the family of six and another couple (who'd swam out to help and gotten caught in the same riptide) struggled to stay above water, the human chain reached them. The people at the front grabbed the two children first, ages eight and eleven, and passed them along to the beach. The mother, close to drowning, was next, and so on.

It took an exhausting hour to get everyone to shore safely. The family's grandmother suffered a heart attack during the ordeal but survived. The crowd on the beach cheered and hugged and cried.

They knew they'd done something heroic and special by coming together. If they hadn't, eight people would have died. Then, that team dissolved and the eighty strangers, forever connected, went their separate ways.[1]

Teams Forming in Crisis

Eighty strangers on a beach is a large team. How about ten thousand? Among the countless heartwarming and heartbreaking stories from 9/11, here's one of the most amazing.

In 1925, Charles Lindbergh was the first person to pilot an airplane across the Atlantic, nonstop, taking 33½ hours in a single-engine plane to go from Long Island to Paris. In the early days of commercial air travel, however, it was difficult for larger planes to make the entire distance from New York City to London or Paris without refueling. Many commercial flights broke up the trip by landing in a remote northern Canadian town

---

1 https://www.theguardian.com/us-news/2017/jul/11/80-people-form-human-chain-rescue-gulf-of-mexico-florida

called Gander. By the 1950s, Gander was the most important airport in the world. The Beatles landed in Gander on their way to New York City. The likes of Albert Einstein, Frank Sinatra, Marilyn Monroe, Elvis and Winston Churchill killed time at the airport bar or restaurant. The locals, who were ordinary, unpretentious people, took it all in stride.

By the 1960s, with the adoption of jet fuel, commercial airplanes became less common in Gander, and its importance receded. The airport was still in use, but its large capacity was a relic of a bygone era. Then with 9/11 that capacity came to the rescue. After two commercial aircraft struck the World Trade Center towers in New York City and a third hit the Pentagon outside Washington, D.C., air traffic over North America was grounded. This put cross-Atlantic flights in particularly desperate straits. With limited fuel and no way to turn back for Europe, where could all those flights land? Gander was one of the airports at the ready.

In all, thirty-eight commercial planes and four military planes were diverted to Gander that morning. The 6,600 civilian passengers and crew didn't know the real reason for the emergency diversion until they landed. Then, the passengers needed to remain on board until security teams could ensure that no terrorists or explosive devices were on board.

The world, horrifed by the events in New York City and the Pentagon, had come to a stop. The passengers in Gander were stranded far from home and unable to return. All flights remained grounded for the next six days.

Six thousand, six hundred people represented 66 percent of the local population in Gander, an enormous influx even in this era of refugees pouring into Europe from Syria and Africa. The ten thousand citizens of Gander could have been excused for feeling overwhelmed. Instead, in a very coordinated fashion, they got to work. They filled gymnasiums and other open buildings with cots, and when the cots filled up, they found families to take the remaining passengers into their homes. Restaurants opened up to give free meals. The locals made sure passengers had access to showers and laundry machines to clean themselves up. They even cared for seventeen dogs and cats and two great apes. Most importantly, they helped comfort people who were far from home, in distress and worried about their loved ones and the future.[2, 3]

When passengers returned to their aircrafts almost a week later, they greeted each other like old friends and traded stories of what they'd been through. They hugged and exchanged phone numbers and email addresses. But mostly they remembered the people they'd met on the ground. As Flight Delta 15 filled up, a passenger asked the captain if he could use the PA system to make an announcement. Normally, this was not allowed, but the captain permitted it. The passenger talked about the amazing hospitality they had all received and said that he would like to set up a trust fund to provide college scholarships for the students of the local high school. He asked for donations of any amount from his fellow travelers. Many of the passengers bonded together, collected $14,000 on the spot, and helped the fund grow to over $1.5 million later.[4]

In a crisis, when chaos or confusion threatens to take over, human beings often reveal their best selves, usually by joining together in common cause. Daniel Aldritch, a political scientist at Perdue University in Indiana, saw this firsthand during Hurricane Katrina in 2005. Though flooding was imminent, officials had not yet ordered evacuation; but local communities, neighbors helping neighbors, immediately took up the task of telling people they should leave and helping those who needed help. Aldritch later conducted research at disasters all around the world and discovered it is almost always ad hoc teams of neighbors who do the most good after a calamity, saving and helping more people than paramedics, firefighters, police and soldiers. As Aldritch observed, "It's this passion for a local community and granular knowledge about who needs what that makes large-scale government interventions ineffective by comparison."[5]

---

2   https://www.nytimes.com/2005/03/20/travel/tmagazine/gander-airport-when-the-going-was-good.html

3   https://www.washingtonpost.com/local/on-sept-11-a-tiny-canadian-town-opened-its-runways-and-heart-to-7000-stranded-travelers/2016/09/08/89d875da-75e5-11e6-8149-b8d05321db62_story.html?utm_term=.1d13762576a5

4   http://mytnnews.com/blog/2012/10/11/delta-flight-15-a-true-story-about-9-11/

5   https://www.npr.org/2011/07/04/137526401/the-key-to-disaster-survival-friends- and-neighbors

In her book, *A Paradise Built in Hell: The Extraordinary Communities that Arise in Disaster*, Rebecca Solnit tapped her experiences living through an earthquake in San Francisco in the late 1980s, and the research she later did at other sites of disaster. During such emergencies, she did not find greed, violence, fear or desperation, but extraordinary stories of teams of people coming together in community, collaboration and caring. As Solnit wrote,

> In the wake of an earthquake, a bombing or a major storm, most people are altruistic, urgently engaged in caring for themselves and those around them, strangers and neighbors as well as friends and loved ones. The image of the selfish, panicky or regressively savage human being in times of disaster has little truth to it. Decades of meticulous sociological research on behavior in disasters, from the bombings of World War II to floods, tornadoes, earthquakes and storms across the continent and around the world, have demonstrated this.... We need ties to survive, but they along with purposefulness, immediacy, and agency also give us joy—the startling, sharp joy I found over and over again in accounts of disaster.[6]

Even distance is no object. Today, in our global era of instant communication, collaborative teams can come together over any disaster. In 2010, when thirty-three Chilean miners got trapped 2,000 feet below ground, the situation appeared hopeless. Yet, teams formed instantly. The trapped miners organized themselves with an unusual level of collaboration, sharing space to stand or lie down, looking after each other's needs, taking shifts. Above ground, teams of engineers and aid workers formed to do what they could. The odds were long. Experts suggested a 2 percent chance that the miners could be dug out after four months. Because the technical capabilities were insufficient, the rescuers put out a call for help from anyone in the world who could assist. People sent important tools and support devices from all over the world. A small company in the U.S., learning about the crisis, offered a drilling rig that could do the necessary work in half the time. It

6   https://lithub.com/rebecca-solnit-how-to-survive-a-disaster/

arrived in Chile three days later. Two and a half months after the disaster, the miners were rescued—all alive. Without many teams all over the world coming together, it never would have happened.[7]

These spontanous teams make sense to us intuitively. People are willing to drop everything and help others, their neigbors, even strangers, even people on the other side of the world, when the need arises. Why?

Because there's no confusion—the purpose is crystal clear. How much more simple could it be? Some people are drowning—let's form a human chain. Thousands need shelter—let's open up our homes and coordinate meals. A group of miners are trapped—let's send our best experts and equipment.

The effect is powerful. Joined in common cause, the elation, camaraderie and collective power is something to behold. The people on a strong team are engaged and feel a deep and driving sense of shared purpose. No matter how traumatic the experience of an emergency or crisis might be, they don't seem paralyzed by anxiety or indecision. And afterwards, studies show, those people experience less grief and post-traumatic stress.

Lost Connections

Why do teams, organized around a clear purpose, make people feel so energized, engaged and alive? Because they get at a deep and often neglected human need. Let me explain.

Ordinary life—going to work, shopping for groceries, taking vacations—feels very different than the experience of being a team in a crisis. It should feel better, you would think, given the fact that our lives are not on the line on an average, ordinary day. But this is not always the case. In fact, our modern existence is often characterized by feelings that are in opposition to the feelings of being on a purpose-driven team. Instead of feeling engaged, energized, focused and powerful, many people often feel anxious, isolated or lonely and depressed. Although not a perfect correlation, more people than ever today rely on anti-depressant and anti-anxiety medication. In the

---

7   http://knowledge.wharton.upenn.edu/article/the-chilean-miner-rescue-a-lesson-in-global-teamwork/

U.S., 65 percent more Americans take such medications daily compared to fifteen years ago. Long-term reliance is also increasingly common.[8]

On a surface level, this development can seem bizarre or counter-intuitive. Everyone likes to complain that the "stress of modern living" is worse today than before. But unless you are living in a war zone, addicted to opioids, a refugee, incapacitated by illness, impoverished or unemployed long-term, chances are you are living a better, higher-quality life today than most humans who have ever been alive.

Still, loneliness and sense of isolation is up. Writers like Robert Putnam in *Bowling Alone* pointed out years ago that our social bonds are not as strong as they used to be. Once, most of us had large, sprawling families. Today, divorce rates are higher, and people tend to live at greater distances from their relatives than they did in the past.

Religious institutions have weakened, too. Attending a church, mosque or synagogue is still common in some countries or cultures but not as universal as it used to be. More people, especially here in Europe, question traditional religious values rather than embrace them whole-heartedly.

In the cities where most of us live, we can be surrounded by people and yet not know our neighbors. We don't have strong ties to our local communities even when we shop, because most neighborhood stores have been replaced by global chains, and the goods and services we consume have likely been produced far away because it's cheaper.

In our jobs, work is also typically no longer a local or community-based activity, but a global one. People move to new cities for their careers. Company headquarters may be in another country altogether. The people we work with on a daily basis on a project or in a department may not be the people we see every day. Virtual or remote teams are less the exception than the rule nowadays. We have fewer chances for casual, relationship-building exchanges.

Even our forms of entertainment and social engagement are oddly detached from the world we live in. Video games are extremely popular, especially among millennials, and massive multiplayer games do involve "gathering" large numbers of people into one universe. But those are usually

---

8   https://www.cbsnews.com/news/antidepressant-use-soars-65-percent-in-15-years/

not the same people we live, socialize and work with in the "real" world. Social media has the word "social" right in the name, but if you notice how many people are staring at their phones while they tweet, post or ping, you also see how little they are engaged in the world around them, how isolated from it they seem.

Are we happier, healthier, more satisfied with our modern lives? Fat chance.

My parents, who have always lived in Greece, had a very different experience of life than I have had—calm, consistent, almost uneventful. My father is eighty-nine years old now and very healthy and happy, thankfully. In his career, he was a public servant with a steady job, but he had very little responsibility and experienced almost no excitement. He didn't make much money, but he was very dedicated to being a good provider, and he was able to earn enough to support a family in a modest home. He wasn't a complete slave to his job. He had friends and hobbies. He occasionally wrote rhymes—he would not call them poems. His biggest priority was to raise his two sons at the highest ethical and educational standards possible. In spite of that "ordinary existence", he's been incredibly happy. In our family, we almost treat his happiness as a joke because it can be so annoying at times. My father laughs and jokes often. His mood is almost always optimistic and positive. Even my daughter finds it too much. She says, "Daddy, why is Grandpa always singing? I don't get it!"

Today, my parents live on an island that could be considered a kind of paradise. The climate is comfortable. There's little pollution. People have enough to eat and do. And they live exceptionally long, healthy and happy lives.

In fact, this island and others like it in Greece are famous as "Blue Zones." There are a number of other such areas around the world where there are many people over eighty years old and some even over a hundred who continue to live simple but healthy, happy and productive lives, even in a world that seems so stressful, dislocated and busy.[9] What's the secret of their happiness and longevity?

Most of the Blue Zone research focuses on diet and lifestyle. Having visited the island of Ikaria, which was profiled in the research, I can

9   https://www.nytimes.com/2012/10/28/magazine/the-island-where-people-forget-to-die.html

understand why. The island is incredibly beautiful and easy to live in. The food is wonderfully fresh and healthy and low in bad fat. The people live more on the "sun-clock" or the "stomach-clock" than the wristwatch. Shops are not open in the mornings, taverns serve you dinner with a smile whenever you want. You can wander to the main square at any time of the day or evening and find people to sit with and talk to. You get lots of exercise just by walking the hills, maybe doing some swimming. On festive occasions, there are fun things like folk dancing, which they proudly call "Ikariotiko".

The easy lifestyle, excellent food and frequent exercise are important for health and happiness. But the research has also emphasized the importance of the strong sense of social connection found in such Blue Zones. It is very easy to be social on an island like Ikaria—in fact, it is difficult not to be social. People are often playing games, dancing, talking. This seems trivial but it's not. Recent studies, especially among aged people, show that loneliness and social isolation is so bad for your health it's the equivalent of smoking two packs of cigarettes a day.

Why would being alone be so stressful and harmful to your health? The work of Johann Hari in his book *Lost Connections: Uncovering the Real Causes of Depression and the Unexpected Solutions* is helpful in understanding. As Hari puts it:

> The umbrella answer is that human beings have innate psychological needs just as we have physical needs. We need to feel we belong, that we have meaning and purpose, that people value us and that we have autonomy. We also live in a culture that's not meeting those psychological needs for most people. It does not manifest as full-blown depression and anxiety in most people; for some people it's just a feeling of unhappiness and a life less fulfilling than it could have been. We've built a society that has many great aspects, but it is not a good match for our human nature.[10]

---

10   https://www.theguardian.com/media/2018/jan/07/johann-hari-depression-brain-lost-connections-book-interview

Isolation and loneliness is a killer, Hari says, because we evolved as tribal animals. If you were isolated or exiled from a group in caveman days, that probably meant you were sick or in great danger and likely about to die. No wonder you would feel stressed, anxious, helpless and depressed.

Many people today work hard to avoid feeling unhappy and dissatisfied with life. They eat well, exercise more, go to occasional retreats for self-care or self-improvement like exercise boot camps, yoga, meditation, mindfulness and so on. Many are obsessed with maximizing everything—our time, our workouts, our brains. We engage in "life hacks" of one kind or another to be more efficient and get more out of our time.

But as Hari and others have pointed out, focusing predominantly on our own personal needs or desires does not necessarily mean we are living happier, more satisfying or meaningful lives. Instead, the real secret to happiness is not to get more but to give more. A study published at Harvard Business School, "Feel Good about Giving" noted the positive feedback loop of those who engaged in charitable or philanthropic activities: "Happier people give more and giving makes people happier ..."[11]

The effect is not only social, it's chemical. The more you do for others, the more serotonin is released into your brain. The recipient of that help gets

---

11   https://hbswk.hbs.edu/item/feeling-good-about-giving-the-benefits-and-costs-of-self-interested-charitable-behavior

a serotonin burst, too. The dynamic is remarkably win-win.[12] Hari points out that helping and supporting other people in any situation makes us feel less isolated, more engaged and more fulfilled. As he put it in an interview, "What heals human loneliness is not getting aid, it's engaging in a reciprocal relationship where someone is giving you something and somewhere down the line you'll give something back."[13]

I have seen this over and over again in my own life and career. In a positive team environment, people give and get all the time. They contribute and are supported in turn. This makes them feel less lonely and isolated and more engaged. When combined with a clear and compelling sense of shared purpose, such as during a crisis or important project, the team is even more powerful because it knows what to do and experiences less confusion or hesitation.

Over a period of time, these teams grow closer and more collaborative. Interestingly, the individuals of the team also grow as people and leaders.

We Better

As I mentioned, I first saw this in Greece when I took over my old home territory. Leading into the economic crisis, I was very eager to develop a strong management team for our business. We developed a vision, shared values and a strategic plan to improve important aspects of the business. The economic crisis hit, and our market collapsed overnight. Suddenly, all of our business plans were meaningless.

Our clear sense of purpose helped us make a lot of decisions. For example, when a downturn comes, the easiest thing in the world would be to let go as many employees as possible, narrow your brands portfolio to the bare minimum, close factories, sell assets, etc. On some occasions, these choices might even be the right ones. But we wanted to be in a better position after the crisis, so we did everything we could to maintain the

---

12   https://www.entrepreneur.com/video/287016

13   https://art19.com/shows/the-ezra-klein-show/episodes/
805c9dc7-ce7d-4238-9e1b-491f138e61e4

brands that would thrive and become our market leaders again and sustain as many employees as possible and keep open the factory that would need to be ready for a new production surge.

We also got closer as a team. Knowing this, when I transferred to Ukraine, I was even more deliberate in trying to develop the performance and closeness of my new team. Our "We Better" vision was a promise that all of our team development work benefit us in every way. By coming together as a team, we would improve our business, develop our careers and grow as individuals.

I wanted to track this growth and development very precisely, so I brought in my leadership coach who had very clear measures for team effectiveness across five critical performance areas. These were:

1. Capabilities and Infrastucture: Whether a team is set up for success by having the members, knowledge, processes and support it needs.

2. Goals and Purpose: Whether a team is focused on outputs and a shared purpose that energizes and gives them meaning.

3. Roles and Individual Expecations: Whether the members of the team are meeting their obligations and support each other in risk-taking and collaboration.

4. Interactions and Team Processes: Whether a team is aligned, efficient, communicates well and handles conflict productively.

5. Learning and Results: Whether a team is growing, developing capabilities and maturing over time.

Each of these five performance areas is divided into sub-factors, which are all measured by surveys of the team members and important stakeholders. The combined scores paint a multifaceted and highly nuanced picture of current team performance capability.

There are also strategies, of course, for developing weak areas over time. If a team doesn't score well on its capabilities and infrastructure, it might need to develop existing team members or recruit different people with the right capabilities to the team. If interactions and team processes score low, then new ways of communicating or holding meetings might be needed, or it might be important to develop team cohesion through intense team development workshops.

Over time, with much focused and precise work, a team can grow in performance capability. The goal is to become a Category One Team.

Category Four	Dysfunctional
Category Three	Adequate to good performance
Category Two	Very good performers but inconsistent or unreliable in sustaining top performance
Category One	Consistently excellent over a sustained period of time

In our first team effectiveness assessment, my management team achieved mostly Category Three level measures with some attributes in the Category Two range. As an ambitious and competitive person, I wanted us to become Category One. My coach told us that it would take two to three years under ordinary circumstances.

Fortunately, or unfortunately, our circumstances proved to be very unordinary. Crisis helped catalyze our development much more quickly.

Meet the Team

As I mentioned in the first chapter, when I came to Ukraine and got to know my team and my business, I discovered that our organization was not in great shape. We were losing market share, our people had no motivation, and my management team didn't have a winning attitude or a sense of urgency and was missing some critical leadership traits. I changed some people around and established a learning path so that we could become even more collaborative and successful in the future.

Individually, my management team was composed of eleven interesting people, each of whom had their own talents and personalities. Let me give you a sense of them by describing three who really stood out.

This is Tatiana

In many ways, Tatiana is a very characteristic Ukrainian woman. Ukraine, like many countries in Eastern Europe, is almost a matriarchal society. The women are highly educated, have strong personalities, and are often the breadwinners in the family. They have a tradition of being tough survivors.

Tatiana is no exception. When she was at school, she earned the opportunity to leave the former Soviet Union on a scholarship to the U.S., but she sacrificed her own advancement to stay home and look after her family.

In the company, Tatiana had already been recognized for her leadership potential and been given a number of challenging assignments abroad. She'd just returned to Ukraine when I arrived in 2012. I was really impressed by her experience and her level of engagement with work. She was in charge of our Corporate Affairs department, and the job was very much in her comfort zone. She loves politics and social issues. She's intelligent, and ambitious, and has strong people skills and a broad network of contacts. She's friendly and people like her.

I saw a lot of versatility in Tatiana and the potential to be a general manager one day, so I moved her into sales, an area she knew nothing about. I figured that experience running our field force would accelerate her development and raise her profile within the company. Like many performance-driven corporations, our company prizes people who can figure out ways to increase revenue and motivate a sales force. So this was a big opportunity for her.

Tatiana responded really well. As we got down to work, it was quickly apparent to me that she was one of the most reliable and hardworking people on my team. She would do whatever it took to get a job done, and she worked nonstop. On weekends, for example, it was almost impossible to get in touch with most people in the company by email or text when I had a question or a concern. Tatiana always replied within 30 minutes. After the crisis began, her response time was even faster. It didn't matter what time of day I checked in or what question I had, Tatiana got back to me almost immediately. I felt total trust in her commitment and her sense of responsibility.

This is Roman

Roman is also Ukrainian. He's young, only thirty-two when we worked together, and holds an MBA from the University of Chicago. He's extremely intelligent, a bit idiosyncratic at times, but impressive in person. He's very creative—the sort of lateral thinker who can be a great problem-solver on any team.

When I met Roman he was the CEO of a small local company. My predecessor had told me about him and suggested we get together. I quickly saw that Roman had skills and ambition we could use, so I recruited him to join our company. I didn't have a position for him at the time, so I sent him to corporate head-quarters in Lausanne to do some projects as part of his onboarding process. He stayed there for a few months and then returned to Ukraine.

After I moved Tatiana into sales, I put Roman into her old position in corporate affairs. It was a good position for him to get a feel for the overall company.

Finally, this is Artem

Unlike Tatiana and Roman, Artem is Russian. He's from Saratov, a rather small-for-Russian standards provincial city. He's also one of the most intelligent people I've ever met. His brain is like a computer. He remembers numbers and can do complex calculations in his head.

From the outside, he looks tough. He's a man of few words, and has an unpolished way about him and sometimes comes across as rude in his demeanor. But I could tell a lot of that was due to inexperience and lack of sophistication. Over time, Artem showed that he actually had impressive leadership skills and a big heart. People found him intimidating at first but came to see him as endearing and charismatic the more they got to know him.

As every manager knows, a team is more than a group of talented individuals. It needs to come together as a unit and function at very high levels of collaboration, trust, determination with a compelling direction, clear guardrails and accountability for execution. Our coach kick-started the team-building process through which we started to gel. The excercises we did together were very interesting and incredibly helpful for what was to come. After I moved a few people like Tatiana and Roman into different positions with heavier responsibilities, we started to click through the normal course of doing business.

The team improved, performance got better. The Ukrainian crisis accelerated that progress dramatically.

Make the Team the Answer to as Many Problems as Possible

Leadership stories tend to focus on the leader, and leave the team as an afterthought. But the leader is not a superhero who can solve all problems independently. As much as possible, the leader should lead and not manage; but to make that judgment, the leader must assess the current capability of his or her team relative to the level or intensity of the crisis.

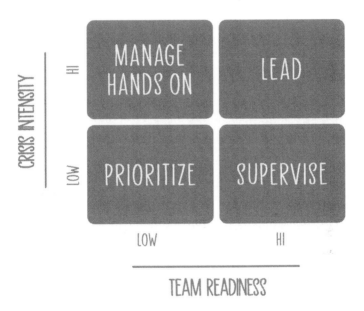

If the crisis level is high but the team's readiness is low, the leader will need to be very hands-on, managing many functions and decisions. But if the readiness of the team is high, then the leader can be more of an orchestra conductor, directing the team appropriately while tapping their experience and expertise.

In Ukraine, each person on my team had different talents and skills, and they also handled their worries and responsibilities in different ways. Some were practical and logical. Others were skeptics who saw important faults in those plans. Some were great at being positive and keeping up morale through lighthearted jokes, stories, and relentless optimism. Others were sensitive and great at looking after those experiencing difficulty. Depending on the circumstances, different people were able to come to the forefront to lead. I never appreciated the diversity of a team more, and it helped immensely that I knew them well and was able to exploit their talents to the fullest.

Disagreements and debate were encouraged. We needed to have a variety of perspectives and opinions to come up with good ideas. We relied on the closeness of our team—fostered by our "tent time"—to have an environment that was safe for innovation and risk-taking.

As leader, I was also there to help the team, and I believed that to be my primary responsibility. I put the good of the team ahead of myself as well as any concerns about my own career and, at times, even the good of the company as a whole. I was there to be a key resource to the team, and to be useful in the most effective ways possible. Sometimes that meant I connected us to other parts of the company to tap critical information, approvals or resources. Sometimes my higher profile was needed to meet with key stakeholders or government officials. Other times my experience and expertise helped improve decisions that were particularly urgent and significant or gave the team the necessary authority. My team came to see that my attitude toward them was sincere, that I supported them in every way, and that I was there for them, not the other way around.

It also helped to have a vision. I think of a vision in a crisis as a belief in the future that goes beyond the immediate confusion and fear. It helped to calm, guide, and motivate the team. In Greece, our vision was openly debated, decided on, and articulated. We wanted to build a company that was better than before by taking advantage of the crisis as a moment to be aggressive in the market.

In Ukraine, perhaps because we were an even closer team, our vision was far less explicit, and yet I felt it was understood by everyone and even more powerful. We aimed to develop the emotional and intellectual experience of the team so that they would be capable of handling the crisis themselves, without me or any other leader. In other words, our vision was to become the leadership team of the future.

For many reasons, it was important to grow close as a team. We needed to believe that we could rely on each other, that the hard work would pay off, and that together, through resilience, fortitude, creativity and luck, we could somehow survive and succeed.

This sense of team camaraderie was critical. We could have fallen apart. Tatiana had a family to worry about, but we also needed her to look after a family of hundreds of salespeople in the field.

Like Tatiana, Roman was a mess watching the conflict tear his country apart. He could have easily left for safer and greener pastures. As a young, successful business person with a great education and a strong network in the U.S., he had half a mind to leave Ukraine and seek a fresh start. And the other half of him—the part of him that was a proud Ukrainian—wanted to join the army and fight. It meant a lot that in spite of this inner conflict he stayed with our organization and worked so hard for us.

Artem, on the other hand, was in a different and very challenging situation. As a native Russian, he basically represented the "enemy". It was hard on him personally to bear that burden. But the pressure didn't affect his work at all, except maybe to increase his dedication. He worked like a dog, practically sleeping in his office, and drinking Red Bull to keep himself going. And he always stayed levelheaded, rational and sympathetic, no matter what was happening. This had a calming effect on others. I watched him grow as a leader before my eyes.

The 10,000

I knew we'd grown a lot as a team in a very short period of time. When my coach assessed our progress at the end of the year period, he gave statistical evidence. From a team that was a Category Three to a Category Two level at the beginning, we had catapulted into becoming a Category One team in record time.

I'd seen this development with my own eyes. My people built rare characteristics and skills not normally called for in corporations, such as rapid decision-making, highly intuitive and analytical thinking, the ability to manage work and life in extreme stress, as well as courage, compassion, and resiliency. As I was preparing to move to Switzerland for a new role, I saw them conducting meetings without me, picking each other up when needed, and reacting to new trigger points with decisiveness.

This was illustrated most clearly one day when we visited our corporate HQ in Lausanne to present our new strategy to the senior leaders of the company. It was a nice break from the pressures of Ukraine, and we were excited to have the chance to review our performance numbers and get some direct recognition for work that had been done under incredibly difficult circumstances. However, in the middle of our presentation, news broke that a Malaysian airliner flying over Ukraine had crashed, killing 283 passengers and 15 crew members.

Almost immediately there were some crazy rumors and fears for the worst. Was it an accident, or had the plane been shot down by the Russians? What if the attackers were one of the anti-Ukrainian militias or the Ukrainian military itself? Did any of those possibilities signal a return to open military conflict or mark the beginning of an outright invasion? My team didn't wait, smartphones in hand, for Twitter to tell them what was going on. Instead, they huddled up and began to develop contingency plans based on various possible scenarios.

Our purpose remained the same. We needed to keep our people safe and achieve our normal business objectives if possible, but the team was a well-oiled machine. There was little fear or confusion and zero delay or hesitation. They knew what to do and how to do it. And they didn't need me to drive or even steer them anymore. They were a high-functioning team of leaders.

The experience of seeing them in action reminded me of a famous Greek story told by Xenephon, who was a student of Socrates and a contemporary of Plato and Aristotle.

Instead of focusing on philosophy, Xenephon wanted to experience the world, so he joined an army of Greek mercenaries that went to battle for a King in Persia that the Greeks admired. The Greeks fought well, but the Persian king was killed in battle. So the leaders of the Greek army met with the Persian leaders to discuss terms for a truce and safe passage back to Greece. During that negotiation, the Persians assasinated all of the Greek leaders. This left the Greek army of ten thousand mercenaries leaderless and stranded thousands of miles from home.

Xenephon was one of three officers elected by the troops to be part of the new leadership team. He made a speech to them that turned their fate around. Xenephon acknowledged that the Greek army had been tricked and deceived. The Persians hoped that by killing the Greek leaders, they would not have any direction, and the resulting confusion and anarchy would finish the job. With our leaders now gone, Xenephon said, we must all become leaders. The Persians will fear us because out of one leader, we will show them ten thousand.

The story of their long and arduous journey home, fighting through enemies and hardship at every step, is called the Anabasis, or the Uphill March, and Peter Drucker called it his favorite leadership story.

Xenephon understood the power of a team to come together by having all become leaders. This is what leadership is supposed to be about. If you are a leader, you are meant to develop the leadership capabilities of the people around you. You're not in a leadership role to ensure that you're indispensable and that your people will need to rely on you forever. Your most important objective and contribution to the organization is to make yourself obsolete.

So, in that sense, I was filled with pride as Tatiana, Artem, Roman and the others jumped into action and made fast decisions in the face of another crisis. Coming out of that ordeal, all three got better jobs. Artem was promoted to sales director in place of Tatiana. Despite being a Russian living in a Ukraine still in turmoil, he became supervisor for a group of five hundred Ukrainians, and is respected and appreciated for his leadership. My successor told me that he'd never taken over such a strong team before.

Crisis catalyzed our growth. Purpose made it possible.

CHAPTER TWO RECAP

■ ■ ■ ■ ■ ■ ■ ■ ■ ■ ■

- Do you have the right troops to fight a crisis? Strong teams are the secret weapon when things go wrong.

- Here are the five areas you need to work in order to build a Category One Team:

  1. Capabilities and Infrastructure

  2. Goals and Purpose

  3. Roles and Individual Expectations

  4. Interactions and Team Processes

  5. Learning and Results

- When dealing with crisis, the way a team works needs to adjust in order to meet the situational landscape. Then, it's all about capabilities and readiness.

- There is no higher responsibility for a leader than to recruit, prepare and develop a high-performance team.

Tools & Resources

Team Effectiveness Assessment

It can be helpful to objectively and quickly assess the capabilities of your current team.

The methodology we used was originally developed by Linkage, Inc.

With such an assessment, you can quickly fill gaps and give yourself specific and overall development goals. The whole methodology and roadmap we successfully followed to transform our team is illustrated on my site www.christostsolkas.com

The Appreciation Tool

During a time of crisis, when people are under great strain, "Appreciation" can be a very useful tool. Diana Chapman, an amazing psychologist and coach, helped me understand the art of appreciation. Here is a short video where Diana explains the secrets of Appreciation https://conscious.is/video/the-four-keys-to-mastering-the-art-of-appreciation.

The process we followed is illustrated on my site www.christostsolkas.com.

CHAPTER THREE

Leaders of Yesterday and Tomorrow

In 2006, a young American named Blake set out to see the world. A lot of young people get the travel bug at some point. Some long to what see what life is like outside their home country. Some want to find themselves. A few are looking for ways to do some good and make a difference. Blake was open to all three possibilities. He was friendly and curious. He wanted to travel at a relaxed pace and spend time in areas tourists don't usually bother to visit. And he was interested in figuring out how to make the world a better place.

In other ways, Blake was not a typical young traveler. He grew up in a middle-class family in Texas, but he was a highly driven person. During high school, he was an exceptional tennis player, and he got a partial scholarship to college until an injury ended his career. Instead of continuing his education, however, he dropped out and started a dry cleaning service for students. The company grew quickly. As soon as he sold the business, he started another company, an outdoor billboard business which promoted country music. He sold that to Clear Channel nine months after launch.

Looking for some fun, Blake and his sister next auditioned for the reality TV show *Survivor*. They didn't make the cut, but they did hear about a new show called the *Amazing Race*, which sent couples on a race around the world. On the show's second season, Blake and his sister missed the million-dollar prize by just four minutes.

Moving to Los Angeles, Blake started a cable company focused on reality TV. The idea was great but the business got squashed by Fox. Blake started two more companies in quick succession before his fateful vacation in 2006.

The decision to visit Argentina came directly out of his experience in the Amazing Race. Racing around the world for the show, Blake and his sister had barely seen the country. This time he would slow down. In a chance encounter, he met volunteers giving shoes to people in need. Traveling with them, he became deeply moved by the poverty he saw. The wheels in his brain started turning. Soon, he had a very big idea that would change his life and the lives of many others.

Today, Blake Mycoskie is famous as the founder of TOMS Shoes, the company that donates a pair of shoes to a needy person in the developing world whenever a customer buys shoes for themselves. This kind of "social entrepreneurialism" is becoming increasingly popular in business, especially among startups. The TOMS Shoes' business model is fundamentally purpose-driven, and Blake Mycoskie is a very new kind of leader.

The Evolution of Leadership

Around 10 million soldiers died in World War I. Two out of three died in combat; the rest from disease.[14] The loss of so many soldiers was largely a failure of leadership. World War I was the first "industrial" war. Weapons were more powerful than in previous wars. Battles were fought more intensely over small patches of land. As trench warfare set in, the kings, queens, generals and politicians in charge did not know how to change mindsets or tactics. They were stuck in a mindset that saw war as romantic and chivalrous. They overlooked the need for organization, clear tactics, risk assessment, and process. Ordinary people paid a horrible price.

---

14   https://www.historyonthenet.com/how-many-people-died-in-ww1

In business, a new breed of managers responded differently as the industrialization age took hold. Henry Ford led the pack. His factories were able to churn out millions of moderately priced cars—cheaply, efficiently and at high quality. Ford's approach to management helped improve society by giving ordinary people access to products that would once have only been affordable by the very rich.

The business leaders who followed Ford continued to refine processes and use resources as efficiently as possible to reduce costs and maximize outputs. Frederick Winslow Taylor studied this approach and how it could be best organized.[15] Taylor's famous "stop-watch" research showed how manufacturing or industrial work could be broken down into precise tasks (called jobs) with procedures that worked best when they were made as standardized as possible. Those jobs were filled with employees who were trained to meet very specific requirements. The jobs were good and well-paying. The overall system was managed by layers of administrators with ever-broader scope of supervisory responsibility, until the CEO at the top—the administrator of administrators.

This approach to leadership was not very different from the oldest hierarchies in history.

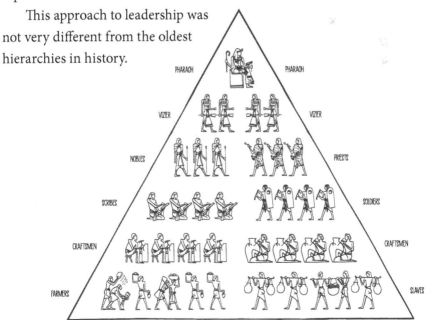

---

15   https://www.pbs.org/wgbh/theymadeamerica/whomade/taylor_hi.html

Such leadership was not glamorous, inspiring or romantic, but it did meet the needs of a rapidly industrializing world. Overnight, the world stopped being ruled by kings and queens and became ruled by men in gray flannel suits.

Managers were effective at getting things done. Society benefited. By the time World War II came around, pragmatic leaders were in charge. Logistics and organization were decisive factors in winning battles. Post-World War II, executives like Alfred Sloan, the CEO of General Motors, epitomized what good management looked like.[16] Researchers like Peter Drucker captured that evolution and articulated the modern theory of management.[17] They defined what good management looked like and showed how it created effective and efficient processes for generating quality, low-cost outputs. The American economy prospered—and most Americans shared in that growth. (Minorities are an obvious group who did not benefit as deeply or directly.)

The MBA, which formalized the study of the management sciences, was a profoundly American invention. Remember that MBA stands for Masters in Business Administration. That discipline focused originally on the core

---

16   https://en.wikipedia.org/wiki/Alfred_P._Sloan
17   https://hbr.org/1964/09/the-great-gm-mystery

processes of running a company which we think of now as functions, like finance, accounting, operations, marketing, and human resources. It had little to do with leadership as we think of it today.

Outside America, management followed a similar track in other countries post-World War II years. In Germany, business evolved from the traditions of medieval guilds, merchant associations, and chambers of commerce. German managers were very cognizant of the concerns of government and workers and yet were at the same time highly focused on the quality of products and the satisfaction of customers. As such, they became extremely efficient at processes. They were often engineers and scientists who turned their attention to the needs of the business.[18]

In France, managers are viewed as a separate and elite class of people defined by their intellect and their ability to solve complex problems.[19] As such, managers are highly networked among the other leaders of French society, including government and the military, and represent the "cream of the crop" of the ruling class. This shows the strong emphasis France puts on business management.

Japan was more like Germany in that it emphasized the improvement of industrial and organizational processes. Japan took the advances of productivity gurus like Edwards Deming[20] and put them on steroids, coming up with such approaches as Lean Production, just-in-time distribution, continuous improvement, Kaizen, and zero defects as ways to organize teams and workflow in order to minimize time, waste and cost while maximizing output and quality. Boosted by such techniques, Japanese manufacturers began to beat American manufacturers in terms of quality and price, most notably in the automobile industry, causing American business leaders to wonder how they had lost their special mojo.

---

18   http://www.photius.com/countries/germany/economy/germany_economy_the_culture_of_
     germa~1394.html

19   https://hbr.org/1991/07/the-making-of-a-french-manager

20   https://www.washingtonpost.com/archive/opinions/1993/12/23/japans-secret-w-edwards-
     deming/b69b8c00-4c5d-483a-b95e-4aeb1d94d2c6/?utm_term=.c48e2b1d9a78

MBA Meets *Mad Men*

John F. Kennedy was only forty-three years old when he was elected president of the United States. He won over Nixon, a very experienced former vice president, by bringing an unexpected skill. He understood style, image, personal brand and the medium of television like no candidate before him. Kennedy's prominence reflected a shift in a society looking for something more than just efficiency and practicality in leadership. That society also wanted inspiration, vision and style. This reflected a broader shift in the way people related to the products and services of business.

In the '50s, '60s, and '70s, as the U.S. and the world became more prosperous, a product's brand became almost as important as its function.

Efficient industrial manufacturing and the development of so many innovative new products generated tremendous economic growth and gave consumers more wealth and purchasing power as those goods also went down in price. At the same time, as more and more manufacturers competed with similar goods, the market became much more crowded. Businesses needed to distinguish themselves in the market to win over customers by convincing them why their products were different.

Branding is the art of differentiation. Iconic consumer products such as Coca-Cola, Campbell's Soup, and Marlboro Cigarettes became hugely successful because of marketing and sales. They made commodities appealing enough to sell widely at profitable prices.

Brands also represented an attempt at connecting with customers and employees through a sense of meaning and emotion. People were drawn to certain products and brands because they stood for something bigger or met certain emotional needs. The TV show *Mad Men* illustrated how effective this could be. Kodak's slide projector wheel, for example, got branded as a "carousel" because it reminded people of childhood memories of merry-go-rounds, which tied into a powerful nostalgia.

Leadership shifted accordingly, from its more "traditional" focus on process and efficiency to an emphasis on marketing and sales. Leaders had once been engineers, scientists or business administrators; increasingly, they were marketers who understood the power of brand. That sense of connection to brand also tied employees to their organizations. You were an IBM man or a GMC man—often loyal to a company for life.

Clarity, Credibility and Competence

By the early '70s, the tide was turning again. The Vietnam War had undermined confidence in American ideals. The oil shocks of the 1970s impeded economic growth. The Cold War intensified. Crime and unrest increased all over the world.

During this era of turmoil, people looked, understandably, for a new type of leader to follow. More than style or charisma, they wanted to be inspired by strength, certainty and simplicity; and they wanted to see results. President Ronald Reagan epitomized this quiet calm and inspiration. By the 1990s, corporations increasingly followed that lead. Jack Welch was the prototypical corporate leader of this era. No one doubted Welch's resolve, determination or follow-through. His clarity and simplicity was unambiguous. He declared that GE would be Number 1 or Number 2 in each of its markets or get out.[21] That was a measure of success everyone could judge and follow.

At the same time, the hierarchy of the organization was becoming flatter. Bosses increasingly had less authority and needed to become better at influencing. Communication and information became more important than ever. Women entered management and had different ways of relating and communicating. Relationships and networks became more important than command-and-control. Leadership got spread around.

Accordingly, good leadership became more sophisticated. A proliferation of leadership development training programs helped create "leaders at all levels" by emphasizing a balance of hard and soft skills. We still measured leadership on hard results, but we understood that those results were more achievable through persuasion, inspiration, charisma, trust, and so on.

---

21   https://hbr.org/1989/09/speed-simplicity-self-confidence-an-interview-with-jack-welch

The Era of Big Vision

The dot-com bubble of the late 1990s started to change our understanding of how to generate business growth and success. Managers who focused on efficiency and incremental improvement couldn't compete against leaders with vision for transformative change and massive growth. Suddenly, profits mattered less than potential, and small pioneers were stronger than established companies. This excitement for everything new and digital hit a wall with the dot-com crash of 2000, and yet the energy and ideas that were unleashed continue to have a lasting impact.

In this "break things and move fast" era, we are all about disruptive innovation. We even try to infuse a startup mentality in new and established businesses. Perhaps Peter Thiel, co-founder of PayPal and author of *Zero to One*, articulated these lessons best:

- It is better to risk boldness than triviality.

- A bad plan is better than no plan.

- Competitive markets destroy profits.

- Sales matters just as much as product.

Founder CEOs like Jeff Bezos and Larry Page do not think small, sweat failure or hesitate to enter new markets. They worry more about "global impact" and gaining and satisfying customers than about any product or profit.

The era of big vision is possible because of seven overarching trends that shape the paradigm of leadership of today.

Everything is Faster and More Connected

Today, the world is changing again, before our very eyes. Everything is interconnected, and information exchange is hyper-fast. Now any event or change can go global instantaneously. This has a profound impact on organizations and the type of leadership we need.

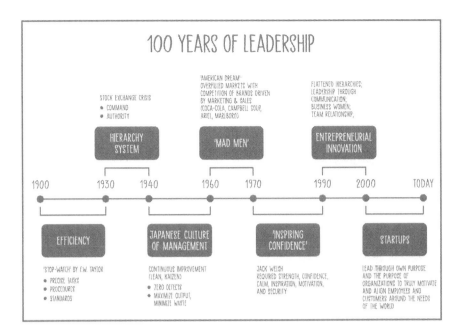

Here's a story to illustrate how fast things can change and how quickly the impact of a crisis can spread. A friend of mine lives in St. Paul, Minnesota. One evening, a few blocks from his house, a police officer stopped a car. The African American driver explained that he had a permit for a gun and reached for his wallet in the glove compartment. The officer panicked and shot him seven times. The driver's girlfriend captured the aftermath of this deadly encounter on her phone and streamed it via Facebook Live as her partner lay dying and a police officer continued to shout at him. Millions watched and the tragic death of Philando Castile, a cafeteria worker at a local school, became an international phenomenon, almost the instant it happened.

In Chaos Theory, there is a famous metaphor that a butterfly flapping its wings in New Mexico can eventually cause a hurricane in China.[22] Today, that's not a metaphor any longer. Anything a company does, or even anything that happens to a customer, can have an overwhelming impact on a business, positive or negative.

---

22   https://fractalfoundation.org/resources/what-is-chaos-theory/

The World is More Transparent

The interconnectedness of information has brought transparency to an extreme. On an individual level, we've gotten used to broadcasting our most intimate thoughts, moments and life stories on social media. Our movements are easily tracked at all times, so long as we are carrying a cell phone or IoT device. As we drive a car, walk down a city street, or enter a public building, it's likely that cameras are watching us. In our homes, an assortment of devices like Amazon's Alexa collect data on our habits, activities, wants and even our moods. Meanwhile, our personal information and the private details of our lives—health records, credit ratings, family pictures—are vulnerable to hacks. The very idea of privacy has been demolished.

Many CEOs and senior leaders are already public figures and subject to intense scrutiny. Like anyone, their personal lives are vulnerable to exposure. Details about compensation and investments are easily discovered by anyone who wants to dig. The things they say or do on the job can be leaked by hackers, disgruntled employees, or colleagues with a political axe to grind.

Some loathe the lack of privacy, others embrace it. Intuit CEO Geoff Colvin is into radical transparency. He believes that transparency is good for business. He creates open platforms for any company, even a competitor, to build applications on Intuit products. And he shares sensitive information to employees as a way of increasing collaboration and trust. For example, every year Colvin emails his own unvarnished performance review to all employees.[23] Colvin gets that it's impossible to hide anything today!

The bottom line is this: Leaders are no longer just people who happen to run a company; they are more than public figures; they are political and cultural lightning rods.

---

23   http://fortune.com/2017/10/20/data-sheet-intuit-ceo-brad-smith/

People (Customers) Have More Freedom of Expression and Choice than Ever

As the Arab Spring, the EuroMaidan movement, and the 2018 March for Our Lives led by American teenagers shows, governments no longer control freedom of expression easily. Social media and smartphones make it possible for anyone to let their voice be heard.

While there are many positive aspects to freedom of expression and choice, there are also downsides. Many people lament the lack of civility on social media platforms. People can say whatever they want with little consequence. Opinions are also, increasingly, more powerful than facts. Recent studies show that fake news spreads faster than truth online.[24] Groups that think alike are more likely to stick together than intermingle with others.

In this Wild West of free expression, people are able to choose what they believe or don't believe. They are also quicker to align themselves more tightly with those they agree with. Where we live and who we see every day matters less and less compared to whose views we side with or what perspectives we consume. This makes a sense of purpose—a directional compass—more important than ever.

Young People Feel Entitled to Lead and are Quick to Assume Leadership

Every generation looks back and criticizes the generation that's coming up behind them. For my generation and older—baby boomers and Gen-Xers—the target of our criticism is millennials.

Millennials get accused of everything under the sun. They are too pampered, too lazy, not practical enough, lack focus or concentration, you name it.

For whatever reason, psychologists believe that millennials have a greater sense of entitlement than other generations. Perhaps they were raised to feel special or unique. Perhaps freedom of expression and choice allow them

---

24   https://www.nytimes.com/2018/03/08/technology/twitter-fake-news-research.html

to feel more powerful than the generation before them did. Whatever the case may be, millennials tend to disregard the rules and assume roles of leadership at an early and, some would say, inappropriate age.[25]

A good example comes from the students of Marjory Stoneman Douglas High School in Parkland, FL. After a shooter killed seventeen of their classmates on Valentine's Day in 2018, the students immediately took a political stance for more gun control. Pro-gun politicians, news organizations and the NRA criticized the students for expressing political opinions when they were so young and unsophisticated. The students cried "BS!" to that put-down, and made their voices even louder, demanding that legislative changes go into effect. Using social media tools they debated critics, pressured politicians and organized fellow students in a march on Washington.

Once upon a time, most people waited to be "senior" enough or experienced enough to assume a position and voice of leadership. A generation of young people today see no reason to wait and no reason why they shouldn't lead. Like all younger generations, they also tend to be more idealistic and "purposeful" than those who are older.

Teams Matter More than Ever

Leonardo da Vinci was a painter, sculptor, inventor, military expert, anatomist and scientist. He did it all, and that's why they called him a Renaissance Man.

That myth of the Renaissance Man lives on but, in reality, they were far from the norm. Most people in the Renaissance were specialists—farmers, soldiers, craftsmen, priests, monks. They specialized in one particular thing. In fact, groups of specialists often banded together to increase their security and power in guilds, monasteries and unions. Early companies were very specialized, too. They manufactured one thing, provided one service or focused on one market.

---

25   https://www.indy100.com/article/young-people-entitlement-disappointed-narcissism-psychology-research-7867961

This continues today. We train and hire for specialization and expertise. We can also access expertise instantly and cheaply. Ivy League schools broadcast lectures on podcasts. Great teachers provide in-depth tutorials on Khan Academy or MasterClass. Anyone who needs to do anything can find a YouTube video explaining how.

As expertise matters less, we increasingly need people from different specialties and areas of expertise to come together on one task, project or cause. They must somehow communicate and collaborate effectively.

Leadership must align teams around a shared sense of energy, direction, cohesion, resilience and creativity.

Value Chains Are Expanding

When a company comes up with some innovative new product or service, it strives to get it to the market quickly so as to enjoy dominant market share as long as possible before competitors come in with a similar product, win customers and cause prices to drop. Everyone knows that product life cycle is now faster than ever.

I had the good fortune and opportunity to study this at Stanford University. Major innovations often occur when companies change previously dependent attributes. For example, the traditional taxi business has a number of dependent attributes which are necessary for customers and drivers to do business. Uber disrupted that process by radically changing existing or adding new attributes. Traditionally, customers call or hail a cab to get a ride, which is an unpredictable and often time-consuming experience. Uber lets you do so by app, instantly, and you can even follow the progress of your taxi on your phone. Traditionally, taxi drivers needed to be licensed and cars needed to be registered. Uber removes those barriers, allowing anyone and any vehicle to participate. Traditionally, when the ride is over you pay with cash or credit card. With Uber you hop out because your ride is already paid for. If you want, you can even rate your driver, too. The driver has the same functionality.

Value chains also change the nature of competiion. Markets used to move up and down verticals within distinct zones of influence. For example, Ford made cars and sold them through dealers. IBM made computers and sold them. In contrast, some new businesses engage with consumers in multiple aspects of their lives. A company like Uber, collecting massive amounts of customer data, knows where you live and many other habits, such as, possibly, how you commute, where you like to go for entertainment and how late you come home. This can lead to a whole range of ancillary services. Uber could get into the tour business or deliver meals or transport patients. In fact, it's doing all those things.

Today, your competitor is not just your competitor. Your competitor may also be your supplier, your customer and even your employee. Customers, partners and service providers can be in collaboration or competition with one another at the same time. The most sophisticated components of any process today can be outsourced, offshored, made and delivered from places that you don't know, and you don't need to know. The goal is the purpose and the customer.

Trust in Leadership Is Down

Even as leaders with giant visions took over industry after industry, another countervailing force influenced our society. For the first time since the 1960s, people have stopped trusting traditional leaders and the establishment.

Even people in the leadership development business don't think leadership is working anymore. A 2018 memo by McKinsey noted:

> The almost insatiable demand for leadership studies is a natural outgrowth of the all-too-frequent leadership failures in government, business, and nonprofits. Few people trust their leaders, according to the Edelman Trust Barometer surveys, among others. Gallup data show low levels of employee engagement worldwide, while the Conference Board finds job satisfaction at a low ebb and executive tenures decreasing. Other research consistently indicates that companies give their

own leadership-development efforts low marks. Leaders aren't doing a good job for themselves or their workplaces, and things don't seem to be improving.[26]

I believe trust in leadership shifted because of the very failures the McKinsey author describes. Think of the chaos we've experienced in the past twenty years. Enron. The dot-com crash. 9-11. The Iraq War. The mortgage crisis and Great Recession of 2008. Financial turmoil in the EU. The collapse of the Middle East. Protests against the 1 percent. Skyrocketing CEO pay. Unemployment and stress. Stagnant wages and wealth growth. Terrorism. The Syrian refugee crisis. Brexit. Fake News. Russia-Gate. Cambridge Analytica hack.

Lack of faith in traditional leadership has intensified as a result of this turmoil and confusion. Leaders were supposed to be our guardian angels, but many turned out to be ineffective at best or villains at worst. All the old attributes of leadership—expertise, experience, practical know-how and charisma—seem less and less believable with each failure or scandal.

As we've lost faith in leaders, we've begun to look for something different. Many are seeking values and principles they can believe in, embodied in leaders who seem to live those values in a pure way. We're looking for leaders with clarity of purpose.

Riding the Wave of Change

Today's old-school leaders are professional managers hired for their competence and rewarded for their results. Their ability to inspire is, at best, a secondary consideration. Most sound artificial, bland and inauthentic.

A new era of business leaders has gained in prominence over the past few years. A generation of CEO/founders is creating movements as much as they are building companies. They are driven by needs beyond business. They put at least some of their focus on "What the world needs" instead.

---

26   https://www.mckinsey.com/featured-insights/leadership/getting-beyond-the-bs-of-
      leadership-literature

A leader like Blake Mycoskie manages to integrate business objectives with a passion for having an impact on the world's problems.

His journey to this end started like a kind of quest. Exploring the world, he collected raw data about needs and problems. Tapping the experiences of others, he turned this data into information and eventually knowledge. Seeing the desperate need for shoes among the poor in developed countries, Mycoskie decided to figure out how to alleviate that need. His first thought was a charity, but his entrepreneurial experience and brain sent him down another tract. Donations could always run out, and charities constantly scramble just to fulfill their mission. But a for-profit business, properly leveraged, could become a shoe-donation machine.

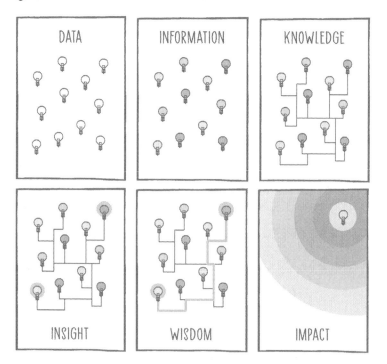

This was Mycoskie's critical insight. He describes the idea as, "Sell a pair of shoes today, give a pair of shoes tomorrow." His wisdom came from understanding human behavior. Mycoskie understood that customers who wanted to help make the world a better place would also be motivated to buy TOMS shoes.

This vision gave Mycoskie even more energy and focus than his previous endeavors. He entered a business he knew little about, solved all problems that came his way, and sold friends, investors and an industry on the power of that story. TOMS shoes grew fast and customers loved that they could help others in need simply by buying something. TOMS continues to expand its "one for one" business model with a new product each year.

This model is not without its critics. Some say that the approach undermines local producers by making foreign goods available. It doesn't have to be that way, and regardless, many companies have followed TOMS with their own "one for one" models. Warby Parker sells and distributes eyeglasses; Roma Boots sells and gives away boots; Nouri Bar donates a meal for a hungry child for every nutritional bar it sells; Sir Richard's sells and donates condoms; KNO Clothing gives away clothes and donates to homeless shelters; Soapbox Soaps donates a month of water, a bar of soap, or a year of vitamins for each soap product it sells, and so on.[27]

Other companies have adopted a variation of this model called the 1 percent pledge. In this approach, companies offer a percentage of their executive time, products, and so on, to those in need.[28] Salesforce, Altasian and YELP are among the pioneers of this movement. But my personal view is that a 1 percent philanthropic gift is less sustainable and less organizationally empowering because the approach is not tied into the business model and success of the company. It's an add-on or a nice-to-have that can also go away.

The model of the new purpose leader is still evolving. But here are some of the attributes that are important.

1. A purpose leader stands for something

Few people would ask a traditional CEO what he or she stands for socially and politically. The answer would barely be relevant. But ask a leader of purpose what he or she stands for and you will get a clear answer.

---

27 https://knowledge.wharton.upenn.edu/article/one-one-business-model-social-impact-avoiding-unintended-consequences/

28 https://pledge1percent.org/

Jane Chen, the co-founder of Embrace, developed a product to help millions of poor premature babies.

Elon Musk wants to reduce the planet's consumption of fossil fuels.

Muhammad Yunus believes in economic opportunity for the poor and developed a microlending bank to help them become business entrepreneurs.

2. A purpose leader has background and personality

Traditional leaders struggle to tell us something about themselves that stands out. They are more about what they do than who they are. In fact, we are suspicious when their backgrounds are too colorful. Purpose leaders have very clear stories with compelling backgrounds. Who they are is part of what attracts and inspires people.

3. A purpose leader tells a story

Today, there's so much noise and confusion that normal messages and brands can't get through. Purpose connects to people by telling stories. Bullet points, details, and even facts are far less important than story. People don't want to listen with their ears and brains, they listen with their bodies. I'm not suggesting that purpose leaders do not have any experience or practical know-how. Far from it. They can be very effective and strategic, but they must also be something more. No era starts with a blank slate. Every new era builds from a foundation of what came before it.

Even though leadership became about marketing in the *Mad Men* era, it still required leaders who could manage processes and operations.

Leaders in the '80s and '90s were a combination of managerial abilities and salesmanship. That's how they motivated and inspired while also running their organizations effectively.

While the idea of servant leadership originated in the early 1970s, it has only really become a popular concept in the past ten years, as leaders began to recognize that their most effective role as leaders was not to serve themselves but to make the people around them successful.

The purpose leader of today retains all of those phases and capabilities while also connecting to people in a much more meaningful and authentic way.

This is becoming essential for success in our modern era. People, especially young idealistic millennials, are very suspicious of inauthenticity and greed. They are no longer seeking employment just for the money but want to contribute to something bigger than themselves, often by helping to make the world a better place. They are looking, in other words, for purpose.

Customers, too, are increasingly looking for something more than just low prices and high quality. They want goods and services that have been ethically made with a sense of environmental stewardship and social responsibility. They want to connect to the brands and businesses they support—not just through the product itself but through the sense of shared purpose aligned with that company and product.

The successful leaders of the future will be different from the past, in that they will not need to craft or design their "authentic purpose" but will have developed and shaped it as a matter of living. They will embody that purpose with integrity. They will not need to try and tie purpose to their business or career but will start or lead their business or cause to make their purpose have broader impact.

The fundamental nature of leadership has changed. It's no longer about competence. Now, it's about purpose. People are looking for meaning, significance, impact and strong emotional connection.

Purpose is the new leadership.

CHAPTER THREE RECAP

- Today many talk about purpose. That purpose reflects and communicates the impact of our work, our business operations, and the essence of our company to others. Purpose-Driven Leadership means we do business while doing good for the world (not only our customers but also non-users of our product or service offering).

- Over the past one hundred years, leadership has gone through different stages—these are the ancestors of today's Leadership model.

- Today's Leadership model is driven by: speed and hyper-connectivity, the need for transparency, the increased freedom of expression and choice, a sense of entitlement (especially of the young), the hightened importance of teams, a change in competition from linear to multidimensional value chains, the lack of strong ideological narratives and the loss of trust in institutions.

- Essentially the new Leadership paradigm transforms the nature and model of business itself.

Tools & Resources

Storytelling

I am a strong believer that stories help us understand organizations and teams, deliver important messages, and help build your leadership persona. Dr. Jennifer Aaker from Stanford University opened my eyes to the power of stories. I recommend spending a few minutes watching one of her videos (on my site www.christostsolkas.com you can see all references).

Generational Changes and Leadership Entitlement

As a Gen-X leader, I need to stay in tune with the attitudes, beliefs and wants and needs of younger employees. Millennials and Gen-Zs, for example, feel a strong sense that they have a leadership role to play, especially when it comes to Level One problems, regardless of their position in the hierarchy or tenure in the organization. This is a major driver in this new era of leadership.

Simon Sinek refers to this as leadership "entitlement". On my site www.christostsolkas.com you can find the link of his revealing talk which helped me understand the whole dynamic.

The Critical Importance of Teams

Teams seem to be more important than ever today. My favorite book about teams describes how teams can achieve success by being fluid, versatile and trust-based. I encourage you to read it.

CHAPTER FOUR

Purpose Drives Growth—Discovering Your Truth

CEOs are highly motivated individuals. But their big job is to motivate other people, sometimes tens of thousands of them, to perform better and ultimately drive company growth. The most powerful means of motivation is purpose. Here's an example.

From its launch in 1975, Microsoft grew like crazy. By 1998, it was the largest company in the world, but by 2000 co-founder Bill Gates was ready to transition out of the CEO role. This is a difficult shift for any company, especially one as successful as Microsoft.

For his replacement, Gates chose Steve Ballmer. Ballmer was an interesting and understandable pick. He was the thirtieth employee ever hired by the company, and obviously knew its business and culture inside and out. He had been a successful salesman, driving some of Microsoft's biggest product wins. He was also highly driven and passionate. His motivational style was legendary, however, and not for the right reasons. His speeches to employees, in which he bounded onto the stage, flung his body around and screamed about how much he loved the company, attracted attention for all the wrong reasons. Videos of his performances went viral.

Still, Ballmer lasted fourteen years as CEO, four years longer than corporate America's average. By many measures, his tenure was a success. He moved Microsoft away from computers and toward services, networks and solutions. He acquired or developed a number of very interesting businesses (though others failed spectacularly). Significantly, Microsoft's revenues also kept growing. The company returned, in 2014, to the very lofty position of world's second most valuable company in terms of market capitalization, behind only ExxonMobil.

Yet, most people view Ballmer's leadership at Microsoft as mixed or even a failure. The main reason was hard to measure yet impossible not to feel. During his reign, Microsoft lost relevancy as a company. Over that fourteen-year period, dynamic competitors like Google, Apple and Amazon rocked the world by creating and then dominating entirely new markets. In the process, they had an enormous impact, changing the way billions of consumers work, live and even think. In comparison, Microsoft was well-run and its business units made lots of money. But the company didn't seem to stand for anything besides revenue growth and operational efficiency. It wasn't an organization that people thought about when they were looking for an answer to some unmet need. It was just Microsoft—too big to be forgotten but not particularly worth thinking about.

Satya Nadella, Microsoft's current CEO, couldn't be more different than Ballmer. An unlikely success story, he grew up in India, got rejected by India's version of MIT and was far more interested in cricket than computers. In America, he studied at a run-of-the-mill college in Wisconsin, not a Harvard, Stanford or USC. Perhaps this background explains Nadella's humble and highly open approach to leadership. As the new CEO of Microsoft, he started by asking some very basic questions: "What is it that we should do? What's the sensibility that would be lost if we should disappear?" Technology trends come and go, but Microsoft needed to stand for something eternal.

One of the answers came out of a difficult personal experience. He and his wife have a child with cerebral palsy. Nadella has spent many nights in hospital emergency rooms as a result. On one of those nights, Nadella looked around at the equipment in his son's room and realized that everything was powered by Microsoft. Suddenly, he felt a deeper sense of meaning in the company's work that went beyond just devices and services. Microsoft was actually changing and improving people's lives. This realization informed his beliefs about the difference the company could and should make in the world. In a very real sense, Nadella discovered (or rediscovered) Microsoft's purpose and made it real for others.

For example, as CEO, Nadella made "accessibility" a big part of Microsoft's new focus. This manifested in inclusion programs for employees with disabilities like blindness and autism. But it also figured into Microsoft's drive for innovation. Artificial intelligence, for example, "completely changes the game around accessibility," Nadella says. Windows 10 is built with gaze-tracking capabilities that can help people who are paralyzed. Microsoft's "Seeing AI" app helps identify objects for the visually impaired. The company's work in virtual reality and holograms supports their video game products, but it has also been applied to tools and services for medical doctors to operate on cancerous tumors and for medical students to learn anatomy. AI and VR, in Nadella's words, can "empower humans to do more, achieve more."

There's no question in Nadella's mind that he developed this sense of empathy for the vulnerable and less fortunate because of his child's serious physical and medical needs. Nadella insists that empathy is not just a nice human quality, however; it's a source of innovation. Most companies listen to customers to figure out how to sell them more stuff. Empathy helps you listen to customers and figure out what they really need to improve their lives.

Today, Microsoft is in business to "empower every person and every organization on the planet to achieve more." To make that happen, Nadella has fostered a very collaborative and open culture that values continual learning and a growth mindset. As a result, Microsoft is doing a better job attracting talent motivated by this purpose, building strategic partnerships and listening to customers. Microsoft is now a growth stock once more, its share price doubling under Nadella's watch, after a long period of stagnation with Ballmer.

Purpose has fueled its innovation and growth.

Searching for Urgency

In Ukraine, I experienced how crisis could ignite a sense of purpose which helped us develop as a team and improve performance. After I left Ukraine,

I wondered how that sense of urgency and energy could be replicated when crisis was missing. Was crisis necessary for purpose? If so, were there different kinds of crises than the one I experienced?

This became a very personal question. When I rotated back to our corporate HQ in Lausanne, all that urgency and energy I felt leading a team left me, and I experienced a lack of purpose in my own life. Like a professional athlete after the season ends or a musician after a concert, I crashed emotionally after my adrenaline rush was over. I had also just tuned fifty and was wondering what to do with my life—a difficult personal combination! If I wasn't sure how to find my own purpose, I also didn't know how to instill it in my new team.

Ukraine was the Wild West. Anything could happen at any time. Lausanne, in comparison, is a peaceful utopia. As I write this book, I'm still living here and I love it. Switzerland is one of the most beautiful, prosperous and progressive countries in the world. Stunning mountains. Beautiful lakes. Healthy people. Vibrant economy. The citizens of Switzerland believe in their country and feel a strong sense of connection and commitment to their society. They work hard, play hard, and live well. What's not to appreciate, respect and love about that?

But my new life was also a little boring at first, and I felt isolated from my old colleagues and out of touch. My change in role was particularly tough. In Ukraine, I'd been a line manager who literally put his life on the line. I loved having a big diverse territory encompassing four different countries with many direct reports, a factory and a large sales force. I got excited by ambitious performance targets and the opportunity to test new strategies and innovations in operations and marketing, knowing that ultimately the success or failure of those initiatives was mine. I appreciated how the pressure of the crisis in Ukraine tested our mental and physical resiliency. I enjoyed the camaraderie of a team in "battle" together, and even the emotional roller-coaster of the unpredictable ups and downs.

Then it ended. In Switzerland, all that responsibility and excitement was gone. My company gave me an impressive title—I was named head of sales strategy for the global sales organization—but there was little substance to the job. Officially, I was now responsible for coordinating and developing strategy, and tasked with creating a new vision for the company in the sales space. My team was there to help develop and deliver those services to our internal customers—the various sales organizations in territories around the world. But we had no authority over those affiliates and only acted in an advisory role as consultants. Suddenly, I went from managing a territory with a significant budget, lots of people and ambitious sales goals to working from a small office at the end of a quiet corridor with a small team, no territory, and no real numbers to hit.

I started wondering, theoretically, how any team could capture or replicate the feelings we'd had during the Ukrainian crisis under more normal business conditions.

This seems particularly challenging in a big company. Although there's always lots of pressure to perform in an established corporate environment, the system tends to dampen strong feelings, excitement and drama. Even when bold ideas or convictions emerge, they often seem to dissipate or become diminished by the bureaucratic processes of the organization. The new marketing strategy gets its sharp edges smoothed off by the lawyers or the middle managers. The customer-first declaration of the CEO gets effectively ignored because the finance function demands that quarterly results need to be hit, no matter what customers really need. It makes me understand why someone like Steve Ballmer might feel the urge to scream and throw himself around the stage: He's trying to cut through the layers of complacency and stir up some passion.

High-performing organizations are very good at doing what they have always done. Producing products. Delivering services. Growing market share. Improving processes incrementally. For many years of my career, this is exactly what I helped do. The game was clear. Our leaders set goals that pushed us hard. We needed to plan, strategize, think, convince, manage, inspire, lead—and some of the things we did felt like "change" because they were slightly different than before. But they weren't fundamentally or radically different, and I don't think their emotional impact was all that powerful—we didn't feel like our lives changed as a result; we weren't inseparable as a team; we didn't grow incredibly quickly as people and leaders.

When I thought about that and looked around at all the different companies I knew, I realized something interesting. Absent a crisis, the closest example of the environment we'd experienced in Ukraine was at startups. Accordingly, I started studying startup culture wherever I could find it, from small companies in Europe to exciting ventures in Silicon Valley. What I learned supported my instincts.

Project Startup

The best startups have an "us against the world" mentality. The people in them work incredibly hard, sometimes for very little reward, and bond very closely, much like my teams in Ukraine and Greece had bonded during our "tent time." People develop rapidly in a startup environment, too. They need to make decisions quickly with little data, so they just go ahead and make them. In the process of shouldering that responsibility and learning from failure and mistakes, they grow as leaders. There's also very little bureaucratic administration in startups to dampen exciting ideas or slow down decisions. On the other hand, there's usually little financial runway to last long if you make mistakes. This ensures that startups, in a sense, are always in crisis mode. The business idea may be great, but the company, for any number of financial, operational, competitive or personal reasons, can fall apart at any moment.

Finally, there's another thing I noticed that startups do well. They're incredible attuned to the outside world. In a big corporation, it's easier to basically ignore the outside world and listen and respond to your own organizational voices instead. Everyone talks about how important the customer is to a business, but most people in big companies are more concerned about meeting internal priorities and demands. In a startup, the customer is everything. You have to figure out what the customer wants, how the customer thinks, what the customer needs in order to have a chance with them. Then you try out whatever service or product idea you come up with and see if it meets those needs. When it doesn't, you ask more questions, get more data, and try again. You become, to paraphrase Nadella, an empathy machine.

This helped me frame a purpose for my Global Sales-Strategy team.

When it came to sales, my view was that our larger company's biggest need was to give more autonomy and decision-making power to people on the front line. Like entrepreneurs in their own company, those people needed to feel a sense of ownership and urgency to be more innovative, make meaningful decisions, and help advance the organization's vision and strategic goals in a much more dynamic consumer world.

I'd seen how that sense of empowerment helped my team in Ukraine. During our crisis, we learned how to take complete ownership over a situation and make fast decisions in line with our vision and goals. We had no sense of "it's not my problem." We were focused externally, on the changing world, rather than internally on our bureaucratic processes and priorities. So that's the spirit I decided we should instill in our global sales team. The question was, how?

Ironically, like a startup, I had few resources at my disposal. I also couldn't tell people what to do or how they needed to change. I could explain why they should change and I could try to persuade them through meetings and presentations, but I didn't have any illusions that this would lead to a meaningful impact. Even if some people were sort of inspired by my talks and wanted to change, they wouldn't be equipped to think differently or adopt new approaches.

What I really needed to do was create a mind shift, and not just in one person or even in the managing directors all over the world, but in many people. In other words, I needed to inspire a culture change in which people would act and think more like the people who work in startups.

How could my team and I infuse that "startup culture" in the global sales force without any resources, authority or mandate? We were just a very small group of strategists occupying an ordinary corridor. The global sales force was the enormous "empire," a huge machine doing what it has done for decades. But, it's also true that startups overturn industries all the time. No one expected Apple and Microsoft to become bigger than IBM, or Airbnb to challenge the hotel industry, or Walmart to overthrow Sears.

Startups start small and change the world. So, I decided to turn my little group into a startup and figure out how to drive that mindset and culture into our larger organization.

Inside the Corridor

I told our team we could have an outsized influence on the whole organization by influencing the culture of the global sales force. Our company needed to change because the world was changing. Outside forces beyond our control were affecting our business. We could serve as a model for how the company should operate and spread that way of working like a virus. Here are the steps we took to make that happen:

Step 1: Adopt the mindset of a founder

The first step was personal. Though our organization is very hierarchical, I needed to act like a founder of a startup to establish a culture that was different than our larger company. I made very practical changes to my leadership priorities as a result.

For example, corporate executives usually want corner offices, big budgets and lots of direct reports. Startup founders don't care about any of that stuff. They have minimal resources, staff and time. They'd rather test ideas with a "minimal viable product" than develop and launch a brand from A to Z.

This can be a difficult shift in mindset for any corporate executive, and requires new ways of thinking about success and progress, but it's also very freeing.

Step 2: Focus less on execution and more on the type of people you want

At a startup, you want creative, empowered people who come up with new solutions on their own initiative. You're creating an ecosystem in which people thrive on hard work, bonding and fun. To recruit talent for my team, I focused on millennials because, according to Gallup, they are particularly inspired by an organization that has a strong sense of purpose they can believe in and that makes them feel their job matters.[29] I also believed millennials would respond better to a looser hierarchy and a more collaborative culture. I tried to encourage my people to think laterally, not linearly, about problems. My motto was, "Think like an artist, not an engineer!"

Step 3: Build the right space

At Lausanne HQ, we built a space where people would enjoy hanging out, using as little budget as possible. We bought IKEA furniture and put in more couches and coffee tables than desks and chairs, and got a cheap foosball table and a stereo. This really changed the way people worked and interacted, and made our office more inviting. We were a lot more social and traded ideas all the time and got up and moved around when we talked, and we encouraged others to come hang out as a way of winning converts with a sign that said, "Coffee & Friends!" People who came for meetings didn't want to go back to their own offices. When team members were transferred out, they didn't want to leave!

---

29   http://news.gallup.com/businessjournal/197486/millennials-not-connecting-company-mission.aspx

Workspace changes the way you think and relate to others.[30] Every time I visit Silicon Valley, I enjoy seeing the different ways American companies help people be more creative, interactive and productive at work.

Step 4: Figure out what customers need

Established companies struggle with innovation because they focus on incremental improvements to existing processes and products. At startups, you start with customer needs first and reverse engineer an approach to deliver those needs. Our customers were the internal sales teams around the organization. We spent a lot of time talking to them. Most of the conversations boiled down to the "5 Whys Technique"[31] which I'll discuss in more detail in Chapter Six. The goal is to start with a problem and follow a chain of questions to determine its ultimate source.

When that doesn't work, I find it helpful to get the customer to tell you a story of a crisis they've experienced, such as a customer relationship gone wrong, a supply problem, a financial scandal, etc. This way, you discover what is important to the customer, and help identify their purpose.

From a corridor to an ant colony

Turning our little team into a sort of startup energized us all and rejuvenated me personally. It gave our team a feeling of power and optimism about the impact a small group can have on a much bigger organization.

Our focus wasn't on a product, but on culture and the way of thinking. Our goal was to be a source of creative disruption to ordinary approaches inside the company. We knew we couldn't order anyone to follow our suggestions, so we had to learn how to market and sell our ideas. This was challenging for me, personally. At times, I was anxious and pushed boundaries by overselling our ideas and plans. Now, I believe that introducing innovation in a big corporation requires timing. Moving too quickly is as

---

30   https://www.economist.com/news/business/21721423-their-eccentric-buildings-offer-clues-about-how-people-will-work-technology-firms-and-office

31   https://www.huffingtonpost.com/mitch-ditkoff/why-you-need-to-ask-why_b_2681958.html

big a mistake as offering up the wrong idea. Startup founders struggle with those things, too. They need to effectively pitch their ideas and passion to investors, suppliers, people and customers in order to have an impact.

Our investors and stakeholders were the people in other departments and geographies. We tried to pass on our message by being an example of what a startup culture feels like and how it thinks, and we also learned how to talk to them about what we were up to at every opportunity, from formal presentations to elevator pitches. We wanted to win "mindshare" to win market share. So, we networked a lot, and in the process our single corridor became connected to other parts of the company, like an ant colony, carrying ideas and people back and forth, and helping to bring change everywhere.

We made real progress.

We created a signature event that helped us reach our sales groups around the world with some simple core messages.

We brought together business thinkers, founders, strategists, academics and specialists on digital and retail strategies as well as automation and robotics. For the first time, our large global organization opened its doors to startups and encountered ideas like Design Thinking, 10X Growth, and Lean innovation. We created a lot of enthusiasm, planned more global events and got great commitment from many groups. We created traction for our existing business model while helping advance a more forward-looking perspective.

There was only one thing we were missing. Our purpose was to change the mindset and behaviors of our global sales force. But this wasn't meaningful enough to really drive innovation and growth. We needed to think bigger. So, in 2016, I asked my team to start researching how purpose can spur innovation and drive growth.

Studying Purpose

To analyze the link between purpose and innovation and growth, we decided to look at a wide range of companies over the past fifteen years, assessing whether their purpose had an impact on their success or growth.

We only looked at companies in the Fortune 500 because we believed it would be easier to verify performance. We started in one sector, Food & Beverage, and then broadened out across eight other sectors ranging from High Tech to Motor Vehicles and Telecoms, focusing on the top three to five companies in each sector. These ranged from established companies to recent startups.

We were looking, in particular, for companies that seemed to have a strong, emotionally resonant sense of purpose internally, as well as a well-developed external focus on the deeper needs of their customers and the world. We analyzed mission statements and the way these companies focused on problems or needs that were linked with their purpose. We also assessed how clearly their business models were aligned with creating impact on their sector, on society or on the world.

The Food & Beverage sector may not strike you as exciting compared to high-growth tech companies like Amazon, Google or Apple. Nevertheless, it was interesting to see that the five largest global companies in that sector, Danone, PepsiCo, Nestle, Unilever, and Mondelez, have deliberately shifted the way they do business to align their purpose more closely with their growth algorithm and strategy.

Paris-based Danone is at the forefront of this change. It has linked itself to health and nutrition from its founding in 1919 with a mission to achieve "health through food" by encouraging healthier eating habits and sourcing practices. Since 1972, Danone has been deliberately applying that ideal to shape its approach to doing business. Specifically, Danone develops, markets and sells products in collaboration with local stakeholders and in consideration of local needs, cultures, and economic circumstances. This helps Danone advance its purpose to reduce world hunger and improve nutrition and sourcing while also achieving growth and market share.

The approach still plays out decades later. In 2006, Grameen Bank founder, Muhammad Yunus, partnered with Danone to develop a Bangladesh-based enterprise, Grameen Danone, launched to develop nutritious yogurt that local populations could afford. The company leveraged local saleswomen to sell an inexpensive product on commission and build interest before developing local production facilities to meet demand. That strategy aligned purpose (reduce malnutrition and poverty) with practice (a workable business model that helped Danone enter and establish growth in a new market). As a result, Grameen Danone developed new products and approaches that are hard for other companies to compete with or copy. The pursuit of purpose, in other words, has helped the company develop and scale an appealing product that not only meets the market need for taste and affordability and improves health and nutrition, but also boxes out competitors.

Danone isn't alone in this. Unilever, a company that shuns short-term profitability over long-term growth objectives, especially in emerging markets, tries to develop brands linked to distinct social causes. It has found that those brands grow at twice the speed of brands without a clear purpose. Putting its money where its mouth is, Unilever also promises to pull its ads from social media platforms that proliferate toxic content.[32]

Nestle has organized its business around thirty-nine commitments to social value, in areas such as nutrition (e.g., reduce salt and sugar in products), rural development (e.g., implement responsible sourcing), water (e.g., increase efficient use and sustainability), the environment (e.g., improve packaging), and human rights (e.g., eliminate child labor). Rather than limit themselves to one purpose, this approach aligns them to many different purposes that impact the world.

PepsiCo has shaped its growth strategy around its "Performance with Purpose" outlook, and is investing in sustainable agriculture and environmental practices that serve their purpose and profitability goals. An example is its LIFEWTR product line and the introduction of Bubly sparkling water.

---

32 https://www.businessinsider.com/unilever-threatens-to-reduce-digital-ad-spend-2018-2?r=US&IR=T

One of Pepsi's goals is to ensure that by 2025 two-thirds of its global beverage portfolio volume will have 100 calories or fewer.[33]

Mondelez, reliant on innovation and talent to win market share in a highly competitive environment, has essentially outsourced its innovation function to a network of startups and retailers to develop new consumer offerings, linking those products more closely to customer needs.

Seeing how clearly these companies leverage purpose in their business, I wondered whether corporations in the Food & Beverage sector focus on socially productive issues because they are vulnerable to consumer and environmental criticism, and closely linked to health, nutrition, and sourcing issues.

Nevertheless, these companies weren't just ticking boxes on a public-relations-oriented CSR effort. They were actively leveraging purpose to motivate employees, meet deep customer needs AND achieve growth, profitability, and competitive advantage.

Purpose and Business Model Together

This was an exciting discovery for us! We realized that companies with a clear purpose not only connect their employees and their customers to something meaningful, they also integrate that with their business model. This outward focus helps them see the world, society and the marketplace differently. It gives them an ability to spot problems and opportunities more clearly, and it actually drives them to become more innovative than ordinary competitors in filling those needs or gaps with urgency. This, in turn, drives higher levels of performance and growth.

Not all companies were equally idealistic, as the examples from the Food & Beverage industry also show. Some companies are very global and altruistic in focus. They openly strive to "make the world a better place." Others are more concerned with immediate customers and market pressures. They want to satisfy customers with better products or lower prices or more efficient processes. This does not indicate a defect or flaw in one purpose

---

33   https://www.bevindustry.com/articles/90919-pepsico-launches-bubly-sparkling-water

or a virtue or strength in another. Instead, the difference is an indication of where that company is strategically focused.

This analysis, which I'll explore in more detail in Chapters Five and Six, helped me resolve some long-unanswered questions. Like many people, I have had "mixed feelings" about corporate purpose for years. What is its function or value? At times I have believed in purpose as a driver of culture, strategy and collaboration. At other times, I have felt downright cynical about the idea, seeing it as little more than a vehicle for public relations or even propaganda, inside and outside the company.

HBR's 2015 report, "The Business Case for Purpose," indicated that such sentiments are widely shared, even among business leaders. That survey of 474 executives found that more than 80 percent of executives believe corporate purpose is important to many key measures of a business, such as employee engagement, success in transformation efforts, customer loyalty, and product quality. Seventy percent also believe it is important to integrate purpose into core business functions. Less than half, however, believe that their organization has a shared sense of purpose or aligns its strategy to its purpose. Fewer than 38 percent say that employees are clear on purpose or that the business model and operations are well-aligned with their purpose. In other words, few leaders know how to think about purpose in a clear and focused way or how to use it to help their people act differently and their companies be more successful.

By dictionary definition, a purpose is an aim or a goal. But corporations already have a concept for that, commonly known as Vision. Vision statements are designed to provide a company with something to strive for, and they also help focus, organize and motivate employees.

Strategy is how you get there. It's the best or smartest path forward. You make decisions about resources, markets, talent, capital, etc., to achieve the vision in accordance with the challenges, competition and opportunities the organization faces. Operations is how you execute and perform. Values are your basic beliefs about "right" versus "wrong", and they strongly influence how you behave.

So where does purpose fit in? It's not the "direction" of the organization, because that's the Vision. It's not the principles of the company, because that's the Values. It's not the culture, strategy or operations, either.

Some people call the purpose of an organization its "reason to exist." Simon Sinek, one of the most influential thinkers in this area, calls it the organization's "Why." Why is the organization in business? What's it for? Satya Nadella touched on this when he asked existential questions about Microsoft.

Legendary business thinker Peter Drucker argued, however, that "The purpose of a business is to create a customer." The clarity of this is powerful. Companies are in business to get customers to buy their products or services. This is how they earn revenue, which is their lifeblood, and it's also how they grow and gain market share. There's a lot of variety in how different companies accomplish such a thing. Some companies build better widgets, others sell them more cheaply. But shouldn't purpose *really* matter? Shouldn't it matter more than *just* business?

Rather than a simple why, as Simon Sinek says, a better question might be "Why is my company in business?" Drucker points to the customer. Others point to the world. A number of fast-growing high-tech companies in recent years declare this very thing. They're in business to "change the world" rather than simply make money. A few, such as Google and Groupon, famously included founder's letters in their IPO prospectuses to declare their focus on long-term purpose over short-term profit. Customers matter to these people, but the world matters more. Or, to put it another way, they're in business not just to sell to customers, but to make their customers' lives better. To them, purpose is not a CSR effort, and it's not a business measure; it's a unique combination of both.

In her book *Becoming a Conscious Leader: How to Lead Successfully in a World That's Waking Up*, Gina Hayden talks about different companies that publicly dismiss the pursuit of profits. As Apple CEO Tim Cook said, "When we work on making our devices accessible by the blind, I don't consider the bloody ROI." They believe that profits come when an organization solves a big problem and makes the world a better place. In other words,

Profits + Purpose = Growth. Moreover, they think this is the moral way for a company to behave. Businesses need to do well by doing good.

In our research, we discovered numerous organizations, often category leaders, that use purpose in a very distinct but deliberate way. First, they define purpose as their company's unique ability to have an impact on meaningful challenges faced by customers in their market or within society or even globally. Second, they leverage that sense of purpose as a core driver of their business rather than as a merely altruistic exercise.

Using purpose in this way shifts their orientation from internal concerns and problems to urgent, emerging or future challenges and needs of customers, society, or the world. The pursuit of that purpose helps them drive innovations that improve or disrupt products, services and strategies and either change the game in existing markets or create entirely new markets. As a result, these companies engage more directly and meaningfully with customers, achieve growth that is directed toward filling more significant or meaningful needs, and distinguish themselves from competitors in a way that is difficult to emulate.

Many startups understand this formula inherently. A sense of purpose is at their core because they were built to serve some need in the world.

To us this was very, very exciting.

Purpose is not just about organizing, motivating or inspiring people to achieve better for the company, it's about innovating to fill some need and make the world just a little bit better. In other words, purpose and innovation are linked. In the following chapters, I will describe how such a connection works.

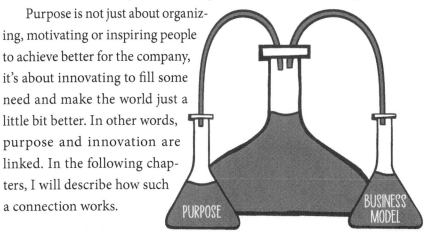

CHAPTER FOUR RECAP

- Evidence from success stories suggests that a clear purpose facilitates innovation and growth.

- Learning from the startup world can pollinate big corporations in the following ways:

  1. Establish a founder's mindset.

  2. Reduce "leadership" and "execution" while tuning-up purpose, team bonding and hard work.

  3. Transform your working environment into a creative playroom.

  4. Connect with real customers in everyday life.

  5. Wait for the right wave to come.

- Companies integrating purpose into their business model create great operational results and increase employee/stakeholder's engagement. Innovation and purpose are inherently connected.

Tools & Resources

The Enemies/Supporters List

This exercise can help broaden your perspective. Usually, companies look only to their customers for feedback and direction. But looking to your "haters" can be invaluable, especially during times of turmoil.

Enemies

1. List your "haters".
   Select an adequate number of them, ideally from different areas.

2. Ask them one-on-one "What are the three top reasons why you don't like our company?"

3. List and group the most frequently given answers.

Supporters

4. Select a few fans of the company (users and nonusers of your product and service).

5. Ask them "What makes our company unique, best in class?" They, especially the nonusers, will likely mention more reputational aspects of your company.

Lessons

6. List and group all the answers.
   Then ask the same audience, the Supporters, a contra question, "What can we do, about it?"

7. List proposed solutions.

This can become a crucial repository of ideas that will help you design your purpose. Remember: Purpose is Impact on Others.

More detailed guidelines of how to do this exercise you will find on my site www.christostsolkas.com.

Determine Your Real Brand Value

During your journey to identify your brand or company purpose, you might be aided by the following visual exercise, tweaked from the original idea of Milan Semelak at http://createvalue.com/.

The real value of your product or service proposition is a combination of three factors. In my view, you don't necessarily need to pick just one. The functional performance or benefits of your company,

HIGHER CAUSE/PURPOSE

REAL BRAND VALUE

FUNCTIONAL PERFORMANCE

EMOTIONAL PERFORMANCE

the emotional content and context, and finally the impact you have on the world, measured by others. Patagonia, for example, might look like 60 percent on Purpose, 30 percent on Emotional Performance and only 10 percent on Functional Performance of its product range. This approach is simple, can be quantified using research and can be benchmarked with your competition. Spend some time with your team thinking about this triangle.

CHAPTER FIVE

Competing on Purpose Inside and Outside the Box

Mature markets are tough. Dominated by long-established players, competition is fierce. In some sectors, products are so similar there's little to distinguish one company's offering from a competitor's. How does ExxonMobil's oil differ from Shell's? Both come out of the ground and get refined through highly technical processes to achieve standards of quality that today's modern engines demand. At the pump, where prices are approximately the same, the big oil companies try to convince consumers that their oil has special attributes. Yet, no car driver could ever tell the difference.

In mature markets, innovation is usually incremental. It's rare for one established company to come out with a new product or a new twist on an old product that is different or compelling enough to leave competitors in the dust. This doesn't mean companies don't try. Many invest a lot into research and development, but it's difficult to build a better mousetrap when the mousetrap industry has been around for a long time. If one company comes up with a tweak to their mousetrap, everyone else copies it pretty quickly anyway.

Michael Porter explained these dynamics in his monumental 1985 book, *Competitive Advantage*. To Porter, companies achieve competitive advantage based on costs, differentiation or focus. This has influenced the operations and positioning of many organizations over the years. Once a strategy mix becomes successful, incumbents build walls around their approach to protect it. Competitors engage in trench warfare to take that fortress on. They chip away at advantage through incremental innovations or improvements.[34]

Yet, it's hard to compete on price or quality when commodity products are similar. Accordingly, companies typically engage in a battle to reduce costs and enhance service. The best ones are highly efficient. They try to execute flawlessly and work to constantly improve operations. This focus on process innovation helps them drive costs down and deliver on their promises to customers. That discipline can become a source of competitive advantage, though it's rarely game-changing and can be difficult to sustain long-term.

Companies in mature markets also spend a lot of money on marketing, for obvious reasons. Customers may value reliable service, but when products are relatively interchangeable, they need additional incentives to continue buying. Companies work hard to develop a distinct brand that encourages customer loyalty. Differentiation is critical. Advertisements, product placement, reward programs and discounts are among the tools companies have long used to encourage people to buy. Today, companies also deploy technology tools and platforms such as apps and social media strategies to engage with customers, collect and leverage data, keep a brand top of mind, and make a product more convenient or easy to buy.

Everything makes a difference. No stone is left unturned. Competition in a mature market is a tough slog and a battle of attrition. Companies in such markets need leaders with a clear strategy, managers with the ability to make the trains run on time, employees who are equipped and able to perform. And if those companies do all these things well—operate efficiently, constantly improve processes, keep costs low, maximize revenues, differentiate from others, satisfy customers—then they will likely be rewarded with more market share and the approval of Wall Street. But for how long? Somebody who has absolutely nothing to lose will disrupt you.

---

34   https://www.thebalance.com/what-is-competitive-advantage-3-strategies-that-work-3305828

Think of how Dollar Shave Club disrupted Gillette. Starting with a single-branded offering and viral marketing, Dollar Shave won over Gillette's target customers with a sense of humor and an acknowledgement of their pain points and built itself into a billion-dollar company. Competing in mature markets is getting harder and harder in a world where purpose also matters.

When Brand and Efficiency Was King

McDonald's is one of the most powerful brands of the past century. Once the company was incredibly innovative. Today, although still enormously successful, its growth path has been challenged by a changing world.

When the McDonald's brothers launched their first restaurant in California in the 1940s, they sold all kinds of barbeque-cooked foods, including hamburgers, and operated like a traditional "carhop" restaurant, delivering meals to car windows. Seeing that hamburgers were their most profitable food item and costs could be further reduced through efficiencies, they reduced their menu selection, switched from car service to self-service, and developed assembly-line processes.

Over the next few years, they continued to hone and refine the McDonald's concept we know today. They developed a restaurant design that was sleek, clean and eye-catching with gleaming stainless steel counters, red chairs and the famous "golden arches." They didn't make the restaurant too comfortable, however, because they wanted people to eat quickly, giving birth to the idea of "fast food." Customers liked the approach, the taste and the prices.

Success breeds success. Realizing their fast-food concept could be replicated systematically, the McDonald's brothers began to sell franchises. They required new franchisees to follow very strict "rules" for how a restaurant could be designed and operated—understanding implicitly that "brand experience" was critical. A milkshake machine salesman named Ray Kroc, impressed by the volume of sales the California restaurants generated, secured a deal to develop franchises across the country. The numbers started small but began to grow. Kroc, who understood the power of advertising, began to leverage the golden arches and distinctive look of the restaurants to draw in customers. Over the next few decades, as franchises were opened in all fifty states and billions of hamburgers were sold, McDonald's constantly tweaked processes and continued to innovate its menu offerings—pre-sliced buns, breakfast meals, drive-through service—generating almost unimaginable growth.

McDonald's was a pioneering company in many ways. In 1961, it opened "Hamburger University" to train franchisees and executives. To give back, the company launched Ronald McDonald House in 1974, providing families a place to stay when their children required extended hospital treatment. The business expanded internationally in 1976, starting in New Zealand. From 1990, the company committed to using recycled materials and reducing waste. In the mid-1990s, it began to include Disney and Pixar toys with Happy Meals. Each innovation seemed in tune with McDonald's promise to its customers. McDonald's was the epitome of fast, convenient, tasty food at family-friendly prices.

The McDonald's formula allowed the company to thrive in a maturing market, despite intense competition, many challenges and occasional ups-and-downs. Over the past decade, however, McDonald's seems increasingly out of sorts with a changing world. Today, customers often spend entire days at a Starbucks, working, taking meetings, seeing friends. Unlike McDonalds, Starbucks encourages customers to think of it as their "Third place."[35] In an environment in which companies are increasingly criticized for not providing a living wage for employees, McDonald's is a target. But most importantly, customers are far more health-conscious today than they have ever been throughout McDonald's long history.[36] McDonald's has tried to respond with healthier offerings, such as fresh beef,[37] but its signature kale salad has more calories and fat than a Big Mac when the dressing is applied.[38]

Today, McDonald's is back on a growth track, thanks to its new strategy, expanded delivery options and apps. Yet its path seems incremental rather than revolutionary.[39] Its "Velocity Growth Plan" involves serving more customers, more often—something that doesn't seem very inspiring, connecting or meaningful in a world that increasingly values purpose.[40] Meanwhile, companies like Pret a Manger (or simply Pret) are gaining market share by focusing on healthy, organic "fast-food" meals and drinks that customers love.[41]

What would McDonalds have to do or change to become a force of purpose-driven innovation again? The company no longer seems to be shaping or leading the world so much as navigating it.

---

35   https://www.fastcompany.com/887990/starbucks-third-place-and-creating-ultimate-customer-experience

36   http://fortune.com/2015/05/15/mcdonalds-anniversary/

37   https://www.eater.com/2018/3/8/17097078/mcdonalds-fresh-beef-quarter-pounders-rollout-operational-changes

38   https://www.cbc.ca/news/business/mcdonalds-kale-calorie-questions-1.3423938

39   https://www.forbes.com/sites/andriacheng/2018/01/31/mcdonalds-is-lovin-it-well-almost/#779d96f75a50

40   https://corporate.mcdonalds.com/corpmcd/about-us/our-growth-strategy.html

41   https://www.ukessays.com/essays/marketing/the-corporate-analysis-pret-a-manger-marketing-essay.php

Performance with Purpose

In contrast, PepsiCo is a company that has taken a more active and deliberate approach to purpose and innovation.

Pepsi was invented around the same time as Coke, another syrupy soft drink that promised to perk you up and boost your health. Pepsi competed with its soft drink rivals on price, but lagged in sales because it lacked Coca-Cola's innovations in bottling, marketing and distribution.[42] In the 1930s, after making a bad bet on sugar futures, the company went bankrupt and changed hands several times, slowly regaining popularity.

Interestingly, in the late 1940s, Pepsi began marketing to the underserved African American population with positive advertising and intensive sales team efforts. As a result, Pepsi achieved dominant market share in that niche. However, those efforts were abandoned following a leadership change in 1950.[43]

In 1975, Pepsi introduced the Pepsi Challenge campaign, which involved blind taste tests to compare preference for Pepsi over Coke. This was the first cannon shot in the intensely competitive Cola Wars. While Coca-Cola's brand identity was stronger than Pepsi's, consumers generally preferred the taste of Pepsi. As a result, in 1985, Coca-Cola launched New Coke, a formula with a sweeter taste closer to Pepsi. This scandalized Coke customers and allowed Pepsi to declare victory in its battle. However, Coca-Cola, realizing its mistake quickly, relaunched its old formula as Coke Classic and regained brand dominance.

Yet, today, PepsiCo, which includes Frito-Lay, Quaker Oats

---

42 https://www.businessinsider.com/coca-cola-vs-pepsi-timeline-2013-1#coke-developed-its-iconic-contour-bottle-got-big-name-endorsements-and-expanded-to-europe-meanwhile-pepsi-went-bankrupt-because-of-wwi-4

43 https://www.wsj.com/articles/SB116831396726171042

and Gatorade, is currently the world's third-largest food and beverage conglomerate, while Coca-Cola recorded one of the largest-ever falls on the Global 2000 list.[44] It's easy to pinpoint the shift as starting in 2006 with the leadership of former PepsiCo CEO, Indra Nooyi. One of the most notable decisions Nooyi made early in her tenure was to reclassify Pepsi products into three categories: "fun for you" (traditional junk food), "better for you" (low fat, low sugar alternatives), and "good for you" (healthy snacks, foods and drinks like oatmeal, hummus and Naked Juice). She also endeavored to improve the nutrition of products in the fun category.

Nooyi viewed innovation as solving a customer need, in this case, healthier alternatives to junk food and drinks. PepsiCo has also been a leader in environmental sustainability. Nooyi, as a native of India, was very conscious of water issues and strove to make operations as conservationally focused and environmentally friendly as possible.

In 2015, PepsiCo launched its new growth strategy based on its "Performance with Purpose 2025 Agenda." To this end, PepsiCo focuses on three purpose-driven areas—Products, Planet and People—which it sees as not just "good to do" but essential for success, profitability and growth as a business.

To improve products, PepsiCo is reducing sugar, fat and salt while shifting its portfolio toward healthier offerings. One of Pepsi's goals is to ensure that by 2025 two-thirds of its global beverage portfolio volume will have 100 calories or fewer.[45]

To improve the planet, PepsiCo is working to replenish water, especially in high-risk watersheds, while also striving to provide more people with safe water access.

To help people, PepsiCo is working with local farmers to improve agricultural practices because half of all people on the planet work on farms. It's investing in training and education of women and girls in local communities because most of those farmers and community leaders are women.

44   https://www.forbes.com/sites/maggiemcgrath/2018/06/06/worlds-largest-food-and-beverage-companies-2018-anheuser-busch-nestle-and-pepsi-top-the-list/#feea4ce1b08d

45   https://www.bevindustry.com/articles/90919-pepsico-launches-bubly-sparkling-water

And it's increasing female representation among corporate management because diversity of perspective and experience is essential for long-term business success.[46]

Likewise, Coca-Cola has taken similar measures. They use their market clout to connect with developing societies. For example, their RAIN initiative is helping African communities get access to water. This is an effective program. Like a number of other major multinationals, Coca-Cola has also launched a plastics recycling project to help sustainability.[47] [48]

In my view, however, when such initiatives remain isolated from the primary business of the company, their impact is limited and ephemeral. After all, it's not likely that mega companies engaged in charitable operations can or will sustain such activities when the financial going gets tough. At the first sign of trouble, big companies find it all too easy to pull the plug on philanthropic business. In contrast, if ethical activities make the company money, you can bet they will be sustained.

Fortune Favors the Purposeful

PepsiCo is succeeding today through a strategy of diversification and a purpose-centered approach to innovation. PepsiCo leadership believes that Performance with a Purpose goes well beyond a CSR program and actually fortifies the company through hard times while giving it the capability to compete more successfully in the future by drawing committed talent and aligning the company's offerings and values more closely with customers and partners.[49]

Even successful and long-established companies are incredibly vulnerable, however. A bad economic cycle, an unexpected scandal or an aggressive

---

46 https://www.fastcompany.com/3066378/how-pepsico-ceo-indra-nooyi-is-steering-the-company-tow

47 https://www.coca-colacompany.com/stories/the-replenish-africa-initiative

48 https://www.beveragedaily.com/Article/2019/03/26/Diageo-Unilever-Coca-Cola-Nestle-launch-Africa-Plastics-Recycling-Alliance

49 https://www.forbes.com/sites/csr/2011/04/07/pepsi-takes-performance-with-purpose-to-heart/#7e09424340b4

new competitor can put a business on life support overnight. Amazon, for example, has decimated many retail businesses such as Borders Books, Sears, and more. But its formidable strength has been in distribution, not Amazon label products. In 2009, it launched its own battery to compete with Duracell and Energizer, instantly taking one-third of the traditional competitors' market share. Duracell and Energizer thought they were just fighting each other; it turns out, Amazon was an even more daunting enemy.[50] Now, Amazon is releasing hundreds of private label products and it has the advertising, distribution and data might to destroy established competitors in those mature markets.

When a company stands for more than just profit and market share, it has more resilience and determination to overcome tough challenges. Its people and customers are more dedicated and committed. Its brand has more stickiness. But the new realization of purpose is that it also helps a company innovate. Purpose brings a business closer to the needs and values of the customer.

When Apple was founded, it basically invented the personal computer market. Then, competitors quickly got into the game and sold machines that were almost as good at much cheaper prices. Apple lost revenue and market share rapidly, and co-founder Steve Jobs was fired. When Jobs returned in 1996, the company was on life-support. Jobs, however, infused the business with a renewed sense of purpose. Apple was not really in the business of building pretty boxes (though it did that very well); instead, it was in the business of helping customers "think different".[51] That sense of purpose permeated and reinvigorated the organization, making Apple a mission-driven and very different computer company.

For sure, Apple also became a very sophisticated company able to combine design, marketing, technology, production, distribution, retail and finance in integrated ways to enable profitability while helping recapture market share. But it was the sense of purpose, embodied in "think different", which gave the company the direction and capability to innovate in bold new ways.

---

50   https://www.nytimes.com/2018/06/23/business/amazon-the-brand-buster.html
51   https://www.youtube.com/watch?v=4HsGAc0_Y5c

Few could have imagined the company Apple would soon become. Although Apple still competes in the laptop market, its innovations, first with the iPod and then the iPhone, allowed it to create and dominate two entirely new sectors, portable music and smartphones. These innovations drove Apple to incredible levels of profitability, making it one of the largest and most successful companies in the world, in only a few short years. Afterwards, computer and cell phone handset companies that once mocked Apple either copied them or became largely irrelevant.

Whether Apple can sustain that level of relevance and innovation going forward remains to be seen. But it rose from the ashes, achieved greatness as a business and changed the world because it focused on "purpose" and leveraged that deep sense of meaning to innovate and grow.

Redefining the Market

If you can't beat them, change the game you're playing. In today's global economy, one way to do that is to expand your appeal in a traditional market by going beyond the product to meet bigger, more universal concerns.

Unilever, the world's largest consumer goods company, operates explicitly in a purpose-driven way. The British-Dutch company was founded in 1930 when a margarine maker and a soap maker merged. Since its founding, the company has grown largely through acquisitions, accumulating over four hundred brands.

Unilever ties its most popular or famous brands to a specific social cause, linking them to environmental, societal or community issues. The company shuns short-term profitability over long-term growth objectives, especially in emerging markets. It also refuses to push ads on social media platforms that proliferate toxic content.[52] Ex CEO Paul Polman believed this adherence to a sense of purpose is critical on several levels.

First, it gives employees and customers a shared sense of meaning that goes way beyond a particular product. For example, Dove focuses on

---

52   https://www.businessinsider.com/unilever-threatens-to-reduce-digital-ad-spend-2018-2?IR=T

women's self-esteem with its "Campaign for Beauty" ads, while the ice cream Ben & Jerry's amplifies social justice issues. Other brands in Unilever's sustainable-living portfolio overtly tie environmental concerns to challenges around mass production, packaging and consumption.

Second, those brands outperform Unilever's brands that are not tied directly to purpose. The company discovered in 2016 that its sustainable-living products generated 60 percent of the company's growth. In general, the company's purpose-oriented brands grow twice as fast as its ordinary brands. In other words, purpose can generate growth and profitability.[53]

Unilever researched this in its landmark study "Make Purpose Pay", which looked at how twenty thousand people around the world made purchasing decisions.[54] Unilever discovered that people interested in sustainability as an issue really do buy products that offer more sustainable choices when offered. When they don't do so it is because they either believe that the claims of sustainability are not genuine, or they worry that the cost is higher. By building up its credibility as an authentically purpose-driven company and keeping its prices competitive, Unilever is able to grow profitability and market share by doing good. This also reinforces the sense of engagement that employees feel for their company and work.

Unilever is so faithful to the importance of its sense of purpose that it resisted and withstood an unwanted merger offer by 3G, a South American company under the Berkshire Hathaway umbrella. Despite the hit to its share price, Unilever worried that its acquirer would not see value in Unilever's purpose-driven innovation focus and might.

Seizing the High Ground and Competitive Advantage

Most established companies compete on operational efficiency and incremental innovation in an existing market space. This makes them vulnerable to competitors that adopt a more global approach to purpose and meaning.

---

53   http://fortune.com/2017/02/17/unilever-paul-polman-responsibility-growth/

54   https://www.unilever.com/Images/making-purpose-pay-inspiring-sustainable-living-170515_tcm244-506419_en.pdf

Such companies simply engage with consumers and employees on a different level. They also seem to be able to innovate and respond to new societal or market issues faster than traditional companies focused more exclusively on profit and share price.

Most companies in the world operate or try to operate like P&G or McDonald's or ExxonMobile. Valuing operational excellence and discipline, they stick to their lanes by focusing on the essential uses of the products they make and sell and striving to meet the basic needs of their customers. They believe that understanding the customer's basic needs allows them to make the sorts of changes and tweaks that will keep their products necessary and appealing.

Today, that mode creates several problems. It prevents companies from being sensitive to big swings in society or strong movements or concerns. A company reliant on a strong brand that it incrementally innovates year after year will be extremely reluctant and risk-averse to changing that brand in a big way when societal expectations or markets change. In contrast, a company that is concerned about more than profit may forego short-term profitability for a larger sense of purpose. But in the process, it sets itself for longer-term and more sustainable growth. Its products will be less static and "packaged" than competitors.

P&G, a formidable, high-quality, strong-performing company for almost two hundred years, is starting to learn that lesson. As former CEO Bob McDonald once noted, "There needs to be an emotional component [to innovation] as well—a source of inspiration that motivates people."[55] In 2004, the company took steps in that direction with its Children's Safe Drinking Water Program, which provides clean drinking water in developing nations. Its water purifier product is specifically tied into this effort and bears the P&G brand name, rather than a specific product brand name.

Also in 2004, the company tried to alleviate issues related to global disasters with that safe drinking program, developing purification sachets to kill bacteria, viruses and parasites in water that may be unsafe due to

---

55   https://www.chegg.com/homework-help/questions-and-answers/p-g-tripled-innovation-success-rate-hbr-case-strategies-innovation-b-bac-k-2000-prospects--q16231705

disasters. The company also developed a fleet of mobile laundromats to do the laundry of people affected by global disasters, an effort welcomed by anyone who has experienced a calamity.

In 2013, the company finally began to address the environmental sustainability challenge by reducing its use of water and expelling of pollutants. Additionally, the company has begun to produce and market other environmentally friendly products like recyclable shampoo bottles made partially from recycled beach plastic. In 2015, the company took an unusually bold step in tying its brand to consciousness-raising issues around "girl power," while tying those issues specifically to feminine products that girls need to buy.

All of those actions count, but they aren't intrinsically part of P&G's business model or growth plan. If it dropped those efforts and returned to the old way of doing things, P&G's operations wouldn't change. In contrast, companies like Unilever focus on global appeal in their innovations, and often outperform competitors that focus more purely on basic operational challenges. When purpose is part of the business model, it gives companies like Unilever something a little extra in the hearts and minds of customers and employees.

As I mentioned in the previous chapter, this research began with a small exercise that my team initiated and established. Together, we looked at eight robust sectors ranging from Food & Beverage to Motor Vehicles and Telecoms, and selected the top three to five representatives of those sectors according to the *Fortune Global 500*. We analyzed their mission statements and purpose to see how clearly they articulated recognition of and service toward some larger societal or global need. Then we analyzed their business model to assess potential impact on those needs. Basically, we were looking for alignment between purpose and business activity.

Then, for comparison, we also looked at a number of small or emergent startups with particularly clear or compelling purpose-orientation.

Existing market spaces were the easiest to define. We found companies clustered into two categories. Some of those companies had a strong operational focus. By way of a hypothetical example, one company we worked with believed that "our role in the world is to become the total food company, satisfying shareholders, customers and employees."

Group A

- AT&T
- China Mobile
- Volkswagen
- GM
- Daimler
- L'Oreal
- P&G
- Exor
- Christian Dior
- Toyota
- Verizon
- Pepsico (marginally)

Other companies focused on broader needs that are more societal (i.e., they improve economic inequality or injustice) or global in nature (they focus on world hunger or environmental sustainability).

Group B

- Unilever
- Nestle
- TOMS Shoes
- Danone
- Warby Parker
- Mondelez

The high-value zone, in my view, is on the second grouping. When products and services are lifted above their most utilitarian elements, they can be tied to a stronger, more resonant sense of meaning. This, in turn, gives those companies a compelling advantage with customers and employees who believe in those values.

But how can a company set itself up for exponential growth and disruptive change of an industry? Is purpose the most important ingredient of that recipe? Instinctively, we assumed that "innovation" would comprise the other parameter. So we started digging into each one of the companies in our sample to see whether they try to achieve differentiation via incremental or disruptive innovation, in existing or completely new spaces. We grouped them accordingly and started plotting the two axes to place our results.

Below you'll see the X/Y axis and where we were headed.

But before we go further, I want to tell you about the two other groups of companies we identified.

CHAPTER FIVE RECAP

- Operating in mature, fragmented markets is tough. Every decimal point of growth takes sweat and blood. By default, any attempt at innovation is incremental. So are the results.

- Companies try to satisfy consumers, stakeholders and shareholders by traditional means. They rarely focus on purpose or global impact.

- Some incumbents try to escape this deadly loop by establishing a broader operational scope and attempting to define a larger purpose. These companies tend to be more successful and impactful.

Tools & Resources

- Collective consciousness helps you understand that you are not in business only for business. A talk by Dr. Deepak Chopra helped me see this. I started a hashtag after watching this video #dobusiness_dogood. Follow it and also don't miss Chopra's video talking about purpose (visit my site www.christostsolkas.com to see the link).

- Read this book by Rita Gunter McGrath to better understand how quickly traditional strategies and competitive advantage can become obsolete and what you need to do to stay alive and win.

CHAPTER SIX

Going for the Unthinkable

In the 1920s, two brothers, Adolf and Rudolph Dassler, began making athletic shoes in Germany. Track runners had long used spiked shoes to gain better traction when racing. The Dassler brothers figured out a way to make those shoes lighter using canvas and rubber. In 1936, they convinced American track star Jesse Owens to wear their shoes in the Berlin Olympics. Owens won four gold medals, and the Dassler brand became synonymous with Olympic glory. Soon the brothers were selling two hundred thousand shoes a year. Their product was so famous that U.S. forces didn't destroy their factory during World War II, even though it had been producing tanks. When the Allied occupation began, all the soldiers of the American army wanted Dassler shoes.

How does a product stand out from the ranks of other, similar products to catalyze the rapid growth of a company? Innovation is obviously key. But innovation, on its own, is not enough. If it were, than any company could spur rapid growth by tweaking or improving existing products. In reality, people don't want something that is merely better than other products on the market. They want something that is "different" in some new and special way. The Dassler brothers, it turned out, were not just selling shoes. They were selling elite athletic performance.

After the war, the Dassler brothers conflicted as business partners and went their separate ways. Adolph Dassler, known as "Adi", formed a new shoe company he called "Adi-das." Rudolph Dassler started "Ru-da", which later became "Puma." For decades, Adidas and Puma dominated the athletic shoe market globally, along with a number of others like America's Converse and the UK's Reebok. Then came a company called Blue Ribbon Sports launched in 1964 in Beaverton, Oregon.

The founders of Blue Ribbon Sports were an odd couple. Bill Bowerman was a coach at the University of Oregon who made track shoes as a hobby. Phil Knight had been one of Bowerman's athletes. Knight was working as an accountant when he realized that his real passion was for entrepreneurship. He saw Bowerman's shoes as a product he could sell. Bowerman's passion was for making better athletic shoes. He couldn't believe the industry still hadn't figured out how to do it right. He kept experimenting with different designs and materials on the theory that the slightest reduction in weight would produce a substantial advantage in speed. For seven years he made incremental improvements; then came his Eureka moment.

The track at the University of Oregon was changing to a new artificial surface. That was the future. Maybe spikes, which were the heaviest part of a shoe, were not necessary when the track was no longer made of dirt, grass or wood chips. But what to replace them with? Bowerman tried all kinds of different ideas until inspiration struck. One Sunday, making brunch for his wife, he stared at the waffle iron. The grooves produced on a waffle looked like a surface that could provide traction. What if Bowerman made a similar pattern out of rubber and attached that to the bottom of a shoe? The rubber tread might function like spikes on an artificial surface, but the shoe would weigh considerably less. Bowerman abandoned his breakfast and heated up some rubber instead, sacrificing the family's waffle iron to create the first rubber-treaded sole which he cut to shape and sewed on to a canvas shoe. The tread worked!

That was 1971. Invigorated by Bowerman's innovation, the company changed its name to Nike, after the Greek goddess of speed, strength and victory, and Knight got to work selling shoes that were unique on the market. They called the first of this new line the Waffle Trainer. Knight drove around the Pacific Northwest and sold Waffle Trainers out of the back of his car to amateur track athletes.

Like Dassler, Nike needed its own Jesse Owens. One of the first converts to the Waffle Trainer was a local track star named Steve Prefontaine. Highly recruited as a high school athlete, Prefontaine chose University of Oregon because Bill Bowerman was the coach. Prefontaine liked Bowerman's innovative approach to training and racing. Bowerman got Prefontaine ready for the 1972 Munich Olympics.

Fans loved Prefontaine's style of running. He was an aggressive competitor, and liked to come out hard, take the lead and stay out front at a time when most runners adopted more "wait and see" tactics. He also was a rebel who seemed disdainful of old rules and traditions. Constantly promoting Nike shoes to other athletes and organizations, Prefontaine became the face of the company and helped make the swoosh logo famous through his racing style. As he put it, "Some people create with words or with music or with a brush and paints. I like to make something beautiful when I run. I like to make people stop and say, 'I've never seen anyone run like that before.'" Then tragedy struck. Prefontaine was killed in a car accident just before the 1976 Montreal Olympics. America and the running world mourned.

Those two legends seemed to embody Nike—the waffle iron and the heroic young runner who fought the establishment and the odds. Innovation meets guts. The Nike culture was one of constant innovation (always trying to make the shoes a little bit better) and a scrappy, highly competitive approach to the market. But what set Nike apart? It did the same things as any other athletic shoe company—designed shoes for performance, reduced costs as much as possible through efficient manufacturing and distribution, and marketed like crazy. It may have been better at marketing than most, and its shoes did seem to offer improvements more often, so is that how

Nike came out of nowhere to become the biggest athletic shoe and apparel company in the world today?

Not quite.

Constantly improved shoe designs, solid business operations, intensive marketing and celebrity endorsements were enough to allow Nike to play the game with the world's global athletic shoe companies like Adidas, Puma, Reebok and Converse. But though the company grew revenues and market share at an exceptional pace, it still struggled to differentiate itself playing by those rules. For instance, in the 1984 Los Angeles Olympics, American Carl Lewis, wearing Nike shoes, equaled Jesse Owens' achievement of winning four gold medals, but Nike did not receive any noticeable surge in shoe sales as a result. People expected athletic shoes to improve athletic performance. That was the old game.

Nike won by playing a new game—shifting the athletic shoe business into a different space. Phil Knight had come to believe that Nike wasn't in the shoe business, but the entertainment business.[56] This changed the way the company viewed products, innovation, marketing and celebrity endorsements.

That vision came to realization in 1985. A University of North Carolina basketball player by the name of Michael Jordan started playing for the Chicago Bears. Drafted third overall, Jordan was electrifying and looked like he had the potential to be a generational player. His ability to leap and dunk seemed to defy gravity. Fans became very excited. The media attention overwhelmed teammates. At the All-Star game, the other players, resenting Jordan's fame, froze him out and refused to pass to him. Jordan kept breaking records in response.

Here's how Nike came into the picture. Jordan's favorite shoes were Adidas, and he wanted a shoe deal that could keep him wearing them. But Adidas was in management turmoil after the death of founder Adi Dassler. During a meeting with the Adidas leadership team, Jordan's agent asked what sort of innovations in shoes or marketing Adidas had planned. Adidas had no answer. Reluctantly, Jordan and his agent met with Nike.

---

56   http://www.espn.com/blog/playbook/dollars/post/_/id/2918/how-nike-landed-michael-jordan

Jordan didn't like Nike basketball shoes, but he was quickly swayed by the company's drive to try innovative approaches to product and marketing. For its part, Nike viewed Jordan's entertaining playing style and charismatic personality as something that would transcend basketball and shoes. So Nike told Michael Jordan they would let him design his own shoe line, and they would build a very different sort of advertising campaign around him that would capitalize on Jordan's personal appeal and excitement.

Michael Jordan's playing career far exceeded expectations. He was perhaps the greatest to ever play in the NBA. As Nike envisioned, he also became a cultural icon whose personal brand went way beyond sports. The shoe marketing deal with Jordan helped launch Nike into a new stage of growth and helped make Jordan very rich. As Nike grew, the company continued to focus on athletic performance, but the energy of the brand focused on fashion and entertainment. Other famous personalities like Tiger Woods, Lance Armstrong, LeBron James and Kanye West helped lift the shoes beyond sports to something bigger—fame, success, revolution. As a result of this premium, Nike could produce more varieties of shoes and sell them at higher prices. Other companies, like Adidas, attempted to follow Nike into the fashion business, but Nike was first and better at it for a long time.

Today, Nike is the largest supplier of athletic shoes and apparel in the world with one of the most iconic brands and slogans of all time. The Nike swoosh and "Just Do It" slogan are strongly linked with quality shoes, competitive athletics and celebrity fashion.

Blue Oceans vs Red Oceans

In existing spaces, competition is fierce. Long-established players fight over every inch of market share through incremental innovation and an obsessive focus on efficiency, cost reduction and margins. In their book, *Blue Ocean Strategy: How to Create Uncontested Market Space and Make the Competition Irrelevant*, authors Chan Kim and Renee Mauborgne describe established markets as Red Oceans because competitors act like sharks tearing each other apart. In contrast, Blue Oceans are new market spaces, free of competitors, waiting to be explored. In those Blue Oceans, pioneering companies grow like crazy.

According to the authors, companies discover Blue Oceans by focusing on new value innovation in products or services while still keeping operations lean and low cost. Companies like Nike differentiate their products or services substantially to create a new game while still maintaining the operational discipline of the old game. In this way, they turbocharge their growth. That's how Nike did it: It shifted its focus from "shoes" to "fashion" while still leveraging its prowess at production, distribution and marketing.

How do Blue Ocean companies figure out which new markets to move into? That magic formula is harder to crack. If it were easy, businesses would do it all the time. According to the authors, Blue Ocean companies get their new ideas by looking across the traditional boundaries of competition. Instead of focusing on current rivals and maximizing the profit of existing products and services, they scan complementary industries with similar products and services where they can apply their expertise and know-how with new customers. Instead of focusing on current trends, they try to shape future trends. Instead of focusing on marginal price competition, they seek products and services that can be priced at a premium because they have an emotional impact with consumers.

Apple is one of the easiest to see that approach come into play. Apple was launched by looking at one industry—mainframe business computers—and seeing how that concept and technology could be adapted for individual consumers: personal computers. They brought ideas and modes from creative industries and embedded them in a highly technical engineering industry. They didn't follow the trends of an industry in development, they constantly tried to get ahead of trends—in computing, digital music, smartphones, watches, etc.—in order to shape or create markets in which they could dominate. Apple's iPhones are produced with incredible operational discipline and designed and marketed exceptionally well, but they can also be priced higher than anything in the market because customers value what they mean.

This is because Apple, like Nike, looks for ways to meet customers' deeper needs and emotional wants, the ones people don't even know exist. Computers and smartphones are not just devices or commodities for Apple, they are ways to help people be more versatile, flexible, productive and creative in their work, life and hobbies without being impeded by cumbersome operating systems or complicated technology. In the process, Apple enables many new markets to flourish, from music, photography and graphic design to advertising, publishing, education, film, and so on.

Note that Apple and Nike are very pragmatic, customer-focused companies. They may have lofty views of their products, but they are still selling commodities. In other words, though both Nike and Apple like to describe themselves as "rebels" or "revolutionaries", they are not trying to change society or the world in a sweeping or transformative way. Instead, very much in the tradition of products throughout the 20th century, like laundry detergent, cars, refrigerators, etc., their purpose is to meet individual consumer needs in a deeper, more satisfying and engaging way.

Netflix is another classic example of a company meeting individual consumer needs in new ways that made it a market buster and category leader.

Throughout much of the twentieth century, people watched movies at theaters or on TV when reruns were broadcast by network television channels. After videotape cassettes came out in the mid-1970s, the entertainment industry started to change. Home video machines began to drop in price, and retail stores were created that let people rent movies and bring them home for a day or two.

By the mid-1980s, there were around fifteen thousand video rental stores in the U.S. Most were "mom and pop" stores or regional businesses. Sometimes these stores specialized by offering different kinds of movies— ranging from more popular titles to more art-house or foreign movies—but generally they all operated the same. Customers applied for a membership card which gave them the right to rent a video and bring it home while making them liable for lost, stolen or damaged videos.

Rentals were not too expensive, a few dollars at most. But the secret to profitability was late fees. When customers were even an hour late returning a movie, they could be charged an extra day. Sometimes customers forgot to bring a movie back for weeks and the fees piled up. Video stores counted on this to make money.

An industry with so many bit players is ripe for consolidation. Blockbuster Video, which originated with one store in Dallas, Texas, in 1985, eventually became that beast. With a solid store concept and lots of financing behind it, Blockbuster began expanding and buying up other regional competitors. By 2004, Blockbuster had nine thousand stores in the U.S.

But Blockbuster's end was already in motion. In 1997, a new movie recording technology, Digital Video Disc or DVD, came out that was less liable to break, cheaper to make and smaller. Soon, DVDs were being rented in video stores alongside VHS cassettes.

To a couple of upstart companies, Redbox and Netflix, DVDs had another advantage. They were small, cheap and light enough to store in a vending machine or send through the mail. No doubt, Blockbuster looked at these competitors in the same way Adidas once looked at Nike: Who cares? When a company completely dominates the market , an upstart competitor with a new approach is just an irritant. But Blockbuster didn't realize the "need" or "want" that Netflix, in particular, was meeting in customers who liked renting videos. Blockbuster thought nobody really wanted to order a video online and wait for days to get it in the mail. Netflix customers liked being able to line up their future movie selections on the computer and avoid spending hours in stores, scanning the shelves. Even more importantly, Netflix customers HATED paying for late fees. Famously, founder and CEO Reed Hoffman launched the company after he was forced to pay $40 in late fees for a movie he'd forgotten to return to Blockbuster. With Netflix mail-delivered DVDs, customers could keep a movie as long as they liked.

Netflix's subscription model was a less obvious innovation that helped the company grow. Stable, growing, monthly revenue is a terrific way to fuel profitability. Slowly, Netflix began to creep up on Blockbuster, and

Blockbuster began to take notice. At one point, the two companies discussed the idea of Blockbuster buying Netflix. Netflix would serve as Blockbuster's online arm. But just as those plans looked like they might go through, the Blockbuster board fired their CEO and rehired their previous CEO, a former 7 Eleven convenience store executive, who dismissed online businesses as fads and doubled down on brick-and-mortar retail stores. Within a few years, Blockbuster had peaked, but Netflix kept surging by focusing on a traditional product in a new market space and meeting deeper customer needs in the process.

The Netflix story would be interesting if that's all there was to it, but Netflix has been remarkable for its drive to stay on top by continuing to move into new Blue Ocean spaces. Recognizing that its mail-delivery model would be made obsolete by streaming video, Netflix went "all in" on streaming video earlier than any other big player. This met deeper customer needs for convenience and ease while reinforcing and growing Netflix's subscription revenue model. At one point, Netflix's streaming movies represented 40 percent of all Internet traffic in the U.S.

Then, knowing that other well-funded competitors were going to eat away at Netflix's streaming service advantage, the company innovated again by getting into producing original content. Their productions of original TV shows and movies met customer insatiable demands for high-quality programming and entertainment. Netflix's competitors, especially Hulu and Amazon, quickly followed suit. Netflix keeps moving into new spaces and competing with existing competitors in new ways. It will be interesting to see if Netflix can continue to do so.

New-Space Machines

A new breed of company has emerged in the past few years that takes Blue Ocean/new-space strategies to the extreme. These companies describe themselves as being "intensely customer-driven" and relentlessly innovation-focused. They demonstrate the power of seeking new spaces constantly, wherever they can be found.

Amazon is the example that most of us know well. Famously, Amazon started as an online distributor of books at a time when "dot-com" businesses were the stock market's darlings, and businesses like Pets.com were valued higher than General Motors. When that speculative market crashed, many dot-com businesses disappeared and a few kept going, Amazon among them.

Amazon's book distribution business, like Netflix's DVD mail order business, met customer needs in new-space ways. Customers like bookstores but they also like the convenience of ordering online, especially when the book costs less. Amazon's distribution model was so profitable, it began to put most brick-and-mortar competitors out of business. From the beginning, however, Amazon wasn't really in the book distribution business. Instead, it was actually a "distribution" company. Starting with books, Amazon quickly moved into other products that could be distributed through its growing system of warehouses and suppliers.

Amazon didn't stop there. Recognizing that discovering "new space" customer needs was critical for fueling growth, the company kept upping the ante. Deliveries got super-fast, from a week or more, down to two days. Today, Amazon has a network of suppliers in most cities that can deliver most things customers order within a few hours. Unlike most companies, Amazon didn't want to charge more for those deliveries, it wanted to charge less. So, it offered a yearly subscription fee model called Amazon Prime, which eliminated delivery fees. Customers loved this and signed up in droves.

Through Amazon Prime, Amazon continued to offer new services that met new needs. Restaurant delivery. Music. Movies and TV shows. Groceries. Shoes. In the process, it entered hundreds of traditional markets but offered new levels of service, convenience, variety and prices that competitors couldn't beat. Whenever Amazon met roadblocks in that service orientation, it quickly adapted and developed new business lines. For example, one Christmas, Amazon's famous two-day delivery service hit a snafu when its distribution partners (USPS, UPS, FedEx) couldn't handle the volume. Rather than see this as a defeat, Amazon just developed its own delivery services and partnered with new delivery partners like Uber.

Amazon's success fueled its growth into new markets that were so outside Amazon's core expertise that observers were surprised. For example, rather than stick with online sales, Amazon bought Whole Foods groceries because it recognized this link between distribution, local convenience and Amazon Prime membership benefits as another leverage point with customers. Needing to build its own server farms to house vast amounts of data, Amazon built AWS services and sold them to other businesses with similar needs, including competitors. Today, that division is responsible for most of Amazon's pure profitability. Not all of Amazon's innovations have worked out. For example, its smartphone, the Amazon Fire, failed to turn customers on. But another moon-shot product, Amazon's Alexa, its in-home voice-activated service, started off slow but now is making great inroads with customers, integrating Amazon services deeper into customers' lives in ways that they value.

Amazon may seem like a one-of-a-kind company, but it is not alone. Its biggest global competitor is a company built very much in the same relentlessly customer-driven innovation-focused model, though it has attacked different traditional markets in different ways. I'm talking about Alibaba.

Alibaba is an "everything" company, almost as if you combined Amazon, Facebook, Yahoo, Google, PayPal, eBay, IBM, Tesla, Orbitz, Sony, Microsoft, Salesforce and so on, into one entity. The company was founded in 1999 as an online marketplace. Its first "new space" angle was the untapped market in China. Basically, it brought online commerce and business services to a market of consumers who desperately wanted them. It was a Blue Ocean rather than a Red Ocean because the big American players were locked out by the Chinese government.

Alibaba didn't stand still on that advantage, however. It kept expanding services from e-commerce to e-shopping to e-banking with consumer-to-consumer and business-to-consumer portals. The focus on innovation is real. Today, Alibaba makes and sells cars that work like computers or robots. It uses facial recognition software to complete transactions that rely on customer smiles. It delivers pharmaceuticals to markets that lack access. It also moved out of China and into two hundred countries worldwide.

In the process, Alibaba has become the largest e-commerce company in the world.

The future of hyper-growth is companies like Amazon and Alibaba. With platforms built to generate customer satisfaction, their purpose is to discover new spaces that meet customer needs. It doesn't matter what the product, service or market might be. These companies will go there to win. In the process, they grow and grow and grow.

Coming back to our exercise as described in the previous chapter, we grouped the companies innovating outside their box/space, operating in a unique way, as listed below:

Group C

- Alibaba
- Amazon
- PayPal
- Facebook
- Netflix
- Nike
- Salesforce
- Airbnb

Hyper-Disruption

Hyper-disruption companies are not for the faint of heart. Because they break the rules and strive for a purpose that's far bigger than business, they can also seem irrational, grandiose, unrealistic, improbable, and even faintly ridiculous. It can take a special type of leader to conceive of and drive such a company successfully. It was said of Steve Jobs that he created his own "reality distortion field."[57] Perhaps Elon Musk is the leader and visionary who comes closest to that characterization today. This is not entirely complementary. Just as Jobs crashed and burned at Apple in the 1980s, so Musk may be on his way to doing the same today. Yet, it's inarguable that both men have had an outsized impact on their industries and the world. Let's look at Musk, an unusual person, from that perspective.

---

57   https://www.theatlantic.com/technology/archive/2012/02/the-steve-jobs-reality-distortion-field-even-makes-it-into-his-fbi-file/252832/

In July 2016, Musk wrote an unusual memo to the employees and shareholders of Tesla Motors. He called it "Master Plan Part Deux." In it, he explained the underlying rationale for Tesla's strategic decisions. The implication was that Tesla's strategic decisions could seem random or counter-productive without an understanding of the bigger picture—the purpose of Tesla Motors.

Unlike most companies, Tesla is not in business to make money or satisfy customers, but to save the planet. Electric cars, Musk implied, are just a "vehicle," so to speak, for accomplishing that goal. This mindset makes Tesla representative of a new breed of company, conceived and operated to achieve something far beyond the scope of traditional business.

Musk started Tesla with a problem to solve. When he was in college, he famously outlined five areas of science he believed would have the most influence on the future of the human species:

1. the Internet

2. sustainable energy

3. space exploration

4. artificial intelligence

5. human genetics

With Tesla and a related company, SolarCity, Musk focused on sustainable energy. He recognized that modern civilization's reliance on fossil fuels puts the future of humanity in peril.

Most people who are worried about climate change or sustainability do very little about it except worry—they see it as a daunting social and economic problem. Most business leaders who care view it as something outside their responsibilities to customers and shareholders. Musk viewed the planetary threat of fossil fuel reliance as a business problem. How do we shift the global economy to a new alternative fuel source? He ultimately came up with a solution that combined engineering and marketing. This was the thinking he outlined in Master Plan Part Deux.

Fossil fuels power our modern world and have done so since the dawn of the Industrial Revolution. Our addiction to them is incredibly strong. Before the Industrial Revolution, wind power, water power, wood and coal (the main fossil fuel of the bunch) were the primary sources of energy we used for transportation, agriculture, heat, etc. After the Industrial Revolution, the need for reliable, cheap fuel grew exponentially—and oil fit the bill because it is relatively inexpensive, easy to find, transportable, storable, refined and adaptable to many different purposes.

Some people have long argued that wind and solar power are cheaper (free, they insist) and more available. But they actually present complex problems as fuel sources. They are not as reliable, easy to store, transportable or adaptable. And until recently, the cost of solar panels and wind turbines was prohibitive. Those costs are finally going down as the adoption of the technologies scale. Weaning off fossil fuels is more possible than ever today but still extremely challenging.

As an engineer, Musk knew that most of our fossil fuels (up to 60 percent) are used in vehicles, especially personal vehicles and transport trucks. And the world has billions of them. This is why, to help convert the world to greater sustainable energy use, he decided to focus on manufacturing electric vehicles. Thus, Tesla was born.

Electric vehicles are not a solution unto themselves, however. They present a number of very difficult problems in any grand effort to increase the use of alternative solar power. Here are some big obstacles:

- **Fuel storage**

   Crude oil, once refined and converted to gasoline, can be stored in tanks. A car can carry its own fuel as it travels, burning that fuel along the way.

   Solar energy can't be carried in a tank but must be stored in a battery. Until recently, batteries for electric vehicles presented a formidable engineering problem. They were extremely expensive and poor performing, offering limited power and range at high cost. Tesla and other car makers helped advance battery technology significantly in the past decade, enabling vehicles with more power and range.

Nevertheless, other problems remained. When a gas-powered car gets low on fuel, it can stop at a convenient gas station and get more fuel, quickly and cheaply. This network of gas stations did not arise overnight but developed and expanded over a century. Such a network is not easy to replicate quickly, especially when the customer base for electric energy is so small.

This is where Musk's other company, SolarCity, came in. SolarCity, an electric solar panel manufacturing and installation company, developed products that would not only power homes and buildings, but electric vehicles, too. Today, SolarCity (founded by two of Musk's cousins but based on his idea) is a subsidiary of Tesla. The vision of cheap, reliable solar power requires a network of solar panels generating electricity, batteries that can store that electricity, and homes and vehicles that use the electricity. Such a network is necessary to convert more of humanity to sustainable energy.

■ Cost and Market Appeal

Cost is another hurdle to widescale adoption and success. There's a reason why the world has so few car manufacturers. Most were formed seventy-five to one hundred years ago. Producing new vehicles is extremely expensive. It takes years of sales to achieve the production scale to reduce costs and compete with other, established manufacturers.

Tesla made their first electric vehicles as cheap as possible, but they knew that would still be far too expensive for most car buyers. So Tesla decided to appeal to early, wealthy adopters, accustomed to fast, smart-looking cars. The first Teslas were stylish high-performance vehicles with distinctive features, like winged doors. They were exciting to drive.

This approach to product development is counter to the strategies of most new market entrants. When cracking established markets, new entrants typically release a cheaper version first. Early cars, radios or TVs made in Japan, for example, were shoddy products but so cheap that people saw them as attractive alternatives. Only later, after achieving market share, did Japanese manufacturers improve their products and raise their prices to match the levels of performance of the established competition. In our own day, new entrants in the smartphone market, like Android, started with cheaper alternatives to the expensive iPhone.

After gaining market awareness and revenue from its costly high-end vehicles, Tesla began to produce and release more affordable mass-market vehicles. This worked as a business strategy and an adoption strategy.

With more car sales, the use of sustainable energy began to grow.

■ Scale and Impact

Still, car sales are just a drop in the bucket. Musk knows that adoption must gain scale to have an impact.

Accordingly, Tesla plans to develop affordable fleets of trucks and buses to begin to supplant existing gas- or diesel-powered transportation vehicles.

It also knows that the market for electric vehicles will only grow if other manufacturers follow Tesla's lead. In line with that view, Tesla did something that no "normal" business would do—it released all its patents. By making the plans for Tesla vehicles and batteries open source and available to all, Tesla is encouraging competitors and adoption.

- **Other Innovations**

Tesla has also been focused on developing driverless technology. This is not just to make Tesla vehicles more cool or even to save lives lost in accidents, but to solve significant problems in fuel consumption.

Traffic jams exacerbate fuel waste. Driverless technology, when present in numerous vehicles, allows those vehicles to coordinate their movements and improve traffic flow.

Driverless cars also allow drivers to do other things while driving, like work, read or communicate, improving productivity.

By turning the car into what is essentially a mobile computer on wheels, Tesla's driverless technology also helps convert cars into data nodes. Car operations and behaviors can be monitored constantly by artificial intelligence. Car performance can be optimized by sending cars new instructions in real time. Cars essentially become nodes in a larger network.

Perhaps this can even reduce the need for cars. Cars can be shared or rented more easily, and arrive when and where you need them, if they are operated by an intelligent network.

These are not normal business strategies. They are the priorities of a business whose purpose is to save the world. Most CEOs would get fired for such audacious plans. Even leaders who might want to save the world would likely keep those grandiose thoughts to themselves. Not Musk. As he put it, Master Plan Part Deux:

> *By definition, we must at some point achieve a sustainable energy economy or we will run out of fossil fuels to burn and civilization will collapse. Given that we must get off fossil fuels anyway and that virtually all scientists agree that dramatically increasing atmospheric and oceanic carbon levels is insane, the faster we achieve sustainability, the better.*

> *Here is what we plan to do to make that day come sooner:*

- *Create stunning solar roofs with seamlessly integrated battery storage*
- *Expand the electric vehicle product line to address all major segments*
- *Develop a self-driving capability that is 10X safer than manual via massive fleet learning*
- *Enable your car to make money for you when you aren't using it*

A New Approach to Innovation

Purpose can seem so intangible or idealistic that some leaders might find it difficult to imagine how they can leverage purpose to actually innovate and solve business challenges. The key is to start with a meaningful purpose and work backwards through the practical challenges (business, technological, market) that stand in the way, while leveraging innovative solutions and business approaches to overcome them. In this way, purpose and innovation become tightly woven with strategy and business model.

As a purpose-driven leader, Elon Musk thinks of business as a means to an end, a tool for solving big, global problems. When Musk identifies problems with critical needs, they seem beyond the scope of individuals or even organizations to solve. So Musk reverse engineers those problems to come up with practical solutions, breaking challenges down into manageable tasks and solving each one in turn. Often this requires lots of money and talent to accomplish. A corporate structure enables Musk to attract investors, hire people, build products, sell them in the market, and move the needle on the global problem he wants to solve.

The process is very similar to the 5 Whys Technique"[58] I alluded to in Chapter Four in which you identify a problem at one level and follow a chain of questions to determine the ultimate source of that problem. Here's how it goes:

- Name a problem you're having

- Ask why it's happening

---

58   https://www.huffingtonpost.com/mitch-ditkoff/why-you-need-to-ask-why_b_2681958.html

- Get an answer

- Then ask why about that

- Get an answer

- Then ask why about that—and so on, five times

When you "reach the bottom", you usually unpack the essence of the problem, the opportunity, the real point.

Musk starts his own version of the 5 Whys Technique with Purpose—the ultimate why. Then he gets to a viable product that will succeed in the market while still helping to achieve his original goal. His analysis looks like this:

- **Purpose (global)**—to reduce CO2 emission levels and help save the planet

- **How**—by (replacing) transitioning energy use from fossil fuels to solar power

- **Through**—increasing use of electric vehicles and making it easier to use solar power in homes

    - **Obstacle**—widespread reliance on fossil-fuel powered automobiles
    - **Solution**—build high-performance electric vehicle

    - **Obstacle**—current battery performance levels poor
    - **Solution**—bring in the best engineers to substantially build a better battery

    - **Obstacle**—customers don't see electric vehicles as appealing
    - **Solution**—focus on speed, style, and brand to increase high-end demand

    - **Obstacle**—to scale and achieve mass consumption, lower-cost models are required
    - **Solution**—build successively cheaper versions and cut out middle-men (dealers) to reduce costs

- **Obstacle**—need competition to spur demand for electric vehicles and associated services. Need open platform to scale
- **Solution**—release all patents for electric-vehicle technology

- **Obstacle**—need to stimulate broad demand for solar power
- **Solution**—build battery pack for home use to allow solar power customers to store and efficiently use that energy

Musk has pressed on through many obstacles and maintained focus on the fundamental problem because of the importance of the purpose in his sights.

PURPOSE-DRIVEN INNOVATION IN FIVE STEPS

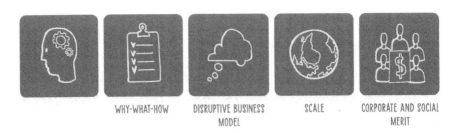

WHY-WHAT-HOW   DISRUPTIVE BUSINESS MODEL   SCALE   CORPORATE AND SOCIAL MERIT

The same thinking and approach applies to Musk's other major company, SpaceX.

Space exploration is one of the five areas of science that Musk believed in college would affect the future of humanity. But space exploration for its own sake is not the point. Rather, Musk believes space exploration is necessary to preserve the viability of the human species. After all, if climate change does make life inhospitable for humans or some other extinction event (like a planet-killing meteor) does occur, then the human species will only survive if it can migrate to another planet.

This may seem like an outlandish and even ridiculous reason to build a company, but Musk has taken a very practical path. Once again, he reverse-engineers the big problem to identify the key challenges in the way and then builds businesses to solve those challenges. In this case, one of the major barriers to interplanetary travel is the cost of rocket technology. Every time NASA sent a space capsule into space, it threw away a giant rocket (essentially a fuel tank). This limited space flights and impeded the kind of delivery of people and resources necessary to build and establish a colony on another planet, such as Mars.

There is, however, a viable market for sending satellites into space. As of 2017, there were 4,635 artificial satellites orbiting the Earth.[59] Most are commercial devices. Musk saw an opportunity to supplant government-funded space programs like NASA by developing cheaper, reusable rocket technology for delivering satellites and materials to space and the International Space Station.

This is a very new way of looking at purpose and business. It's not for every leader, but at a time when leaders (especially young leaders) are more idealistic and purpose-driven than ever, it is becoming a more common way to build, fund, staff and run a viable business.

Such companies are focused on global needs in areas that are not being served by businesses or with technologies and approaches that are not being applied to those problems. They are disruptive in the sense that they are driving innovations that haven't been seen before while also bringing benefits beyond the boundaries of their sectors or markets. A mix of startups and established companies occupy this space; though, typically, the more established companies had internal startup engines driving their innovations. Success for these companies is measured through disruptive growth that also helps improve global problems.

Here are some other examples:

Grameen Bank/Kiva

Muhammad Yunus, mentioned in the Grameen Danone example, was a banker who wanted to alleviate poverty in Bangladesh (a purpose with global need). Yunus observed the impact that small loans could have on helping launch and support small businesses. He decided the most effective solution would be to offer microloans to female entrepreneurs specifically because that gender is under-employed, highly motivated to support their families, and lacking in access to capital. Yunus' Grameen Bank hit multiple objectives: It funded new business growth, alleviated family poverty, and saw a return on its investment.

Inspired by Yunus, Matt Flannery and Jessica Jackley launched Kiva Microfunds which enables people to give money to entrepreneurs in developing countries via a network of field partners. This brings the power of microfinance to greater scale with more expansive reach. Like Grameen, most of Kiva's loans go to female entrepreneurs. Loans are also made to enable students to attend higher education or to support refugees.[60]

BIONIC/G-Star Raw

G-Star Raw is an environmentally focused Dutch designer-jeans manufacturer founded in 1989.[61] Initially, G-Star specialized in using raw denim, which means that the cotton is unwashed and untreated by harmful chemicals. In addition, G-Star Raw sourced organic cotton, grown sustainably, for its clothing.

This would have been another example of a business competing in an established space with a higher purpose by adopting more sustainable practices. In 2014, however, the company joined forces with BIONIC, a company co-owned by musician and producer Pharrell Williams.[62] BIONIC is a raw material manufacturing company, launched on the principle that "a company can successfully marry purpose with profit." BIONIC focused on using plastic pollution recovered from the oceans and coastlines as the source of its fabrics and materials for any number of applications, from clothing to furniture and cars and industrial uses. The goal is to alleviate the massive problem of plastic pollution—an island of plastic the size of Texas floats in the Pacific Ocean. G-Star Raw made the decision to use BIONIC recycled materials in its jeans.[63] This required the company to completely

---

60   https://www.bizjournals.com/columbus/news/2018/07/26/social-entrepreneur-kiva-expanding-access-to.html

61   https://www.inverse.com/article/15182-for-g-star-raw-the-hottest-fashion-trend-is-recycled-plastic

62   http://bionic.is

63   https://www.forbes.com/sites/zackomalleygreenburg/2014/02/10/from-blue-to-green-inside-pharrells-latest-fashion-venture/#57570d5754e4

overhaul its sourcing strategy and adopt its factories. The new product has helped G-Star Raw enhance its brand with many celebrity endorsements and good press while expanding its market with new stores around the world.

Impossible Foods

Impossible Foods, founded by Stanford biochemistry professor, Patrick Brown, is one of a host of companies trying to alleviate global reliance on CO_2-producing cows by converting meat- and cheese-eaters to delicious plant-based substitutes. Approximately 30 percent of arable land is devoted to farming animals. Brown claims that Impossible Foods' technology uses 95 percent less land and 75 percent less water than beef. He notes that, if the world switches away from animal-based meat and cheese and to plant-based meat and cheese, the impact on the planet's plant biomass will be "easily visible from outer space."[64] Impossible Foods also has numerous celebrity endorsements and is gaining traction in grocery stores and restaurants, including fast-food franchises.

Uncharted Power

Uncharted Play was launched by Harvard grad and Nigerian-American dual citizen, Jessica O. Matthews, to help bring electric power to underserved communities around the world. The first product was a soccer ball called the Soccket that generated electric charge as children played with it. The ball could then be used to power lights.

The idea was inspiring, the objective admirable, but the business faltered. The balls themselves did not last long and distribution problems impeded sales. As a top executive of Coca-Cola told Matthews, "you have to become a business so people can do business with you."[65]

So, Uncharted Play pivoted. They realized they were not a maker of soccer balls or jump ropes but of a technology that enables microgenerators to harvest energy. Partner companies could make the devices for those

---

64   https://www.bloomberg.com/news/articles/2018-04-20/impossible-foods-quest-to-save-planet-draws-environmentalist-ire

65   https://medium.com/@jessicaomatthews/unchartedpower-dfd781a2f19

microgenerators. This helped Uncharted Play broaden the scope of its ventures beyond "play" objects. In 2016, its technology was used to generate power through vehicular traffic. The company soon changed its name to Uncharted Power.[66]

This shows the centrality of purpose to Matthews and her company. It might have been easy with praise and funding to pivot in a more purely commercial direction, but the company stayed true to its goal to democratize the availability of power.

Khan Academy/Udacity/Coursera

Nonprofit organizations can also disrupt existing industries while endeavoring to solve global problems. Education is one of the great disparities between the well-off and economically deprived people as well as people from developing countries. Access to quality education can significantly impact the prospects of any individual. MOOCs, or Massive Open Online Courses, threaten the exclusivity of expensive academic institutions but democratize learning at unprecedented scale.

Organizations like Khan Academy, Udacity and Coursera were launched as ambitious, world-changing initiatives. Though each has narrowed its focus to specific market niches, these companies are still striving to make advanced education and learning available at global scale.

We thought that this new breed of companies that both innovate in completely new spaces while addressing global issues belong to a separate category, and this is how we grouped them:

Group D

- Uber
- Tesla
- GE
- Uncharted Play
- Khan Academy
- G-Star Raw
- Impossible Foods
- Space X
- Google
- Grameen Bank
- Embrace

---

66   https://medium.com/@jessicaomatthews/unchartedpower-dfd781a2f19

Beneath the Bottom Line

Purpose-driven businesses enhance their appeal by focusing on problems or issues that their employees and the customers of their products and services care about. The "loftiness" of their purpose dictates the space in which they play.

Plotting these ideas on an innovation vs purpose context diagram (the X/Y chart described in Chapter Five) we ended up with the below picture:

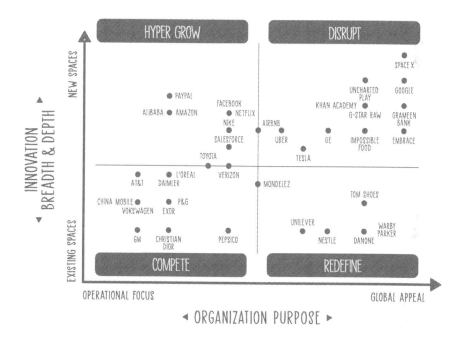

Companies with an operational focus in an existing space (Compete) are focused on delivering service, price, and/or experience their customers value. Their fundamental goal is to satisfy customers while serving as a good corporate citizen—fortifying communities, enhancing diversity, operating ethically. This is Quadrant 1.

Companies that compete in existing spaces with global appeal deliver the same kinds of products and services, but they are also cognizant of larger needs their products can help fill. They recognize that businesses use and may even exploit resources, labor and economically undeveloped areas, for example, and strive to operate in such a way that the world (not just the customer) is better off because of their business, rather diminished by it. They sit in Quadrant 2.

Companies with an operational focus in a new space (Hyper-Growth) want to delight customers, rather than merely satisfy them, by meeting their needs in ways that exceed traditional expectations for service, experience, convenience, price, etc. They believe the customer is the highest good and the focus of all innovation, and will sacrifice short-term profit to meet customer needs. Most probably revenue and scale is their primary focus, and they are located in Quadrant 3.

Companies that focus on global concerns in a new space are more idealistic and ambitious than traditional businesses. They are trying to save the world by leveraging the structure, operations, funding and revenue models of traditional businesses in service of some great cause. This is clearly Quadrant 4.

All purpose-driven companies attempt to live by a higher standard or code than mere bottom-line concerns like maximizing profit or growing market share. The degree to which they strive for higher aims depends on their quadrant. Does this approach to business make a positive difference? We've tried to show that it does, because purpose-driven companies typically outperform traditional competitors. Purpose can be linked to more discretionary effort on behalf of employees and more intense brand loyalty from customers. It may not be top of mind all the time but it's there, beneath the bottom line. Purpose also provides direction and focus for innovation. The performance of such companies shows that purpose supports profits.

Purpose-driven companies are also more resilient over time. During moments of crisis, scandal or failure, a strong and clear purpose reinforces commitment to the company and helps leaders guide people through choppy waters. In effect, it gives companies extra credibility and latitude with customers and employees. No one expects those companies to lose money deliberately or to not operate fundamentally like normal businesses. But the companies stand for something more, and they have relatively clear values or moral lines.

Indeed, companies cross these lines or violate their customers' and employees' expectations at their peril. It's one thing for a finance company like Wells Fargo to rip off customers with extra accounts, service charges and improper foreclosures—Wells Fargo does not have a sincere reputation as a purpose-driven company. However, when purpose-driven companies or purpose-focused leaders seem to violate a lofty reputation, the public repercussions can be severe.

For example, in 2018, cracks began to show in Elon Musk's glowing reputation. With investors (especially analysts and short-sellers) and others, Musk revealed erratic and occasionally vindictive behavior unbecoming of a planetary savior. However, the true believers of Telsa (customers, employees and investors) are holding on, perhaps because Musk's overall purpose remains strong, and he has yet to violate the values they want to see in him.

There are advantages to being a purpose-driven business today, but there are hazards, too. Authenticity and integrity must be demonstrated. Purpose-driven companies and leaders must speak and live their truth.

CHAPTER SIX RECAP

- Innovating in unchartered territories that are new to the industry and new to the world is an alternative way to overcome incrementalism and achieve hyper-growth. The stories of Nike, Apple, Netflix, Amazon prove it.

- The secret is to discover and address the needs of your customers that they do not even know they have.

- To achieve hyper-growth, innovation alone does not suffice.

- Disruptive companies do not just break the existing rules, they expand the business to address global societal needs and do it in an organized, step-by-step approach.

- A purpose-driven innovation model embraces the goal of exponential and disruptive growth.

- The innovation-purpose matrix can help you define your strategic pursuit of growth.

Tools & Resources

- Read the continuous innovation article by Ash Maurya. It nicely illustrates how the innovation process has changed over the years, until today when it is intrinsic to every company's continuously evolving business model. Visit my site www.christostsolkas.com to check out the link.

- Get familiar with the innovation process through the use of Ideation Templates. It is an innovation process enabler developed by one of my favorite teachers at Stanford, Dr. Jonathan Levav. Here are the titles of his five templates:

  - Subtraction—useful for complex products or to control costs

- Task unification—when aiming to control costs

- Division—for simple quantitative improvements

- Multiplication—for simple quantitative improvements

- Attribute dependency—useful generally, but hard

Visit my site www.christostsolkas.com to watch the video where Jonathan explains the theory with examples.

- Similary, Business Model Innovation (BMI) is very nicely presented and taught at St. Gallen University. The thinking is based on the underlying assumption that all business models are consisted of distinguishable patterns. Innovation, therefore, comes when these patterns are creatively reassembled in different combination.

  Visit my site www.christostsolkas.com to read a very comprehensive paper of BMI.

CHAPTER SEVEN

Pick a Global Problem, Any Problem

On December 7, 1972, the Apollo 17 spaceship was launched. For a few hours, the space capsule orbited the Earth's atmosphere, then its third-stage rocket was ignited to break the spaceship away from Earth and establish its trajectory to the moon. Almost two hours after departing from orbit, astronaut Jack Schmitt did something that the spaceflight's tight schedule did not authorize him to do. He pointed a camera at Earth, lined up his shot and took a picture.

That photograph was the first to capture the whole planet in a single, non-composite image from outer space. To the astronauts on board and the countless millions who've admired it since, the image is awe-inspiring. The Earth looks like a beautiful "Blue Marble" afloat in a black and infinite sea.

Many had longed for such an image for some time. A counterculture leader named Stewart Brand had lobbied NASA through the 1960s to release a picture of the Earth from space because he believed it would inspire a more planetary consciousness. Brand had used a composite image of the moon on the very first edition of a new magazine he published in 1968 called *The Whole Earth Catalog*. He used other images of the moon for the covers of subsequent editions. *Whole Earth* was an eclectic collection of essays, articles and product reviews which aimed to promote a view of the Earth as a single planet, not a collection of different countries and people. Brand and his readers believed that global challenges such as environmental pollution, overpopulation and the threat of nuclear destruction could only be tackled if more people understood the holistic, shared nature of the Earth. As futurist architect and scientist Buckminster Fuller put it at the time, "people perceived the earth as flat and infinite, and that that was the root of all their misbehavior."

Apollo 17 was the last manned spaceflight to leave the Earth's atmosphere. Five years later, in September 1977, NASA launched an unmanned robotic spacecraft called Voyager 1 to study the solar system. It was a bold goal with unlikely chances of success. Even if Voyager 1 reached Jupiter or Saturn, it was very possible human beings would lose contact with the spaceship and never know what had happened to it.

In 1980, Voyager 1 achieved its primary objective by reaching Saturn and viewing the planet and its moons from perspectives never before seen by humans. Then, in accordance with its original flight plan, Voyager 1 built up enough velocity to escape Saturn's orbit and set off for interstellar space. This would take it farther than the engineers and scientists who built Voyager 1 ever dreamed.

Although Voyager 1 was on a mission to explore the universe, Carl Sagan insisted that Earth should not be forgotten. He pushed hard for the NASA team to turn the spaceship's camera around one last time and take a picture of Earth from the far reaches of the solar system. Despite the technical challenges and the possible danger to Voyager 1's systems from the sun's powerful radiation, Sagan was successful in his argument. On February 14, 1990, the spaceship rotated and took a photograph of Earth.

From such a great distance, Earth was no beautiful Blue Marble filling up the image. Instead, it was a pale Blue Dot in a sea of indistinguishable stars.

After that, Voyager 1's cameras were powered down, and the spaceship continued its journey into the beyond. It still travels through space today, over forty years later.

In 1994, in a speech at Cornell University, Sagan said,

Our planet is a lonely speck in the great enveloping cosmic dark. In our obscurity—in all this vastness—there is no hint that help will come from elsewhere to save us from ourselves. It is up to us. It's been said that astronomy is a humbling, and I might add, a character-building experience. To my mind, there is perhaps no better demonstration of the folly of human conceits than this distant image of our tiny world. To me, it underscores our responsibility to deal more kindly and compassionately with one another and to preserve and cherish that pale blue dot, the only home we've ever known.

The idea that there are global problems to solve is a relatively new concept for human beings. The possibility that businesses are the best tool for solving those problems is newer still.

Global problems threaten existence or quality of life. I define them as Level One problems because they are both urgent and almost too massive to conceive of resolving. Ironically, they also offer the greatest opportunity for business growth. Any company that points itself toward a Level One problem and delivers a viable market solution that can be brought to scale is likely to achieve exponential growth.

It's a very new thing, however, for a Level One problem to be tackled by business. For most of our history, when human beings have managed to face such a threat, they have done so through the vehicle of government. How can a business leader identify a global or Level One problem and develop a solution or a market approach that can galvanize a company (including shareholders) and be successful with customers?

Addressing Global Problems—the Institutional Approach

World War I, known then as the Great War, created such horrendous suffering at such scale that many wished or believed it would be forever known as the "war to end all wars." The savagery of war, the fear of disease, even injustice did not stay within one country's borders. Problems in one country affected other countries, too. People of all nations, we now understood, shared a common enemy.

Crisis motivates purpose and channels energy. The new thinking around ending war evolved quickly in the lead-up to the peace treaty negotiations. U.S. President Woodrow Wilson, in preparation for the negotiations, developed a list of "Fourteen Points" that envisioned how a more peaceful and just world could be secured. Wilson's plan included the establishment of a general association of nations guaranteeing the security and political independence of each state.

By 1920, a League of Nations had been formed. Its goals were to prevent wars and settle international disputes through negotiation while also addressing issues like labor conditions, mistreatment of native peoples and minorities, and global health problems. The League failed to gain a hold over world affairs as many nations, especially the United States, did not join. "America First" became a slogan among the nationalists in the U.S. who did not want to get involved in other countries' problems. Thinking of today's political ambient, it sounds ironical but also scary. Fascism began to emerge in Germany, Italy and Spain.

In opposition to the ultranationalist trend, however, stood the communist movement. Centered in the new Soviet Union, universal communism held that all workers, regardless of national origin, belonged together in common cause against the ruling and capitalist classes. It was a very purpose-driven view of the world, close to religion. Yet, like most religions, it was also highly conflict oriented and saw those with contrary views as enemies.

World War II brought global conflict back again. All nations and regions of the world were affected. The League of Nations was dissolved in 1943 and replaced with a new United Nations, in the hope that some day the world could begin to strive for peace and problem-solving again. The development of the atomic bomb made such a global perspective all the more urgent. Suddenly, the total destruction of the world was possible. Other problems like pollution, explosive population growth and famine were almost as threatening. These sorts of challenges and crises could not be addressed by single nations or even alliances because they crossed many borders and regions. They were global problems.

This gave even more energy and sense of purpose to global organizations like the United Nations and the World Bank. Though somewhat independent of nations, these are essentially political organizations that reflect the values, strategies and priorities of their member states. As such, the solutions they offer to global problems are often ineffective or hampered by political disagreements or alliances. For example, a war in the Middle East might threaten global peace, but attempts to intervene could be blocked by Security Council members that don't want to upset a client state or a delicate strategic balance.

To address global problems and crises more directly, non-governmental organizations (NGOs) like UNICEF, the International Red Cross, Doctors without Borders and so on, have arisen. These organizations are less hampered by politics but also less powerful because they are not backed by a government or nation. Instead, they rely on donations, expertise and political skill to achieve their goals. Typically, they focus on a specific type of global problem—like disaster relief, hunger, education, urgent care, blindness, malaria, etc.

For example, when the dreaded Ebola virus broke out in the Congo, both the Congolese government and the international community were unable to respond effectively to the crisis, perhaps due to the fear of the virus spreading. The international NGO Doctors without Borders/Medicine sans Frontiers went anyway. An emergency care team flew into the capital. Helicopters were unavailable, so they rented cars and drove three days into the jungle to the grass hut town where the virus had shown up. The DWB's team built an isolation ward within 24 hours and began testing the villagers for the virus. They had to overcome the reluctance of people who feared being tested. When they learned of deaths in nearby villages, they went to those bodies immediately, isolated them, disinfected everything and transported the bodies back to their base. Battling Ebola is a race against time. DWB care teams were willing to do whatever it took to help people in need.

NGOs have advantages. They are built to provide a solution that fills a deep need in the world, and their employees and donors are more likely to care passionately about that cause. This can make the purpose-driven organizations. Since they are not affiliated with a particular government, they can address cross-border or global problems more easily. Unfortunately, they often lack clout or resources as a result. They are frustratingly limited in their ability to solve the causes of problems, and instead tend to focus on alleviating the effects.

Can business possibly hope to tackle global problems more effectively given the limits of market capitalism and its focus on profit?

Enter technology.

Technology Speeds Up Globalization

Technology has always played a huge role in giving people a more global perspective. The printing press made the mass production of books and newspapers possible and launched the international circulation of information and ideas. The steam engine launched the Industrial Revolution, creating great opportunities for manufacturing, necessitating global trade, increasing the speed of transportation, and enabling the expansion of nations and businesses around the world—for good and bad.

Electronic communication increased the speed of globalization and deepened global ties. The telegraph, the telephone, the radio and then the television began to eliminate the distance between peoples, and facilitated more sharing of ideas, news, information, culture, events and, yes, problems, too.

Airplane travel made physical distances smaller. When Charles Lindbergh crossed the Atlantic by plane, he opened up the possibility that people could move about the planet more freely and conveniently. When the Soviet Union launched the Sputnik space satellite, it galvanized America to develop its own space program. Speaking to a crowd in Texas, the American President John F. Kennedy gave one of his most famous and inspiring speeches which focused on the sense of purpose a mission to the moon would bring:

We choose to go to the Moon... because that goal will serve to organize
and measure the best of our energies and skills, because that challenge

is one that we are willing to accept, one we are unwilling to postpone,
and one we intend to win...

And on the last of those Apollo moon missions, an astronaut aimed his camera at Earth and took a picture.

When the *Whole Earth Catalog* put the photograph of the Earth taken from outer space on its cover, it captured the minds of many global young visionaries at the time. Steve Jobs noticed. In his famous 2005 commencement speech at Stanford University, Jobs described the *Whole Earth Catalog* as the first Google because it introduced curious people of his generation to ideas and possibilities they could find nowhere else. *Whole Earth Catalog* founder Stewart Brand seemed to have that vision in mind when he founded the WELL (Whole Earth 'Lectronic Link), one of the world's first virtual communities. WELL started as an electronic Bulletin Board System (BBS) before the development of Internet browsers, then became one of the first ISPs when commercial traffic on the Internet was permitted. In the WELL, topics of conversation were divided into sub-categories, much like REDDIT today.

The Internet changed everything, of course. The emergence of giant companies like Amazon and, especially Google, enabled globalization to take a quantum leap. Devices like smartphones gave mobility to computer power and the Internet. Use of the Internet expanded from idea exchange to business exchange. Even small businesses have become global in our technology-enabled world. Users have become customers, and those customers can be found everywhere.

Now, as a result of technology, people and businesses can influence events in other parts of the world and be influenced by them in turn.

The Business of Business Is Changing

Today, for the first time in history, organizations are stepping up to meet the challenges that governments and international organizations can't seem to resolve. Until recently, corporations put little focus on problems not related directly to their business. Shareholders and even customers insisted that corporations concentrate not on social problems but on making desirable products and services as cheaply and efficiently as possible. Any attention paid to global problems should occur through philanthropic funding and activity.

That's changing for the reasons I described in Chapter Three. If a customer buys a shirt in America today, they want it to be inexpensive, but they are also concerned that it be manufactured under humane labor conditions. Likewise, a company producing a refreshing drink or a smartphone had better deliver that product as cheaply and conveniently as possible, while also not exacerbating any environmental problems around the world. Companies can no longer outsource or offshore their bad behaviors.

Today's new generation of founders and CEOs take that sense of corporate responsibility even further. They believe in the power of business to do good while also doing well, and they know this can be channeled to help propel their businesses to greater success.

They understand how purpose can motivate, satisfy and align people like few other sources of meaning.

Some companies seek to do good by dramatically improving business operations in line with a sense of purpose or mission. These are the companies in Quadrant 3. Often they do this by increasing efficiency and access while reducing prices and friction. Amazon, Nike and Netflix took traditional business models and turbocharged them on behalf of customers, scaling their offerings to another level compared to competitors. This enables them to reach more customers, provide better service and earn more revenue which gets fed back into customer service and efficiency. The result is a dramatic enhancement of value, operational efficiency, access to global markets and improvement in customer satisfaction and experience.

Some companies seek to do good by leveraging their business models and processes in a more purpose-driven way to benefit individuals, communities and the world. These are the companies in Quadrant 2. Danone, TOMS Shoes and Patagonia are among the companies that provide traditional goods and services but tweak their business models to improve people's lives, often beyond their customer base. Danone helps improve the sustainability of farming and water. TOMS Shoes delivers footwear to those who are too poor to afford it. Patagonia is trying to improve sourcing practices and help the environment. No analyst would say these efforts are "good for business" or the bottom line; and yet, when such companies live by a sense of purpose, they create goodwill, commitment and enthusiasm among employees, customers and communities, that pays significant dividends.

For companies that wish to be purpose-driven, Quadrants 2 and 3 offer clear paths forward. Such companies are offering products and services aligned with commercial demand.

If there is a problem with Quadrants 2 and 3, it is this: Those arenas of innovation are getting increasingly crowded. Twenty years ago, with the dawn of the popular Internet, a great wave of startups strove to "dot-com" existing business models. Amazon transformed brick-and-mortar bookstores with its digital platform and then moved on to overwhelm every other retail product distributor. Netflix out-competed brick-and-mortar video stores and later attacked traditional cable channels. Nike elevated the brand of a shoe and linked it to the passion for athletics and competition. Today, creating room in this space with a new company or a new twist on an existing sector is daunting. There is limited Blue Ocean to explore.

Same goes for Quadrant 2 companies. Given the success of Patagonia, Danone and TOMS Shoes, more companies will increasingly integrate their philanthropic or corporate social responsibility initiatives into their business models. To the extent that they are sincere about improving lives, communities and the world, this trend will be a good thing. The planet can use all the help it can get. But it will be increasingly difficult to differentiate companies that leverage their business models to do good and achieve greater ends. Perhaps, however, it will also become the norm.

The area with the most Blue Ocean or white space is Quadrant 4, where organizations are specifically built and directed toward solving a global problem or meeting a global need. Traditionally, this has been outside the interests of for-profit business. NGOs and global organizations, supported by governments and donors, have been able to provide services without the need for profits. In recent years, for-profit enterprises have begun to move into that space, but most are either very small or their transition to profitability remains far off.

Yet, in the future, this is where the action will be. The potential scale and need is enormous. This is the new realm for massive growth. The question is: What crisis will you focus on? What urgent global need will your business seek to fill? And in that sense, what is the use case you are working on?

Identifying Level One Problems

In his book, *The Better Angels of Our Nature*, Steven Pinker says we are living in the most peaceful period in the history of humankind. Our likelihood of being murdered, dying in a war or losing a child to a fatal disease is lower than ever. Compared to previous eras, millions more people than ever live above subsistence levels and are able to afford luxury items like electronic goods and vehicles. Access to education has never been more widespread. Intolerance and systematic repression is less prevalent, despite the attention such problems receive in the media. By most normal standards, life today is very good, even though many people may not feel that way.

The irony is that we are also living in one of the most dangerous periods in human history. Much of that danger is a direct byproduct of our technological progress, economic development and the social institutions and systems that seem at a breaking point. Nuclear war. Climate change. Social media platforms that manipulate the public. Algorithms that restrict choice. Authoritarian governments with high-tech monitoring capabilities. The social injustice of unfair financial or voting systems enabled by digital technology. The list of potential threats is long, complex and varied.

How should we define Level One global problems and crises that can or should be tackled by business? I examined many different lists put forward by many thoughtful groups. There were plenty of commonalities and some interesting differences. For example, almost every list noted climate change and war. This is understandable since we are experiencing great disruption from storms, weather patterns, conflicts in the Middle East and the migration of refugees. But millennial survey respondents, unlike other demographic groups or populations, focused almost as heavily on social justice, government accountability and economic opportunity.[67] No doubt this is because millennials worry a lot about the challenges of making their way in a world where they are not yet established in their careers, and worry less about the challenges of growing old or sick. The U.N.'s list was more comprehensive, covering many issues, from water and food to refugees, international justice and the status of women.[68] However, that list was excessively long and was more random in terms of its categories.

Finding less overlap than I expected, I decided to identify my own short list of significant problems. I made the categories as broad as possible (Level One problems) so that I could include other, secondary problems as outgrowths or consequences. Here is my Top Three:

1. The Destruction of the Planet

The human impact on the global environment is profound. We see this through the many manifestations of climate change and the devastation due to waste and pollution.

Destructive forces that afflict the environment also threaten communities, safety, security, agriculture, livelihoods, health, etc. Rising sea levels. Arctic melting. Severe drought. Intense flooding. Hurricanes. Wildfires. The spread of disease-bearing insects. A surge in allergies. Oceans filled with plastic and human waste. Lakes and reservoirs poisoned by farm runoff.

Environmental degradation can even be linked to war, displacement and political upheaval. Scientists believe that rising temperatures, for example, contributed to the number of Syrian

---

67 https://www.businessinsider.com/world-problems-most-serious-according-to-millennials-2017-8/#10-lack-of-economic-opportunity-and-employment-121-1

68 http://www.un.org/en/sections/issues-depth/global-issues-overview/

refugees fleeing that war-torn region for the EU.[69] In turn, that surge in refugees contributed to the political destabilization of Europe and inflamed anti-immigrant sentiment in the U.S. Similarly, in Honduras, El Salvador and Equador, climate change encouraged the spread of a fungus to coffee plants which devastated crops and the local economy and put hundreds of thousands of laborers out of work.[70] The severe conditions led to political instability and the rise of gang activity.[71] Fleeing that hardship in 2016, tens of thousands joined caravans of refugees heading to the United States, influencing U.S. politics and the 2016 midterm elections.

2. Illness, Quality of Life and Death

Modern medical science and clinical care is a miracle. Hearts, hands and faces can be transplanted. Countless diseases can be treated with sophisticated drugs. Genes can be altered inside cells. Babies can be operated on in the womb.

Yet, basic health and wellness remain a challenge. Too many people around the world lack access to affordable care. The Silver Tsunami (the wave of baby boomers turning sixty-five) will bring a massive increase in chronic disease, dementia and costs. Mental illness, drug addiction, obesity, diabetes,

69   https://www.theguardian.com/environment/climate-consensus-97-per-cent/2018/jan/15/study-finds-that-global-warming-exacerbates-refugee-crises

70   https://www.mcclatchydc.com/news/nation-world/world/article24749563.html

71   https://www.huffingtonpost.com/entry/migrant-caravan-honduras-trump_us_5ad68870e4b03c426da93a2c

heart disease and social isolation are rampant, especially in the developed world.

Communities, families and society pay an enormous price (economically and socially) when people lead lives that are less healthy, engaged and productive. Those problems show every sign of growing.

Why do people still die of malaria? Why can't we yet cure cancer or eliminate hunger? Surely, there's breakthrough growth potential for companies that help people live longer and healthier lives, and die quickly and painlessly when the end has come.

3. Lack of Economic Opportunity and Social Justice

In many ways, the world has never been more prosperous and free. Yet, barriers and threats to economic advancement and abundance are everywhere.

The wealth gap is high. Extremely wealthy neighborhoods, regions and nations can exist near very poor ones. Race and economic status can influence how much access people have to education, employment, services (like grocery stores, banks and the Internet) and even good health. Exacerbating those problems, corruption in governments and institutions remains stubbornly common today in spite of enhanced transparency and access to information.

These forces can diminish freedom, individual rights, security and prosperity. What can we do about planetary inequality, and the growing global gap between the poor and the rich? It does not seem sustainable or desirable from environmental, economic, political or ethical standpoints. With so much wealth on the planet, how can we take better care of those in need? Is a global or universal income a solid solution?

If we don't address these problems in a meaningful, market-driven way, then I fear we will pay an enormous price. Political strife, war, terrorism, refugees, disease, death … all those horrors are only likely to intensify and will undoubtedly threaten the prosperity and quality of life of the wealthy and prosperous, too.

Strategies for Addressing a Level One Problem

No company can solve a Level One problem. It is not feasible or practical for a business to end climate change or eliminate economic disparity.

A company can, however, build a practical, feasible market solution to address a sub-problem in one of the outer rings. In doing so, it can contribute to helping alleviate a Level One problem. This imbues the market solution with a very direct and real sense of higher purpose.

Tesla, as we've already discussed, did just that. Climate change is the Level One problem it has always aimed to address. Yet, climate change is too massive, global, complex and nebulous a problem to address directly. So Tesla founder Elon Musk directed innovative energy, engineering talents and business acumen to solving a secondary problem that contributes to climate change—the increase in carbon gas in the atmosphere. He then built a commercial product and a business to make that happen.

In a very similar way, Google addressed a Level One problem as its foundational purpose. Essentially, Google came into existence to make information accessible for the benefit of humankind. As CEO Sundar Puchai put it in the 2018 letter to shareholders, "Today, our mission to organize the world's information and make it universally accessible and useful is as relevant as it was in 1998."[72] Its first product was a browser. But, even as Google expands into a dizzying array of other ventures, products and services, the company continues to hew very closely to its original sense of purpose.

---

72   https://abc.xyz/investor/founders-letters/2018/

Scanning every book in the world. Mapping every street. Building smartphones and AI assistants. Offering video content through YouTube. Organizing emails. Leveraging healthcare data. Providing Internet access to rural communities. Google's purpose is supported by a wildly profitable business model built on advertising sales. As a result, Google has the financial fuel to do whatever it wants. It's very telling that Google stays aligned with its purpose "despite" its success.

Starting with Level One problems creates a pathway from purpose to solution via a product or service offering that can drive a business. The Level One problem creates the North Star, the greater purpose worth pursuing. It allows the company to say, "We're in business to solve X" even if it actually makes a product or service that is less grandiose. In fact, the process of breaking down Level One problems into sub-problems actually makes solutions to that problem more manageable.

The below chart illustrates how some businesses start with a Level One problem, then break that down into more practically manageable problems that they can finally address with a business solution.[73] For example, if the world's two largest bottled drink companies, Coca-Cola and Pepsi, really want to impact the Level One problem of plastic waste, that power is in their hands. I have no doubt they can build a Use-case for making that a profitable or sustainable part of business operations.

WHY ↓ WHY ↓ WHY ↓

GLOBAL PROBLEM LEVEL 1	GLOBAL PROBLEM LEVEL 2	GLOBAL PROBLEM LEVEL 3	GLOBAL PROBLEM LEVEL 4	FINAL PRODUCT OR SERVICE	BRIDGING MECHANISM (HOW)-EXAMPLES	COMPANY
CLIMATE	OCEAN POLLUTION	DISPOSAL OF PLASTIC	RECYCLING	CLOTHES, APPAREL, MADE OF RECYCLED PLASTIC	RPET REPREVE FIBER (UNIFI) ECONYL (AQUAFIL) BIO-DERIVED MATERIALS	PATAGONIA H&M G-STAR RAW DGRADE HAMILTON PERKINS TIMBERLAND COSMOS STUDIO

73 https://www.knittingindustry.com/creative/making-textiles-and-clothing-from-recycled-plastics/

Here is an even more powerful example. Allbirds is a shoe company. They engage in a holistic view of their environmental impact and they go beyond recycling with the astonishing vision that "shoes should function like trees, [leaving] a net positive to the climate," clearly stating they are on a mission to put plastics and petroleum out of business. Sustainability, they say, is not enough anymore. It should be replaced by Accountability because "our planet deserves better".[74]

More and more companies are now following this path from Level One problem to commercial product. In the process, they are pursuing purpose in a very forceful and galvanizing way. Below are some specific ways to address the three Level One problems we've discussed.

Level One Problem: The Destruction of the Planet

Pollution is a planet killer. To alleviate it, companies can find better ways to reduce or eliminate the use of plastics. One way to do so is to turn recycled materials toward better uses. As previously mentioned, G-Star Raw uses recycled plastic in the manufacture of clothing that helps alleviate climate change with a practical solution and its own very different profitable business line.

Other companies are using recycled fabrics as raw materials to alleviate global waste. Apparently, most clothing (80 percent or so) that is donated actually ends up in landfills or incinerated. But brands like Eileen Fisher, Patagonia and Kaillo make a point of serving customers while reducing that waste, aligning purpose with a global problem.[75]

Level One Problem: Illness, Quality of Life and Death

Around the world, developed countries face a massive healthcare problem. Costs are soaring, particularly among patients with chronic illness, such as diabetes, heart disease, kidney disease, mental health problems

---

74 https://fortune.com/2019/10/07/allbirds-founders-why-we-need-to-eliminate-plastics-for-good/
    https://www.allbirds.com/

75 https://earth911.com/business-policy/clothes-recycling-4-brands/

and addiction issues. Such groups can account for 50-80 percent of total healthcare costs for a nation.

In the USA, the chronically ill and poor fall through the cracks because of the lack of universal healthcare coverage and a robust social welfare system. While Medicare and Medicaid might cover their care costs, they often lack the basics that take priority over care, such as adequate food, transportation or shelter. Without regular care or support, they may frequently seek necessary care at hospital emergency rooms, which is even more costly and fixes only immediate needs, not long-term ones.

For traditional hospitals and physician clinics, there is little incentive to care for these patients. But a new breed of for-profit healthcare company has recently emerged in the U.S. to fill this gap. Absolute Care, based in Atlanta, Georgia, actively seeks the sickest of the sick, the people that most healthcare organizations hope to avoid. They work with health insurance companies to identify those patients, then contract with the insurers to provide the patients with care for a certain cost. If they can produce quality care outcomes cheaper, Absolute Care earns the difference as profit.

Absolute provides better care by doing things differently. Most doctors see patients in 15-minute intervals with little time to understand the patient's deeper needs or issues. Absolute wants to see patients as much and as long as possible to understand them fully. They deploy care teams for each patient that include physicians, therapists, social workers, nutritionists and drivers. They transport patients who need to be brought to the clinic. They make sure people have appropriate food and housing, even supplying people with a place to live if needed.

These extensive services actually reduce overall costs by an average of 26 percent. They improve care outcomes dramatically. And they change lives, not just for the direct patients, but for their children and grandchildren, helping to revive and restore communities to health and economic productivity. In the process, Absolute Care makes a healthy profit which it uses to fund its growth and expansion to more clinics and cities in order to help solve the nation's overall chronic health crisis.

That's a perfect marriage between purpose, product and profit.

Level One Problem: Lack of Access to Economic Opportunity and Social Justice

Providing access to economic opportunity may seem like a pipe dream for a corporation. Yet, in some ways, it's as old as business itself. When Henry Ford started the mass production of automobiles in Detroit in the early 1890s, he knew his business could be an engine of transformation for America, helping bring the country out of an agrarian past and into an industrial future. He paid his workers the very high wage of $5 per day because he wanted to retain them and because he wanted them to be able to afford the cars they made. This linked Ford's success as a business with America's success as a nation, combining purpose with profit.

Today, lack of a living wage remains a huge barrier to economic opportunity for many people. Another barrier is access to banking, especially among the poor or "unbanked", as they say.

Worldwide, 39 percent of the world's population are unbanked (no access to banking) or underbanked (inadequate access to financial institutions). In the U.S., the unbanked and underbanked are 27 percent of the population.[76] This is a serious barrier to life in our modern world. It prevents people from getting paid, paying bills, establishing credit, transferring money to loved ones or getting loans.

In response to this massive global need, a variety of fintech and financial service companies have emerged. Business models vary, but many are based on Blockchain technology and access to mobile phones. Taiwan-based GMobi was founded in 2011 and currently reaches around 200 million users, predominantly in the developing world. In India, it launched Oxymoney, a mobile wallet that enables users to add to their cell phone credits and transfer money. This allows rural laborers to send money to their families. If those families lack access to computers or banks, they can pick up their money at local stores.[77]

---

76   https://hackernoon.com/how-to-overcome-poverty-by-helping-the-unbanked-723f8c915d62
77   https://techcrunch.com/2017/06/19/banking-the-unbanked-in-emerging-markets/

A Mexican fintech company called 4UNO focuses on providing needed banking services to domestic workers, as well as benefits like health insurance that employers can purchase for their employees. The insurance covers life and accident, unlimited medical phone calls, annual health checkups and four doctor visits for about fifteen cents a day.[78] Philippines-based Coins uses digital currencies to enable cross-border remittances, by which laborers working in a foreign country can send money to their families securely. Over $600 billion in remittance payments are made annually around the world, making this an enormous market with great need.[79]

Build a Better Mousetrap

The saying goes, "Build a better mousetrap and the world will beat a path to your door."

In 2019, if you link your business to purpose by focusing on a Level One problem, you can gain access to massive new markets while engaging talented employees, attracting purpose-driven investors and filling needs for committed and engaged customers. The best approach is to think big (Level One) and work backward to the product or service that can meet that need—then go build, operationalize and market it.

But this is not just a game for idealistic entrepreneurs. Increasingly, in a more purpose-focused marketplace, established companies will need to think about how their businesses impact Level One problems.

As with Patagonia, this may require performing a Level One audit on the company's business lines. Is it, through its products, processes, operations, sourcing practices, etc., acting in some way that negatively impacts a Level One problem? If so, this presents an opportunity to galvanize your workforce, investors and customer base in line with a greater purpose.

For example, to address the problem of pollution, the Danish beer company Carlsberg developed a simple solution. Rather than rely on plastic

---

78   https://medium.com/f4life/two-problems-one-solution-how-fintech-is-boosting-access-to-banking-and-insurance-for-domestic-1f728c259f60

79   https://techcrunch.com/2017/06/19/banking-the-unbanked-in-emerging-markets/

rings to secure six packs of beer together (the industry norm), the company has developed eco-friendly drops of adhesive that are strong enough to join beer cans together but weak enough so that customers can easily separate cans at home. The idea was developed by a Carlsberg designer who took it on himself to develop the adhesive at home one weekend, then videotaped the solution and emailed the CEO. The new "Snap Packs" are expected to reduce Carlsberg's plastic use by 1,200 tons a year, the equivalent of 60 million plastic bags. Carlsberg wants the approach to become the new industry norm. Now the same company goes one step ahead and presents its latest designs of Green Fibre Bottle made from sustainably sourced wood fibers, which it claims is fully bio-based and recyclable.[80]

How much this benefits Carlsberg financially remains to be seen. Indeed, its simple and cost-effective answer to a massive global problem may be so easy to emulate that Carlsberg eventually loses some of the credit in the market. But the employees of Carlsberg will always be able to look at a six-pack on the shelf or the "paper" bottle and know that they helped alleviate climate change and spread the benefits broadly. That is a powerful feeling for anyone associated with a company. It may also spur Carlsberg employees to embrace innovation in other opportunities, creating a culture of purpose-driven improvement.

In addition, by talking about its advancement publicly in the right way, Carlsberg can help "own" the issue. Carlsberg can transition from a traditional beer maker to a trendy product that is tied to efforts to save the planet. That's not a bad space to be in for a world of millennial consumers.

---

80 https://www.businessgreen.com/bg/news/3082507/paper-beer-bottles-carlsberg-toasts-world-first-sustainable-drink-packaging-designs

CHAPTER SEVEN RECAP

■ ■ ■ ■ ■ ■ ■ ■ ■ ■

- Despite the explosion of science, technology and knowledge, massive problems plague the planet and jeopardize its future.

- I call these Level One problems. In my view the three biggest are:

  1. The Destruction of the Planet

  2. Illness, Quality of Life and Death

  3. Lack of Economic Opportunity and Social Justice

- Global nonprofit organizations, as we know them today, have not proved fully capable of addressing these problems.

- By focusing on these very problems in a methodical way and embedding them as variables in a company's business canvas, for-profit organizations can help. There is a methodology to do so.

- Alleviating global problems epitomizes the purpose-driven leadership model and may constitute a new path for capitalism.

Tools & Resources

Here are some indicative lists of **urgent global problems**—call them challenges or dilemmas, as identified by various groups. The detailed content of the lists and the references can be found on my site www.christostsolkas.com.

- What millennials say list:

  1. Climate change/destruction of nature (48.8%)

  2. Large scale conflict/wars (38.9%)

  3. Inequality (income, discrimination) (30.8%)

4. Poverty (29.2%)

5. Religious conflicts (23.9%)

6. Government accountability and transparency/corruption (22.7%)

7. Food and water security (18.2%)

8. Lack of education (15.9%)

9. Safety/security/wellbeing (14.1%)

10. Lack of economic opportunity and employment (12.1%)

- 80,000 Hours Club list:

  1. Risks from AI

  2. Promoting effective altruism

  3. Global priorities research

  4. Improved institutional decision-making

  5. Factory farming

  6. Biosecurity

  7. Nuclear security

  8. Developing world health

  9. Climate change

  10. Land use reform

  11. Smoking in the developing world

- World Economic Forum List of five top risks

  1. Weapons of mass destruction

  2. Extreme weather

  3. Natural disasters

  4. Climate change

  5. Water crisis

CHAPTER EIGHT

We Have the Technology

In December of 1944, a Japanese soldier named Hiro Onoda was sent to an island in the Philippines to fight the Americans. Like all Japanese soldiers, Onoda was told that surrender would be dishonorable. So he soldiered on and on and on.

I read about Onoda's remarkable story in Mark Manson's book, *The Subtle Art of Not Giving a F*ck: A Counterintuitive Approach to Living a Good Life*. Onoda had a strong personal code, a sense of purpose. He also ended up slipping between the cracks of history, and waking up on the other side. This allowed him to see the world with fresh eyes, and truly notice how much technological, cultural and political change had occurred. It also forced him to question all he believed in.

A few months after he was stationed in the Philippines, American forces took the island, capturing or killing most of Onoda's compatriots. Onoda and three others hid in the jungle and continued to harass the American war effort in any way possible. That summer, the most fearsome technological advancement in human history was unleashed on the Japanese Empire when the American forces dropped the atomic bomb on Hiroshima and later on Nagasaki. Onoda didn't know anything about that. He and his companions continued to live as primitives on their island, fighting the Americans.

Even years after the war had ended, Onoda fought on. The governments of America, the Philippines and finally Japan tried to convince Onoda and others like him that the war was over. They dropped leaflets and messages everywhere. Onoda and others like him believed these were lies and fought on. The American forces were gone now, so Onoda fought the locals instead, burning their fields and buildings, stealing their food. Eventually, people believed that all the lost Japanese soldiers had been found or killed. It did not seem possible, decades after the war, for anyone else to be still out there in some jungle. Then, Onoda was found in 1974 by a Japanese adventurer who had been searching for him. This man, Suzuki, finally convinced Onoda the war was over and helped him to get home. Onoda returned after spending more than half his life in the jungle fighting a war that was long over.

He didn't seem to mind that loss. He had lived and fought for a purpose—to protect his country. The country he returned to did not seem to be the one that was worth fighting for, however. Japan had changed. Indeed, it was well on its way to becoming one of the most technologically and economically advanced countries in the world. Despite the luxuries and marvels such as TV, Onoda didn't like this new Japan. The emperor was a figurehead. America, the enemy, was now an ally. People were more worried about buying cars or consumer goods than honor or pride. Onoda did not feel at home anymore. He moved to Brazil and died there a few years later.

On the other side of the conflict in World War II, a French engineer named Pierre Boulle served as a spy in Singapore, helping resistance movements across South Asia. When he was captured by the Japanese, he was sentenced to hard labor in a jungle camp. Few people survived these terrible conditions. After the war, Boulle wrote a novel about his experience as part of a prisoner of war troop forced to build a bridge. He called the book *The Bridge Over the River Kwai*, and it was made into a movie that won Academy Awards and became a classic.

Boulle wrote other novels, but the work he became best known for was a science fiction story published later in life under a false name. Boulle called the book *Monkey Planet*. Later, it was retitled *The Planet of the Apes*. In that story, astronauts leave Earth to travel to another world. One of the astronauts, played by Charlton Heston in the movie, is cynical about the planet they're leaving behind, despite its technical advances. Earth is too prone to war and conflict. When the spaceship crash-lands on a new planet, the astronaut is shocked to find it populated by intelligent apes who capture and herd human beings as if they are animals. It is a great shock, and a terrific moment, when he discovers that the planet he landed on is actually Earth. In the aftermath of a man-made catastrophe, apes rose up and took the place of humans, turning his former home into a dystopian hell.

If we were to disappear into the jungle or fly into space for twenty or fifty years, what kind of world would we return to? Surely, in that time, technology would have changed and influenced society, perhaps dramatically. In a cynical vision, like Boulle's, that technology might be a destructive or negative force, creating a culture of want and need. In a positive vision, the world might be a better, safer, more equitable and productive place. Which world is more likely? Which technologies will shape that world most profoundly?

In this chapter I want to explore nine technologies that seem potentially influential on our future. I make no claim that these nine are the most likely to affect humanity. They are only meant to spur thinking about how technology can and will shape our world. If the stories of Onoda and Boulle are to be heeded, it will be important that technology have a clear purpose if we are to create a better future.

Technology #1: Blockchain

In five or ten years, we may look back on 2009 and view it as one of the most important moments in the history of information technology, on par with the rise of the personal computer, the emergence of the Internet, the development of search engines, the evolution of smartphones and the reliance on the cloud. The advancement I'm talking about is Blockchain, something so nebulous and unusual most people don't really understand what it is or does.

Blockchain is a virtual ledger that records transactions and data. The ledger is transparent, decentralized and public, and represents a complete historical record of all transactions associated with an event, a product or service. Those records cannot be altered, destroyed or hidden; therefore, they function as a permanent "source of truth" that does not rely on being located in any place. As a result, the record is accessible anywhere, anytime. While this approach to recording information may sound simple or unnecessary, it is actually a breakthrough in cryptography. Blockchain enables transactions that are completely safe and secure. It creates "trust" in anonymous Internet transactions where no trust existed or seemed possible before. Most importantly, it decentralizes and democratizes control of an individual's information. It puts "you" in charge of your own data, eliminates the need for middlemen (like banks), and creates the kind of transparency that will shine a bright light on the world's darkest corners.

Today, Blockchain has many practical uses.[81] For example, it can help health plans or drug manufacturers trace a drug from production through distribution and sale to the end-user, allowing the companies involved to determine whether that person actually takes the drug or how they are affected by it, positively or negatively. Similarly, Blockchain is used in many other supply chain situations. For example, the world has a huge problem with food fraudulence—the expensive fish or extra virgin olive oil you enjoy in an unpscale restaurant may actually be substitute products—and food wastage. Blockchain can help securely verify the provenance of an item, so you know where it came from and where it's been along the way. Likewise, Blockchain can help us understand how or where food is going uneaten, opening the way to transforming waste on a global scale.

For those who have heard of Blockchain, chances are that happened because of Bitcoin. In fact, Bitcoin is only possible because of Blockchain, its underlying technology. Bitcoin is a truly virtual currency, stored only in

---

81 https://www.telegraph.co.uk/connect/better-business/business-solutions/blockchain-applications/

the cloud. At first, Bitcoin was largely attached to dark web activities, such as occur on Silk Road, an online service for selling drugs. Later, as early adopters proliferated, digital transactions normalized and the currency became more mainstream. The value of a Bitcoin rose and fell (sometimes sharply) like the value of any traded commodity. This alarmed observers and reassured them that Bitcoin followed some conventional rules after all. Yet, there was also something enticing about its magical power to exist outside financial institutions. The mainstream is beginning to catch on, and sophisticated economies like Singapore, Dubai and Iran are experimenting with cryptocurrency while Canada, the UK and Israel are researching the possibility. On the other hand, Germany, Switzerland and Japan are among the countries that have experimented with and rejected cryptocurrencies.[82]

Bitcoin and Blockchain represent a potentially seismic shift in the control of economic resources and information. They eliminate the need for intermediaries. Since the 1500s, financial transactions have been largely channeled through financial institutions like banks. This makes these institutions centers of power. The powerful control them. The powerful access them. And they exert great power over national economies and the state. For the first time in history, Bitcoin and all other cryptocurrencies shift some of that power away from centralized banks or governments and into the hands of individuals.

One of the biggest problems in today's world is the mobility of money. Worldwide, over 2 billion people do not have adequate access to financial institutions.[83] Banking is also costly. Transaction fees, late fees, handling fees, etc., may be small but they add up, and banks seek to manipulate processes to maximize those fees and extract billions from customers. Crypto transactions have no fees or miniscule fees. They free users from paying to spend and deploy their own money.

The impact on access to economic opportunity is profound. Mobile money has been around for some time, and in many ways has revolutionized the

---

82 https://cointelegraph.com/news/state-issued-digital-currencies-the-countries-which-adopted-rejected-or-researched-the-concept

83 https://medium.com/@connectjob_/fintech-vs-blockchain-be8acfedcc5c

economies of developing nations and communities. But even mobile money is based on established financial institutions that control those transactions and charge fees. Crypto allows anyone to transact with anyone else, safely and virtually for free. This can enable people to pay their bills, save money, lend money, start businesses, buy goods and services without fear or cost.

As I mentioned, Blockchain goes well beyond cryptocurrencies in that it revolutionizes the way information is stored and exchanged. Think of how this might help us overcome some of the data challenges of today. For example, one of the biggest problems in healthcare is the power to control and access patient health records. Billions of dollars have been spent in the United States alone building record and transaction systems that can allow access, coordination and flow of data. They are costly, insecure, vulnerable and do not function well. Most do not communicate well with one another. This is an enormous problem that makes healthcare more expensive and less safe.

Blockchain decentralizes those records and enables easy communication across different digital platforms. It is also more secure and less vulnerable to hacking. And since Blockchain is a transparent historical record of all transactions associated with that data or that person, it lends itself to creating a lifetime health record for an individual, one that is not trapped in a single institution but follows the patient wherever he goes. This is the long-imagined dream of health information. And it puts the power of that data in the hands of the patient, not the institution.

What other applications can you imagine for Blockchain? What societal problems will it solve? What business models can emerge? Can you imagine a world without banks and health plans? What organizations or services would emerge into that vacuum that people would gain more value from?

Technology #2: CRISPR/Cas9

On July 25, 1978, a baby girl was born in England. Although approximately 335,996 other children were born that day, Louise Brown was special. Her cells were cultivated in a petri dish in a process that became known as in vitro fertilization. Once the cells had grown, they were implanted in her mother's womb, and Louise was born nine months later—the world's first test-tube baby.

The media went crazy over the sensational story of an "invented" baby. Police security was needed at the hospital and at Louise's home. Even the pope criticized the decision of the parents to tamper with nature. Although Louise was a normal baby and child in every other sense, her fame followed her everywhere. In 2018, Louise turned forty. She still receives hate mail occasionally.[84] In the meantime, over 8 million babies have been born using the same technology.

In November 2018, a Chinese scientist named He Jiankui used in vitro fertilization technology to conduct another scientific experiment. He applied CRISPR, a tool for "editing" genes in cells, to change the genetic code of two babies. Specifically, he manually disabled a gene associated with AIDS/HIV to make the girls resistant to the disease. The scientific community was outraged by this manipulation of human DNA and the creation of "designer" babies.

CRISPR stands for "clustered regularly interspaced short palindromic repeats." These genetic sequences are found in bacteria. Cas9 is an enzyme that uses these sequences to cut specific strands of DNA from genes in other organisms. Scientists can apply Cas9 very deliberately and directly to edit genes as they wish.

The uses of CRISPR seem limitless. CRISPR potentially could:

- Rid malaria from the mosquitos that transmit the disease to humans

- Repair the deterioration of muscular dystrophy

- Eliminate a patient's cancer genetically, without applying toxic chemotherapy or drugs

- Create organs in pigs that can be transplanted to humans

- Develop new designer pharmaceuticals

---

84   https://www.independent.co.uk/news/health/test-tube-baby-40th-anniversary-world-first-reaction-ivf-louise-brown-a8454021.html

- Treat blindness

- Edit humans[85]

Bluntly stated, humans have never had more power to change life. Does this represent the ultimate threat to humanity, or the biggest gift or both? Will the ethical considerations override the scientific possibilities? Imagine a company finding a way to leverage CRISPR to improve human health. Perhaps a disease-free, super-healthy, super-intelligent being will be born in the next few years. Perhaps people, with a ready supply of genetically modified organs, tissues and body parts available, can essentially become immortal. What other previously insurmountable problems can CRISPR finally solve? What businesses will make those solutions commercially available?[86]

Technology #3: The Internet of Things/Internet of Bodies

In 1964, an obscure Canadian philosopher named Marshall McLuhan wrote a book called *Understanding Media: The Extensions of Man*. McLuhan believed that all tools are extensions of the human body. The hammer is an extension of the hand. The flashlight or telescope is an extension of the eyes. The car is an extension of the legs. The computer is an extension of the brain.

Writing about McLuhan's theories, the American academic John Culkin observed, "We shape our tools and thereafter our tools shape us." Human beings, in other words, quickly develop a reliance on their tools that makes those tools indispensable. Who, these days, can imagine being without their smartphone for even a few hours? A tool that we didn't even have twenty years ago is now an essential part of our lives, shaping our habits, brains and even our personalities.

85   https://www.popularmechanics.com/science/a19067/11-crazy-things-we-can-do-with-crispr-cas9/

86   https://singularityhub.com/2019/05/02/crispr-used-in-human-trials-for-the-first-time-in-the-us/

Prepare for tools to become extensions of the body in an entirely new way. Thanks to the Internet of Things, billions of devices are now connected to the Internet. This means that almost anything can be turned into an intelligent digital device. A refrigerator, a pen, a car, a plant vase … all can become nodes of data, monitors and robots doing what we ask them to do. A smarter, more efficient, more interactive world awaits.

The Internet of Bodies is around the corner. People can swallow pills, equipped with sensors and processors, that will monitor their health internally. They can put on smart contact lenses that monitor glucose levels and help diabetics manage their conditions with a new level of precision and ease. Devices inserted into the ear or the heart or the spine can help a deaf person to hear, monitor their heart condition or walk again despite paralyzed limbs. Of course, with data breaches a daily occurrence now, concerns about personal data privacy are understandable. Perhaps new implanted IoB devices will be vulnerable to hacking and even control by outsiders. Yet, the power of technology to improve, enhance or heal the human body is incredibly tantalizing.

Imagine a microscopic device that can exist inside your body, constantly monitoring you for disease or adverse health conditions.[87] Imagine your car driving you to work and picking up your groceries and children while you're at the office. Imagine your smartphone, taking time away from you when you're not using it, to apply its computational power to solve massively complicated problems that improve life on the planet.

What approaches to this technology will solve the biggest problems and have a powerful impact on the market? What businesses will be able to take advantage of these opportunities?

---

87   https://singularityhub.com/2019/07/10/cancer-killing-living-drug-is-made-safer-with-a-simple-off-switch/

Technology #4: Artificial Intelligence and Robotics

In 1770, a Hungarian author and inventor named Wolfgang von Kempelen built a chess-playing machine called the Mechanical Turk. Sitting across a chessboard, the turbaned mannequin battled human opponents by moving its own pieces. The level of play was quite strong, and the Turk won more than it lost. A spectacle of amazement, the Mechanical Turk toured much of Europe and America over the next seventy-five years playing chess champions and such notable figures as Napoleon and Benjamin Franklin. Although many suspected there was some trick or hoax involved, the mechanics of the machine were extremely convincing. It was only much later that researchers figured out that a chess-playing human sat inside the Mechanical Turk and used the levers to create the illusion of artificial intelligence.

Two centuries later, IBM built a computer actually capable of beating the world's greatest chess player. When Big Blue defeated Gary Kasparov 3½ games to 2½ in a 6-game competition, it signaled to the world that artificial intelligence had finally arrived. Kasparov, who detected real intelligence and creativity in some of Deep Blue's moves, suspected IBM cheated by inserting human decisions and interpretations into the play. He demanded a rematch, but IBM retired Deep Blue and moved on to developing other applications of AI. Kasparov might have had a point. Twenty years later, Big Blue, IBM's AI cancer-diagnosis computer was accused of very poor results in diagnosis and treatment suggestions, which were corrected by further input from its human handlers.

When I was an engineering student thirty years ago, AI was considered a very promising technology. Back then, we wrote algorithms that attempted to imitate how the human brain works. Trying to code that way proved to be impossible, and AI didn't progress much. In the last ten years, that approach has changed. Now, instead of replicating human thinking, we've realized that the best way for AI to learn is to let it observe. So we've combined computer processing with sensors, monitors and other mechanisms for data input. We don't try to define the difference between a cat and a dog, for example; we feed the computer lots of images of cats and let it write its own rules. This kind of self-learning capability is at the heart of the AI explosion; and when it is combined with enormous quantities of data and tremendous computational power, we create the possibility of a machine that can make predictions about the future far more quickly, cheaply and accurately than humans.

After all, human beings can't process, remember, interpret or draw patterns from such large and fast-moving streams of data. We need algorithms to do the work for us. An algorithm is a step-by-step process that produces insight or can even make judgments or decisions. Computers rely on the complex interplay of many algorithms to do the work we want them to do. From the beginning of the computer, we've wondered whether that network of algorithms could become so intelligent that it would seem human. Alan Turing said, "Suppose non-conscious algorithms could eventually outperform conscious intelligence in all known data-processing tasks—what, if anything, would be lost by replacing conscious intelligence with superior non-conscious algorithms?" His Turing test posited that we could assess whether machines can actually think by engaging them in conversation. If they're indistinguishable from a human conversation partner, then real thinking is taking place.

Today, machines may not be able to "think" like a human, but thanks to AI, they can certainly learn. That's the promise and threat of the rise of AI. Yuval Noah Harari, the author of *Homo Sapiens* and *Homo Deus*, says that all living organisms are already made up of algorithms, from humans to dogs to viruses. The only difference with machines is that living organisms rely on biochemical algorithms which have "learned" through evolution over millions of years. Questions about the difference between AI machines and humans, Harari says, come down to confusion between the nature of intelligence and the nature of consciousness. Intelligence gives us the ability to solve problems. AI is exceptionally good at that, and becoming better than humans. Consciousness is the ability to feel things in an intelligent way. Humans are still distinct from AI in that sense. Superintelligence without consciousness is the likely future of AI.

According to HackerEarth, AI is currently being applied in five different areas.[88] These are:

- Reasoning—solving problems through logic

- Knowledge—forming conclusions based on data

- Planning—setting and achieving goals

- Communication—interacting with humans through language

- Perception—taking in information through sounds, visuals and other sensory inputs to draw observations and present insights

In essence, then, AI helps make predictions and suggest actions. The applications of these capabilities are limitless and pervade our world. AI is integrated today into almost all areas of human endeavor and business. It's part of finance, healthcare, distribution, supply chains, transportation, manufacturing and entertainment. AI is responsible for making stock trades, diagnosing illnesses, moving goods more efficiently, driving cars automatically, making complex machines, and even choosing the movies, music or food we should buy or select.

If AI might replace or augment human thinking, robots leverage that intelligence to potentially replace or augment what humans do or would like to do. Kate Darling of the MIT Media Lab defines a robot as "a physical machine that's usually programmable by a computer that can execute tasks autonomously or automatically by itself."[89]

Why are robots so exciting? Because robots can move about and perform tasks like humans, it must feel like we are creating a type of life. Certainly, robots are valuable to humans because they can free us from mundane, dangerous or precision-driven tasks, and do them much better.

Robots are working in factories, warehouses, farms and mines. They're operating as retail service workers, soldiers, pharmacists and brain surgeons.

---

88   https://www.hackerearth.com/blog/innovation-management/applications-of-artificial-intelligence/

89   https://www.wired.com/story/what-is-a-robot/

They're cleaning houses, defusing bombs, operating drones and caring for the elderly and physically disabled.

The ability of robots to do tasks better than humans is tantalizing. The potential of robots to replace humans in all manner of work, even work that seems to require uniquely human capabilities, from pharmacy to journalism, worries many of us. If robots can be put to work to solve our biggest problems, what would those problems be? In the environment, robots could potentially help us clean up pollution that humans can't or don't want to go near. In terms of access to economic opportunity, perhaps robots can help the disabled function physically so they can participate in the workforce, or help an otherwise struggling farmer or a business owner be more productive at lower costs.

In 2016, a robot named Sophia was activated by a Hong Kong-based company. She can manage fifty different facial expressions and engage in conversation. That ability to connect through language and reflect or project emotion makes a major difference in the sense of humanity in the robot. In 2017, Sophia became the first robot to become a citizen of a country. She now has seven siblings.

Plenty of storytellers have looked at robotics and imagined a dark future for humanity. Just think about the *Terminator* movies. AI may be an even scarier prospect. Before he died, Stephen Hawking warned that humanity's biggest threat was AI. "Whereas the short-term impact of AI depends on who controls it, the long-term impact depends on whether it can be controlled at all." Hawking didn't think the real risk was in AI becoming malevolent toward humans, but that it would be so competent humans wouldn't be necessary anymore.[90]

Imagine a different future in which AI and robotics help foster a better world rather than limit our potential.

---

90   https://www.vox.com/future-perfect/2018/10/16/17978596/stephen-hawking-ai-climate-change-robots-future-universe-earth

What can we do to turn AI and robotics towards solving humanity's biggest challenges and problems?

Technology #5: 3D Printing

3D printing has been around in some form since the early 1980s. The basic technology that is used today, called fused deposition modeling, was invented in 1988. In the thirty years since, 3D printing has been impeded by technological challenges and high operating costs. In the past few years, the technology has improved even as the cost has dropped dramatically.

The excitement of 3D printing is that it eliminates the need to manufacture at scale, and enables the economic production of a single product when and where it is needed. Theoretically, a farmer in need of a tool, a doctor in need of a prosthetic, or an entrepreneur in need of a prototype could design and manufacture that item with absolute precision. This gives any individual with access to a 3D printer the power of a factory and the resources of a manufacturing company. 3D printers can also solve the problem of distance. Remote communities and developing countries seem poised to benefit the most.

The applications of 3D printing are probably limitless. Manufacturers use 3D printing to develop prototypes and parts or even produce and sell products while customers wait. 3D printing has powerful educational possibilities, allowing students to learn how to design and build objects on their own. The technology could even find its way to space, allowing a space station or planetary colony to build what it needs, despite the lack of raw materials.

On a social level, 3D printing democratizes manufacturing, making it more possible for more people and communities to produce what they want, cheaply. No doubt, this distributed technology platform will empower people to get what they need to do their work or live their lives while also unleashing great entrepreneurial potential. A 3D printer could print a house, for example, in twenty-four hours. Another potential impact will be the rise of creativity and do-it-yourself design and invention. Once, only highly trained architects, engineers, industrial designers and craftsmen could design and create buildings, machines, elegant devices, and so on. Now, any individual of any age or experience can become his or her own designer with the ease with which children can manipulate photos today.

The downside of 3D printing may, like robotics, lie with the people who no longer are needed to work in factories or in stores. To counter the global problems with inequality that will likely result, do we need to implement a minimum universal income? The ideal purpose of technology is to help solve problems, not create new ones; yet, "creative destruction" has always gone hand-in-hand with innovation. Where there is change, there is the need to adapt.

Technology #6: Virtual/Augmented Reality

In the popular TV show, *Star Trek: The Next Generation*, one of the great sources of escape and play on the spaceship was the Holodeck. In this virtual reality room, the ship's crew could do or experience almost anything. They could go back in time to visit an ancient ruin while it was functioning. They could participate in a famous story like Sherlock Holmes as though they were living the drama. They could generate a world or an environment or an adventure that was unplanned, and let that experience unspool naturally.

Historically, radio, film, TV and computer games have introduced us to the experience of artificial environments that felt increasingly "real" to the beholder. Virtual and augmented reality seem likely to be the next stages in that evolution. The giant tech companies sure think so: They're making enormous bets through their investments.

VR has powerful possibilities to offer. As a tool for gamers, it can create an immersive game-world that will "place" players into the game worlds they long to inhabit. As an educational tool, VR can help students experience life in another point in history or explore a great museum on the other side of the world or interact with a program of a great philosopher like Aristotle as if he is the guest lecturer. As a training tool, VR can let surgeons practice on virtual patients or explore complicated procedures or even the body itself, while also enabling pilots and soldiers to train for realistic and dangerous scenarios. As a communications tool, VR can enable people to interact with each other "in person," despite great distances, while saving time, resources and reducing energy use and pollution.[91]

Imagine the changes that can come in many different industries—travel, movie watching, wilderness trips, sports, education. Suddenly, you wouldn't need to experience something directly; you could do it virtually. The way we work together might change, too, as physical offices become irrelevant. People might visit hospitals virtually first to be diagnosed, preventing exposure to germs and disease or greatly alleviating the stress on emergency departments.

On the downside, virtual reality is a potentially highly addictive technology that might suck users in while making the "real world" seem a humdrum and unfulfilling place. We've already seen the impact of social media and smartphones on people's attentions.

Technology #7: Social Media and Global Connectivity

Even before the World Wide Web, since the early use of the personal computer, people have congregated in virtual communities. The first such communities were known as bulletin board services (BBS). They allowed people from around the world to "dial in" to a particular server, and participate in a text-based chat discussion on any number of subjects or themes. They became very popular as ways to access information and engage with people interested in similar topics. More than anything, they created a sense of community among the members and participants. Some of those early communities like the WELL were passionate places for debate, sharing, information exchange and activism.

The early Internet browsers made this experience even more vivid and easy, while moving communities away from single servers into the broader network. Businesses like Friendster, Myspace and, eventually, Facebook became the new iteration of online communities. Facebook

---

91   https://www.nytimes.com/2017/07/27/climate/airplane-pollution-global-warming.html

emerged as the behemoth, linking friends, acquaintances and interested strangers across a web of connections while also serving as a platform for countless communities focused on specific issues or shared interests. Other services like LinkedIn, Twitter, Reddit, Second Life and Instagram offered specialized experiences or forums for different purposes or types of people. For example, LinkedIn focuses on the professional aspects of our lives, while Second Life allows people to escape their lives by presenting themselves in avatar form. Reddit is largely text-based, while Instagram is almost completely visual.

In their early days, modern social media platforms were considered a frivolous but surprisingly intimate way to connect with other people. Old friends from high school. Colleagues around the world. Fellow researchers, artists, and so on. Starting with the Arab Spring uprisings in Egypt and Tunisia and later in the uprising in Ukraine, social media became viewed as a great enabler of grassroots democracy. Resisters of authoritarian regimes could communicate through unofficial channels, share information, learn news and make plans. During the 2016 U.S. presidential election it became apparent how vulnerable social media networks were to manipulation, hate, extremism and fake news.

Are social media platforms good or bad? Do they facilitate communities or undermine society? Can they be productive not only in a social sense but in solving humanity's problems or enabling economic and political solutions?

Whichever way social media goes, there will be much room for growth of services, uses and numbers. How can global connectivity facilitate serious crises handling? How can purpose-driven businesses leverage such platforms to solve big problems? Students of subjects can gather to improve their knowledge and understanding of a subject. Professionals can advance their insights into less-explored areas of their field.

The potential and the pitfalls of social media and global connectivity remain very real.

Technology #8: Growing Food

Food production, distribution and waste are immense problems today, putting pressure on society, the economy and the environment. Technologies that alleviate some of this pressure are now increasingly available.

Today, half the world's population lives in cities. By 2050, that will rise to 70 percent.[92] How will we feed 2 billion more people than now, most of whom will live in urban centers, far from food production?

Today, large-scale agricultural production on farms is very hard on the environment, especially in the developing world where most population growth is occurring. Agriculture often starts with clearing land for crops or livestock, which contributes to climate change because of deforestation. Agriculture is also hard on soil nutrients and composition and requires enormous quantities of water, which may not be readily available and may become even more scarce soon. To supplement soil and grow healthy produce, farmers use highly toxic (often petroleum-based) fertilizer as well as pesticides. This increases pollution and inefficiency. Some of the most environmentally intense produce, like cows for dairy and beef, and corn for corn syrup and oil, are the very things we consume the most. An argument can be made that cow flatulence, for example, is more harmful to the environment than vehicle exhaust.[93] Agricultural animals consume almost as much produce as people.

That's only the first stage. Once produce is ready for market, it must be transported. This means moving refrigerated and highly packaged goods long distances to sell in urban centers. More fuel is wasted with the transportation and refrigeration. More pollution results from all of the plastic packaging. The quality and taste of food also degrades when it is stored, distributed, repackaged, shelved in stores, brought home and refrigerated.

---

92 https://www.un.org/development/desa/en/news/population/2018-revision-of-world-urbanization-prospects.html

93 https://animals.howstuffworks.com/mammals/methane-cow.htm

Then there is food waste during and after delivery. One third of the food that is produced is wasted every year, enough to feed 2 billion people. In the wealthiest countries, consumers throw out 40 percent of all food that is wasted.[94] Some countries are trying to regulate food waste. Diverting food would have as big an impact as changing diet. Overeating is also a major source of food waste.[95]

Technology is helping and will have an increasing impact going forward. GPS technology, for example, can make farming much more productive and efficient. Lab-grown meat holds the promise of an alternative that is far less burdensome on the environment, ethically sounder and perhaps able to give more people needed protein one day.[96]

Another approach to growing food might be even more sustainable and scalable. A number of new investor-backed startups are experimenting with hydroponic technology that allows people to grow produce very quickly and efficiently in cubes in their own kitchen. With four or five cubes, a family could grow enough vegetables to consume a salad every day of the week. The vegetables would replenish rapidly, providing a constant supply of food.[97] IKEA is currently marketing these vegetable production tools for home kitchens.[98]

This system would help reduce reliance on large farms and inefficient distribution and retail channels. It could also reduce overall waste. The system is potentially intelligent as well. One intelligent hydroponic cube can "learn a lot" as it adjusts light, nutrient and soil conditions for optimal growth. Hundreds of thousands or millions of cubes, connected together through the cloud, can learn very quickly and potentially make substantial leaps in productivity and efficiency. Grocery stores are also getting in on

94   https://www.nytimes.com/2017/12/12/climate/food-waste-emissions.html

95   https://www.sciencedirect.com/science/article/pii/S0308521X16302384

96   https://www.washingtonpost.com/national/health-science/burgers-grown-in-a-lab-are-heading-to-your-plate-will-you-bite/2018/09/07/1d048720-b060-11e8-a20b-5f4f84429666_story.html

97   https://www.voanews.com/a/smartphone-grow-vegetables-indoor-cube/3185347.html

98   https://www.independent.co.uk/extras/indybest/house-garden/gardening/best-home-hydroponics-kits-gardening-indoor-herb-garden-a8461671.html

the act, growing produce in stores or on top of buildings, to reduce waste, inefficiency, pesticides, water use, etc.[99]

Technology #9: Solar Power

Since the conversion of coal-fired ships and the arrival of the automobile, the world has been addicted to fossil fuels. In the century since, oil has driven our economy. It has made great fortunes, caused economic booms and busts, catalyzed regional conflicts, inspired unlikely alliances, changed society and polluted the atmosphere to such an extent that extreme global climate change is likely irreversible. Our addiction to oil has been so over-powering that rather than save the planet by turning our attention urgently toward alternatives, we continue to seek new ways to extract and use fossil fuels as though nothing was wrong.

For centuries humans have pondered how to tap the sun's energy as a source of fuel. An efficient, cost-effective conversion mechanism has been lacking until recently. Solar power has been around since the late 1800s, but it only began to take hold as a potential alternative in the 1990s. Worried about peak oil, the environment and lingering fears of the next oil shock, solar panels were adopted by many large office and industrial buildings. They were expensive, bulky and difficult to take advantage of, however.

In the past decade, despite cynicism of those who thought it would never be cost-effective, solar power has begun to take off. The industry is high-growth. The number of people employed by the solar industry has doubled since 2010, while prices for solar panels have dropped by around 60 percent.[100]

As solar cells become cheaper and more efficient, their use will continue to spread. Perovskite solar cells, an alternative to silicon, promise to be cheaper still, once they become available for commercial production. As technology improves, solar panels may become ubiquitous. Conversion

---

99   https://www.businessinsider.com/infarm-creates-a-mini-lettuce-farm-for-grocery-stores-2016-4

100   https://www.cleanenergyauthority.com/blog/the-future-of-solar-energy-01232017

cells could be "painted" onto the surfaces of walls or cars. They could power smartphones, computers and every vehicle or tool we use. It's conceivable that oil will be made anachronistic very rapidly as the solar economy takes over.

Imagine what business opportunities could result. As humans become more reliant on solar power and less addicted to oil, they will need a new infrastructure of energy filling stations, batteries, and power sources. Perhaps roads could be equipped with electricity recharging pads. Maybe a few entrepreneurial types in a community will find ways to service the electricity needs of their neighbors, supplanting the local power utility.

"The Cause of and Solution to All Our Problems"

Human beings have always used technology to solve urgent problems and achieve critical goals. The hunter-gatherers developed weapons and tools which helped them kill larger, faster animals and forage for food more effectively. The first agrarian civilizations harnessed cows and developed hoes and irrigation systems to grow crops more productively. The Romans built a network of roads and aqueducts to serve the needs of their empire. Those constructions still influence the locations of cities, the prosperity of regions and the flow of trade two thousand years later.[101]

Until today, however, nothing in human history compared to the Industrial Revolution in terms of the explosion of technology, innovation and change. Over the course of several centuries, the world became replete with new devices, technologies and systems. Steam engines. Factories. Giant trade ships. Extensive railroads. Communication systems like the telegraph and telephone. Financial systems like banking, currency and stocks. The electric power grid and countless electric devices. All of these technologies burst into prominence because they served important needs. All of them got exploited and accelerated by new businesses that grew fast and large, almost overnight, many of which still exist today. Societies

---

101 https://www.dailymail.co.uk/sciencetech/article-5673247/Roman-roads-contributing-spread-prosperity-scientists-claim.html

transformed under the pressure these new technologies exerted. Lives changed, families changed, communities changed. The impacts were never always or completely positive. Sometimes different solutions, technologies and rules were necessary to correct problems that resulted. Sometimes those new solutions and technologies led to still more problems.

Consider the need for light. As the Industrial Era took hold, work changed. People who once relied on daylight spent more time inside or in the dark. Candles and oil lamps were the primary source of illumination. The cheapest candle wax and oil was rendered from animal fat. But animal fat exuded unpleasant odors, spewed thick smoke and spattered grease. The quality of the light was also poor, and sometimes house fires resulted. The best available alternative, we soon discovered, was whale oil.

Almost overnight, the traditional whale hunt became an industry. In America, long-standing whaling communities in Massachusetts and Cape Cod suddenly emerged as global centers for thousands of fishermen and many prosperous merchants and financial collectives. The well-stocked ships they funded set out on voyages that could last two to five years while the fishermen on board chased giant sperm whales around the world. When those fisherman finally encountered a whale and the hunt began, the garrison of fishermen turned into soldiers and launched attacks on one of the largest creatures ever to roam the Earth. After the fight was over and the dead sperm whale was tied to the side of the hull, the whaling ship turned into a floating factory, and the fishermen carved out the blubber and rendered it into oil in a giant furnace on the deck. The flames of that furnace burned brightly for many nights. Then the whaling ship would move on, and the whale's carcass would be left behind to float away.

The world's first oil crisis developed because sperm whales became scarce. The majestic beasts became harder to find, even as the number of whaling ships increased. No doubt, extinction loomed. Then, in 1854, at the height of the whale hunt, a chemist in Canada named Abraham Gesner invented a new type of fuel called kerosene. Gesner's process distilled kerosene from coal and later from petroleum. The American oil industry started because of the industrial world's insatiable demand for light.

Kerosene's reign as an illuminant was short-lived. Edison's light bulb and the electricity grid took over the market because it was easier and safer to turn on a switch than light a lamp. We quickly found other uses for kerosene, however, in a new industry.

Henry Ford was credited with "inventing" the automobile. But he was one of many thousands of inventors striving to produce a "horseless" carriage in the late 1800s. Some versions used steam power, others electricity. The diesel- and gasoline-powered engines were late to the game. But finding a solution was becoming a necessity. In part, this was because horses were an environmental disaster. The horse crisis.

The world's major cities were clogged with the horses that transported people in carriages and trollies. Horses created traffic jams, but unlike cars, they also produced waste and disease. In 1900, New York City streets were polluted every day with 40 dead horses, 2.5 million pounds of manure and 60,000 gallons of urine. When the automobile came along, it was seen as a environmental savior.

In other words, just as the invention of kerosene helped save the majestic sperm whale from extinction, so the invention of the automobile made living in major cities, at least for a time, healthier and cleaner.

This is the story of technology. Crisis leads to solution. Solution leads to business model. Successful business model grows in scale as a brand-new market opens up. Modern global giants like Standard Oil (Exxon) and Shell emerged to meet the global need for kerosene and later for petroleum, just as the great car manufacturing companies rose out of Ford's innovation. Yesterday's savior, however, can become tomorrow's threat. Today, millions upon millions of gas- and diesel-fueled cars and trucks are responsible for a significant percentage of the pollution and greenhouse gases that threaten to cause devastating global climate change. Temperatures are rising. Wild fires are burning. Drought, flooding and disease are forcing millions of people around the world to become refugees. It will only get worse unless something changes.

What will we do to save the day now? Maybe the electric car will prove to be the answer, or perhaps some other technology will offer a very different kind of solution, capturing carbon from the atmosphere or giving us the ability to turn environmental pollution toward some productive use.

The point is that technology takes off when crisis is at hand. The biggest opportunities arise because of the greatest need. Right now, I believe our biggest problems, as I discussed in the previous chapter, concern environmental challenges, health challenges and access to economic opportunity. Are there technologies in existence right now—like kerosene or the automobile—that can alleviate those needs?

The impact of technology is notoriously difficult to predict. Assessing a particularly new and exciting technology, it can be easy to overestimate its potential for changing the world, just as it can be easy to miss how that technology might "turn against us." Given the global scale of the problems we face and the urgency of our need for solutions, the technologies described in this chapter may present significant opportunities for new high-growth businesses—the Standard Oils, General Electrics and Fords of the future. Hopefully, they will also save us from ourselves.

CHAPTER EIGHT RECAP

- Technology can help address Level One problems in a multitude of ways.

- There are nine technological streams with transformational potential:

  1. Blockchain

  2. CRISPR/Cas9

  3. The Internet of Things/Internet of Bodies

  4. Artificial Intelligence and Robotics

  5. 3D Printing

  6. Virtual/Augmented Reality

  7. Social Media and Global Connectivity

  8. Growing Food

  9. Solar Power

- Today, the potential of technological enablement is so profound we can best capture it in a simple phrase: "Whatever you can imagine, you can do."

Tools & Resources

To better understand the role technology can play in seeking solutions for our Level One problems, below are some good places to go (for all links visit my site www.christostsolkas.com).

- Read *Fast Company*'s article "5 Ways Artificial Intelligence Can Help Save The Planet". It talks about

  - Autonomous energy and water networks

  - Climate modeling

  - Real-time data dashboards

  - Disaster resiliency and response

  - Earth bank of codes

- Read a very interesting paper from WWF Australia published in 2017 that talks about smart cities, the IoT, VR and AR, Blockchain, Electricity Generation and Storage, AI, Autonomous Vehicles, Agri Tech, Food Tech, Ocean Tech and the Sharing Economy.

- Read a ZDNet article by Greg Nichols tackling the top 10 technologies which can help the planet.

- Get the e-book from Singularity University titled *Feed the World: How Exponential Tech Can Create an Abundant Future.*

- On the preventative side, Machine Learning and AI can help us to anticipate and better manage future disasters, according to an article of Seth Guikema in *Scientific American*, you have to read.

CHAPTER NINE

Putting It All Together

A few years ago, I spoke about purpose, crisis and innovation at a conference in Europe. It was a big event with some world-famous people as keynoters. I was humbled but excited to be sharing the stage on one of the days. The talk went well. I could see people nodding, smiling, taking notes. They asked questions. They got it. Here are the titles of the PowerPoint slides I used:

1. **Crisis**

   Where purpose is born

2. **Innovation**

   = Purpose x Crisis

3. **Growth**

   = Purpose and innovation at scale

4. **Business Model**

   Purpose ⟺ Global Problems ⟺ Customers ⟺ Innovation

5. **Technology**

   Helps you get there/Operationalizes innovation

6. **Leadership**

   Purpose is the new leadership

7. **Impact**

   How success is measured

8. **Performance**

   It pays your bills

In my talk, I gave examples of different companies that are following this approach, many of which I have discussed already in this book. I spent much of my time talking about leadership, particularly the challenges leaders face today in motivating employees and winning in the market, and the way purpose is the foundation of lasting impact and real significance.

In the reception afterwards, two people approached me with questions. The first was a young woman from Sweden who'd trained in agriculture and food science. I'll call her Ilsa. She'd always been idealistic about food and sustainability, but her education had really focused on making the old system function more efficiently. That didn't seem like a big enough goal for her, given the world's global problems. A year ago, however, she'd met some people online who were developing an artificial meat process and wanted to form a new company together. They'd asked her to come on board. She'd hesitated before, but now she wondered if she should give up her old job and join them. She was clearly excited about this idea, and I could understand why. You don't have to be a vegan to recognize that the production of meat, particularly beef, is brutal on the environment. By many estimates, cows are one of the main global contributors of CO_2 to the atmosphere because of their flatulence. And creating pasture land for cows by clear-cutting forests and jungle in developing countries continues to devastate the environment. An innovative business selling artificial meat that tastes great and is affordable could save the planet while helping to solve the problem of hunger, too.

Ilsa was fired up by my talk but still overwhelmed by the practical business side of that challenge. How do you change the world when you're just three people with big dreams, a very alternative idea and no clear path to market?

I asked her where she fit on my quadrants.

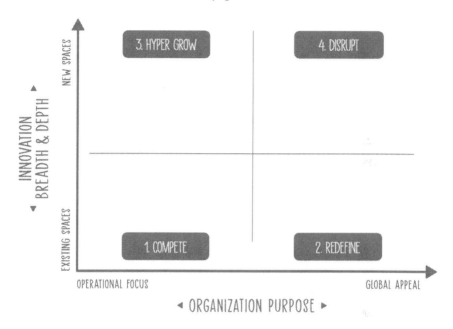

She said that she initially thought the company was very much in the quadrant that focuses on global need in a white space area (Quadrant 4). However, when she really thought about the market she realized she was still competing against more traditional organic and specialty food suppliers. If she couldn't play their game well, her company wouldn't make it. In a few minutes, I helped her come up with some focused questions about what her customers want, how big the market might be, and how the product could reach them. Very quickly, she felt as though she was armed with a way to develop a business model that could support their purpose and compete with a commercial product in the real world. This put her business closer to the quadrant of global appeal in an existing space, but still "high" up in the quadrant in terms of white space and innovation.

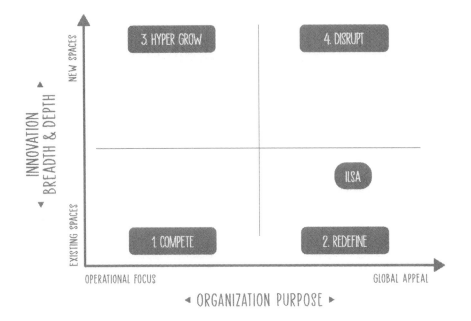

Seeing this on the chart calmed her fears quite a bit. She and her partners could still change the world, but their idea wouldn't seem as "out there" or "radical" to investors who wanted to support something that could make them a return. In fact, she was beginning to think bigger than ever in terms of the company's potential valuation and how much funding they should seek. I wished her luck and told her I looked forward to seeing news of her company in the years to come.

The second person who approached was not a millennial in hip clothes. He was a tall man in his mid-forties from Germany, wearing a poorly fitting suit. He introduced himself as Max, the CEO of an engineering company with around eight hundred employees. As a very left-brain thinker and practical manager, Max wanted to know how he could bring to life a sense of purpose for his company. Business was good. You could say it was booming. But like many good CEOs, he also worried about what he couldn't see coming, and he had a sense that what I was saying about purpose was a blind spot for him. His company wasn't facing any particular crisis, at least not a direct one. He was somewhat worried about political issues, including Brexit, a new administration in Germany, and the possibility of global trade wars.

But he didn't see how his company could shape, change or even prepare for those possibilities. He was more curious about purpose. Could he bring purpose into his company and make a big difference on growth, market share and impact?

I asked him what the purpose of his company would be. He thought about it for a second and said, "Maybe our purpose is to have happy employees." In Germany, this made sense. German companies are a lot more employee-centric and -empowered than in the U.S. and Britain. Happy employees could lead to even better results. As former Southwest Airlines CEO Herb Kelleher often advocated, if you hire good people, make sure they care about the same things you care about (safety, service, doing the job right) and let them have fun, your business will be okay. Your employees' engagement and willingness to solve customers' problems will lead to substantial competitive differentiation and long-term success. This didn't feel right to me, though, so I said to Max, "Is that why you lead this company—to make your employees happy?" As he considered my question, I pressed him again. "Do your highly talented engineers come to work for your company to be happy?" No. He agreed that this wasn't the case.

He tried another tact: "Maybe our purpose is to develop the best engineers in the world." I understand why he went there. Talent is hard to come by. Driven people with technical expertise (whether salespeople, marketers, physicians, engineers, etc.) have a tendency to seek organizations that continue to develop and build their skills. They are hardwired to learn and grow through on-the-job problem solving and professional development. Yet, that didn't feel right to me either. "Is the purpose of your organization to be a school?" I asked. He agreed that it was not. And insisted that he would keep thinking, and let me know if he came up with anything.

A few weeks later I got a message. He wrote that after much soul-searching and discussions with his executive team and key employees he realized something. As a contractor, the company doesn't really have a product or a direct impact on the world. But the company's clients actually do. Reviewing clients, it was easy to see which ones operated in areas that made his people feel good and which didn't. A car parts manufacturer client, for example, was an industry leader in environmental sustainability. Helping that company meet its goals made the people in his organization feel great. Another client made military hardware which it sold mostly to the Middle East. Despite the revenue, no one in the organization felt good about that relationship, especially given the extent of recent military conflict.

"We decided we're in business to help **our clients** make the world a better place," he wrote me. "So, we're going to be a lot more choosy in the future about the clients we work with and the projects we apply our talents to. We've started to develop a list of industries we work in and how our clients can have an even bigger impact on the world. We also developed a list of companies we might prefer to drop because they are not focused on global problems. When I socialized this with our teams, I got some pushback about lost revenue, but most people were extremely enthusiastic. I'd say it energized us a great deal. Now we have to figure out the details. But we've already come up with some interesting ideas and approaches that we've never tried before. I'm excited about that, and even the holdouts seem willing to try."

I felt good about this development and the previous conversation with Ilsa. Very quickly, two organizations were now thinking differently about their work. They were energized by that change. It was creating new pathways and possibilities. By drawing a line between business and global impact, they were also strengthening connections with their people, customers/clients and investors.

Personally, I believe both those companies will be more successful financially and socially as a result. Now, let's dig into the path your company can consider following.

1. Crisis

Crisis is where purpose is most often born.

It was through crisis that I learned about purpose. But in thinking about this book and, in particular, this final chapter, I debated whether purpose should be first or whether crisis should be first. While it's obvious a company should have a clear sense of purpose before any crisis, in practical reality, it often doesn't. Crisis can focus a company on what really matters.

John Kotter, the incredibly influential business thinker, laid out this formula thirty years ago. In his 8-Step Change Model, Kotter declared that change only really takes effect when some underlying crisis forces people, companies and customers to adapt. In my business career, I've seen the truth of this from many different levels and perspectives. Try motivating anyone, even yourself, to change without some cause or need to do so. Chances are, whatever your best intentions, you just won't follow through or feel the motivation to stick with it. Think about motivating and shifting an entire organization to a new software system or a new accounting system or a revamped product design or better manufacturing processes without some fear or urgent opportunity driving the change. You might as well practice herding cats first.

Crisis can spur change. But it's also a powerful motivator to seek out a meaningful purpose. If a crisis is big enough, you might need a clearer sense of purpose just to survive. As I described at the beginning of this book, I was "lucky" twice in my career to confront a crisis as the leader of an organization. First in Greece and then in Ukraine. In both cases, economic and political forces well beyond our control completely overturned our normal business plans.

In the case of Greece, I discovered the power of purpose as I lived through the crisis. I was in despair before then, and my people felt lost as our business profitability evaporated overnight. To manage that confusion and lack of direction, I turned to purpose and brought in some ideas and approaches that helped us focus on a meaningful path, develop courage and resiliency, and formulate a plan to take steps to save our company and our jobs.

In the case of Ukraine, I brought that understanding of purpose into my new role as head of that territory. We got to work right away on developing our purpose. The crisis at that time was sort of an ordinary business crisis. We weren't reaching our business goals. I recognized that many of my leaders did not have a lot of motivation. And we didn't feel united or aligned. Developing a clear purpose for the group helped us come together and begin to speak a common language and feel closer as a team. It also helped me identify and position key people in leadership roles that stretched and developed their skills. These people became my most valued lieutenants later on.

Then the BIG CRISIS hit in the middle of that work when the protests became violent and the Little Green Men invaded. This threw Ukrainian society and our company into turmoil. Suddenly, the purpose that we'd come up with around business goals and team alignment didn't serve our more urgent needs. We needed to develop a new, more relevant purpose around keeping everyone safe and attempting to sustain normal business operations. I believe that the second purpose was built on the first. If we hadn't done the work of introducing the power of purpose earlier, it would have been harder to do it later. So I'm grateful for the lessons I learned in Greece that I brought to Ukraine.

Crisis helps. It's really difficult for human beings (as individuals and in organizations) to truly and deeply understand the need for purpose until they confront a crisis. Until the crisis comes, the need for purpose is more academic than urgent. We may believe or think that purpose is morally or ethically a good idea, but we don't necessarily see it as a lifesaving need or a desperate solution.

There are a few simple reasons why:

- We tend to coast when the going is good. We get very busy managing the day-to-day and can't always see the forest (purpose) for the trees (business objectives, daily challenges). When the crisis hits, we are suddenly confronted with very big questions like,

  "What really matters?"

  "What (resources, people, plans) do I need to save and what do I need to let go?"

  "Why is it important for me, my team or the organization to keep working so damn hard during this very difficult time?"

  The answers point to purpose.

- Sometimes we believe we are working or living with purpose but we are really not. This is not our fault. It is, again, human nature. It takes real discipline, daily practice, and lots and lots of awareness to live, work or operate according to a greater purpose without losing track of that purpose, forgetting about it or falling away from it. When the crisis hits we get reminded in a hurry. We either realize that purpose has been missing or we discover that we've wavered. The crisis serves as a reminder. All the difficulties are conspiring to help us figure out what's really important.

- The purpose we're living or working by is not actually your real purpose, or maybe it's no longer valid. This happens all the time. Companies get very lofty ideas when they determine their purpose, but when they operate and make decisions in the real world, they often do so in ways that have little relevance to that purpose. When the sh*t hits the fan, they don't turn to their purpose because it's not actually real, or they realize that their purpose no longer feels relevant. What's a company to do? Well, if purpose really does help a company navigate uncertainty, change and threats, then it's time to figure out what that purpose should be. Once again, crisis can be a gift.

A sense of purpose is not intellectual or ethereal. You feel it in your guts. You rely on it frequently, like a touchstone, to make good decisions. You use it to gain clarity when there is confusion all around.

The good thing about a crisis is that it interrupts old patterns of thought or ways of living and doing business. A crisis makes it necessary to question everything that used to work and figure out new solutions and new ways forward. When the old ways suddenly don't work anymore or don't mean as much given new realities, we need to get real (authentic, genuine, clear-hearted) about what actually does matter. Alcoholics Anonymous talks about hitting bottom. Seth Godin says entrepreneurs reach the dip. That's the point where you look up (often in despair) and say "What *does* matter?" Organizations, communities, leaders and people

.he same moment of truth. Some, of course, would argue "Why wait foɪ ᴜ crisis? Just do it now."

2. Innovation = Purpose x Crisis

Crisis can help define the problem you need to solve. For me and my team in Ukraine, the crisis made it very easy to decide that survival and business-as-usual should be our purpose. For a financial firm during an economic crisis, a new sense of purpose might mean evaluating and changing current business practices. For a mature-beverage manufacturer, the crisis might be that the processes of manufacturing and distribution the company has relied upon for many decades threatens the environment. As we discussed earlier, this could be related to excess water use or the problem of obesity because of sugar or the devastation of pollution generated by so much plastic. Adding to that hypothetical crisis, maybe the government starts taxing sugar, eroding the company's profits.

Facing a crisis, even if it doesn't directly and immediately threaten the organization, inspires a response. If the crisis is serious enough, however, that response is likely to change current business practices. When crisis meets purpose, innovation is almost always the result.

When my team and I looked at purpose-driven startups, we stumbled across the link between purpose, crisis and innovation. Studying larger companies next, we quickly determined that the same formula applied. I think it's an intuitive concept to understand. As we discussed above, people find it hard to change and grow without a crisis and a renewed or new sense of purpose. In the same way, a person might struggle to lose weight until they face a severe health crisis. Recognizing that they really want to stay living for years to come, that purpose becomes a powerful force for changing an old path. For an organization, that's the definition of innovation.

The classic startup motto is: "Give me a problem and I will find a solution."

The world certainly has plenty of problems today. In 2015, the United Nations came up with its list of Sustainable Development Goals. In 2018, a

Danish company called Sustainia turned those goals into a list of business problems. They included reducing global inequality, reducing consumption and production, preserving the oceans and slowing down climate change.

What can businesses do to address such global challenges? As *Fast Company* noted, companies "can actually create solutions that improve lives and develop new markets. In other words, being responsible isn't some moral choice, but rather it's smart strategic planning."[102] Solutions to global problems can be drivers of innovation and growth.

A report by CB Insights, "2019 Game Changers", focuses on startups that are making a mark by tackling global problems.[103] The startups chosen are "high-momentum companies pioneering technology with the potential to transform society and economies for the better." Categories included AI, superbug killers, ecosystem engineering, autonomous vehicles, net-zero buildings and defense against disinformation. CB Insights identified three startups in each of those twelve categories that it saw as having the potential to be game changers.

Massive global problems represent massive market opportunities. Think about the problem of plastics. Much of the effort put into recycling plastics is useless, researchers now believe. Two-thirds cannot be recycled at all. Seventy percent ends up in landfills.[104] Growth in plastic waste will be overwhelming in the next thirty years if we don't do something about this problem now. Will regulations, policy and public education be enough? It hasn't been so far. Instead, we need the innovation and ingenuity of thousands of companies that can profitably convert or divert our need for plastics toward better, more environmentally sustainable ends. Likewise, companies like Adidas that pledge to use only recycled plastic can have a huge impact on the environment, improve the bottom line and connect better with customers.[105]

---

102 https://www.fastcompany.com/40526823/4-of-our-biggest-global-problems-are-big-business-opportunities

103 https://www.cbinsights.com/research/briefing/2019-game-changing-startups/

104 https://www.independent.co.uk/voices/plastic-waste-wish-recycling-bins-black-environment-green-shopping-a8548736.html

105 https://money.cnn.com/2018/07/16/news/adidas-using-recycled-plastic-only/index.html

FORECAST OF PLASTICS VOLUME GROWTH, 2014-2050

	2014	2050
PLASTICS PRODUCTION	311 MT	1124 MT
RATIO OF PLASTICS TO FISH IN THE OCEAN (BY WEIGHT)	1:5	>1:1
PLASTICS' SHARE OF GLOBAL OIL CONSUMPTION	6%	20%
PLASTICS' SHARE OF CARBON BUDGET	1%	15%

SOURCE: WORLD ECONOMIC FORUM, 'THE NEW PLASTICS ECONOMY', 2016

3. Growth = Purpose and Innovation at Scale

Innovation is about where you are going, but exponential growth comes from bringing purpose and innovation to scale. Take another look at the quadrant to see how using purpose to move up the Y axis can lead to significant market expansion or the establishment of entirely new markets.

The vast majority of established organizations find themselves by default in the lower left quadrant. They are competing in existing spaces by attempting to raise their game operationally. So, MacDonald's is trying to sell more burgers than Wendy's. Or Ford is trying to earn higher margins than Toyota. Even Apple, it seems, despite its renown for innovation, is just trying to make more money by selling slightly better smartphones than competitors. Frankly, when it comes to the handset, Apple has stalled out. Markets get crowded. Customers lose excitement. The money can still be great, but it's unlikely that the connection between people, product and customer will stir the passions in quite the same way. An explosive surge in growth is unlikely. There's no reason for it to happen.

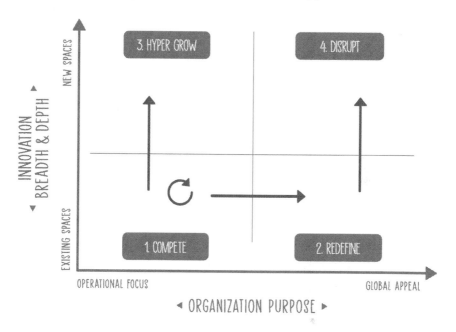

So, what's a company in a mature market to do? For years Apple has been rumored to be coming out with a new kind of TV or an Apple car. Would these products fire customers up? Maybe they'd help Apple surround the customer more than ever, but I doubt they would charge the company with the kind of energy that shot its valuation and brand prestige into the stratosphere starting with the iPod and continuing with the iPhone. No doubt, Apple CEO Tim Cook knows this, too, and he's under tremendous pressure to continue Steve Jobs' legacy of exciting innovation.

Cook is a bit inscrutable in this regard. Though an incredibly competent CEO, he cannot possibly replicate Jobs' personality and passion. However, if there is anything Cook has spoken passionately about, to my knowledge, it has been health. Steve Jobs' death from pancreatic cancer seems to still move him deeply, and certainly Apple was shaped by Jobs' life and death.

I find it fascinating, as a result, that Apple's boldest move in recent years has been its entry into healthcare. That move started slowly and relatively quietly (for Apple) with the introduction of the Apple Watch which had some health monitoring features. Behind the scenes, Apple kept making low-key moves in the healthcare space, developing new technologies, bringing in influential talent, acquiring some related companies. Recently, however, Cook spoke boldly of Apple's bigger plans in a statement that was genuinely Jobs-like in its radical quality. "If you zoom out into the future," Cook said, "and you look back, and you ask the question, 'What was Apple's greatest contribution to mankind?' It will be about health."

Now, that is a bold pronouncement for a giant company known for IT, entertainment and creativity. But if you take Cook at his word and think about what that means for Apple, you can recognize that he's talking about shifting out of Quadrant 1 (where the market for handsets is now) and into a new area. How far will Apple go? Does its move into healthcare represent a shift into Quadrant 2 with a redefinition of existing product lines for more global appeal? I would argue No. If Apple stopped at the Apple Watch and promoted a health and wellness campaign for employees and customers or somehow attached Apple's products to healthy lifestyles or more efficient hospitals, that might be the case, but it doesn't appear so. Likewise, Apple is not inventing an entirely new product category suitable for Quadrant 4. Instead, Apple seems to see tremendous growth potential in bringing its data and interface technology to the healthcare industry as it already exists. In this way, just as Amazon disrupted distribution companies or Airbnb threw the hotel accommodation industry into turmoil, Apple seems bent on bringing tremendous efficiencies and customer focus to healthcare customers. As a result, I would put Apple's new healthcare business line squarely in Quadrant 3.

How big should your innovation be? It depends on what quadrant it falls into. If it's a new twist on an existing product line, that's Quadrant 2. If it's a total new way of doing the work, that's Quadrant 3. And if it's a whole new offering that few have introduced or considered before, then you're getting very close to Quadrant 4.

Where do the biggest opportunities for you lie? I've argued that shifting upwards in the quadrant is essential for exponential growth. As I also already suggested, positioning your company in Quadrant 4 is a tough game. It may be where the world's biggest problems or needs can be found, but that doesn't mean it's where you'll find the biggest business opportunity in the short-term. Even Apple's most prominent innovations were variations on existing products. It's always played well in Quadrant 3. Apple's move into healthcare seems consistent with Apple's long-standing tradition. Such an approach, if successful, would no doubt satisfy investors, disrupt the healthcare industry, and delight patients.

4. Business Model is Purpose ⇔ Global Problems ⇔ Customers ⇔ Innovation

A successful purpose-era business model brings your purpose, global problems, innovations and customers together. Here's a simple story about a very small problem that had the potential to become a practical idea with the right business model.

An experienced executive I'll call Monica returned to her company's headquarters in Rome after a long assignment in the U.S. At the office, she discovered that parking in the center of the city is a daily stress. Everyone wants a company parking spot but there are only so many to go around, and those spots go to the top executives first. All the rest of the employees need to find spaces on the street nearby or deal with public transportation.

One day she had an idea. Even though all of the company's parking spaces were assigned, she noticed that many spaces were often open because executives travel a lot. It seemed silly to let those spaces go to waste when others need them, she thought. In her own small team, for example, there were four assigned parking spots, but fifteen additional people had nowhere to park. Why not develop a small project to monitor when assigned spaces will not be used and let people who need a spot know? She asked a couple people on her team to come up with a simple system and test it with the group.

She figured they would jump on her suggestion, but the people she had asked to work on the problem didn't do anything. When she checked back a few months later, they agreed to get right on it, but nothing happened. About a year after that, she learned that a rival company in the same city had come up with a similar idea and acted on it. Now, businesses in the downtown area were regularly using a parking share app that was attracting customers and capital.

This really frustrated her! Her people had an opportunity to do something innovative but procrastinated and blew it. Why? Because an idea that potentially met a need lacked a business model.

Services like Airbnb and Uber create value by using resources more efficiently. But this concept is not just for second homes and family cars, it applies everywhere. Parking spaces are a good example. Wherever there are "givers" and "receivers" or "owners" and "renters", there is an opportunity to create a two-sided market where both benefit.

I read an article recently on "Platformization" which recommended turning existing products, processes or services into revenue-generating platforms. The authors talked about reimagining a global fulfillment process to look more like Amazon and less like SAP. Pretty much any sharing economy business model could become a platform.

Automakers are transitioning from being primarily manufacturers to becoming mobility solutions companies, focused on car sharing, bike sharing, and public transport to help them grow deeper connections with customers in the future, while transforming vehicles into smartphones on wheels. Amazon Web Services has been a huge growth engine for the company functioning as a platform service for supplying data storage in the cloud for customers and competitors alike.

I understood Monica's frustration at seeing "her" idea get executed by another group. I've often felt the same way. Today, business innovation doesn't always follow traditional rules. Good ideas can show up unexpectedly. If you don't follow up on those ideas, somebody else with more time, initiative or motivation will beat you to it. Execution is the difference between great ideas over coffee or beer and the next big business concept or growth sector.

To move her idea for an app prototype toward a platform, Monica would have required more knowledge, expertise, budget and pairs of hands. For every Facebook or Dropbox, there are dozens or hundreds of companies that simply didn't scale fast enough to turn their good idea into an awesome product.

Here's the really funny thing. Why did Monica's group fail to execute on her suggestion? It turned out, the people she asked were already monitoring spaces and using them occasionally for themselves! As a result, they were reluctant to develop a more public, open system and lose their informal benefits. People are not always resistant to change merely because ideas are new. To understand how to motivate them, you need to determine what they actually value and what matters to them.

How do you get them to think even bigger and go far beyond the problem-at-hand to solve related problems? The team that developed the parking space app at the rival company didn't stop innovating. They built their app to help convert drivers to greener commutes by increasing carpooling and public transportation. Making a positive impact on the company and even the community got them excited because it gave them a sense of purpose.

Why stop there? A parking app promoting green living could easily promote healthy living and wellness. It could encourage biking, tie into wearables like Fitbit, and create an online marketplace for healthy businesses or services to market to employees.

Money, aligned interests and incentives help, but the kind of extra effort, brain power and entrepreneurial zeal needed to build a brand-new business is catalyzed by a sense of greater purpose. Purpose-driven innovation can help people connect the problem they're trying to solve to much bigger community, societal or global problems. As the scale of focus grows, so grows the scale of opportunity. By tying a parking app to a real purpose, you can eventually create a dynamic platform that makes the world a better place.

Here's how I would advise someone like Monica to come up with a business plan in the future:

- Identify a two-sided need that many people share.

- Figure out the real market drivers for the "buyers" and "sellers".

- Scheme out a platform that will help bring buyers and sellers together.

- Identify what other related needs those buyers and sellers might also have ... build the ecosystem.

- Develop a scaling model.

- Tap into something bigger—a sense of purpose shared by your buyers and sellers—that your idea can fulfill to motivate you into action.

With those questions answered, you may have enough ammunition to convince others—partners, employees, investors—that this is an idea worth pursuing.

The big shift for established corporations is to stop thinking about purpose as a philanthropic or social responsibility campaign—and start thinking about purpose as the key to critical innovations and massive potential growth. Purpose can be woven into your business model in a variety of different ways. Here are some suggestions:

- **Buy One Give One**

  Companies like TOMS Shoes pioneered this approach. Customers buy a product knowing they are also buying something for a person in need.

- **Replace Purposeless Assets**

  A company begins to transition from a harmful product to a product in line with purpose. For example, car manufacturers can shift from gasoline combustion engines to diesel or electric vehicles.

- **Employ Those in Need**

  Some companies focus on giving jobs or education to people in need. Intel, for example, trains refugees to be coders.[106]

---

106 https://www.fastcompany.com/40529447/the-intel-foundation-is-betting-it-can-transform-refugees-into-tech-workers

■ **Lead a Trend**

Purpose can be tied to business model by taking a stand and setting a positive trend: a tech or garment manufacturing company that won't employ labor in unfair conditions, for example, or an influential clothing designer like Stella McCartney who won't use leather.[107]

■ **Impact Investing**

Capital was once viewed as neutral, its only duty to seek positive returns. No more. Impact investors leverage capital to achieve purpose-driven change in the world. For example, SolarHome was founded to supply cheap, renewable electricity to people in developing countries who lack access.[108]

■ **Partner with Charities**

A company can leverage its core competencies to focus on social sector issues. For example, Salesforce employs a 1-1-1 philanthropic model that leverages technology, people and resources to improve communities.[109] They view this work as a growth market, and measure progress like they would any business line. They also actively support other businesses, including startups, in pledging 1 percent of their people, technology and resources in similar ways, enhancing their impact and reputation.

■ **Offer Free or Inexpensive Versions for the Needy**

Some companies offer extremely expensive products and services at reduced costs to needy consumers. For example, Ivy League colleges that charge up to $100,000 per year for tuition often offer free education and certification to students around the world via MOOC courses.

---

107 https://www.peta.org/videos/stella-mccartney-takes-on-the-leather-trade/

108 https://kr-asia.com/greg-krasnov-of-solarhome-on-southeast-asias-solar-energy-opportunity-startup-stories

109 https://www.salesforce.org/pledge-1/

Likewise, pharmaceutical companies that charge high prices for drugs in the U.S. may offer free or price-reduced versions of those medicines in the developing world.[110]

5. Technology Helps You Get There

Today, technology is no longer a barrier to making an idea happen. If you can think it or dream it, you can probably find a technology to do it.

In Pittsburgh, for example, cameras and proximity sensors monitor traffic flows to adjust traffic lights and thereby reduce traffic jams which waste fuel and harm the environment.[111] In healthcare, a startup called Cota Healthcare crunches immense quantities of data to develop better treatment paths for patients with cancer.[112] The energy industry uses drones to inspect pipelines and wind turbines, report on emergencies and even deliver supplies to hard-to-reach areas.[113]

What can a food company do to combat obesity, diabetes and other related chronic illnesses? Nestle decided to bring the power of personalized medicine to bear on its customers' nutrition. The Nestle Wellness Ambassador platform allows customers to send pictures of the food they eat to Nestle, along with DNA and blood tests to assess susceptibility to chronic illnesses. With that information, Nestle provides personalized nutrition advice and supplements. When such services are conducted across millions of customers, the data promises to provide deep insights into the connections between nutrition, lifestyle and genetic code.

Some years back, a food technology company called Linfa developed because of the marriage of three technologies. The original idea was to grow vegetables in the home using elegantly designed hydroponic chambers. These could be stacked in a kitchen, allowing the person at home to grow a substantial amount of produce year-round. The purpose of the company

---

110 https://www.ncbi.nlm.nih.gov/pmc/articles/PMC5725781/

111 https://sustainablebrands.com/read/product-service-design-innovation/how-ai-machine-learning-are-solving-global-problems

112 https://www.cotahealthcare.com

113 http://info.industrialskyworks.com/blog/how-to-solve-the-biggest-problems-with-oil-and-gas-projects-using-drones

was to enable fresh vegetables to be grown anywhere with minimal environmental impact from fertilizer, soil erosion and transportation. The problem was that the hydroponic chambers depended a lot on the quality of the light and the skill of the grower.

So, the team wedded their hydroponic idea to a second technology for data-generating light. With this sophisticated LED system, the quality of the light in the chamber could be monitored exactly and altered to improve growing results. Suddenly, Linfa turned a device for dedicated hobbyists into something with more mass-market appeal.

Then, it took it a step further and developed a way to share data among all customers. In this way, the hydroponic system could become smarter, figuring out from thousands of sources what approaches to growing vegetables (light, soil, nutrients) worked best.

Most companies spend some time worrying about which technologies will disrupt their industries. Technology has advanced so quickly that the question is almost meaningless. The real question should be, what urgent global problems do your customers want you to solve? Once you have clarity around purpose, the technology will likely be easy to find.

6. Purpose is the New Leadership

Today, trust in traditional leadership is at an all-time low. People view CEOs and politicians with suspicion—not in spite of their professional experience and competence, but because of it. Maybe this is because they associate traditional leaders with the devastating financial collapse of 2008 and all the job losses, corruption and tough times that went with it.

In contrast, people are more enthusiastic about leaders who are clear about their purpose. Such leaders stand for something meaningful, and they are able to create a deeper connection between their own aims and their followers/employees and customers. On top of that, they are often keen to disrupt business-as-usual and fuel growth. This feels exciting and significant to be around.

Although I am not a supporter of President Donald Trump and his populist agenda, I recognize the power of his very simple, purpose-driven message: Make America Great Again. It's hard to tell how real it is for Trump, a master brander, but he delivered that message repeatedly to his core supporters and electrified them. In contrast, Hilary Clinton could not really move her supporters with any specific emotionally charged agenda outside of her own historic attempt to become America's first female president.

Trump also connected better with his supporters because he knew emotions are always more energizing than facts. Steve Martin, the author of *The Science of Persuasion*, says that although we all think we are influenced by facts and coherent arguments, we are actually far more influenced by what we believe others around us are doing. For example, the way hotels use arguments about environmentalism to try to convince guests to reuse their towels is less effective than telling guests that most customers in this specific hotel, or even room, reuse their own towels.

In a similar way, Trump appealed to voters by pressing emotional triggers. Corporate CEOs who rely on traditional speeches, marketing ads and memos that pass through legal are unlikely to connect with employees, customers and even shareholders going forward. No one is interested in the same old narrative. They want a human touch with next-door-neighbor kind of messages.

Ricardo Semler became CEO of his father's Brazilian company, Semco, when he was only twenty-one. Semler tried to reinvent his family-owned business by doing lots of management consulting-type things. He broadened the portfolio by acquiring new businesses, and he fired all the old managers and brought in new ones who had very tough performance standards. It worked—for a while. But Semler didn't think it was sustainable. Nobody liked working for the company, even him. It was too stressful.

So Semler did something really different—even crazy for the corporate status quo. He turned the company into a purpose enterprise that put people first. To show he was serious, he got rid of all the rules and let the people take over. No set working hours. No project plans. Total transparency. People could decide what to do, how to do it, when to get it done by, and how much they should be paid. They even gave their managers performance reviews, not the other way around.

Amazingly, Semco became successful. It grew every year for twenty years, became a more profitable business, and the people were happy.

In its own way, a company like Google has done the same thing. Give people purpose and let them be free. This takes a special type of leadership. All the old attributes of leadership—expertise, experience, practical know-how and position—seem less credible and meaningful today. As people have lost faith in leaders and leadership, they've begun to look for something different. They seek values and principles they can believe in, embodied in leaders who seem to live those values authentically. Customers want the same from the companies whose products they buy.

The desire for meaning can be dangerous. Followers can be attracted to powerful ideologies—such as Nazism and ISIS. Yet, followers are also attracted to ideas and people that drive positive change. Purpose-driven leaders are not satisfied with small goals; they want to make moon shots happen. If they don't have the expertise, resources, or talent to do it, they go find it.

As more employees, customers, investors, and influencers are drawn to this type of leadership, it will be important for all leaders and decision makers to understand and compete in the marketplace for purpose.

Companies and leadership programs are already starting to get organized around this theme.[114] The movement has begun. The world is ready. Leadership is dead. Purpose is the new leadership.

7. Impact is the New Measure of Success

In an economy that increasingly elevates and rewards purpose-driven companies, how can you target objectives and measure success? There is clearly one key metric that stands before all others: Impact. How much impact is your company having on alleviating the urgent need it has set out to resolve?

This starts, first, by identifying that urgent need. Then you must assess how far you go toward meeting that need. To think in this way, I like to flatten out my four quadrants by focusing on customer-focused needs versus

---

114   https://teams.movingworlds.org

global or human-focused needs. Placing those on an X-Y axis, it becomes easier to identify where purpose-driven companies cluster.

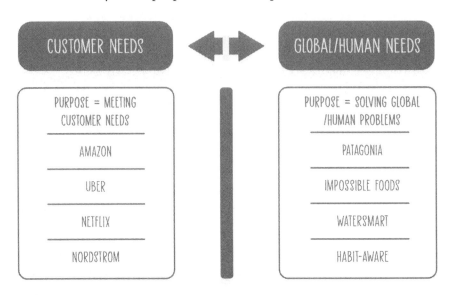

Let's look first at companies meeting customer needs. Almost every competitive company claims they are in business to serve their customers. Their notion of the customer can be defined broadly, to range from B2B to B2C. Few companies truly move the needle for customers in a transformative way. Most rely on a conventional mix of providing some service or product in an existing market while using branding, marketing, sales and attentive service to push that product or service to customers. Even though customers might feel strong brand loyalty or preference for one product/service over the other, the offerings and the companies are relatively interchangeable.

This is old-school capitalism. In this new purpose era, companies meet customer needs at a whole new level. Amazon is the face of this movement. According to Amazon's own purpose statement: "Our vision is to be earth's most customer-centric company; to build a place where people can come to find and discover anything they might want to buy online." It's easy to prove that Amazon has succeeded marvelously in that regard. The self-described world's most customer-focused company stops at nothing (including profitability) to deliver new services that delight customers.

Uber transformed customer expectations for transportation conve...
and ease, gaining huge market share in the process. Netflix did the same for
TV entertainment. Nordstrom has transformed the customer experience of
retail by combining customer data, digital technology, creative local stores
and personalized services.[115]

On the other end of the spectrum, there are purpose-driven companies
that are worried less about the customer's market demands and desires, and
far more about their human needs or the needs of the planet as a whole.
For example, Patagonia, the clothing and outdoor equipment manufacturer
and retailer, has always been at the vanguard of environmental activism.
More recently, it has put "saving our home planet" front and center as
its corporate mission. Patagonia's HR is empowered to hire people who
are committed to that mission. Sourcing strategies have been revamped
to serve rather than impede planetary needs. Politically, the company is
backing candidates with committed environmental strategies. And the
company continues to vigorously support grassroots activists and public
land-conservation efforts.[116]

It's not easy for a legacy manufacturer and retailer to have a transformational impact on a global or human need because such companies still must
compete in the old world. The closer your business model aligns with the
need you seek to alleviate, the more likely you will be at achieving impact.
This is why it's easier for new companies to find the technology, market,
funding and business model that helps it target those purpose-oriented
needs directly.

Impossible Foods, mentioned in Chapter Six, is a company that has
developed plant-based meat substitutes that taste so much like real meat
customers find it easier to switch over. By satisfying customers' taste for
meat with a meat substitute, Impossible believes that it can drastically reduce
environmentally inefficient use of land and water and the production of
environmentally harmful emissions. Recently, Impossible Foods launched

---

115 https://www.forbes.com/sites/blakemorgan/2019/03/26/the-10-keys-to-nordstroms-digital-
     transformation/#1476fd564aa0

116 https://www.fastcompany.com/90280950/exclusive-patagonia-is-in-business-to-save-our-
     home-planet

a new burger, the "Impossible Whopper", through fast-food giant Burger King. Not only does this give Impossible a giant new customer with lots of new revenue, but it significantly advances the goal of broadening the consumption of meatless burgers—helping to save the environment and improve human health.[117]

WaterSmart is a software service that assesses water use, predicts demand and helps identify and track waste. The company uses sophisticated analytics and AI to analyze the consumption patterns of millions of users. This could well turn out to be invaluable information in reducing waste. Investors have backed the idea with a recent $7 million raise. Whether WaterSmart can achieve its purpose remains to be seen. However, it's powerful to see a purpose-oriented company identify a significant global need, address it with sophisticated technology and satisfy a base of customers (in this case utilities) willing to pay for that service. This is business model meeting purpose in action.[118] As TechCrunch notes, "The good news is that the commercial market for water solutions is bigger than you might think, and that venture-stage companies in water perform better than many investors and entrepreneurs realize."[119]

HabitAware tackles a problem on a more human level. Millions of people have self-harmful body-focused repetitive behaviors like hair pulling or skin picking. Traditional medicine and therapy does a poor job helping the sufferers alleviate their problem. A husband and wife couple with direct experience developed a simple bracelet and software solution that enables its customers to track their behavior, interrupt those patterns and rewire their brain. Filling an important need, the company has been remarkably successful raising money, gaining public attention and support, developing an intuitive and powerful product, and marketing and selling it directly to consumers. Another example of purpose-driven business plan in action.[120]

---

117   https://www.nytimes.com/2019/04/01/technology/burger-king-impossible-whopper.html

118   https://www.watersmart.com/about-watersmart/

119   https://techcrunch.com/2015/06/22/turning-water-problems-into-business-opportunities/

120   https://habitaware.com/pages/about-habitaware

Over the past five hundred years, the world has changed dramatically. It has probably changed just as much in the past twenty years. All of that change has accelerated because of technological advancements. Though many worry about change, the problems of the globe have never been more solvable. What are the "impactful" challenges that remain to be solved? War, disease, violence, hunger, thirst? If you can dream a solution today, you can find a business model and a technology to fix it.

The great thing about this approach to business is how much enthusiasm it engenders among shareholders, customers, employees, stakeholders and observers. Think of the "goodwill" and share premium that Elon Musk, Tom Mycoskie, Steve Jobs or other visionary purpose leaders have generated for their businesses. Stakeholders want to create new legal frameworks for you. Regulators want to help you. Banks want to finance you. Consumers and customers seek out your products or services. Talent seeks out your organization for employment. You are in the news more often.

Marketers understand this link well. (Perhaps this is why genius promoters like Musk and Jobs have been so far ahead of the curve.) They see and leverage the connection between purpose, customer need, brand and business model—to a T.

8. Performance Pays Your Bills

A close friend of mine taught me a lesson many years ago. He had just graduated with a degree in pharmacy and was expected to begin work at the family drugstore business. Success meant making dad's small enterprise grow faster, maybe by opening up a couple of new stores … That's it. My friend George, however, had noticed the growing market for homeopathetic medicines. In his view, people were looking for milder treatments with less toxic effect on the body. This became his new passion.

George developed therapeutic and beauty solutions that didn't include any chemicals except for botanics. He leveraged the beauty and bounteous nature of Greece and its ancient history of medicine in his marketing. Because of his deep knowledge of drug commercialization, he decided to avoid grocery stores or supermarkets. Instead, he started small, just selling his new products to independent pharmacies. His friends from university and his personal network of pharmacists became his biggest allies.

Consumer response was fantastic. Within a couple of years, he proudly showed me his revenue graph and how he'd manage to double his sales year over year. I was amazed. Enthusiastically, he told me that this had been his plan from the beginning: every year to double sales.

Ten years later, he developed his brands so nicely, both in the domestic but also in the export markets, including the U.S., that he was able to sell a majority stake of his business to a Chinese fund, and he is now one of the most successful and well-recognized entrepreneurs in Greece. In addition to his natural talent to build brands, I think his "never give up" mentality proved to be one of his biggest assets.

Today, some of the highest-profile leaders and CEOs engage in social and political causes, following a "purpose-driven" strategy over bottom-line results. Many of those leaders have stepped down from their roles because of poor company performance. While they were successful in creating a purposeful brand and vibe around a special cause, they failed to meet bottom-line promises and forecasts. WeWork, eBay, Uber are among the latest examples.[121] Other companies with grandiose claims that they are helping the world include Lyft, Snapchat, Etsy and others. Salesforce, on the other hand, offers a contrary example. Marc Bennioff's company has enjoyed stellar growth both organically and through acquisitions, while also contributing meaningfully to its social agenda.

Clearly, putting purpose uniquely above and separate from other concerns is a recipe for failure. But some people insist that business performance must come first, and social impact and sense of purpose is a luxury that can be indulged in accordingly. In my view, performance and purpose must be balanced and integrated. Performance pays the bills. Purpose feeds the commitment and energy. Delivering on both can be measured by revenue and social impact. If they both get achieved, then purpose has been effectively integrated into the business model, into the DNA of the whole organization. Such businesses, I believe, are the ones built really to last and thrive.

---

121   Source: https://www.nytimes.com/2019/09/28/business/wework-juul-ebay-ceo.html

Putting It All Together

It's one thing to believe in purpose, define it, and dream about it. It is another thing to put purpose into action. How do you bring it all together and get started?

INNOVATION AND PURPOSE – HOW TO REINVENT YOUR COMPANY

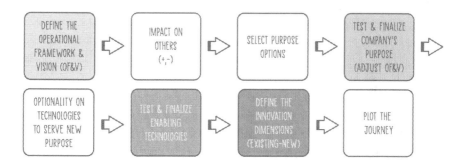

When I work with founders and top executives, I bring them through the following eight practical steps:

Step 1. Determine Location

Decide where you currently operate in the quadrants. Is that where you want to be? This is the start of the larger journey, and it helps to tie purpose to business model to market together from the beginning.

Step 2. Admit Current Impact

If you're in an "old-school" business this isn't going to be pretty. What is the current impact of your product or service? Honest answers only. My soft drink, for example, doesn't deliver happiness; it contributes to obesity. My plastic cases don't just help customers get their products in top condition; they help pollute the world. In all seriousness, you may have good impacts and bad impacts. Start with the truth and you can find your truth.

Step 3. Develop Purpose Options

If your business or company is going to do something very different to maximize positive impact, what would that be? Can your automobile reduce CO_2 emissions? Can your plastic company change the way plastic is used or recycled?

Step 4. Road Test Your New Purpose

If your new purpose is to reduce harm, for example, do you have the technological and business means to do that now? If not, what will you need to do differently? Perhaps you will need to hire new scientists or reengineer your manufacturing processes or work closely with customers to meet their critical needs.

Step 5. Adopt Technology Enablers

Often, transformational purpose requires technology. What will you need to help you get where you want to go? The Internet, AI, robotics, Blockchain, solar power … you name it. Come up with a list of gaps that only technology can solve, then go out and find the technology. It's waiting for you.

Step 6. Test Again

Does your new formula work? Does your business plan fit your purpose? Have you identified the right customers and markets? Are you meeting those needs with impact? Do you have the technology in place to make it happen?

Step 7. Set Destination

Now that you know where you are and the impact you want to have, where do you want to go on the growth quadrant? Does it make the most sense to play in existing spaces, or should you venture forth into new spaces?

Step 8. Plot the Journey

You're ready to get started. You know where you want to go and you know why. So what do you need to get there? The most important thing is to find and attract the right people. As leader, you will need to communicate your message of purpose and impact over and over. You will also need to continue to assess and adjust your action plan. Often, this involves small tweaks every day. But you also can't be afraid of major pivots. Startups understand this better than established corporations, but it's hard no matter what. It takes a great deal of vision, conviction and persuasion to enable an organization to change its business model or approach to the market, even for the right reasons.

The most important piece of the puzzle, however, is you. Do you want to lead with purpose? Once you answer that question, you can find your answers for all the other questions.

More CEOs and leaders are taking social matters seriously.[122] There's no question that the times have changed. Have you changed, too? You can gauge this by assessing what really matters to you.

Maybe what matters is your family or your health or your passionate hobbies. In such cases, you might choose to step out of the business arena and devote yourself to a personal pursuit. Perhaps you're burned out, or just not feeling it anymore or there's something else that you really want to do to feel right. There is nothing wrong with that. Everyone deserves to be happy, engaged, fulfilled and to feel a sense of significance and compassion in their lives.

On the other hand, maybe what matters to you is something external and bigger than you. If that purpose is a problem or a quest that only a business or organization can solve or a need or a potential that only a business or organization can meet, then you have a different kind of answer. You might need to become what I call a purposeful leader. This is someone, at any level of the organization, who inspires, motivates, organizes, strategizes,

---

122 https://hbr.org/2018/02/more-and-more-ceos-are-taking-their-social-responsibility-seriously

coaches and directs the people around him or her to accomplish a larger, purposeful vision.

This is not an easy road. Companies that are striving to embrace purpose must undergo significant change to get there. It also creates a tangible dilemma. Being purpose-driven sets a company apart from competitors in a broad sense and helps them be more dynamic and innovative. I believe it is a source of real competitive advantage. However, companies that are purpose-driven are viewed differently by customers, employees and the stock market. Because they are purpose-driven, people assume they should always act with values and ethics in mind. It almost doesn't matter whether their purpose is aligned with a particular issue or not. Perception and expectations count more.

Purpose, in other words, can make you a target. If your purpose-driven company fails to take a position on controversial issues, customers can get very emotional and criticize you. If you take a public stand, you can get attacked by other customers. In particular, navigating areas where societal, political and business priorities clash is incredibly difficult. As the world becomes more chaotic, uncertain and polarized, this need for meaning and purpose will only grow. Accordingly, societal, political and business clashes are likely to increase.

As the great Peter Drucker said, "Free enterprise cannot be justified as being good for business. It can be justified only as being good for Society."

Purpose is a very serious business.

In fact, I believe it will be the most serious challenge you have ever taken on.

It will also be the most fulfilling, supported and connected journey of your life.

CHAPTER NINE RECAP

- Hey, did you like what have read so far? Do you want to move forward?

- If you have not bumped onto a serious crisis yet, why wait? Discuss about the issues you face (i.e. enemies and supporters exercise in Chapter Four) with your people and brainstorm on possible purpose directions.

- Assess where your company stands today and how it impacts the world. Reverse the negatives. Can you become good by attacking one of the Level One problems that looks relevant to you? Integrate it with your business model.

- Where do you want to be in the future? Do you want to go for moon shots or short jumps? Brainstorm to identify relevant technological enablers. Check your assumptions with employees and customers. Refine. Craft your plan with phases and a few metrics.

- Join the team of believers, changers and likely disruptors.

Tools & Resources

Purpose and Business Model Matrix

As discussed in this chapter, there are various ways to attack Level One problems or subcategories of them. After selecting a problem and integrating it with your business model, you will encounter the critical question "HOW?" For example, I am the founder of a software company, and I would like to help communities in need to prosper through job opportunities. In the below 2X2 matrix I have plotted four different ways to do that.

PURPOSE & BUSINESS MODEL MATRIX

LEVEL ONE PROBLEM: ACCESS TO ECONOMIC OPPORTUNITY

1. **Give money.** In any form, from charity to a 1 percent pledge. While a traditional approach, impact is minimized in my view, making sustainable success less likely.

2. **Lend money.** Lending to local software entrepreneurs in very affordable terms can operate like the famous microloans pioneered

by Muhamad Yunus and described in Chapter Six.[123] This creates more sustainable development, but impact is still light because some loans will fail and contribute to a cycle of poverty. Funds might also be misused.

3. **Give jobs.** This is in line with what Leila Janah has done with her company Samasource https://www.samasource.org/ which is nicely described in her book *Give Work*. She offered classroom training of people in Africa and India on coding with the aim to create outsourced jobs. Another good example is the Intel Foundation, which just gave the International Rescue Committee $1 million to retrain one thousand German-based refugees for technology-related jobs.[124]

   It is a very impressive idea and hard work. It can certainly have impact and some sustainability. The weak spot is that the work that needs to be done by intermediaries or NGOs to organize, funnel and maintain the flow of training and outsourcing.

4. **Create jobs.** In my view, this is the most powerful way to deal with inequality and unleash opportunities for people to access growth and prosperity. It is based on the assumption that this very objective is part of a company's business model and operations. As a result, it can be potentially highly impactful and sustainable. The greater the success of the company, the more jobs this can create.

Think about these two dimensions and design or repurpose your organization accordingly.

---

123 https://godmoneyme.com/2013/04/16/five-problems-with-microlending/

124 https://www.fastcompany.com/40529447/the-intel-foundation-is-betting-it-can-transform-refugees-into-tech-workers

EPILOGUE

For the last five years or so—coincidentally, the same period that I have been working on this book—I have been trying to go deeper into my life, examining, among other things, the trail that we each leave behind. Is it important to leave something behind or not? What is the role of luck in the way our life unfolds? Can we help our trajectory in a positive way by being prepared and ready to grab opportunity when it appears?

I've also reflected on how our experiences shape us, and what bad luck actually means and whether that's something to be avoided or embraced. For example, I have had a lot of "bad luck" in my career, so much so that one of my colleagues used to call me a "black swan", because wherever I went, a crisis soon followed.

Through my experiences, reflections and the writing of this book, I've concluded that crisis is not bad luck, but good luck. It's a gift, and your best trainer. Whatever doesn't kill you makes you far better than before. It makes you think. It forces you to turn off the autopilot we can all tend to rely on and hold the steering wheel yourself. Sometimes it pushes you to rediscover qualities from your youth that were sleeping while you pursued a professional career. It reacquaints you with the importance of risk taking, companionship, experimentation, play, positivity and the sense that "anything and everything is possible."

Ultimately, crisis may be the biggest gift any of us ever get because it helps us discover our inner self.

For a team, crisis helps teach that each member has special qualities beyond their résumés and assigned roles that might go unused, untapped or unrecognized otherwise. In overcoming emergencies, you get pushed to use everything and everybody in the best possible way. Hierarchies and organizational structures just don't matter suddenly. You put together new, simple systems that actually work. You need to be fast and effective. And beyond everything else, you develop a sharp and vital sense of purpose. It doesn't need to be there forever. A team's purpose can alter. But for a time, it matters very much.

For an organization, crisis teaches that the collective group can have an important role to play in a broader context, maybe even globally. Together, you can have an impact on the world. The bigger the crisis, the bigger the gain. The more people you positively affect, the larger the opportunity to grow and flourish. There is a kind of magical reciprocity in that formula: The world pays you back for the purposeful efforts you make. And we have more than enough problems in the world these days to tackle. Just pick one.

Next comes the how: the operationalization piece. What approaches can you use to fulfill the needs of your current customers, understand their wants that are not yet expressed, and serve them in ways that will benefit the general public and even the planet? It is not always obvious. It takes courage, "tent time", imagination, and science to come up with quality answers. Being innovative for the sake of innovation is a short and unfulfilling trip. It won't take you far.

For sales, entering new markets or white spaces might feel scary at first. But there are ways to start small, prototype and test prior to selecting the final shots. There's no need to be afraid.

Chances are technology will also be necessary. We are lucky to live during the heart of the Fourth Industrial Revolution. I am a firm believer that today "whatever we can imagine, we can do."

Technology decentralizes and democratizes decisions, relations and transactions. It creates personalized products, goods, services, even medicines without human hands. It connects people, brains and bodies in unthinkable ways. It uses the gifts of the sun. It enables you to use your senses remotely and to live experiences without being there. It facilitates the production of food and other essentials of life without burdening the planet. It corrects nature and helps us to realize the eternal dream for a longer life. What a world has become possible! Just need to grab hold and make it happen.

Am I being too visionary? Maybe. But I see such things happening around us all the time. We just need to move out of our self-limiting beliefs and write new stories with new rules. If we use some of these ideas, we can build the world anew. In the process, we'll live happier lives and leave a better planet to our children.

If not us, then who else? If not now, then when?

That's a question I hope you answer, starting now.

■ ■ ■ ■ ■ ■ ■ ■ ■ ■ ■

Oh, before I forget. I want to give you an update on my colleagues from Ukraine ...

Tatiana got promoted as a managing director in a large territory in Latin America. After significant achievements, she left the company to create her her own future back in Ukraine.

Artem, promoted twice, now serves as an area vice president in Saint Petersburg, Russia, managing huge resources and challenges.

Roman advanced in two consecutive jobs, attaining number one status in territories of greatest importance and responsibility and then left the company to pursue his own dream.

And me, though I still live in Lausanne, Switzerland, I've left the company, too, in order to forge my own path in business and, hopefully, the world.

ACKNOWLEDGMENTS

In the beginning it was a speech and an article in HBR, then a blogpost, and another one, and so on. I was encouraged by some people I respect very much to continue writing even though the corporate environment I worked in at the time was not accustomed to one of their executives engaging in such a public and honest dialogue. I put all of my writings together on a website, without any agenda or objective, just hoping that like-minded people would read my thoughts and engage with me in return.

Eventually, the volume of material grew and took on a sense of direction. I began to feel I had something larger to contribute. Should I write a book? Could I? I asked my friend and collaborator, Keith Hollihan, for his opinion. He was positive. Keith is an amazing person with whom I share similar life stories and he was at least as crazy as me. Thank you, Keith, for this amazing journey.

The next problem was the storyline. I soon realized that putting together a variety of thoughts, ideas and stories does not make it a book. My friend, coach, and mentor, Phil Harkins, sat next to me to help, offering not only his sharp, experienced eye but also his natural empathy and his willingness to be there for me unconditionally. Thank you, Phil, for your support, friendship and insights over the years.

My teams in Athens, Lausanne and Kiev helped me to become a better professional and person. Their help and support are reflected in each and every line in this book. I am listing their names below in no particular order, though I fear I might forget somebody. Thank you ALL. *Chapeau!*

- Athens: Vasilis Nomikos, Christos Harpantidis, Costas Salvaras, Jackie Taylor, Leonidas Tolis, Vassilis Nomikos, Nikitas Theofilopoulos, George Partsakoulakis, Romina Siaterli, Walter Veen

- Kiev: Tatiana Karpova, Artem Krivtsov, Andreas Mosel, Roman Khrushch, Natalya Trifonova, Nataliya Davydova, Piotr Cerek, Malcolm Healey, Victor Borovkov, Denys Strobykin, Liviu Vornicu, Nadezhda Redkina, Emil Krustev, Iryna Zhukova and Iaroslava Tereshkova

- Lausanne: Hugo Vilchez, Klavs Berzins, Christos Kiritsis, Tyrone Kearvell, Darek Kiersztan, Magda Drag, Anil Turan, Joao Costa, Aldo Podesta, Christian Rivette, Mike Halparin, Philip Goldhammer, Alexandra Gorra

I want to express my heartfelt appreciation for all the friends who gave me precious feedback on ideas, concepts and even full chapters. Margarita Albanezou, Romina (again), Anil (again), Andrii Kladchenko, Sushim Gupta and Bohdan Nahaylo. I cannot forget you.

Also, huge appreciation for all my followers in social media and from the website.

Ellie Bakopoulou from MILK Athens, and Alina Bonn from Agency 94 took excellent care of logos and looks. Alina was the cornerstone of all marketing and PR activities related to the book.

Without B.G. Dilworth for coordination and advice, Ronda Rawlins and Michele DeFilippo from 1106 Design for the whole publishing process, Sheri Gilbert for all approvals required, and Andreas Aggelopoulos my favorite cartoonist illustrator from Patras who designed all sketches and charts, publishing wouldn't have been possible.

Finally, I would like to express my love and gratitude to my family, Stanka, Dimitris, Elena, my little Sebastian, Yannis, George and Eleni, with whom I not only share a name but a life, too.

ABOUT THE AUTHOR

Christos Tsolkas is an Independent Business Advisor and Entrepreneur.

He has spent more than 25 years in positions of significant responsibility (General Management, Sales & Marketing) with multinationals in the Fast-Moving Consumer Goods sector, leading senior teams to achieve high performance and change. His educational background is Chemical Engineering & Business and he is dedicated to continuous learning.

Christos has had the unique opportunity to lead organizations in the midst of extreme crisis, not once but twice, including when the Greek Economic Crisis of 2010 unfolded rapidly and when the Ukrainian Crisis of 2013/14 devolved into violent geopolitical conflict. In both cases, Christos stabilized business operations and maintained the morale and security of personnel while positioning brand portfolios for strong growth. Most importantly, he leveraged each crisis to catalyze the development of his management teams, enabling the organization to not only weather those storms but thrive.

Christos is a turnaround specialist and a creative thinker, keen on internal startups and digital platforms. He is driven by the potential of new ideas to transform businesses, grow markets and inspire people. An author, blogger and passionate speaker, Christos was born in Athens, Greece and has lived, and worked across Europe. He currently resides in Lausanne, Switzerland.

Visit his personal blog www.christostsolkas.com
✉ contact@christostsolkas.com
in https://ch.linkedin.com/in/christostsolkas
🐦 @ChTsolkas

Printed in Great Britain
by Amazon

39400158R00145

The
Endeavourist

The
Endeavourist

How one man tried to beat extreme
poverty in Kenya

Kenneth King

RedDoor

Published by RedDoor

www.reddoorpublishing.com

© 2017 Kenneth King

The right of Kenneth King to be identified as author of this Work has been asserted by him in accordance with sections 77 and 78 of the Copyright, Designs and Patents Act 1988

ISBN 978-1-910453-44-5

The events described in this book actually happened, though some names of people and places have been changed. For the sake of the story, some sequences of events have been simplified and some individuals have been represented by one composite figure

A CIP catalogue record for this book is available from the British Library

Cover design: Rawshock Design

Typesetting: Tutis Innovative E-Solutions Pte. Ltd

Print managed by Jellyfish Solutions Ltd

I dedicate this book to the most profound and positive influence on my life, my father, John F King, known to his family and friends as Jack and to me as my wonderful and loving Da.

And to absent friends…

Thanks

I want to thank my mentors, guides and editors, Ian Shircore and Dr Sarah Burton, who have put up with my stubborn and often reluctant acceptance of their professional and passionate advice about what would work and what would not. Ian and Sarah, you have never flinched over the years in which I have twisted and turned the chapters, their content and indeed the scope and direction of the entire book. I will forever be in your debt for your patience, energy, creative input and professionalism.

I owe a special thank you to Olive Foley for her dedication in meticulously reviewing the text and critically checking facts and chronologies, and for her suggestions and advice.

To Alan and Norman King, whose support and timely interventions in this story were very settling to me in those moments, but were mostly, as ever, brotherly and caring.

I also want to thank sincerely Sheila Jayarajan, who made me think again about what sort of book this should be, and helped me to bring more life to some of the characters and scenes.

To my publishers Clare Christian, and Heather Boisseau and to all the team at RedDoor Publishing, in particular Sadie Mayne, whose guidance and support has made real the dream of professional publication.

THANKS

To Jason O'Callaghan, whose leadership, advice and support on PR and marketing have contributed enormously to the launch of this book.

To Nadine Soares Lino, for your insights, ideas and advice... thank you.

Alan, Clare, Heather, Ian, Jason, Nadine, Norman, Sarah, Olive, Sadie, Sarah and Sheila, this book would not be what it is without you. I really appreciate all your support and patience. Thank you.

To Monique Legair, for your practical support with Hong Kong, thank you. To Hugo Bänziger, Colin Furniss, Hugh Hughes, Konrad Joy and Neil Smith. Thank you for your belief in me over all the years, for the key opportunities at key moments, and for your enduring friendship and professional support.

To my Navan Road gang, thank you 'forever and ever'.

To my cherished Mon, and to Sue and Chloe Brown, Liam, Sean and Orla Foley, Abbie, Grace and Ben King: Without you all, I would be lost. Thank you for all your welcomes and your smiles throughout all the weathers of life.

Ken, July 2017

1

How I became a bastard

'Voyager upon life's sea,
To yourself be true,
And where'er your lot may be
Paddle your own canoe.'

Sarah T Bolton, 'Paddle Your Own Canoe'

I'd ordered a Porsche. It was a blue 911 Convertible and almost perfect. The dealer had spent a month fitting the extras I wanted – the special wheels, the seats and the sound system. When it was finally ready and I went to pick it up, I was tingling with excitement. It was a sunny Saturday morning and I couldn't wait to be out on the road.

When I walked into the showroom, it looked magnificent. But there, alongside it, looking even more magnificent, was another car, another Porsche, the coolest car I had ever seen. A metallic black 911 Turbo with matt black wheels, a double hand-stitched black leather boudoir interior and a huge whale-tail, it crouched there like a dark muscular shadow. It was a one-off, specially imported from Germany. It was, quite simply, the most beautiful car I had ever set eyes on, and it was within my reach.

'You'll easily find a buyer for the convertible,' I told the dealer. 'Let me take the black one instead.'

'Come on,' he laughed. 'You've paid for the convertible and it's got all those extras you wanted. Let's do the paperwork.'

'No. I'm serious. I must have the Batmobile.'

'And I'm serious, too. We've done a deal. I've spent weeks getting the blue one just how you wanted it. It's yours. You're committed.'

I was in love. I was insane.

'I'll take them both.'

'You'll do what?'

'I'll buy both cars from you. Now.'

I handed him my black American Express card.

* * *

In the marble and glass towers of London and Manhattan, energy, intelligence, ingenuity and stamina can be lavishly rewarded. This had become my world during the 1990s. I'd developed my skills, first in IT and then, more broadly, in project management. In the years since I'd moved from Dublin to London, I'd moved from insurance into the high-risk, high-reward business of investment banking. I found it fascinating, and I quickly gained a reputation as a person who could take on the big global projects and get results. The truth was, the bigger and more awkward the project, the more I relished the task. No project – nothing – intimidated me. I was measuring myself against the biggest challenges I could find and coming out on top, time and time again. I was feeling good about myself. And I was getting noticed.

One morning, a few months after I'd started a new job as Global Re-Engineering Director at an investment bank, on what I thought was a fabulous salary, my American boss called me into his office.

'We want you to stick around, Kenny,' he said. 'You're a key part of the leadership team and I don't want any distractions getting in the way of that. Congratulations.' He handed me an envelope.

When I opened the letter I saw that my bonus had been set at a minimum of 100 per cent of my annual salary, guaranteed for the next three years. They were doubling my income. I'd now be making more in twelve days than I'd been earning in the twelve months before I left Dublin as a systems designer.

I had been in England for eight years. But now I had really arrived.

'Don't thank me. You've earned it. Now fuck off and do what we pay you to do.'

The extra money wasn't that important, except as a means of keeping score. What mattered to me was the feeling that I had put my early doubts and failures behind me. I'd done badly at school and only started to take charge of my life when after three years I went back to night school, re-sat the school-leaving exams and won myself a place on a four-year evening degree course in computer science at Trinity College, Dublin. That had paved the way for a succession of jobs in the insurance industry, the move from Dublin to London, and, eventually, the switch into the world of investment banking.

Now I felt in control, appreciated and duly rewarded. And if the money wasn't everything, I certainly wasn't going to turn down the luxuries it offered me.

I bought myself a home in London – a five-storey townhouse near Buckingham Palace. I bought cars, took luxury trips, invested in a few works of art. I worked ferociously hard, putting in the seventy-hour weeks the job demanded and shuttling backwards and forwards between London, Frankfurt and New York, often flying the Atlantic twice in a week. I ate finely, drank too often and too much, and felt proud of my ability to manage projects and find solutions to the tricky problems in a way that no one else seemed (to me) as able to do quite as well. I was the archetypal spoiled City banker. I became demanding and intolerant. The rhyming slang for a banker was spot on: I was becoming a not very nice person.

Around this time, the top investment banks were desperately competing for the individual talents they thought could transform their company's performance. This was the period when the Big Swinging Dicks of the City were negotiating astonishing salaries for themselves as they switched loyalties and sold their souls to rival employers. Stories abounded of 'two-for-three' deals and 'three-for-twos'. A two-for-three guaranteed the employee £2 million a year for three years, regardless of that individual's performance. A three-for-two meant higher pay, but less long-term security – just £3 million a year for two years.

Although I wasn't in that league, I was doing very well for a son of Dublin's Northside. I was continuing to show that I could deliver what the banks wanted from me. Problem-solving was my game. At my best, I was sometimes able to anticipate problems way ahead and solve them before they caused any difficulties.

When my bank introduced 'FTKP', as a way of weeding out low performers, I could see what was coming. FTKP stood for 'Failure to Keep Pace'. In practice, it meant that all of us who managed large teams were forced to identify the worst-performing 10 per cent of our staff. Individuals classified as FTKP would get no bonuses at all. They would be put on three-month improvement action plans – 'three months to shape up or ship out' – and ruthlessly culled unless there was a radical improvement in their performance. It was brutal, but it had been seen to be effective in other industries, especially at General Electric, where GE's legendary CEO Jack Welch had pioneered this notorious 'rank and yank' approach.

Across the departments I managed, it turned out that almost all the poor performers were concentrated in one particular unit. That made it fairly easy to deal with. I decided that we should outsource the entire function, letting these least effective 10 per cent go, and solving the whole underperformance problem at a stroke. My boss loved the idea. Within a few months, by the end of November, the outsourcing was complete and I had almost no low-performing staff left.

A few weeks later I was called in to see the new boss, who had the list of all the year-end performance ratings for my global teams spread out on the desk in front of him.

'What's going on, Ken?' he said. 'Your group hasn't been FTKP-ed.'

'Well, we covered all that with the outsourcing we completed last month. The vast majority of my low-performers have already gone.'

His brow furrowed.

'But your list is not FTKP-ed.'

'I know. It's OK, though. Most of the poor performers were taken out in November.'

He frowned and lowered his voice menacingly.

'What part of "your list is not FTKP-ed" do you not understand?'

I couldn't believe my ears. His displeasure was clear and my card had just been well and truly marked. If I didn't show that I was complying with his stupid, dogmatic interpretation of an arbitrary rule, I'd end up on my boss's own FTKP list.

Faced with the choice between dumb obedience and a career threatening refusal to do it, I called in fifteen of my staff, one by one, and told them I was reclassifying them as among the lowest 10 per cent of performers. Their performance would need substantial improvement, I explained, and they had been nominated as FTKP. Their bonuses were gone and their jobs were at risk. Their stunned expressions spoke volumes. Now I was well and truly swimming with the sharks.

Of course, if I'd been half as clever as I thought I was, I'd have seen this coming and delayed the November outsourcing project for just a couple of months. If I'd done that, the problem wouldn't have arisen. I should have FTKP-ed those guys, then outsourced their jobs in January, which would have left the other fifteen perfectly good staff unaffected. They could have collected their bonuses and remained safe in their jobs and I would not have fallen foul of the big boss.

But no one gets it right all the time. I'd seen people who'd produced outstanding results escorted out of the building with their belongings in a black bin bag when the tide had turned and they were suddenly out of favour. When people's incomes depend heavily on large bonuses and everyone's playing musical chairs because of the imposition of policies like FTKP, it doesn't encourage team players. People are in it for themselves and you can hardly expect them to muck in and put their differences aside to get things done. It makes for a slippery, highly politicised environment, and sooner or later it will be you in the cross-wires.

Eventually, my turn came. I was beginning to feel burnt out, mentally, physically and emotionally, though I worked hard to ensure that nothing showed on the outside. I was still working ridiculous hours, scrambling on and off planes for meetings in Frankfurt, New York, Singapore, India and Tokyo, but the hunger to achieve had been sated. I was beginning to wonder if there was something else I should be doing with my life, and I was having to put in huge amounts of effort just to stay afloat. My results dipped, and I realised the blood in the water was my own. Investment banks can smell self-doubt and they are not forgiving.

All too soon, the call came. I was told my services were no longer required and given an hour to collect my possessions, say goodbye and leave. I'd get six weeks' money and that was the end of it. I was unemployed. Worse than that, I felt finished. My precarious new position and declining demeanour soon impacted on my very recent marriage, which was more fragile than maybe either of us had realised. I couldn't see how on earth I would ever be able to pay off the mortgage. I felt lethargic, angry, sad and fearful. I was worried about my health, about my lack of energy, about having no reason to get up in the morning. I could see myself ending up alone and drunk and desperate – and I didn't like what I saw.

After a serious disagreement about money and family, there followed a sudden separation and then lawyers' letters with a demand for half my assets. The dream had become a real nightmare.

We had once been so close. Soon there was a legal battle raging over the house we shared in Pimlico, the house I had bought before we had got together. That house was the symbol of my climb from nothingness to owning Porsches and fine art and a half-a-million-pound job. The divorce lawyers' battle lasted two years, as long as the marriage itself.

It was now 2008, the year that I felt at my lowest ebb. Divorced, useless and broken. Devastatingly shattered on the inside. As the financial crisis swept the world, all the banks began laying off their staff. There were thousands of ex-bankers in London like me competing for the same handful of jobs. Having been a workaholic, I would wake up in the morning and wonder who I was. I felt like a has-been. One day, walking down Oxford Street alone, it especially hit me – all of the loss, all of the pain. I went down a side street into some dark doorway and found myself hunkered down on my knees sobbing uncontrollably, my face in my hands, tears oozing between my fingers. I could sense passers-by giving me curious looks but I didn't even care who saw me. I was beyond caring at that point. I had felt in control of everything for two decades, but now it was all gone or crumbling away – the job, my marriage, my house, my esteem, my health, perhaps even my sanity. I must have cut a pretty sad figure on my own in that doorway.

Where was there left to go in life? This was some midlife crisis. My choices seemed stark: either find another banking role, or sell the house I loved.

But property prices had crashed too. I knew I had to sell the house, but I couldn't even do that.

It was time to take stock of what I did have to offer the world.

What could I do? Where could I go?

I wiped my eyes and carried on through the swell of humanity down Oxford Street, thinking hard. When there's nothing left inside, you need outside help. I needed a purpose, a direction. I needed a strategy to get me back on track, something that would help me look forward rather than back. If I could sell the house, I was more than prepared to invest it in anything that would lift me out of the slough of depression. And it was just when I was at my lowest ebb that I remembered Anthony Robbins.

Robbins is a world leader in the life-coaching industry, a bestselling author of books like *Awaken the Giant Within* and a fantastic speaker. I'd been a fan of his methods for years and I knew he held a huge (and expensive) week-long 'Date with Destiny' seminar every year. I needed to be there, I decided. I needed to be swept along in all the noisy, energetic, feel-good razzmatazz of a big all-American event like this, in the hope of finding what I was looking for. So I booked my place, flew to Florida and found myself in a hotel ballroom packed with 2000 people who'd come to get a piece of the Robbins magic.

I'd checked in my reservations and most of my inhibitions at the door, but I still felt the urge to turn and run. As a European, this wasn't my kind of thing. Yet, within an hour, I was climbing onto a chair and rocking back and forth, whooping and cheering along with this mass of hopeful humanity. The voice inside me was telling me this stuff was way too over-the-top and in-your-face American – that it was all too brash, too staged and mechanical. But Robbins knows what people need.

'Go with it,' I told myself. 'If it means putting up with six days of this rah-rah shit, that's what you've got to do. If it doesn't work, you've got the rest of your life to try something else.'

So I listened, and clapped, and high-fived my neighbours, and went with the flow. By the end of day one, my face was aching from smiling so much. By the end of days two, three and four, I realised I was having a good time, whether I liked it or not. And by the end of day five, I suddenly found I knew what I wanted to do. The big man had delivered. I was going to do something useful in the world.

And it seemed, according to Tony Robbins, that I had actually, unwittingly, been in training all my life for this Eureka moment. Tony Robbins taught me how to work out what I was uniquely qualified to do.

So, I figured, I have expertise in running large-scale complex projects, I have unusual freedom in that I don't have to raise children and don't have an intimate relationship to nurture. I have some remaining savings, and I hope to raise cash from the sale of my house. How can I draw upon these factors to make something of my life? Plus, I have a fourth element – natural vitality, if I could just re-awaken it.

In that Florida hotel ballroom, I surmised, the purpose of the last twenty years of my life had been to prove to myself that I was good enough. Why did I want a five-storey house around the corner from Buckingham Palace, two Porsches, a 7 series BMW and fine art on the walls, in the first place? To prove to myself that I am not inadequate. That mission has been completed. So, I conclude, what would be the point in re-walking that path for the next twenty years of my life?

Think big, Tony Robbins encouraged. Belief in limitations has to be cast aside, he extolled. What does my life to date uniquely qualify me to do? What future destiny would make sense of all that has gone before? Every experience, good or difficult, enjoyable or painful, that has happened in my life to date, has led me to this very place, to this very moment, when I will decide my destiny.

I go into a corner with all these exciting perceptions, and come out two hours later not with an answer, but with a big question.

Could I use my unusual freedom, my financial resources, my experience in professional project management of difficult global challenges, my understanding of business and finance and my natural vitality and dogged determination to go headlong into Africa and try to devise a new highly structured, private sector, self-sustaining method for alleviating extreme poverty? Even become the Henry Ford of poverty alleviation. The thought made me radiate with hope. And chuckle. Why the hell not?

So I decided that I would find a way. I would go to a struggling African country to see for myself – not as a poverty tourist, but as a man with an idea. I had been reading about microfinance, the concept of lending very small amounts to budding entrepreneurs in the developing world, as a first step out of extreme poverty, and it had really inspired me.

Personally I would never have bought my first car and I couldn't have got through university without the help of loans. So I completely believed in credit as an essential stepping stone for everyone.

Maybe I could put microfinance at the very heart of a project to endeavour to beat extreme poverty in a small trial somewhere. And if it works, who knows the future? – the impact could be dramatic and wonderful.

I knew I couldn't predict whether I would be in Africa for a year or five years or forever, and at that point, I didn't much care. I didn't have a long-term plan for my life anyway, so I would just go.

The plan was simply to give it everything I had.

2

First impressions

'The Earth was made round so that we would not see too far
down the road.'

Karen Blixen, *Out of Africa*

It's all very well having a blinding flash of inspiration and deciding
that you'll go to an impoverished African country and do something
that will make a difference.

Now I knew what I wanted to do, the next question was obvious.
How? How, exactly, was I going to make it happen? I needed to know
a lot more about what needed to be done. I needed to know what had
been tried already, what had worked and what had failed. I'd read
about the UN's Millennium Development Goals, the bold, ambitious
eight-point plan, beginning in 2000, that aimed to eradicate poverty
and hunger and improve health and education opportunities across
the developing world by 2015.

But I'd also heard that progress had been slow. Some money that
had been promised had not yet come through. I collected all the
books, articles, videos and reports I could find and hurled myself

into an intensive programme of reading and research, including a little Penguin paperback from 2005 called *Our Common Interest: An Argument*, written by a group called the Commission for Africa.

The front cover quote by Bob Geldof grabbed my attention.

'If our plan is adopted,' it said, 'this could be the decade when Africa's fortune turns.'

A plan? I thought. Believing I knew a thing or two about plans for transformational change projects, I wondered what structure and approach Bob Geldof's plan had envisaged.

I settled into a critique of the plan for achieving the impressive ambition stated on the back cover: 'Changing a continent. Saving the world'. But I soon came across a single sentence that stopped me in my tracks: Referring to the eight Millennium Development Goals, it stated 'Already those noble ambitions are receding into the distance.'

What? How could this be?

The book was written only five years into the project! The target for achieving the UN's eight Millennium Development Goals had been set at fifteen years. How could confidence in achieving these fifteen-year goals already be receding into the distance after just five years? Were the goals themselves utterly unrealistic? Or had the shaping, organisation and execution of the UN's big project to deliver them not been up to par? Or was it something else? What could be going so badly wrong?

For sure, the Millennium Development Goals looked difficult to fund, to plan, to steer and control. But at heart it was still just a huge human-based project. And there were a lot of good things going for this project – very clear objectives and scope, clearly articulated measurements of success and an unambiguous timetable. Plus, it had massive global support at the highest levels.

Presumably it also had an experienced leadership team, professional project management and a good handle on the major underlying issues in each area. Had they sought and achieved a consensus approach to the project in each region, integrating the efforts of institutions, governments, charities and foundations? The Millennium Development Goals (the MDGs for short) must surely have had financing arrangements in place, perhaps with the World Bank, for access to funds while the pledged funding was in the pipeline. Surely the project must have forged a matrix of global and local roles and responsibilities and put in place the necessary management and governance structures for planning, engagement, communication, spending controls, logistics and risk management?

Or maybe not?

I was intrigued. Why the hell was the world so far behind schedule on this vast project that was crucial to a billion of the world's poorest people?

One key element in the UN's approach to the MDGs had been the appealing idea of creating 'Millennium Villages'. The theory was that development aid efforts should be focused on selected villages in several African countries that could be supported to lift themselves out of poverty and achieve the Millennium Development Goals for themselves. Based on the methods developed in these pioneering villages, the concept would then be implemented in neighbouring communities. Local people would be able to see for themselves what could be achieved, and donors and governments around the world would be inspired to support a growing network of Millennium Villages across the continent.

The village of Sauri, in western Kenya, became the first ever Millennium Village project, in 2004. During the project, there had been a big increase in maize production, malaria dropped sharply, and the local primary school jumped from an outside ranking to the top ten. Progress wasn't perfect, and some of the advances might have happened anyway, but still I felt hugely inspired by the whole concept. This was exactly the sort of project I felt drawn to. I had the energy, the desire to do something valuable and the planning and project management skills to play a useful role. I wanted to get involved, and I decided to offer my services to the UN. I didn't really have a plan but by now I was on a mission.

For weeks, I made calls and fired off emails, trying to offer my services free of charge. But nothing happened. That's not, apparently, how it works. You don't just go and knock on the front door of the UN. I didn't have any contacts in the worlds of international aid, development or politics. It seemed it's not a system designed for individuals but for institutions and I couldn't find a way in. My frustration grew as I bounced from pillar to post. I couldn't break through and make contact with anyone who could help get me to my ultimate target of finding and talking to someone with authority to take a decision about including me.

I was sure the Millennium Village approach was right, though.

So I'm lying in bed wondering what to do if I can't do that. And something inside me says: who says you can't do that? No one *owns* the Millennium Goals. As far as I know, no-one's *copyrighted* the

Millennium Village. So why don't I just set up my own? It's just a project, isn't it? And isn't project structuring and leadership what you do?

There would certainly be some advantages to working outside the framework of the UN. True, I wouldn't have the benefit of the UN's tried and tested systems and experience. But I would be able to move fast, to use my own money and take my own decisions without having to refer back to committees or adhere to pre-ordained policies. I'd be able to do what was right for the people and the situations I found in one particular area, with a flexibility that no big organisation could allow.

'Fuck it!' I decided. 'I'll just damn well go to Africa and create a Millennium Village project myself, then. And I won't lose five years with delays to get started either. Houston, we have fucking lift-off.'

It was stark raving bonkers – a batty, preposterous, perhaps even deranged scheme to establish a Millennium Village project myself in order to advance the UN's inspiring Millennium Development Goals.

But it also felt like one of those life-changing moments.

As the spring days passed and the trees outside my window came into leaf, bursting with growth and renewal, I became more and more determined. The more I stared out the window and thought about it, the more attractive this crazy scheme seemed. My personal life was in a pit. My house was on the market. At dinner parties I'd drift off into my own thoughts. I'd never been lost for words, but now I had little to contribute when friends were talking about their careers, their families or their houses. I sensed that I was at an impasse. The prospect of stepping out of my familiar life, my comfort zone, was both scary and exciting – and just seemed too crazy an idea to bring up in South West London over the dessert wine.

Under the UN timetable, a Millennium Village project was supposed to take five years. I had already reckoned I could cut that time, perhaps by up to a third. I could design and write my own customised project methodology, implement it without looking over my shoulder, decide for myself what risks were worth taking and make adjustments and corrections on the fly if circumstances changed. And if it didn't work out, it would only be my effort and my money that would have been wasted.

Ah yes, my money. My limited remaining savings wouldn't cut it. That wouldn't be enough to bring about a revolution in some remote spot in Africa. If I invested some or most of the proceeds of my house, that could work. But what if the money didn't even touch the sides?

But I wasn't going to fail. I was going to go it alone and make it work.

But where? My initial research suggested Tanzania as a possible candidate. I'd been there briefly and had been fascinated by the country. It had vast natural resources, a good climate for agriculture, millions of acres of fertile farming land and fantastic tourist attractions – from Kilimanjaro and the Maasai Mara to the exotic spice island of Zanzibar and hundreds of miles of wonderful white sandy beaches, facing the Indian Ocean. Why isn't this place already economically wealthy, I had wondered? Despite these advantages, though, the country had been ground down over the decades by corruption and mis-management to become one of the poorest countries in Africa. Now it had a new, reforming government and the signs of economic growth and regeneration were everywhere as you drove through the bustling capital. Buildings were going up, new cars and trucks packed the busy streets and new shops and businesses were opening up every day. But how much of this was going to spread out to the rural areas? What would it all mean to the ordinary people far from the main cities?

It seems to me blindingly obvious that access to credit is essential if people are going to lift themselves up economically. Most of us have needed bank loans at some point in our own development. Families in our North Dublin parish depended on the local Credit Union, and small loans had enabled my little world to stay afloat while I tried to build myself up in my twenties.

It was obvious to me that for any African individual or family to rise from extreme poverty into the lower middle class, then credit, and definitely microfinance, would have to be available. This meant it was vital for me to choose a country for my project where the microcredit sector was already strong, investing heavily for the future by developing its staff, its branch network, its technology and systems, and, crucially, growing rapidly in rural towns.

One of the key mechanisms to help people start their own businesses has to be microfinance. Tiny loans of $50 or $100 could allow would-be entrepreneurs to buy the equipment needed to open a new food stall, a barber's shop, a bicycle taxi service or a small hut with a start-up tailoring business and set themselves on the road to a better life. It worked, and it had been proven time and time again, throughout the developing world. Indeed, when the global financial crisis hit in 2008 and the big international banks were having to write off bad debts left, right and centre, start-up entrepreneurs in Africa and Asia kept on steadily repaying their loans. Microfinance banks didn't need bailouts.

I'd studied microcredit in New York and attended conferences about it in London and Geneva. I believed it was likely to be a crucial part of any Millennium Village project. But I found that Tanzania's microfinance sector wasn't sufficiently developed for my purposes. What I was trying to do would be difficult enough anyway, and that would make it even harder. So I reluctantly crossed Tanzania off the list and turned my attention to neighbouring Kenya, where many of the banks were already committed to growing microcredit as a tool for developing business in rural communities.

Kenya offered some practical advantages, besides access to microloans for small businesses. My younger brother, Alan, an accountant with a multinational company, was already working in Nairobi on a one-year assignment, and would certainly help me find my way around. He had all the trimmings of business success – a big house provided by the company, a chauffeured car, a maid, a cook to prepare his breakfast and evening meals, and a team of gardeners. Plenty of room if I want to come for a visit, he offers.

I was soon exchanging emails with a promising-sounding charity, Haven Kenya, which looked as if it might be able to help me find a suitable location for my Millennium Village project. On the other hand, there were concerns about ethnic and political tensions, still simmering after the murderous violence that followed Kenya's disputed election in 2007, and about the reportedly epic level of corruption in Kenya. I had read enough to know that the culture of *kitu kidogo* – a small bribe, or, literally, 'a little something' – was a massive problem and a serious barrier to economic change and development. I guessed that Kenyans were frustrated by it, but figured it was a necessary way of getting through life. How would it affect a relatively wealthy *mzungu* – originally a word applied to European traders, but now the common term for any white person – like me?

I was impatient, though, and nowhere in the developing world, almost by definition, was going to provide the perfect setting for what I wanted to do. So I bought a pair of glare-reducing Oakley sunglasses, booked a flight from Heathrow to Nairobi and looked forward to seeing my brother. Apart from Alan, my only contact in Kenya was the woman I had emailed at Haven Kenya, Mama Jayne, and I was going to try and take it from there. I just needed a single hook.

* * *

I realised how little I actually knew about the geography of Africa as I watched the animated map on the plane, tracking our progress. Algeria and Libya alone seemed to cover an area the size of Europe. As we flew over the vast plains and mountains of Sudan, I knew I had only the sketchiest idea of what I was letting myself in for. But whatever I was expecting, it vanished when we landed in Nairobi.

I found a small, neat, calm airport. A pleasantly sunny day, with no searing heat, no teeming, noisy crowds. Alan was there to meet me, with a broad smile and a big, air-conditioned, chauffeur-driven

4x4. Long leisurely avenues through the city brought us to a gated housing complex with a communal swimming pool where gardeners were tending the orderly shrubs and hedges.

'This is Karen,' my brother, Alan, grinned, 'the Land that Time Forgot. Make the most of it. Not all of Kenya's quite so comfortable.'

Karen is an affluent area on the edge of Nairobi that was once the farm belonging to Karen Blixen, whose autobiography, *Out of Africa*, was made into a big romantic movie starring Robert Redford and Meryl Streep. It's a gently hilly area, with a cooling breeze by day and few mosquitoes at night, and it had long provided an oasis for ex-pats and Nairobi's wealthy families. Cocktails at the Karen Country Club were followed by dinner, served by waiters in stiff uniforms, while my brother's driver waited dutifully outside. It felt like stepping back a hundred years to an unreal world of languid colonial luxury and privilege.

But this was Sunday. Monday morning brought the real Africa.

Crazy traffic. Lunatic drivers. Toyota mini-buses designed for twelve or fourteen with almost twenty commuters crammed inside. These private *matatus* are not an alternative to the main transport system; they *are* the main transport system. The conductors hang out the side doors, shouting insults at each other, and the drivers push and nudge forward into every hint of a gap in the chaotic traffic.

The bus station was a sea of sounds and colour. As a *mzungu*, I was instantly surrounded by street sellers peddling a bewildering array of goods. Watches, of course, but also belts, underwear and, particularly, padlocks. This was more like it! Noise everywhere.

People everywhere. Smells and movement and confusion and a lot of laughter.

My bus journey to Bungoma took nine hours. It was hot and tiring, but every minute of it was a feast for my hungry eyes. We trundled through the Rift Valley, where fertile pastures stretched away as far as the eye could see. And as we travelled for hundreds of kilometres, crossing the equator as we went, a vast patchwork of tiny plots, rich with crops, unfolded – green, lush and unexpectedly reminiscent of County Kildare.

Green and lush? But this was Africa. I wasn't expecting green and lush. Where was the cracked, scorched earth from which no green shoot could be coaxed? Where were the malnourished children, pestered by flies, staring out hopelessly from their prehistoric huts? Again, I was relying on the snippets of 'Africa' I'd got from the news. I'd clearly been standing behind the door when any real education on this stuff was being handed out at school. I realised – and was duly chastened by the fact – that should I choose to send a postcard home I would struggle to fill it with what I knew about the real Africa, not the economic one I had been studying.

There were small children, of course. Lots of them. But they looked cheerful and energetic. Definitely a bit ragged, and barefoot, too, but also smiling and laughing as they played, waiting for the older children to come home from school. The introduction of free primary education in 2003 had had an enormous positive impact. But the term 'free schooling', I learned, is a misnomer. It can cost parents at least $50 per child for compulsory uniforms, parent–teacher association charges and exam fees. Not much to us, but a huge financial commitment for families who earn under $1.25 a day. And secondary schools, with a vastly higher level of charges, are a distant dream for a majority of rural families.

If the children generally looked surprisingly happy and healthy, the houses along the route were more in line with my expectations. Some were mud huts, with families cooking, eating, sleeping and bathing in a single room. Others were two-room dwellings – one room for cooking and sitting, one room for sleeping. The more luxurious homes had brick walls, divided rooms and a corrugated iron roof on a timber frame. I tried to imagine how hot a house like that must be to live in, but it didn't bear thinking about.

I wondered about the small farms I saw all along the route. Were they wholly dependent on rainfall, or was there some other way to get water to the crops? We didn't cross many bridges, so rivers and streams had to be few and far between. People must rely on seasonal rains to grow food, I supposed. No wonder they went hungry when the rains failed. Surely a method to get water from rivers or wells onto the crops must be one of the first essentials for feeding local people? Irrigation. The word stirred a distant memory. We must have done irrigation in geography, but I must have been staring out of the window. I was here to learn, though, and I stored up all my questions for later.

My destination was Bungoma, a major town in the Western Kenya province. Weeks back, I had found a charity near the town, called Haven Kenya, who could house me and would be my first hook into rural Kenya.

Bungoma couldn't have been more different from Karen. My first impression was of a chaotic little town with low-built buildings, blazing sunshine and clay dust blowing through the streets. I felt as if I'd arrived by stagecoach on the set of a western movie. But instead of John Wayne striding down Main Street to meet me, there was a short, plump, welcoming woman with a round face, a huge smile and wearing a bright pink suit. Her husky voice, rounded ankles and aura of homely authority immediately brought to mind Mammy Two Shoes, the African–American housemaid in the Tom and Jerry cartoons.

'Mr Ken King! Mr Ken King! I am Mama Jayne. Welcome to Bungoma. Welcome to Haven Kenya. You must be tired after the journey. Come and have some tea.'

What can I say about Mama Jayne, except that your immediate instinct is not to resist her? I knew that Haven Kenya was a small charity with a long-established programme which brought volunteers from America to work on projects in Western Kenya. What I didn't know at that time was that it all revolved round Mama Jayne, whose energy, effort and enthusiasm were by far the charity's biggest asset. I'd arranged to stay with Haven Kenya for a week, while I looked around for a possible location for my Millennium Village project, but I had no idea how much time and enthusiasm Mama Jayne – who flatly refused to be addressed by any less familiar name – was prepared to hurl into helping me.

'I'll be your African mother while you're here,' she told me, without a trace of anything other than utter sincerity. 'I'll take you round to meet people and see whatever you need to see. And if you need anything, just ask me. It's great to have you here.' I was instantly smitten.

My home for the week turned out to be a little thatched mud hut in the Haven Kenya compound, with two wooden bunk beds and no electricity or running water. The diesel generator would run for a couple of hours from 8 p.m., providing light for the communal area where the volunteers gathered in the evenings. And if I wanted to freshen up in the morning, I could collect some warm water from the smokehouse, top my bucket up with water from the borehole and use it to take a 'shower' in the row of cubicles lined up along an outdoor wall. It was all pretty raw and basic, and I realised, with a start, that the ancient Greeks and Romans had probably enjoyed more creature comforts than this.

But comfort isn't everything. And no light means no light pollution. That first night, I looked up and saw a million stars, winking and twinkling against the dark velvet cushion of the sky. It took my breath away. I'd never seen so many stars, never consciously thought that so many existed. I stood staring silently upwards for ten minutes, until the crick in my neck and the ache in my back reminded me how long and tiring the day had been. I stepped into the hut and lay down on the narrow thin mattress. Africa. I was here, in the middle of it, and my adventure was beginning. I slept like a peaceful baby.

In the morning, I was the last to get going. I could hear noises and voices all around as I gradually surfaced and remembered where I was. I pulled on some clothes, experimented with the shower bucket and met a few of the American volunteers over a quick breakfast of cornflakes with tepid long-life milk, white bread with melted margarine and milky chai tea.

After breakfast, Mama Jayne and I sat in her office while I explained what I was hoping to do in Kenya. She was quick, alert and helpful, and I knew at once that I had found a valuable supporter. I was lucky: Mama Jayne would prove to be my pivotal link into Africa.

She was scheduled to visit several small community groups over the next few days and she invited me to go along to learn more about local people.

Haven Kenya's old and battered Nissan van looked as if it would hardly make it out of the gate. But we set off, clunking and bouncing over ridged and potholed roads and eventually turning off to strike out over rough tracks and fields.

The first extended family we visited had built up a flock of about a hundred chickens. They aimed to sell these birds as meat and use the money to build a large flock of laying hens that would provide eggs for sale and give them a steady income. An uncle had died recently and they were going to convert his dwelling into a coop. The plan was to start by buying 30 good-quality chicks at 200 shillings ($2.50) each. They'd done their sums and worked out the rate of growth of the flock and the number of eggs that could be expected per month. It all made sense, and I was impressed by their knowledge and determination.

Then came the crunch. Would I like to help by providing the $75 needed to buy the chicks and get the project going? What could I say to that? What could anyone say? It was relatively small money, that gave an opportunity to improve their lives at a stroke. I handed over the money, prompting gleeful celebrations, whooping, hollering and impromptu dancing.

For the next few days, we went from one group to another. We saw women's groups, youth groups, neighbours who had formed self-help groups and started some business project or other that would, they hoped, lift them clear of the constant hand-to-mouth struggle to survive. Tree nurseries, poultry farming and tailoring were the most popular ideas. It proved increasingly difficult to get away from any of these groups without making some form of donation. But I was learning from every one of these encounters.

It was clear that many of these groups needed training as much as they needed money. Most people let their chickens run free on the farm to eat scraps of leftover corn. Great, I thought. Free range and organic – that's got to be good. But apparently not. That's Western thinking. Out here, free range meant literally that: the chickens were running wild and free, with no kind of enclosure. They'd lay their eggs anywhere they liked, somewhere out in the maize crops. You couldn't find the eggs, so you couldn't sell them. If you did find an egg, there was no way of telling how old it might be. And the meat was a big disappointment. All that running around made the birds fit as fleas, tough and wiry, with very little breast meat and stringy, muscly legs. You had to be gracious about it when a family killed one of its precious chickens to give you a welcome feast, but, to be honest, it was a bit like sitting down to tuck into a portion of Paula Radcliffe or some other well-honed Olympian.

The chickens themselves were easy prey for dogs or foxes, so a lot of them simply vanished. Some families made small wicker coops to keep a brood together, but confining them brought its own problems. Infections spread quickly, wiping out all the chickens in a coop. I noticed, too, that these families hardly ever sold a chicken, or ate one. Their aim was to build up a flock for a big bulk sale – a one-off payday that, to judge by what I saw in front of me, might never come.

I asked Mama Jayne if she knew anybody who was qualified to give them advice about how to do it better, and said I was willing to fund that, at least as a first step. Jayne explained all this to them in the local dialect and they seemed happy. Not whooping with joy, like the first lot, but accepting. Would I come back later to visit and to pay for a proper coop? Yes, I thought. That seemed fair enough. I agreed to come back in a few months and see how they were doing.

Back at Haven Kenya, I was shown the primary school they had built up over the years through donations. They claimed to have an excellent educational record, which, if true, was an extraordinary achievement when each class had about fifty students and very few books. They took the children as far as year 7, I was told, but not through year 8, the final year of primary education. After year 7, the students scattered to other schools or dropped out altogether. Haven Kenya lost touch with the children and lost the authority to pressure parents to stretch to afford a secondary education for them. Having a year 8 class would make all the difference. It would enable the school to take the kids right up to their final primary school exams and then work with the parents to shepherd them into high school if at all affordable for them. Could I assist Haven Kenya with a year 8 classroom? A few thousand dollars would build and equip it.

Within a few days, I was already committed to spending money right, left and centre – and I hadn't even begun my own project yet. I'd have to be more disciplined than this. But I reflected that if everything else went wrong and I achieved nothing else in Kenya, these would be good things to have subsidised. I learned eighteen months later that the first class of eighth-graders had graduated and all but three had gone on to high school. Maybe they'd have made it anyway. How could I know? I was told that two local students were ranked in the top ten in the county that year. One extra classroom was just a drop in the ocean, but I knew that at least it was something real and tangible that could have a long-term impact. It felt like a tangent from what I came to do, but a good and enjoyable one.

My week in Bungoma had been an eye-opener in so many ways, and I owed much of it to the flying start I'd got through Mama Jayne's help. I'd made a new friend and a valuable contact, so I went to see her and give her a little thank-you present before I caught the bus back to Nairobi.

As I walked across the yard towards her office and saw the schoolchildren playing outside the building, I remembered I had a few bags of toffees and chocolates I'd put in my holdall for the long journey to Bungoma. No point in carrying them back with me to the capital. I might as well give them to the kids. In a matter of seconds, there was a swarm of children buzzing around me.

'*Mzungu*! *Mzungu*! Me, mister!'

Small hands reached out towards me as other kids came running from all over the schoolyard.

The gate-porter rushed over and shouted at the eager kids to form a queue. But that wasn't going to happen. I watched, appalled, as he pulled out a small whip, like a jockey's crop, and set about the children, literally whipping them into line.

'Hey, cut that out!' I shouted. 'Stop it. Don't hit them! It's only a few sweets.'

But he was warming to his task.

'STOP IT!'

The porter stopped and stared at me, but he didn't seem to believe that there was anything wrong with beating these youngsters for disobeying him. He shouted at a few more children in a desultory way, but you could see his heart was no longer in it and he sloped off back to his chair by the gate. I appeared to be more upset than the kids were, so I quickly handed out the rest of the sweets and went in to say goodbye to Mama Jayne. I didn't mention the assault on the children to her, but I kept turning it over and over in my mind on the long bus ride back to Nairobi. Would the kids tell their parents about the porter, or was that how some of them were treated at home? Heavy corporal punishment was still a feature of life in Kenya, and smacking kids hard was standard. Or was it my fault for having created a free-for-all?

On the whole, my week in Bungoma had been successful. I felt I'd found the right general area for my Millennium Village, though I had yet to identify a specific community. I'd learned a lot about the practical problems facing extremely poor people in rural areas, and

I'd got some glimpses of their hopes and dreams. I'd need to do a lot more reading and research to help clarify my ideas, but I'd be coming back, next time, with a far more focused notion of what I was looking for and how I might go about things. The jolting of the bus gradually lulled me to sleep, and I must have been right out of it for two or three hours when I woke up with a start.

I'd been dreaming about the porter and his whip and the children, irresistibly drawn to my bag of sweets while the whip rained down on their heads and shoulders. It was a kind of allegory, or maybe the makings of a sort of parable, I realised.

Those children had just been muddling along as usual, doing whatever they were doing, before I turned up with my bagful of treats. Some kids were happy to get one sweet. Some got two because they were smart and quick enough to scuttle round and pop up again on the other side of the crowd. But, however you cut it, I'd only had enough in my bag for a small proportion of all the children who wanted a sweet. In the end, more kids were disappointed than were made happy, and some had suffered a whipping into the bargain. Would it have been better to keep the sweets out of sight and let the children get on with their lives without introducing a new factor and a new competition in which some of them, inevitably, would lose?

Was this what would happen with my Millennium Village? If I came swinging in from the clouds, bringing training and economic opportunities for the people in one particular community, helping them lift themselves out of lives of poverty and uncertainty, how much good would it do?

How would people in the neighbouring villages feel when they got nothing? Would that lead to resentments that never existed before? That was the dilemma, right there. If you can only do a limited amount – and inevitably disappoint those who see it close up but don't benefit – is it right to proceed for the good of the few?

Having thought it all through, I returned to my initial conclusions. Setting up a project in this remote backwater of Eastern Africa wouldn't be like working in an international bank where you had endless meetings and conference calls and boxes to tick. Here I could be nimble, use my money wisely. My fellow countryman, the eighteenth-century philosopher Edmund Burke, once wrote: 'Nobody could make a greater mistake than he who did nothing because he could do only a little.' But I didn't come across that quote until much later. At the time, it just seemed clear to me that if everyone gave in to the kind of doubts I was entertaining, nobody would ever do anything. So I resolved to cut out the philosophising and get on with it.

3

Finding Siboti

'I'm not a do-gooder. It embarrasses me to be classified as a
humanitarian. I simply take part in activities I believe in.'

Gregory Peck

The weeks I spend in Africa, researching my new project, are becoming
longer and the weeks in London are getting shorter. I'm living on my
own in the house in Pimlico, which is still on the market. I look out
the window at neighbours striding off to work under a grey sky as
I sip my morning coffee and wonder where my choices are leading
me this time. I can only watch as the value of the house continues to
plummet.

After a few weeks at home, working out the fundamentals of
how I can fund this thing from the comfort of my study, I am keen to
leave my sad memories behind and get started on the Siboti project,
using the last of the cash I have in the bank. This time I'm going to
need a car of my own to enable me to get around and find the right
location for my Millennium Village project. Bungoma doesn't strike
me as the sort of place that would have an Avis office, so I figure

I'll have to rent a car in Nairobi and drive four hundred kilometres across the country just for starters. That's going to be an adventure in itself, and I'm looking forward to it.

'You want to watch yourself,' says Alan, when I call him in Nairobi. For some reason, my brother is none too keen on the idea of this long solo drive across country.

'Oh, it'll be fine, it'll be grand.'

'Hold on,' he says, and gives me a contact number. 'I'll arrange for my company's security chief to be on the alert in case you run into any problems. Call him if you need anything.'

'Thanks Alan,' I say, repressing a smile. The younger brother turns parental guardian. But I don't mind. I'm grateful. It means I have someone looking out for me while I'm in Africa, and that is a reassuring feeling.

I go online and order a road map of Kenya. When it arrives, though, it prompts a nervous laugh. It looks deceptively simple, like a map drawn by a four-year-old. Just a great big central blob, Nairobi, with a road – *the* road – running in a straight line north-west across the heart of Kenya. It doesn't inspire much confidence. I don't remember the road being like that. I'm pretty sure the bus made a few turns last time. Better get myself a satnav, too.

* * *

After the nine-hour flight from Heathrow back to Nairobi, and a couple of sundowners at the Karen Blixen resort hotel, I wake up full of energy and raring to go.

Once in the car, I buckle up for my day-long jaunt. What a wonderful feeling it is, being in a totally different world. My empty house in Pimlico feels like another planet as I pass through the western outskirts of Nairobi.

I'm less than two hours from that city when a smartly uniformed officer waves me down at a police checkpoint – known by ex-pats, as I'll later learn, as a 'police cashpoint'. He's polite and apparently friendly.

'Good morning, sir. Are you aware that you were travelling at well over a hundred kilometres per hour?'

Er, no. I was doing maybe sixty or seventy kilometres per hour. You'd risk your life doing a hundred on these uneven roads, and, anyway, he has no speed gun. He's just making it up. He decides I'm going to have to pay him a fine. We haggle a bit and eventually agree on a figure of 4000 shillings (worth about $50 at the time). But as I reach into my wallet, he catches sight of a US ten-dollar bill and his eyes light up.

'How much is that worth in Kenyan money?'

'About 4000,' I say, knowing it to be worth about 800 shillings. I was never a good actor but I try to look and sound sullen and fearful.

'I'll take that.'

'But that's not fair,' I whine. 'I need...'

'I'll take that and you may proceed.'

He pockets the note and waves me on, dismissively. I've had my first brush with police corruption, but at least he'll only get its face value when he tries to change my ten-dollar note – a small revenge. And I'm on my way towards Bungoma.

I can't cross the equator line again without stopping. The guy at the tourist information stall insists on giving me a scientific demo. Take water ten metres south and it swirls away clockwise. Walk ten metres north of the equator and it drains away anticlockwise. I'd heard of this phenomenon but never seen it. Apparently the water of every bathtub in the southern hemisphere drains away clockwise, while every bathtub in the northern hemisphere drains anticlockwise. It's to do with the Coriolis Effect and the Earth's rotation, I'm told. It looks indisputable, an amazing natural phenomenon.

As I stare at the swirling water, I'm suddenly struck by the idea that I've been sitting in an office for years, not connecting with what is going on in the natural world. I'm blown away by the concept. I'm on a planet, spinning in space. As I look at the grains of Kenyan soil beneath my feet I have the sense that my psyche is opening up like a flower in spring – opening up to the atmosphere around me. Before, I was mainly interested in working and climbing the ladder. I just got on with stuff in my little life. Now, looking up at the brilliant blue sky, I get a glimpse of my own utter insignificance in the greater scheme of things, but at the same time feel a new and acute sense of purpose: that I've somehow graduated into another world. Bungoma lies before me, shimmering in the heat.

Later someone tells me that stuff about the water is all bollocks – just not true. But it doesn't matter what they think, because I've got the message. There is another world outside the one I have known all my life.

I've passed through Nakuru and left the equator behind me as I head north-west. I'm making good progress now, with less than

150km to go. The countryside is reeling past on both sides and I'm seeing a lot of detail I missed before. There's not much sign of wildlife, but after a while I glimpse a flicker over to my left and realise I'm passing a small group of zebras. It's hardly a herd – maybe just half a dozen animals, loitering in the bright sunshine – but I'm delighted to see them. If those are zebras, this must be Africa. Apparently the collective noun for a group of them is a dazzle, and you can see why.

When I talk to a wildlife expert about them later, I'm surprised to learn that zebras are actually black animals with white stripes, rather than white ones with black markings. That's not what I'd have assumed, but the evidence is there in their DNA. And they are rather magnificent creatures, with their Mohican haircuts, their legendary stamina and their stubborn, untameable independence. I'm glad I've seen them in the flesh. For the next few miles, I'm keeping an eye out for lions or giraffe or three-metre pythons, but there's nothing spectacular to be seen and I soon find myself leaving the countryside behind and driving through the outskirts of a noisy, bustling town.

Eldoret, 7000 feet above sea level, is one of the largest towns in the Western Kenya province. It's the 'Home of Champions', wealthy with the winnings of many great Kenyan athletes, including Olympic gold steeplechaser Ezekiel Kemboi. It's the fastest-growing urban area in Kenya, but shadowed by the memory of the brutal massacre in 2008 in which more than thirty people were burned to death in a church after the disputed elections. I inch my way through the trafficked streets and eventually emerge into open country again.

I've almost reached Bungoma when a back tyre explodes. Bloody wonder it didn't happen earlier, on these rough and rutted roads. But

I'm hardly out of the car when five guys appear from nowhere and want to help. How kind, I think, as they rally round and start trying to change the wheel.

It takes a minute or two to catch on that they don't have the faintest idea what they're doing. They don't have cars. They don't know about cars. When I realise they're trying to take the wheel off without jacking it up, I shoo them away from the vehicle and change the wheel myself.

My helpers all want payment. Five more men have gathered to watch and offer their advice. No thanks, I'm fine. I give the first five, who had tried to change the wheel, a hundred-shilling note each. The second five, who had just watched and talked, are not happy. I'll soon learn that you can't please everyone and remain solvent.

I get going again and I'm bowling along at a brisk pace, looking forward to arriving in Bungoma, when I hit the mother of all potholes, a jagged trench stretching right across the road. Both front wheels blow out instantly and the roadside ditch starts coming at me far too fast for comfort. Adrenaline rushes through my body and time slows to a snail's pace. If I brake now, I won't be able to keep this car from lunging in whatever bloody direction it decides to go. It bucks and lurches and I wrestle with the steering. Somehow I keep it more or less straight and I grind to a halt on the road.

When my pulse stops racing, I call Mama Jayne. Her driver at Haven Kenya, Kizito, is a great guy with a lot of local connections. He manages to find a breakdown truck that will come and rescue me. The tow into central Bungoma is about fifteen kilometres but the truck driver wants $200. That's roughly six months' wages in this area. He must have been rubbing his hands with glee when he heard a *mzungu* was stranded out on the main road. I suck it up and hand over the cash.

I leave the car in Bungoma for the night and squeeze myself and my luggage into a *matatu* for the ride to the Haven Kenya compound. It's been a long day and I am happy to reach my mud hut at last and see some friendly familiar faces.

The next morning, Mama Jayne is full of plans and ideas. I've asked her to set up lots of meetings for me and assign me someone to help me find my way round and to translate for me – either from Swahili, or one of the local languages. But she's not having any of that. She's cleared her own diary and she's going to be with me for the whole week. We're going to start by seeing another chicken-breeding group, but first I need to get new tyres for the car.

It takes two hours. By the time the tyres are fitted, we are already running very late for our first meeting, but Jayne is totally unworried. 'Relax, Ken. It's Africa time, you know. It's no problem.'

We talk to the chicken breeders, then a group who are doing turkeys, and another group who see ducks as the key to a brighter future. The duck people say there's a strong and growing demand. They have a hand-dug well in their compound, with lots of murky water that's OK for ducks but not for humans. Jayne confirms their claim that the ducks are more hardy and disease-resistant than chickens.

Within an hour, I'm helping to design a duck enclosure. I'm getting into this. I've spent the last two decades working in huge offices and now I'm standing in the middle of rural Kenya, giving advice on accommodation for ducks. Granted, I did take the opportunity, before leaving last time, to spend an hour with the poultry adviser I had hired for the chicken groups, but that doesn't quite make me an expert. I'm serious, though, and so are they. Together we work out how much it'll cost to build an enclosure that'll include a small swimming pool. Apparently, ducks need the water for fertility. In the car, Jayne and I discuss the love-lives of ducks and giggle like teenagers all the way home.

I realise I'm happy. When was the last time I felt like this? I've felt fulfilled in the past in my house, with my family, in my job, with friends, with my wife – but all that has changed. This new happiness is unfamiliar. It's an ancient feeling. Had I forgotten what it was like to feel truly happy, I wonder?

The next day begins with a trip to see two youth groups, in an area west of Bungoma, towards the Ugandan border. These two groups – the Siboti Pioneer Youth Group and the Breathe Hope Youth Group – have come together to launch a number of projects. They've built a coop and started breeding chickens. They've bought saplings, grown them and sold them for a profit. They've organised football tournaments and other community activities. And they've worked together on an ambitious project to dig out a huge reservoir. The government made the land available, but there's no money for mechanical tools or diggers. The youth group leaders have mobilised their own members and other local youngsters and dug out this vast reservoir by hand, one spadeful at a time. Now it's almost ready and they're planning to build a small run-off pond and start a fish-farming business.

They're impressive, these young people. They're working to help themselves and their community, and anything they receive from outside sources – government or charities – is simply giving a hand up to people who are already willing to do as much as they can to improve their lives.

'Hand-ups, not handouts,' says Mama Jayne, and the young men beam at me, their white teeth flashing, leaning on each other's shoulders. They can see I get where they're coming from.

'I wish I could understand the language,' I say to her, and she smiles too.

'They understand,' she says. 'They see you.'

I'm becoming increasingly confident that this is the way to go.

Our next stop is a visit to the middle of nowhere, or slightly beyond. It's the local polytechnic, and we get there by bumping our way down a barely recognisable track and then hacking straight across the open fields. Plenty of other people make their way to this remote spot, though, and the college offers an impressive range of courses in everything from carpentry and tailoring to mechanical engineering.

The polytechnic building was originally provided by the government, and they tell me that 60 per cent of the teachers' salary bill is also funded from government sources. The community is responsible for equipping the college and the balance of the teachers' salaries is supposed to come from tuition fees. But, as I soon learn, few of these students can afford any fees at all, so the teachers end up working for 60 per cent of their notional pay. It's a wonder they don't just pack their bags and leave, but rather than being daunted and defeated by the lack of funding, the teachers we meet actually want to expand the polytechnic's activities by running evening classes.

It's a great idea, but being stuck out here in the back of beyond means there is no electricity supply. No electricity means no light, and no light means no evening classes. I begin to feel that familiar sensation – an appeal for assistance – coming on. I'm beginning to recognise the signs by now.

Could I, by any chance, do something to help the college install solar-powered lighting? The request – like so many others – is so reasonable, and it demonstrates the resourceful thinking and determination to improve the opportunities for young people that I'm seeing everywhere I look. I really could go round all day, every day, and find well-thought-out and deserving projects that would make a huge and immediate impact on people's education, health and incomes. You could take them all on, and they'd all be worthwhile. All you'd need would be several million dollars.

I know I can't make a commitment to provide a major solar power installation for this place. But the project goes into my mental filing system. A new seed has been planted. Maybe I can find a way to make it happen at some point down the road.

Later, near the polytechnic, I meet the Gancata Youth Group. Most of the members are not actually as youthful as I was expecting, but that's because the group was formed twenty years ago. Their faces are a little lined and there are flecks of grey in their hair, but they're still full of energy and optimism. The Gancata group had started off breeding chickens, selling eggs and poultry meat, and had gradually amassed enough to buy one cow, and then another. The profits from the chickens and cows had financed the opening of a hairdressing shop, and then a second. No one is getting rich here, but I realise it is just another testament to the initiative, drive and determination, in good years and bad, of these people. They are natural entrepreneurs and great role models for the newer local youth groups – and for everyone else around here who is prepared to get stuck in and make the effort to clamber up out of the clinging quicksand of extreme rural poverty.

I like what I'm seeing today in this area. Siboti is a small rural community, quite close to the Ugandan border. It's not too big – fifty or sixty square kilometres – so I'd be able to get around it all right. And it looks promising. The people I'm meeting seem friendly and responsive and there are enough natural resources to start my Millennium Village project with a reasonable chance of success. I've got to be realistic and I know that what I want to do wouldn't work in some godforsaken, war-torn region with barely any rainfall or rivers, no fertile soil, no roads and access to markets. But this place isn't like that. There are many, many people living in grinding poverty, but it's a place with potential.

If Siboti will work with me, I think I can work with Siboti. I'm beginning to feel I've found what I'm looking for.

I'm encouraged, too, by the fact that I haven't seen any sign of the big white 4x4 Toyota Land Cruisers favoured by the international aid agencies and other multilateral bodies. People have told me there are lots of NGOs in East Africa but I haven't seen any in the area. Even in Bungoma, the nearest big town, I rarely see Westerners. I reason that this is a good thing: Siboti will be a blank canvas for me.

I'm not likely to run into any problems caused by overlap with or interference from existing aid projects. So the signs are good, and the next thing I need to do is find out whether I can get the necessary enthusiasm and commitment from the community and its leaders.

Will people be willing to take a chance on me? Will they be ready to get stuck in and really engage with the project? And will their community leaders provide the active and enthusiastic support I need? There's only one way to find out. I need to ask the people of Siboti.

Mama Jayne agrees, and she sets about arranging a big community meeting for the day after tomorrow. I've already seen signs of her organising talent and am confident she'll ensure a respectable turnout.

On Friday, Peter Wanyama, the principal of the polytechnic, opens the meeting with a prayer and what he calls a few words of introduction. I'm waiting in a room off the main hall and can hear him. It's quite a few words. Once he gets going, there's no stopping him. But eventually, his stamina flags and it's time for me to have a turn.

'This man has come to talk to us about a big opportunity that he wants to offer us,' he says. 'Let us all listen carefully.'

This is it. I'm on. Mama Jayne is going to translate for me, so there won't be any language problems. I'm just ready to get going, though, when the scale of what I am about to embark on hits me right between the eyes and almost stops me in my tracks. Jesus, if this meeting works, this place is going to be the focus of my life for years to come. I've got what I wanted, the opportunity to find a way to alleviate extreme poverty. But if I blow it now...

I pull myself together. Don't ramble, Ken. Keep it simple. Keep it strong. Just speak directly to the point, add a bit of motivational bait and see if they bite. I walk through the door into the main hall, and I'm amazed at the true size of the crowd Mama Jayne has assembled. I know now what they mean when they talk about a sea of faces. Hundreds of people. Community leaders, teachers, men, women, youths, babes in arms – they're all here and every bench is filled. I've made big presentations hundreds of times – but nothing like this. I feel hugely nervous. I breathe deeply and I'm ready to begin.

'What I have in mind is a partnership,' I announce. 'My door will be open to anyone here who wants to work with the project to help his or her family escape extreme poverty. I can create opportunities and provide a certain amount of funding, but it's up to you to make it all happen. Are you interested in that? Do you want to take a chance with me, take a chance on me, to work together and build a way to beat the deep poverty in this area?'

I look around and I can see the answer in their eyes. There's a buzz of excitement. At the very least, I've got their interest.

Then come the questions – lots of them. The audience gathers momentum until it feels like a fully-fledged firing squad of benign bullets coming at me from all directions. I feel overwhelmed and relieved in equal measure. There are questions about water for drinking and irrigation, schooling for the children, health and medicines and opportunities to make money. I'd like to tackle all these things to some degree, I tell them, but we can make progress together only if we've got the community and its leaders firmly on board.

'No problem,' one of the younger farmers says. 'We'll tell the Chief about your plan and tell him we want it to go ahead. He'll be as pleased as we are that you've come to Siboti.'

That's a big breakthrough. The Chief is very much the leader of his community. What he says goes. If he hears the plan presented in a positive light by his own people, my first meeting with him stands a much better chance of getting us off to a good start.

For now, though, I need to know more about the people here. I need to get a better idea of how they live and what they care about. And I need facts. How much do people earn? How many of the children ever get to go to school? How many children are orphaned? How bad are infant and maternal mortality rates in the area? How many people die from the three big killers – AIDS, tuberculosis and malaria?

With my old work hat on, I've put together a questionnaire covering these key issues. I'm going to need a team of four or five people to carry out this mini-census over the next few weeks. I ask for volunteers and within a few minutes we have a team of three guys and two girls to collect the information I want. There seems to be no official source for this kind of data so it's down to them to gather all the facts we'll need. It will take a few weeks but at the end I will be a walking oracle on Siboti.

Before the meeting is over, I want to take advantage of this huge gathering to see how deep the enthusiasm for my proposed project is likely to run. I know the people down at the front are in favour, but what about the silent majority? Will the community as a whole really engage with the project?

I decide to test the water. I take a punt.

'Next week,' I say, 'I am planning to go to Uganda for another meeting, just like this one. Please understand, I can only do one project. So I will have to choose between doing the project here or over the border in Uganda. Over the next few weeks, I need to see how much you want it to be here.'

That does it.

'Are we going to let this opportunity go to Uganda?' a voice shouts from the back of the crowd.

'No!' shout back a few voices around him.

'Are we going to show this man we are serious people?'

'Yes!' shouts out a big group.

'This man is a saint. He has been sent to us by God. Are we going to let down God?'

'Nooooo!' wails the entire assembled mass of humanity.

Oh, shit. This is already getting out of hand. I wanted them to buy into me but I don't want to be revered as some kind of deity. That's just way too weird. I'm certainly no saint, but at least they are interested in starting a millennium village type of project. I can worry about the fine-tuning and make it clear that I'm not a prophet or a messiah some other time. And, anyway, right now, belief of any sort is certainly what this project needs.

There'll be more prayers to close the meeting. But beforehand, Peter, the principal, announces that one of the children, an orphan will recite two prize-winning poems she has written.

The first poem is in Swahili, so I don't know what the girl's saying. But she delivers her poem with such intense, raw emotion that it gives me goose bumps on my arms and neck. When she's finished, the crowd is totally silent for a few seconds, her words hanging, echoing, in the air. Mama Jayne leans over, a tear in her eye, and translates for me what the girl has said and I feel the power of this child's grief. Her second poem is in English.

'When a wily fox grabs the carefree chicken, it is my fault, her caning birch explains,' recites the girl, referring to her uncle's wife, who is now reluctantly responsible for bringing her up. You can tell that this poor child's problems have really started with the untimely death of her mother. Her poem is about the sadness – and the anger – she feels at being left motherless and unwanted. She's not the only one. She's one of hundreds of children in this small community whose lives have been blighted by the loss of their parents. Orphans here are often treated as second-class children in the families that take on the task of bringing them up.

That does it for me. Something clicks inside. This is the kind of moment when the reality of poverty in these communities strikes home.

Disease, accidents or death in childbirth can happen anywhere in the world. But, of course, they don't happen nearly as much to people who have even a tiny bit more than the basic subsistence income these people survive on. They don't happen so much in places that have access to healthcare and medicines. They don't happen so much where HIV and malaria are seen as preventable diseases, rather than random acts of god. So adults and children die, directly or indirectly, of poverty.

The number of children that die astounds me. Our own population survey of Siboti will prove heart-rendering. There is a funeral for a child under five almost every day in Siboti – more than three hundred times a year. My mind boggles. These children are not being savaged by lions, trampled by elephants or bitten by poisonous snakes. Half of them die of malaria, pneumonia, AIDS or diarrhoea. In Britain or Ireland, they'd be treated and survive. Here, that doesn't happen. These children live, and die, in a community where many people's earnings are well below the United Nations' definition of extreme poverty of $1.25 a day. That's not enough. It leaves people short of food, clothes, shelter, education, medicines and hope, at the best of times. And it leaves them no leeway at all when anything goes even slightly wrong.

Where poverty walks, death stalks close behind. My aim of alleviating extreme poverty, of helping rural families haul themselves up off the bottom rung of the ladder, is not about economics or politics. It's about existence. It's about life. To get the chance to make some impact, in such an amazingly direct and practical way, is a privilege I'm very aware of. Listening to this girl recite her poem, I know what I have to do with my life, for the next few years, at least.

Siboti has touched me already. I feel like I have no choice now but to focus every sinew of my ability in this place. So Siboti it will be.

4

The big idea gets bigger

'Despite the hundreds of non-governmental organisations
and the continued outpouring of foreign aid, East Africa
remains a region overwhelmed by extreme poverty.'

Jacqueline Novogratz, founder of Acumen,
a non-profit global venture capital fund

I'm back in London, in the world I know, to hatch my plan for Siboti.
It's the height of summer and it's been raining for two days.

On the surface, life seems normal. I've learned to rein in the
urge to give all my friends and contacts a blow by blow account of
everything I've done or am trying to do in Kenya. I'm starting to
understand what they really mean when they smile and nod politely.
It's not that they're not interested. Some of them definitely are. But I
am utterly obsessed, and I can't expect everyone to share that.

I'm still processing the hundreds of images and incidents I carry
round in my head. I've seen lots of positives and lots of reasons for
optimism, but I've also glimpsed some chilling examples of what
life on the poverty line really means. There's no safety net, and bad

situations rapidly get worse and worse. On one of our day trips, Mama Jayne had introduced me to Kwashi, a teenage girl who'd had an accident at home. She was an epileptic, and she'd been hit by a seizure and fallen into an open fire while her parents were out, suffering terrible burns to her right leg. I don't know whether better treatment and careful rehab could have saved her leg, but in the depths of rural Kenya that was not an option. The leg had been amputated and soon she had to drop out of school, after discovering that Siboti's rough and rutted tracks made getting there on crutches practically impossible. Without an education, and in an area where youth unemployment was a problem for even the fittest youngsters, she stood no chance of leading an independent life. In the Western world, of course, her accident would never have happened in the first place; her epilepsy could easily have been controlled with a single daily pill.

Kwashi was surviving, and when I talked to her she was remarkably cheerful about her fate and her life. But meeting her and seeing how she and so many others lead lives that are entirely dictated by their inescapable poverty has jolted my perspectives. I see things differently now. I buy a coffee while waiting to meet a friend, and can't help thinking that this small latte represents half a week's income for someone in Siboti. I'm living in two worlds, and they might as well be on different planets. I can't wait to get back to Kenya.

Walking down Chancery Lane, dodging the taxis and the puddles and picking my way through the crowds of city workers and Chinese tourists, I wonder how the five young people recruited after our big meeting at the polytechnic are getting on with the Siboti survey project.

The deadline for completing the survey has been set for the end of this week. I have asked the team to use the polytechnic as a base and fan out from there to survey the surrounding hamlets and settlements in this particular part of Siboti, counting the people and noting the basic facts about the way they live, until they have built up a sample of about 3000 local residents. They'll be asking about family size, the proportion of children attending school, the number of orphans and the prevalence of health problems like HIV, TB and malaria. They'll also be keeping their eyes open for signals that will help us estimate incomes within the community.

If a home has a corrugated iron roof, for example, rather than an improvised thatch, that's a sign that the family living there is more prosperous – or less poor – than the neighbours. Another clue is the existence of toilet facilities – usually a pit latrine consisting of a hole dug in the ground, a few yards away from the house, with some bits of fencing around it to give a semblance of privacy. Crude as these rough and ready toilets are, they are a lot better than nothing. For the majority of the people in Siboti there's no option but to find a corner of a field or wood and do what you have to do there. It's called 'open defecation' in formal development terms, and it's a major problem in many parts of the world. According to the UN, nearly a billion people still have no choice. In India more people now have a mobile phone than a toilet – and it's probably the same in rural Kenya.

Once the work has been done and Mama Jayne has collated the results and sent them to me in London, I will have all the facts at my fingertips to start planning my big project. I will be able to think in terms of real numbers. I'll be able to calculate what resources I'm likely to need to really make an impact on these 3000 lives.

Why 3000? Well, you have to start somewhere. And you can't just get involved in an open-ended commitment, if you have limited resources. I know that each of the UN's Millennium Village projects in Africa aims to cover a rural population of about 5000 people. I don't exactly know yet why the United Nations chose 5000, rather than 1000 or 10 000, but I'm assuming that figure is based on UN research and experience – and that's good enough for me.

Privately, I'm expecting my nominal figure to creep up to 4000 – maybe even 5000. I want to be flexible about drawing the boundaries of my project. I'd rather be able to talk to families on the edge of the project zone and say 'Sure, you're welcome – come on in' than have to draw a line and say 'Not a soul beyond this point.' So we're surveying 3000 people, planning for quite a few more, but keeping a realistic lid on the scale of the project.

By the end of the week, I am hopping from foot to foot, barely able to resist grabbing the phone and calling Mama Jayne. She's got a big job on her hands, collating all the information from the survey team, and I know she'll get it all across to me as soon as she possibly can. But this suspense is almost unbearable. I call up my lovely, long-suffering friend, Mooli, take her out to our favourite Spanish restaurant for tapas and cava and waste the whole evening hardly eating, hardly talking, locked in a chatter of internal dialogue that I dare not share with her. With anyone else, an evening like that would probably spell the end of a beautiful friendship. But Mooli knows me well and understands how preoccupied I am.

'Don't worry, Ken. I know the signs of when that head of yours is at work. Go home. Try to get some sleep. And let me know what Mama Jayne comes back with.'

Sleeping's all very well, in theory. But the motor's whirring tonight and it'll take some stopping. I'm sitting in my house in Pimlico, but I might as well be back there in Siboti.

My theory is beginning to take on a definite shape. The way forward is beginning to reveal itself as a commerce-based, self-sustaining approach to alleviating extreme poverty. It will need a certain amount of funding to get it going, but if it works the way I want it to in Siboti, it can in time become self-financing. It can be sustainable and repeatable, a model that could be implemented later in other areas nearby, and potentially rolled out further, the whole of Western Kenya, perhaps – maybe to elsewhere in Africa or other parts of the developing world.

I'd need all the elements to work together – training, microfinance, improved farming techniques and better marketing of the products the community produced, all held in place by a professional project management framework. But if we get it right, we'll have a practical, systematic method that will bring prosperity, and with that food, health, education and real prospects for a better future.

I sit there for hours with my laptop and coffee cups piled up on the desk, making notes, setting up spreadsheets and googling everything I can find about the successes and failures of various

African poverty alleviation projects. By the time I finally crawl into bed, it's 4 a.m.

When I wake up late the next morning, unkempt and drowsy, I find my way to the kitchen, make myself some strong black coffee and prepare to face up to the laptop.

And there it all is. She has delivered. My inbox is full of text files, scans, spreadsheets and pictures.

Back in Bungoma, Mama Jayne has virtually taken over West FM, the town's favourite internet café. She's been there for hours, pumping through the results of the survey and a torrent of other helpful information and observations. If she's been wondering why she's not had an instant response from me, she's far too polite to comment. I must email her straightaway, if only to confirm that it's all coming through successfully.

'Fantastic,' I type. 'This is wonderful. Thank you so much for all the effort you've put into this Mama Jayne. Please tell the team I am really grateful for all their work. I'll see you all again very soon.'

The printer starts churning out the file marked 'Siboti Survey – Main Results'. This is the moment I've been waiting for.

Wait a minute, though. This isn't quite making sense. I've got various assumptions in my head about what the numbers will show, and they don't tally at all with what I'm seeing in front of me. I look at the bottom right of the spreadsheet, where I'm expecting to see an aggregate figure of something like 3000 people. But it reads: 18 243.

What's that supposed to mean?

Then it hits me. These earnest, conscientious youngsters have been so keen to help that they have surveyed the whole Siboti area.

They've ignored, or forgotten, the plan that said we would cover the 3000 or so people living nearest to the polytechnic. Or maybe they just thought that if a survey covering 3000 people was good, a survey that covered six times as many would be six times as good.

A few individuals here and there have probably slipped through the net, but these surveyors have basically set out to talk to everyone – women's groups, youth groups, self-help groups, churches, pastors, elders and families – in the whole of Siboti. They've pushed out in every direction to the very edge of the official administrative area. They've asked all the questions I wanted to cover, and a whole lot more besides. I've got a mountain of information, an ocean of facts and one big, unanswered question.

How big should this project be?

Should I stick to my original idea of trying to help 3000 people? Or should I, could I, start thinking in terms of extending the project to cover the whole population of 20 000 or so?

A quick calculation tells me I can't possibly assist the development of the whole of Siboti. The UN's best guess at the cost of helping each person in a Millennium Village project is $50 a year. If I try to work with the whole community of 20 000 people, over a period of, say, four years, I am going to need about $4 million. It's out of the question. I don't have it, so it's not even worth thinking about.

But then again, that UN figure is bound to be what the accountants would call a fully loaded cost estimate. It probably includes a share of the expenses of running a UN office in the local town, the salaries of a platoon of field officers and admin staff, the provision of those Land Cruisers – maybe even the costs of hotels and flights to Nairobi (or even New York) for consultations, conferences and training courses. Compared with all that, I'll be running my operation on a shoestring. I won't be taking a salary or paying for an office in town and my transport will be a little motorbike (a 2x1, I suppose, rather than a 4x4).

I don't know what the cost per person will be for doing it my way, but I'm pretty sure it's going to be a lot less than $50 per head per year. How much less, I can't begin to guess. But I do know that if the income-generating components of my project start to deliver, there will be an element of sustainability that will quickly reduce the need for outside funding.

My philosophy is to develop the idea of private sector-led poverty alleviation, based on solutions that are commercially sustainable, durable and replicable. Otherwise I can't afford it, and it would be a handout. And then you're just waiting for the next handout, and another one in ten years' time, and it will all go on as it has done for the last fifty years since independence.

For many development experts, international aid is now seen as a dubious blessing, simply because it has failed to create the changes everybody wants. With fast-growing populations and economic and political stagnation over the last few decades, parts of Africa have been going backwards, with the poor getting poorer and more numerous.

One of the most outspoken leaders of the anti-aid movement is the controversial Zambian-born economist Dambisa Moyo, once named by *Time* magazine in its list of the world's 100 Most Influential People – and once accused by Bill Gates of 'promoting evil' through her books. Moyo's first US bestseller, *Dead Aid: Why aid is not working and how there is another way for Africa*, was published in 2009 and sparked furious arguments around the world. But it certainly helped me refine some of my own ideas and it prompted Kofi Annan, the Ghanaian-born former UN secretary-general, to say it made 'a compelling case for a new approach to Africa'.

Prudence tells me I should stick to just 3000 people.

Instinct tells me I should go for broke and try to cover the whole population of 20 000.

But it's not as clear-cut a decision as it might seem. If I work with everyone in Siboti, I'll avoid the inevitable resentment and complaints from those who are excluded from my plans. There'll be less of the 'Why them and not us?' jealousies that are bound to arise if I focus on a small minority within the community. And, by going for the bigger ambition, I should be able to count on the backing and support of the Chief and all forty-two of the community leaders, the village elders. Surely things will go better if I have all of these influential local leaders on my side?

I can feel the fear of failure, a tight knot in my stomach that's urging me to play safe, to take on only what I believe I can do well. Be sensible, Ken. You know the dangers of spreading your resources too thin. What if you run out of money? What if this ambition to help everyone means you fall short and fail to make a real difference to anyone? What if? What if?

I come from a background of metrics and spreadsheets, methodical risk assessments and measured, carefully considered decisions. If I were still at my banker's desk in London or New York,

I'd be weighing up the pros and cons and I'd probably be settling for the smaller-scale option.

But I'm not in that world now. And I'm not the same person. Kenya has already changed me. My motivation is different. It's stronger, deeper, more visceral.

I've seen up close the cruelty, the ugliness, the dangers and the sheer injustice of extreme poverty. It's fucking horrible. And I know that the greatest crime of all is that it's avoidable. Don't we have an absolute and moral obligation to use our skills, experience, technologies, resources and energies to do what we can to put an end to it? And I have an obligation to these people. I feel it. I know it. I can't duck it. If there's any reasonable prospect of success, don't I have to go for it, on the most ambitious scale I can?

I'm more than prepared to give my time and my effort for the next few years. I'm more than prepared to put in a substantial portion of the money I will receive after I've sold the house in Pimlico – hopefully as a medium-term working capital loan. If all goes well and I can make profitable the core businesses that will be needed at the heart of the Siboti project, those businesses can pay back that loan. If not – and I have to face this possibility head on – I'll have kissed goodbye to hundreds of thousands of pounds.

As I look through the survey figures from Mama Jayne again, I tell myself I still have to make up my mind. The decision is still in the balance. But there's a limit to how much I can kid myself. I know which way I'm being tugged. Unless some new factor comes up that I haven't thought of before, it looks as if I will be going for the big one and facing up to the challenge of trying to help all 20 000 people.

I must get back to Siboti and meet the Chief. He'll have a key role to play, and I need to know whether he's someone I'm going to be able to work with.

* * *

I've already seen enough of Kizito, the driver who ferries Mama Jayne's Haven Kenya charity volunteers around, to know he is going to be a valuable ally. Within hours of arriving back in Western Kenya, I find myself chatting with him and one of his friends, Edwin Matua, about my next steps, including making my first contact with the Chief.

'That's easy,' says Kizito. 'Edwin can fix that up for you, Mr Ken.'

'You're welcome to call me Ken you know,' I say.

Both men nod and smile. It's not a *mzungu* issue, I've established: any man in a position of authority in Siboti is a mister. It's a cultural difference. People here seem to feel more comfortable calling me Mr Ken.

'No problem Mr Ken,' says Edwin. 'I can do it. The Chief is my uncle. Let me call him and inform him we are coming. Yes. We will see my uncle at his place. He will be very happy for your visit.'

He's as good as his word. The next day, Kizito and Edwin pick me up and we go to see the Chief, bumping and lurching our way up the boulder-strewn track over Siboti Hill and down a narrow, potholed ravine on the other side until the land opens out and we find ourselves at the Chief's farm. It's a big place, by Siboti standards, a substantial house built of rough-cast local bricks, with a roof made of corrugated iron sheeting.

The Chief is waiting outside to greet us, and my first impression is entirely positive. The Chief and his two assistant chiefs have a wide range of powers under Kenya's system of local government, and they are appointed by the appropriate ministry in Nairobi. But this chief has an aura of natural authority. He's tall and imposing – at six foot three inches he's certainly the tallest man I've seen in this area. He's in his late forties, I guess, slim but powerfully built, with a strong, serious face that cracks suddenly into a warm, open smile. His name is Fredrick Wanjiku, but he is only ever referred to as the Chief.

'Welcome,' he says. 'I've heard a lot about you. We've got a lot to talk about, Mr Ken, but first let me show you around my *shamba*.'

The *shamba* is a large and well organised five-acre farm. The chief grows maize to feed his family and also raises a variety of cash crops – bananas, onions, tomatoes and sweet potatoes – which his wife sells at the local markets. There's another, smaller compound, further down the hill, with another two acres of rich, fertile soil.

'My other wife lives down there,' he says proudly.

Kenya's forty-two tribes have a centuries-old cultural tradition of polygamy, but 'plural marriage', as it is also known, is not all that common these days among the Christian people in this part of Western Kenya. The tradition is very much alive in other areas of the country, though. (Kenya's most famous polygamist, Ancentus 'Danger' Akuku, married 130 wives and fathered 210 children, living into his nineties and dying peacefully in his sleep in 2010.) Responsible polygamy requires the husband to provide for all his wives and children, and there are not many men in Siboti with the resources to do that. I have a suspicion that Fredrick Wanjiku's ability to support two wives somehow adds to his air of power and authority.

He's proud, too, of his prowess as a farmer. He shows me his grain store, a little shack made of bamboo and reeds that sits on stumpy pillars, knee-high above the ground, to keep the rats and mice away from the maize.

'From what I've heard, you are going to help us market our crops and put Siboti on the map,' he says. 'I like the sound of that, Mr Ken King. You are going to make me a millionaire, I think.' He's smiling broadly. He's pulling my leg, but how hard?

I'm a bit alarmed by his comment. Perhaps he actually believes that, and I sincerely hope he doesn't. Shall I put him right? I decide it's best to bite my lip and let it pass.

We make our way back to the house and file into the Chief's living room. It is surprisingly formal, with a large wood-framed sofa and lots of chairs, each with an ornate lace doily draped over the back. I take my place on the sofa and look up. There's no ceiling and the corrugated sheeting of the roof extends out far beyond the tops of the rough-hewn walls, leaving a wide gap through which a cool breeze blows in. We are introduced to the Chief's wife and his two daughters and the Chief opens the meeting with a brief prayer, thanking the Lord for his goodness and asking his blessing for my project.

'And we pray that God will bless our special visitor and help him to help us beat the challenge of our poverty,' he ends.

Amen to that, I think. If this is going to work, I will need all the help I can get, human and divine.

As we settle down to begin our meeting, the Chief's daughter brings us drinks. There are six bottles of soda – Fanta, Coke and Sprite – rolling around on the tray as she walks. Oversize bottles, I notice, twice the usual size. Well, I suppose he is the Chief.

I start by explaining who I am and why I'm here, how I come to be in Siboti and what I'm hoping to do. I make it very clear that I don't see myself as a saint or a miracle worker and include a lot of diplomatic compliments about the qualities I've already seen in the people of his community.

The Chief is watching me carefully. Maybe I've already gone too far with this gentle flattery. Despite my genuineness, perhaps his bullshit detectors are starting to twitch. So without any more flannel, I tell it straight and focus on the essential role he must play if we are to succeed. This project is going to need a strong, high-profile leader, someone who is trusted and respected, who can inspire commitment, represent the people of Siboti and take decisions on their behalf and who can arbitrate if any disagreements crop up. This bit isn't flattery. It's the plain truth. If he's not prepared to lead from the front, there is no one else who can do it. Without the Chief's wholehearted backing, I might as well pack up and go home.

For a few moments, I can't tell what Fredrick Wanjiku is thinking. Then that broad smile cracks his features.

'Mister Ken, I am happy. I am very much happy. I heard already much of what you have told me, but I wanted to look in your eyes and hear it from your own mouth. My people need a project like this. We must have a *barassa* meeting with my assistant chiefs and the elders to inform them of your wonderful vision for our people.'

Great relief. Now we can talk plans. Every project needs a good steering committee that can test and, if necessary, challenge the project plan, monitor progress and represent the interests of all the stakeholders. The assistant chiefs and the forty-two village elders will be our steering committee. Having a committee that large may make for long meetings, but it should guarantee that every part of the community is kept closely in touch with what's going on.

We can't afford to have any misunderstandings. The Chief and I must both know exactly what we're talking about. He's absolutely clear that he wants this project to happen and that he will do anything and everything he can to support it. But is he, despite my denials, holding me up as some sort of one-man transformation machine? I need to stress again that I can only do so much.

I can outline a way forward and structure the multiple projects. I can help start the core businesses that will be needed, bring in all the necessary agricultural experts, business trainers and health advisers and provide the start-up funding. But it will be the people of Siboti who will have to do the work, lifting themselves out of poverty with their own energy and effort. They will have to improve the agricultural methods and grasp the new economic opportunities. All I can do is to create an environment in which change can happen.

'We are ready,' says the Chief.

I look at his resolute jaw and his level, determined gaze and I know we have a deal.

But what have I agreed to? We haven't had any discussion yet about the possibility of starting the project on a small scale, with just 3000 people, as I'd originally intended. The Chief has just assumed

– or maybe he has been told by his informants – that what's talked about as The Mr Ken Project is coming to Siboti as a whole, not to one small part of his jurisdiction.

'Just one thing, Chief,' I begin. 'How many people are there in Siboti, in this whole official location?'

'Nobody knows for sure,' he says. 'Maybe 18 000? We're waiting for the government census results. I won't be surprised if it's much more. Maybe 22 000.'

I'm on the point of blurting out that I haven't decided yet whether to start with 3000 people or 20 000 when I realise I already have.

The die is cast. I know what I have to do. It's the whole community or nothing. Siboti or bust.

5

Rain and funerals

'Sure, I always knew you'd go far, Kennit – just not that far.'

Noeleen King (1939–98)

'Hi, how are you, Da? How are things?'

I'm phoning home, the dutiful son, asking for news. But I know what's coming.

'Oh, you know, Ken. The usual. Rain and funerals.'

Talking about the weather is a luxury reserved for the English. The Irish talk about the rain.

'Sure, it only rained twice this week,' my father continues. 'Once for three days and once for four days.'

The Eskimos may, or may not, have a hundred words for snow, but the Irish have only ever needed one for rain. It confidently exists in every tense: past, present and future – and a new one – the unconditional. It rained yesterday. It is raining today. It will rain tomorrow.

It rained throughout my childhood. It rained on my adolescence.

I am about fifteen years old, a skinny, bespectacled, sensitive boy, doing my school homework, sitting on a stool at the kitchen table. My mother is in the living room, watching television, getting up now and then to make us all tea or bring the nightly treat of chocolate biscuits or homemade apple tart. My father, a police officer, is busy, intense, 'writing dots', scratching away with black ink and an old-fashioned wooden dip pen, crafting musical scores for Ireland's police band, the Garda Band, at the same round table.

He is picking apart by ear the melody, harmonies and chords of *Dallas*, which he has recorded from the television with his cassette tape recorder. He allocates parts to clarinet, trumpet, trombone... thirty players, thirty parts. A TV theme tune converted into a rich big band arrangement that will surprise and delight. All written out by hand, dot by dot, neat and tight and obsessively right. This seems to me an amazingly scientific and skilled process for creating music. When it's complete, he will take his new *Dallas* score into band rehearsal, hand out the individual parts, lift his conductor's baton and listen intently while they play, halting periodically if he hears a musical utterance defined by his pen but unintended by his pitch-perfect ear.

When Irish police officer Dick Fallon was gunned down in a bank raid in 1970, the first murder of a Garda since the 1940s, Ireland was in shock. My dad sought permission to put a band together of serving police officers, who marched and played at that sombre funeral. His great achievement since then had been advocating that Ireland should have a full-time police band that would perform in schools and at events around the country. It would present a new and benevolent face of policing, particularly to the tough kids in rough neighbourhoods who might naturally have a highly sceptical view of the police.

Tonight he is delivering on his promise, arranging music for the new Garda Band, of which he is sergeant-in-charge. The band has shelves full of arrangements and many are his work – his creations. He is dedicated to two causes, the excellence of his beloved band, and providing for his family. He seldom drinks alcohol, and uses every penny he earns to support us. Every night when he is not out working to try to make ends meet, he writes dots at the kitchen table, studious and absorbed. Then, as now, I feel a huge respect and admiration for him. I desperately want him to notice me. I want to feel the warmth of his attention. But this is a house of its time. Displays of affection by grown men are not the norm. Our house feels like everything a home of the period should be – solid, reliable, consistent, safe, warm and caring. We are a family, like so many others, of good citizens, decently and diligently making our way through life.

Another evening. It's raining again. On the radio, Tony O'Reilly is delivering a speech to a celebrity audience that's howling with laughter. Dr AJF O'Reilly is a giant of Irish business and society. He grew up just four miles from our house in north Dublin and has risen to become first an international rugby star and then CEO of the mighty Heinz food company. At weekends, he flies back to Ireland from the US, as he is also a pioneer of oil exploration in Irish waters, proprietor of our biggest national newspaper and founding director of a large business conglomerate on the Irish stock exchange. He is also a dazzling, irresistible raconteur.

To me, at fifteen, O'Reilly is a hero. Tony O'Reilly is everything I feel I'm not – talented, intelligent, funny, gifted, popular, athletic, admired by everyone and hugely successful at everything. Into his tales and yarns he weaves the names of many of those who make up his illustrious audience tonight. For months afterwards I wonder whether I'll ever do something or be somebody to warrant an invitation to an event like this, maybe even a mention by my hero. Probably not. I will most likely finish my mediocre schooling at sixteen, get a menial job and grow up to envy and begrudge the big boys, not join them. At this moment, the scope of my ambition reaches no further than this room; outside is only gloom and a pre-ordained path to disappointment. My personal cloud of adolescent inadequacies presses in on me, as incessant and inevitable as the rain.

Some people facing the future I envisage for myself at fifteen would take life by the scruff of the neck and set about knocking it into shape, working hard at school, furthering their education and experience by taking every opportunity that presents itself. Not me.

At school, I set myself low standards – and consistently fail to meet them. Becoming eligible for the world of work, with poor grades, low confidence and few options, I'm lucky to get even one job offer, as an insurance clerk. So I am not to be cast straight onto the scrapheap, then. I can find my own way there, slowly and gradually. I have just turned seventeen, and I take the job.

For some reason, though, I can never get excited about the work. Occupational pension benefit calculations don't inspire me. I sit pounding a calculator all day, in a grim office full of smoke and sullen silence. There are no desktop computers, of course, and as you shuffle over the yellow nylon carpet, the metal filing cabinets spark with a bolt of static electricity whenever you go to touch them. But they can't jolt me out of my rut. There is a kind of comfort in mediocrity. It is effortlessly achieved and easily maintained. Yet, at twenty years old, after three years of being a not-very-good pensions clerk I feel something unexpected stirring inside me. The desire to escape, at first no more than a vague restlessness, grows within me until it becomes all-consuming, and not in a good way. The predictability and limitations of my future prospects only serve to fuel my nagging self-doubt.

I am young and desperate to jump off the track I am on, fearful of what will happen if I don't act. I am haunted by the spectre of my sixty-year-old self, sitting at an Irish bar, with only a pint and my regrets for company.

'If only,' the spectre muses, 'if only I had – when I was young, when I had the chance – beaten a path away from this place.'

If you can overlook hating the work, the poor pay and Ireland's early-1980s income tax level (even as a junior entry-level clerk I am paying almost 60 per cent), Irish Life Assurance in Dublin is a great place to be. There are great people and the after-work social life is fantastic.

But I need to escape my current rut. Desperately. And the only way to get out and up is to do something that will require a lot of work. So three years after starting as a clerk, I bite the bullet and enrol at night school to retake Ireland's school leaving exams. Three nights a week, as I travel to Plunket College, just round the corner from where Tony O'Reilly grew up, I imagine I am on a path to becoming a bit more like the big man. The very idea propels me to get the grades I need and secure a place on an evening degree course in computing science at Trinity College, Dublin. This, in itself, seems to impress my bosses at Irish Life. I get a transfer into the computer department, first in an admin role and then as a fully-fledged trainee computer programmer. This is more like it. Computing is a fast-moving field. There've been lots of young guys down here on the second and third floors who have moved on, taking their expertise off to New York and making a small fortune. This is a job with prospects, and I'm not going to let go of the opportunity. For four years, I keep my head down and work hard. I put in long hours, and as my skills and confidence develop, I'm starting to feel I belong.

But then it's back again: a sense of restlessness growing inside me. There's that gnawing fear that if I take my foot off the gas, I'll just slide back into nothingness.

I know what lies in wait for me if I stay in Ireland. I'll spend my whole life carrying around with me the feeling that I have successfully graduated one step from my feeling of being a third-rater. But there's no way of knowing what my fate could be beyond Ireland's shores. In the wider world, nothing will be impossible. Anything might be achievable. I want to prove to myself that I am really capable, that I can make something of myself, to build my self-esteem, to become worthy. I'm not out to prove it to anybody else. That doesn't matter. Just to myself. For myself.

I don't want to emigrate, to leave my friends and family, but I know I have to go or else be damned forever with a nagging guilt that maybe I could have become somebody or done something significant out in the world.

I feel I have no choice. I have to leave.

London seems easier than New York. I could get home more often to see family and friends. That's about as far as my logic goes. I will move to London.

I buy a few recruitment magazines, contact agents in the big city and fly over for two days of interviews. By the time I come back to Dublin, I have a job offer that doubles my take-home salary and includes a company car. I hand in my notice and throw a farewell drinks party. In July 1990, I pack my things into my car, say farewell to the family, board the ferry and leave Ireland.

* * *

The next few years are a whirl of activity. I'm climbing fast, taking on more and more, shifting my focus from pure IT to project management. I make the leap from insurance into investment banking, and suddenly I'm playing with the big boys. The projects are huge now, and the stakes are so big you daren't even contemplate failure. These are huge, complex transformational change management projects on an international scale, with big budgets and impacts reaching into the tens of millions. These projects seek to change a company's methods, working practices and systems across the globe. The stress is insane and the travel is incessant.

The pressure suits me though. London, New York, Tokyo, Frankfurt. I'm flying every week, and flying high. It's a mad world all right, but I can handle it. As the years roll past, it becomes more and more intense. Monday is always London. Every second Monday, it's out to Heathrow airport with colleagues for the 8.30 p.m. flight to New York. Taxi to Manhattan, hotel check-in then out for drinks with my fellow travellers. Bed at 2 a.m., which, given the five-hour time-zone difference, is 7 a.m. according to my body clock. Four hours sleep and in to catch the boss at 6.30 a.m. Work until 8 p.m., then out for a steak dinner and lots of drinks until at least midnight. Wednesday is a repeat of Tuesday. Thursday at 4 p.m., take a taxi to JFK airport. Board the 7 p.m. return flight. Grab four hours sleep on the plane. At 7 a.m. Friday morning, hit the British Airways arrivals lounge where they iron a shirt and a suit while I take a shower. A bank car is waiting to take me to the office. Arrive by 10 a.m., work till 7 p.m., go home, change and then out to catch-up with friends. Midnight, home and fall happily into bed.

During a bout of heavy turbulence over Siberia one Friday evening, on the way back from a business trip to Tokyo, I watch the British Airways flight attendant precariously navigate the first-class cabin to rescue my jittering glass of vintage champagne. I recall last week's management conference in the Loire of France where I had regaled colleagues with my own tales and yarns, as I had heard my countryman, Dr AJF O'Reilly do over the kitchen radio decades before. Today is all a long way from upstairs on Dublin's number 39 bus, with its steamed-up windows and the smeared oval porthole wiped clear by my rain-soaked leatherette gloves. I suddenly realise the mission I set myself all that time ago has been fulfilled. I am no longer a third-rater or a second-rater. I brim with success and confidence. This evening, staring out at another oval-framed view of the outside world, I relish this new and liberating feeling. A feeling that is decades late showing up, but still very welcome. After all this time, I realise, I no longer need to prove myself. I am happy and confident. I feel peace. And closure.

* * *

Back home in Dublin, my mum is also thriving in her way, but possibly not surviving. Cancer has struck. Her hair is going and her physical pain is excruciating. It's so hard to witness. My dad has recently retired and he's spending all his time looking after her. He has dedicated himself to her care, sleeping when she sleeps, staying awake through the night when she needs him. They've fallen in love all over again and, despite her illness, she has never seemed happier. She goes round the house singing James Brown's 'I Feel Good'. She is so very determined to beat this.

On the eve of my Dad's sixtieth birthday, as we are all preparing to go to his formal Garda retirement dinner, we hear the sound of music in the distance. Curtains are pulled back, blinds are raised and doors are flung open right along our street, as all the neighbours come out to see what's going on. Ollie, my sister, is the first to realise what's happening.

'Dad, it's your band,' she squeals in delight.

All thirty Garda Band members have turned out in full uniform for the occasion. They've parked their cars at the top of our road and lined up in formation. Now they're marching crisply towards our end-of-terrace house, in a surprise tribute to my Dad, playing at full volume, reading the musical dots he scribed years earlier onto stiff cards that can be clipped onto marching trumpets, clarinets and drums.

My Dad, now risen to the rank of Garda Superintendent and the title of Musical Director, is already dressed in his business suit, ready to leave for the dinner. What a pity he's not in his officer's uniform, in tunic and cap, with his cherished Sam Browne belt that signifies his elevated rank. He takes my mum's hand – the first time I've ever seen him do it – and they step together down the short garden path to the roadside pavement. She's dressed in an emerald-green suit, her once-flowing mane of black hair now cut short and coloured sandy blonde. As they watch and wait and the Garda Band approaches the house, he puts his arm around her and she leans into him, and I feel like bursting with joy at the closeness I see between them. The band halts in front of the house and the musicians pivot towards my dad. When the music stops, the conductor gives him a formal salute. My dad snaps to attention to take the salute, and salutes back.

'Hip-hip,' shouts the conductor.

'Hurrah,' cheer the band members, the family and all the neighbours.

'Hip-hip.'

'Hurrah.'

'Hip-hip.'

'Hurrah.'

There are tears in my eyes. I am thirty-four years old and I desperately want to give my dad a big hug, and to get one back. I'm so proud of him and I want to feel totally close to him. If not now, in this poignant moment, then when? But I can't do it. It's not our way. I go up to him and shake his hand firmly instead.

'Congratulations, Da,' I say. 'Isn't this great? You've earned this.'

'Thanks, Ken,' he replies, proudly, as the neighbours cluster round to shake his hand. They're shaking my mum's hand, too, but I can see she's wincing in pain. I ask her to come inside, but she's having too good a time. Despite the pain, her smile is beaming brightly.

Dad's colleagues have organised a surprise Garda motorcycle escort from the house to the retirement dinner. So we all jump into the waiting cars and we're whisked off in a cavalcade of flashing blue lights. As we pass the terraces and houses that have been the backdrop to my childhood, I gaze out of the darkened car window, a smile on my face from ear to ear. I'm overcome with pride at my father's achievements, my parents' love and the respect my dad's colleagues have shown for him and for us as a family.

* * *

A few months later, I am in a big meeting on the thirty-sixth floor of the bank's New York office when someone tells me there's an important call for me. I excuse myself and take the call. It's my brother, Alan.

'Ken,' he says. 'Sorry to disturb you. It's bad news. I've just been talking to the hospital and Mam's not going to make it.'

I've been going to Dublin to see her regularly, often on the way back from my fortnightly trips to New York. But now she's at death's door and I am here, stuck in the middle of some bloody project kick-off meeting in mid-town Manhattan. There's nothing I can do. I put the phone down and go back in to complete my presentation, focusing intently on the job in hand for two hours that feel like a lifetime. I feel I've earned a year's money in that two hours. All I want is to be alone. I take a cab back to my hotel, hit the cocktail bar and gulp down four stiff gin and tonics. Then I stagger up to my room, puke yellow bile all over the bathroom and collapse on the white marble floor.

As I lie there, alone in the depths of my misery and sense of overwhelming loss, I have no idea that something of world-wide importance is happening just a few blocks away. Kofi Annan and his advisers at the United Nations are busy formulating the ideas that will, in due course, shape an important part of my future and form the basis of my salvation.

Within two years, the UN will be announcing the eight Millennium Development Goals that will win the acceptance of the world's leaders and set the ball rolling for the biggest effort ever made to fight disease, hunger and poverty. The fifteen-year project, starting in the year 2000, will engage governments and non-government organisations in a massive global programme aimed at raising the very lowest incomes, erasing hunger, enabling a primary school education for all and providing relief from deadly diseases for millions of the world's poorest people.

At the time, none of this seems remotely relevant to my life, but the seeds of my destiny are being sown while I'm slumped there on the bathroom floor. The noble vision the UN is developing will, in time, save me from myself, and from a creeping reliance on alcohol to cope with a life that revolves obsessively around the driven, pressured, narrow realities of the investment banking world – a world in which I've been struggling to see any value or purpose beyond the money it pays me.

6

On the road without a map

'At independence Kenya's economic indicators were equal
to those of South Korea, but forty-five years down the road,
Korea's economy is forty times that of Kenya. The mediocrity
of leadership is across the continent.'

Raila Odinga, prime minister of Kenya 2008–13

Getting to know Siboti properly – how it works, who the people are
and how they live their lives – is my top priority now. I've got to get
out there and see more for myself, to learn the lie of the land. Mama
Jayne has seconded Kizito to me as my guide and my interpreter,
and I've already seen enough of him to know that he's going to be
a tremendous asset. He's smart, trusted, cheerful and well-liked and
I'm certainly lucky to have him on my side.

'OK. I need to get my bearings. Where can I get a good map of
this area?' I ask him.

Kizito laughs.

'There isn't one, Ken,' he says.

'Yeah. I understand. If there's not a good map, then we'll get an
old one and I'll mark updates on it as we go along.'

'No. There isn't an old map, either. There's no map of Siboti, I think. I've never seen one.'

That's not something that would have occurred to me. Everywhere is mapped now, surely. We can use Google Earth to get a bird's-eye view of the most hostile, remote and godforsaken places on the planet, from Wall Street to the top of Everest, from the middle of the Sahara to the deep ocean canyons. So nowhere's a mystery any more. And yet nobody's drawn a map of Siboti, an area with 20 000 inhabitants, hundreds of farms and scores of small settlements? I'm thinking that maybe what I'm doing in Siboti might one day put the place on the map, but I didn't think I'd be doing it quite so literally.

So we set off, armed with our clipboards and notebooks, to take stock of the place and put together a basic map for our own use. It's not going to be the world's greatest. I used to try to draw maps of Ireland when I was in primary school and the land of my birth always came out looking suspiciously like a tracing of a Chicken McNugget. But I do need to have something that shows me the names of the villages and hamlets and where the boundaries, roads and streams are, along with the locations of the Chief's house, the district officer's building, the police station, marketplaces, schools, churches and other local landmarks.

We end up with a map that's a bit like the map of the London Underground. Everything's present and connected, and roughly in the right place, but with no accurate representation of distances. I grow to love that little map. After a while, I transcribe it onto a bigger sheet of paper and hang it proudly on the wall of our office, where it is added to and enriched month by month. It feels like an Indiana Jones treasure map, and it makes me smile.

More importantly, though, this initial assessment of the area is aimed at getting me tuned in to the routines and realities of local life. Once I know more about these, I can start to design a customised project methodology that will fit the Siboti project's goals and circumstances.

I'm beginning to notice all sorts of things that no one had pointed out to me before. For example, whenever we roll up in one of the tiny villages, we have conversations in three different languages, with Kizito acting as interpreter. Many people speak English and Swahili and their own local dialect, Bukusu, switching effortlessly backwards and forwards from one to the other. Yet many of these adults never went to school. Who knows what enormous potential and brainpower is going to waste as these untaught linguists scratch a living, at or below the poverty line, in this far-off corner of Western Kenya?

Whatever the language, though, it doesn't take long to spot the common themes in most of our conversations. Parents are concerned about the cost of sending their children to school, for example. Even though primary education is supposed to be free, there are uniforms to buy and there's a fee to be paid every year to the school. This may be only $25 or so, but many families in Siboti live on incomes of $300 per year. And the $25 fee is per child, so school fees for a family with three children can take a quarter of the year's money. If you allow for one new $25 school uniform a year – with the used uniforms handed down from one child to the next – that leaves just $200 a year for the family's food, clothing, fuel, medicines and everything else. In practice, that modest $25 fee is often the difference between a child going to school or not – and many don't make it.

All over Siboti, there are children whose attendance at school has been cut short by their parents' inability to pay the school fees. I realise, with a jolt, that if I can help these families out by removing this barrier, I can make a big difference for just $25 per child. If I want to make an impact on primary education in the area, the quickest, most cost-effective way of doing it is to help with the costs of attending school. There are hundreds, probably thousands, of children in the area who are unable to go to school because there's no money to pay the dreaded school fees'.

If I could help, say, twenty-five children back into class at each of Siboti's nine schools, that could start to make a useful difference. I'm doing the sums in my head and it's a no-brainer. In a matter of weeks, I can get 225 children back on track towards a proper education. And that's exactly the kind of quick win I need to get people on side for this project. It's a momentum investment, an opportunity to get things moving with a bang.

The other topic that crops up all the time is water. I've already noticed how much pride and effort goes into washing clothes and school uniforms, the women sitting for hours pounding and wringing out the laundry in plastic basins with just a few inches of cleanish water. Drinking, cooking, washing and making sure the chickens have water are the other priorities. But the crops in the fields and smallholdings have no irrigation systems and are not watered. They rely entirely on the rain – and in bad years, when there can be an extra month or two with no rain at all, the parched crops don't stand a chance in the teeming heat. For families that may have no other source of income, this can be catastrophic. Subsistence farming is a dangerous occupation, hoping that nothing goes wrong that will trigger a disaster.

We are travelling around talking to people one day when I spot a big blue water storage tank and a pumping station, obviously unused. It was installed by the Kenyan government several years earlier as part of a grandiose scheme to bring a better water supply to the area. But they don't work, Kizito tells me, and they never have done.

The idea was that water would be pumped to these storage tanks via long pipelines from Kalamisi, several miles away. Contracts were awarded and the tanks and pumping stations were duly built. But the contractor responsible for the pipes decided to boost his profits, so the story goes, by fitting pipes that were cheaper and narrower than the plans specified. And the cheaper pipes weren't up to the job. Once it was obvious that the system wasn't working, the contractor realised he had a problem. But instead of going back and fitting wide-gauge pipes, which would have left him with a loss on the project, he chose an alternative solution. From what I've been told by a senior employee who claims to have been present at the time, the contractor found the right person in the public works department and slipped him half a year's salary as a bribe to sign the work off as satisfactorily completed.

When it came to the day of the grand opening ceremony in Siboti, with the local MP and a high-ranking government minister in attendance, everyone involved was a little concerned about the fine details – like the absence of water in the main storage tank. It could have been embarrassing, a water storage tank with no water. So someone recruited scores of local youths and told them there was 200 shillings on offer for a day's work to turn up with a bucket and spend the day getting water from wherever they could find it to fill up the tank. A small army of youngsters turned out, very happy to earn $2.50, and bucket after bucket of water was poured into the storage tank. Of course, even after this, it was nowhere near full, but when the ribbon was cut and the tap was turned on, a dribble of water trickled out. Honour was satisfied – and that was all anyone seemed to be bothered about. The politicians went away again, and the tanks remained unused forever.

While this grim farce was going on, the people of Siboti had watched events unfold with their usual resigned fatalism. No one had really expected the government to solve the water problem, so no one was particularly surprised by the outcome. Everything went back to normal, the women spending half of every day fetching and carrying water from distant streams and waterholes as usual.

Stories like this are quickly ceasing to surprise me. I'm already getting used to hearing about this kind of thing: Kenyans' ability to endure. It's an admirable coping strategy to manage hard times, but could it also be counterproductive if it means there are no expectations to meet? Whatever, if I am going to start building momentum and credibility for a substantial project here, I need to do something that will really improve the water supply. I'm beginning to understand why local people might be sceptical, might refuse to believe anything until they see it actually working. The hugely positive response at the first community meeting showed that a lot of people are optimistic about my plans for Siboti, but the looming bulk of the old blue storage tank is a monument to past failures. I need to show that I can deliver real improvements, quickly, in areas of people's lives that really matter to them.

I have two key issues underlined in my notebook now – school fees and access to clean water. If I can make an impact in either or both of these areas, I'll win a lot of credibility for the project.

I ask Mama Jayne and Kizito to arrange a *barassa*, a big public meeting, where I can talk to the people of Siboti and ask them what they think are the main reasons why the area is so poor. We borrow benches from St Peter's Catholic church and a cheerful crowd of more than 200 people gathers outside, sitting in the shade of the tall trees and drinking the bottles of Coke, Fanta and Sprite – universally referred to as 'sodas' – that we've supplied.

I ask the people to tell me why they think Siboti has so much poverty. I need to hear from them, in their own words, what they believe the issues are and what they think can be done about it.

What follows is fascinating – perhaps the most interesting discussion I have ever heard. An honesty emerges that flattens me with its frankness and insight.

'People here want prosperity', translates Mama Jayne, 'but they are convinced that no one, outsider or insider, can really get to grips with some of the underlying causes of poverty in Siboti.'

I look around at the watchful faces before me and try to compose my expression. People have emptied the precious 'sodas', for the most part, and they lean forward. The warm air feels electric. They seem genuinely fired up by the group discussion (or maybe it's the sugar hit). Perhaps it's the opportunity to be given a platform. When life presents you with few opportunities, perhaps it just feels nice to be listened to?

A man stands up and begins to talk quite quickly.

'For instance,' Mama Jayne jumps in with a translation for me, 'the farms are too small. Families are large and the land is always divided between the sons when the father dies, so the farms quickly become too small to support a family.'

'OK, OK,' I say to the man, 'so what happens then? What about jobs outside the farms?'

Mama Jayne and the farmer exchange some words. After what feels like a long speech, he sits down.

'Industry and jobs are non-existent,' she says, fanning herself with the notebook I have discarded on a bench, 'so people try to supplement their farming incomes with small shops or stalls. There is no irrigation, so the crops are entirely dependent on the rains, which don't always arrive on time, or at all. Siboti has a few rivers and several seasonal streams, but there's no easy access to clean water for drinking, cooking or washing. Boiling water to purify it is time-consuming and means having to forage for firewood, so people take short cuts and use unboiled water, which causes health problems. With no electricity, people cook indoors over charcoal fires and, for light, use smoky paraffin lamps that cause serious respiratory diseases, especially among the children.'

'Ok, thank you,' I say to her. 'That's a lot to take in.'

On the other hand, it seems there are also some very positive and encouraging messages. These people really can grow crops, and they are proud of their prowess as farmers. If a few things were fixed, they say, they could make a much better living from the land.

'Such as?' I ask, sensing that the secret of unlocking the path to prosperity may be about to be revealed.

'We need markets,' Mama Jayne translates for me. 'We need to be able to sell our produce at fair market prices. Instead, we're trapped here, forced to sell to the brokers, the outsiders who come here on motorbikes and give us almost nothing. But there's no choice. We have to take what they offer. We have no transport, so how can we get our products to the markets?'

That makes sense. What else?

'And we need good-quality seeds, and fertiliser, but they are too expensive.'

'And we need irrigation, but we have no money to pay for it.'

'There is no industry here. Nobody has any money, so there are no good buyers for our goods locally. We have to sell to outsiders, and we are cheated.'

'Yes. Cheated. We are always cheated.'

As they talk and encourage each other to speak up, I am hearing exactly what I need to do if I'm going to help these people.

I quickly realise how it could all work out. If I can create some kind of commercial co-op that will train people, get them the seeds and fertiliser they need, using microfinance loans, and guarantee to buy from them in bulk, we might have ourselves a really workable income generation project. I would need to know that I could sell or use all the produce, of course. That would be critical. But I'm already beginning to see how it might be possible to create the conditions for greater prosperity here, based on helping Siboti's residents to make the most of what they have.

'So, Mr Ken, how are you going to help us escape poverty? How can it be done?'

People are clearly eager to know more, so I ask for half a dozen volunteers to come up and join Mama Jayne, Kizito and me at the front. There's something I want to show them. I grab a notebook and go quickly down the line, noting down the names and occupations of each of the volunteers. Then I shuffle them round into a suitable running order and begin my explanation.

The first man in line is Titus. He grows chillies to sell. In the chit-chat before the meeting began, he's already told me that what he needs most is a steady market and a fair price for his produce.

'OK, Titus,' I say, turning to the crowd. 'This is how it will work. Let's say I've found a businessman in Nairobi who sells chilli spiced chicken to the big supermarkets. He needs a regular supply of high-quality chillies and he's said he will buy large quantities from the farmers here in Siboti.'

I take a 100-shilling note from my pocket and hand it to Titus.

'This 100 shillings is part of his first payment to Siboti's farmers. So it's new money coming into Siboti from outside, and this is your share.'

Titus looks pleased.

'OK. Now, Titus, are you a good husband?' I ask.

To my surprise, there is a sudden outburst of hilarity in the crowd. Maybe Titus isn't the world's greatest husband. I didn't think the question was all that funny, but our audience obviously knows a thing or two that I don't.

'All right. Never mind. You don't have to answer that. Just tell me, now you've got this money, will you be giving it to your wife to buy food for your family?'

There's another ripple of laughter and I hear one or two sceptical comments from Titus's friends and neighbours, but he looks solemn.

Yes, he says, that's just what he would do. He'd give the money to his wife straightaway for the kids' food.

'So let's pretend this lady is your wife,' I say, ushering forward Aichene Sumuli, a short, confident woman who looks as if she'd eat Titus for breakfast. Aichene has already told me that she's a seamstress and that it's her sewing machine that brings in a little extra for her family.

Titus, who seems a little reluctant to get involved with this formidable woman, quickly hands her the 100-shilling note.

'Now, Aichene, do your kids like tomatoes?' I ask. She nods vigorously. 'Let's give them all a treat. I want you to use the 100 shillings to buy a box of tomatoes from Dorcus here.'

Aichene does the deal and hands the money over to Dorcus, who grows tomatoes in one corner of her family's smallholding. There's not much of anything to spare in her life, but Dorcus would dearly love to get her hair done, for the first time in months. She wants to spend the money to go and see Rose, the best hairdresser in Siboti.

'Go on. You've earned it. Treat yourself,' I say. Even though we're only acting this out, there's a huge, wide grin on Dorcus's face as she turns to give the 100 shillings to Rose. I'm struck, as so often in Siboti, by the gleaming Hollywood-white teeth that make these smiles so infectious and disarming. How do men and women who have never been near a dentist in their lives – and whose diet is dictated purely by what happens to be available – have such wonderful teeth?

The crowd likes the idea of Dorcus enjoying the unusual luxury of a proper hairdo. Rose is quite a local star and she acknowledges the applause, bowing briefly to left and right as she takes the money.

'What are you going to do with the 100 shillings, Rose?' I ask.

'Oh, that's easy. I'll be going to visit my best friend, Reginalda, who I haven't seen for many months. She lives a long way away, so I'll be getting George here to take me there on his *piki-piki*.'

George Mateyui, the next in line, is a farmer who owns his own motorbike and makes his living by running a *piki-piki* taxi service. He'll be happy to carry Rose up hill and down dale to see her friend and to wait and bring her back, if it takes all day.

Especially, in fact, if it takes all day. George likes the days when he can get out on the motorbike and earn some proper cash. The rest of the time, his usual transport for trundling around Siboti is a battered pushbike that's seen much better days. The old boneshaker urgently needs a visit to the little workshop behind James Mobutu's house, so that's where George will be spending the money. James is the last of my volunteers and he's a man who can keep any clapped-out old bicycle going year after year. When he gets the 100 shillings from George, James explains, he'll be putting it towards a new school uniform for his daughter, courtesy of Aichene and her trusty sewing machine.

I look around at the crowded meeting. They get it. Our little enactment has made the point in clear, straightforward terms that everyone can understand.

The people in the audience can see for themselves that the original 100 shillings of new money has gone round and round within the local economy, giving Aichene her tomatoes, Dorcus her haircut, Rose her *piki-piki* fare, George his bicycle overhaul and James's daughter part of her new uniform. That single 100-shilling note has been passed from hand to hand and helped a lot of different people earn some cash and get what they want for themselves and their families.

Eventually, of course, the money will be lost to the outside world (perhaps when somebody uses it to take a *matatu* ride into Bungoma). But in its wake there will be a lot of extra business activity that would never have occurred without the 100 shillings of outside money that has been brought into the area. The new money will generate real growth in the local economy, with a direct positive effect on living standards.

There is a lot of nodding and smiling and some laughter. I look back over my shoulder at James. He's the very picture of innocence, so I know something's going on.

'Ah, right. I think I'll have my 100 shillings back now, James, if that's OK.'

He grimaces, shrugs, mimes a tear or two and hands me back the money.

'So what have we seen here? How much new money from outside did we bring into this area?'

'A 100 shillings,' chorus the massed ranks in the packed churchyard.

'And how many business transactions happened in total?

'Five or six? That's right. And what's the total value of all those business transactions? Yes. Five hundred shillings was spent in this community by *other* people because of the hundred shillings that one farmer earned by selling his chillies through our project to a company in Nairobi. A lot of good things can happen here when new money comes in and then goes round like that.'

A 100 shillings isn't a fortune, of course. My ambition is to get every adult in Siboti up to an annual income of $1000.

'You will begin with a contract to grow cash crops for this Siboti project. Those who do well will become High Achievers. Then I'll know who is serious about escaping from extreme poverty. The high achievers will have extra opportunities to make money, and more privileges. More education for you and your family, and a recommendation to the bank to finance irrigation kits and other things you need.'

I can see this is going down well.

'The High Achievers who make $500 with our project will become silver members. We will help these serious farmers go on to the final stage, gold medal status, which will mean they'll make $1000 per year with us. That's 85 000 shillings.'

After the initial gasp, there's a few seconds' excited chatter and then the meeting falls oddly silent. Given that the average low-income family in this area earns about $300 a year, it's clear why. People look stunned, as if they can't conceive of ever earning that much money. Then they turn to me with a new light in their eyes. Some look disbelieving, others almost joyful. What might it mean to them, for their children, for their future prosperity? Am I a madman or am I talking sense?

'If the farmers of Siboti are serious about working with me and my team, I promise I will try to create new opportunities for everyone who lives here.'

I look at the crowd around me, and I know I have their ear.

'This is real,' I say. 'I know precisely how much external money our project will need to bring into Siboti to allow everyone at this meeting to make 85 000 shillings a year. Do you think we can make it?'

'Yes, we can make it,' the cry goes up.

Another pause. A woman's voice rings out, strong and clear.

'With God's help, we can make it.'

With every fibre of my being, I believe I can do my part to make this work. Will they do their part? What do I know? But I have to believe we are really on to something. It should be possible to get a project going here that will help people lift themselves out of extreme poverty once and for all.

After the meeting, I'm riding my rented motorbike down Siboti Hill, in the bright afternoon light, the sunshine hot on my arms.

I'm happy, almost ecstatic, just to be alive and doing what I'm doing. The goal has to be to raise these wonderfully warm local people out of extreme poverty, to elevate them to a basic level of prosperity which will enable them to live with the dignity and security enshrined in the UN's Millennium Development Goals. After all the pain of the last few years I'm doing something meaningful with my life. It feels amazing.

A U2 song starts up in my brain, and Bono's voice is ringing in my head.

'EL-EV-A-TION.'

Why fight it? I'm not the world's greatest singer, but I love this song. I pull down the visor of my helmet to muffle my voice and shield the countryside from my euphoric shrieking as I give it all I've got.

'EL-EV-A-TION.'

I've never really thought about that song's lyrics before. I'm not even sure they make any kind of sense. But that one word certainly means a lot to me now.

The song is for me, at this moment, as much as it is for the people of Siboti. I am elevating myself in many ways here, too. We're all in this together.

I belt out my own version…

'I know now why I'm here'

'EL-EV-ATION'

'Oooh-ooh. Oooh-ooh-ooh. Oooh-ooh. Oooh-ooh-ooh.'

'EL-EV-A-TION'

7

Water is life

'In Kenya women are the first victims of environmental degradation, because they are the ones who walk for hours looking for water, who fetch firewood, who provide food for their families.'

Wangari Maathai, Nobel Peace Prize Winner 2004

'Do you know about the boreholes?' Kizito asks me the next day.

'Boreholes? What boreholes?'

'We have boreholes for water here, Ken. Ten of them. Only they don't work.'

I simply don't have the money – nor the permissions – to replace the inadequate pipes that had been laid for miles to supply the big blue unused tank I've been shown. But maybe I can do something to get these boreholes working again.

I've already seen for myself how women and children spend hours every day carrying water, walking long distances, trudging back with buckets on their heads, or carrying five-litre jerrycans, and then turning round to go back and do it all over again. A family will usually need twenty litres a day for drinking, cooking, washing and other purposes, so that's potentially four round trips to the river or the waterhole. It's a momentous waste of time and effort, and it's something, I realise, that I can get to grips with straightaway.

For once, though, Kizito's information is not precisely accurate. Only nine of the ten are completely useless. The tenth borehole still manages to produce a reluctant, erratic trickle that's enough for just a handful of families.

Nearly thirty years ago, I discover, the government of Finland had co-operated with the Kenyan authorities to organise and fund the digging of ten boreholes and provide simple, robust manual pumps to bring the water to the surface. They didn't have to go very deep, as there is plenty of water in aquifers just a few metres down, and soon Siboti had the benefit of the best safe water supply for miles around.

But then, one by one, over the years, the pumps had begun to fail. For the last few years, there has only been the one borehole still in use. From what Kizito tells me, the general attitude seems to have been that if everyone waited patiently enough, the Finns might come back and get the pumps working again. But the Finns have never returned, so getting these boreholes back into action might offer a good opportunity for me to be seen to be getting things moving for the community.

Fixing ten boreholes and replacing the pumps will cost maybe $50,000. But getting the water flowing again will be a big step forward. The sale of my house in London is finally going through and I feel safe enough to eat into my savings to fund the boreholes and pumps. Perhaps a thousand families can be freed from the daily grind of walking miles to fetch water and will be able to spend their time productively tending their crops. So there will be a direct economic impact on the community. And if I insist that the contractor I choose uses local Siboti labour to re-dig the boreholes and lines them with locally kilned red bricks to stop the sides falling in, that will provide a few jobs, at least for a short time. Borehole water doesn't have to be boiled, unlike the dirty, muddy water the women have been carrying back from the streams, and that will save time and resources, too, as a lot less firewood will need to be collected. People's daily lives will take a turn for the better – and I will have the quick win I'm looking for.

It still bugs me, though, that these boreholes have been left in that state for so long.

'Water is life' is a phrase you hear every day in Kenya, but it seems that no one has taken the initiative to get the water supply in Siboti up and running again. I'm used to working with Brits, Americans and Europeans, and they would surely have got something organised to fix a problem like this for themselves before now. Can you imagine a bunch of Germans sitting around, hoping that the charitable Finns might reappear one day to sort out the wells and mend the pumps? They'd find some way of sharing the cost, and they'd just get on and get it done.

On one level, their sheer, dogged perseverance is admirable. But on another, it makes me want to scream: 'It doesn't have to be like this!'

I realise, though, that any new pumps I provide are no more likely to last for ever than the ones the Finns installed. If I refurbish them, I'll need to get local people to take responsibility for the boreholes and the pumps, so that they feel they own them and are able to move quickly to fix any problems before they get expensive.

'Life's hard. You just have to persevere,' I hear people say.

But, in this case, the persevering is effectively delegated to the women. 'Delegated perseverance' is part of a woman's lot, and the men don't seem to be in any great hurry to share this particular burden. So it makes sense to try to create a structure where it is the women who are actually in charge of the new water pumps.

Over a lunchtime soda, perched on a bench by a local market stall, Mama Jayne comes up with an inspired suggestion. We should try to persuade the women to set up a neighbourhood water committee that can run each borehole. These committees could collect a tiny fee – it would only need to be 20 shillings a month, about quarter of a US dollar – from each of the hundred or so families who will use the pump. That way there'd be about $25 a month going into a maintenance fund for each of the pumps – not a fortune, but enough, as the reserves built up, to deal with all but the most catastrophic breakdowns. It's the women who will be around the wells most of the time, so they are the people who are best placed to check that everyone who uses the water pays the fee. And because they are the ones who will feel the immediate benefit of having a good water supply on hand, without the need to spend hours fetching water from far away, they will understand that this is 20 shillings a month well spent, even for the poorest families. They will be collecting the money, managing the pumps and taking the decisions.

This is starting to sound good. We will get every one of the hundred or so members of each water group to vote in elections for the committee, which will consist of a chairperson, a secretary and a treasurer.

We try the idea out on Kizito's mum and her friends over tea at her house the next afternoon, to see if they think it will work. They love it, but they suggest that each group should also have an elected water pump attendant.

These water pump attendants can take on the routine task of locking the pump handle every night and unlocking it every morning, so there will be no opportunity for outsiders to come along and help themselves to water without contributing to the maintenance fund. To give the right prestige and authority, they want the water pump attendant to be an elected member of the committee. We all agree and drink more tea.

To me, the most sensitive and critical role on each local committee will be that of the treasurer. Treasurers will look after the money, something that has never normally been done by women in this society. This may well turn out to be a sensitive issue. If a treasurer's husband tells his wife, 'Money is men's business – you've got to hand the money over to me and I'll look after it', the woman has to be empowered to stick to her guns and resist that pressure. I will need to make sure we have full support from the community leaders on the big steering committee – the Chief, the two assistant chiefs and the forty-two village elders – as this is an innovation that some of the men will possibly see as undermining their authority and status within the family.

I line up a steering committee meeting where the elders will be able to talk about the plan and raise any problems or concerns they have about it. The date is set and I wait, fingers crossed, to see how many of the elders will turn up and what level of opposition there'll be to what I'm proposing.

In the back of my mind, of course, this isn't just about water. I've got my own undeclared agenda in the background here, to do with another of the UN Millennium Development Goals – moving towards gender equality. For the economic side of the Siboti project to be a success, we will need the women in the community to start taking on new income-earning projects in the future – trying out alternative crops, for example, or setting up beehives and producing honey. All the most successful microfinance projects I've studied have mobilised the untapped potential of women in traditional societies, and I have already seen for myself how hard these women are prepared to work to support their families. I can see this structure of ten women's groups built around the boreholes forming the basis for all sorts of other activities that have nothing to do with water, from setting up new micro-businesses to delivering financial education and advice about HIV/AIDS and other health problems.

I hope I'm not naive enough to think it would be wise, or even right, to come blundering in like some nineteenth-century missionary trying to impose my European perspectives on the people of Western Kenya 'for their own good'. But that risk is in fact very real and present. Provoking a backlash from Siboti's disgruntled males would virtually guarantee the failure of the whole project, and it would probably do the women no favours either. Any progress we can make on this front will have to be gradual and based on a general agreement that what we are doing benefits everyone, men and women alike.

I'm hoping for a big turnout of elders for the steering committee meeting. It will be my opportunity to talk and listen and fine-tune my planning. The Chief keeps reassuring me that everything will go well, but I'm definitely getting nervous about it. When I wake up on the morning of the meeting, I realise this is going to be a make-or-break day. If the elders aren't interested enough to attend, or if they argue fiercely against the idea of forming the local committees and putting the women in charge of the pumps, it's going to be a major setback.

We gather in a large mud hut beside St Peter's church in the middle of Siboti. Almost all the elders are there, and as they listen to what I'm proposing, their interest is definitely sparked.

'So I'm suggesting we give the women the opportunity to look after the pumps,' I announce. 'After all, they're the ones who usually collect the water.'

After Kizito has translated my words, I look around at the men's weathered faces. A couple of them nod. Some of them glance at each other but nobody raises his hand to object. They lean on their sticks and wait for more.

'I believe the women will do a good job,' I continue. They will look after the water pumps and they will look after the money. No one will cheat the families when the local women are in charge. The women will know if they do, and they will talk.'

This seems to strike a chord. There is a murmur as the men turn to their neighbours for a brief exchange of views. Then they turn back to me and the Chief nods.

'Yes,' he says. 'This is good. Thank you, Mr Ken.'

Now the men show toothy grins and more of them are nodding.

We wait as the elders discuss the proposal further. There are a lot of questions, laboriously translated for me by Kizito, which is fair enough, but everyone seems to appreciate that getting all ten boreholes working again can do nothing but good for the whole community.

'Great,' I say. 'Should we proceed?'

'Yes, Yes' they respond.

I can hardly stop smiling. Part of me is astonished that no one objects to the formation of the women's groups to look after the water. This is a world where patriarchy is alive and flourishing. It feels like a mini victory. Kizito, too, is happy.

'You see, Ken,' he says, beaming. 'We need you here.'

We've got the green light to go ahead. It's thrilling. Now all we have to do is make it real.

Over the next few days, I take the first steps. I'm trying to find the right contractor to work with us on the boreholes, and I'm meeting all kinds of charlatans and bullshitters and receiving all kinds of different quotes for doing the work. But I strike it lucky when I get a quote from Joseph Wakesa. His numbers make sense and I like him immediately. He runs an established construction company and he's done a lot of wells and boreholes. I can see he doesn't seem to exaggerate or overpromise, and I think I'll be happy dealing with him.

As far as I can see, Wakesa is straight. But he's something of an exception, as the construction industry seems to be riddled with sharp practice. At the top of the heap are the cement barons, who include some of Kenya's richest multimillionaires. They are sitting pretty, as everything needs cement. From roads and buildings and other government infrastructure projects to building a village school or lining the walls of a newly dug well, cement is always the first essential. It's the same throughout the developing world. As soon as rural societies start to move from mud huts to brick-built houses, cement becomes a key element, the route to wealth, power and influence for those who are in a position to profit from it. The cement bosses rule the roost. Many are tied in with the politicians, often enjoying lucrative positions as monopoly suppliers.

At the next level down from the cement barons and their cosy political relationships, there are the distributors and local suppliers – and, no doubt, another web of connections with local politicians and administrators. From top to bottom, the construction industry is a minefield, full of traps for the unwary and problems that can only be resolved by paying the right person at the right time. I don't know how Joseph Wakesa navigates his way through all these complications, and maybe I don't want to know. I'm just delighted to see how fast his preparations for re-digging the wells, re-cementing the walls and installing new pumps are moving ahead.

My next move is to offer Kizito a job. His energy, honesty, local knowledge and cheery good humour are just what I'm going to need. I've got the blessing of Mama Jayne, who is sorry to lose him but believes this is a great opportunity for him to spread his wings and show what he can do.

Kizito is the first person I've ever employed on my own account in almost thirty years of working, so it's a strange feeling for me.

I've bought him a motorbike like mine. It's just a little TSA Star with an 80cc engine, but it's cheap (and reliable) and a huge status symbol as well as a practical tool for getting round our patch. Together, we bump and skid our way around Siboti, visiting every one of the disused boreholes, explaining to the local women that we need to talk to everyone who will use them when they're repaired and promising to come back at a particular time two days later to explain the plan.

When we return, it's the same story at every stop. Whatever time we've said, the women don't begin to turn up until an hour after that. It's nearer two hours after the specified time before we have everyone there. But this isn't a sign of opposition – or even lack of interest. Once the women are assembled, there is plenty of enthusiasm and they ask some pretty penetrating questions. Why am I insisting on putting the wells in the hands of the women, rather than the men, the traditional heads of the families? Why must people pay 20 shillings a month, and who will the boreholes belong to? Does the plan really have the full support of the Chief and the elders?

These women are hearing the details of the plan for the first time. They are mainly from the older generation – the ones who grew up before 'free' primary education came to this part of the country. Many can't read or write, and can only speak the local Bukusu dialect, with a little Swahili and no English at all. I talk to them in English, telling them about the Siboti project and how repairing the boreholes and installing new pumps is an important first step, and they listen and nod politely, without understanding a word I say. Then Kizito steps up and translates for me. There's a buzz and a chatter as he's talking, and when he's finished everyone's smiling and asking him for more information about how it will all work.

I step forward. 'We've got full backing from the Chief and all the elders. Each of the new pumps will be owned and operated by a local women's group, so you must get together and form a committee and elect a chairperson, a secretary, a treasurer and a water pump supervisor. We'll put your groups in touch with the manager at the Equity Bank in Bungoma, who will set you up with a bank account for the water fund. Each committee will own its pump and the 20 shillings a month each family chips in will ensure that there's always money available for any repairs or maintenance jobs that are needed.'

Taking a seat on the bench, I watch the women's expressions change while Kizito translates. They are surprised, I can tell. This is a tense moment for me. It's a deeply traditional society in this part of Kenya, and these women are not used to being put in charge of their own destiny. I know some of these women are bound to face resistance from their husbands, who usually control the money.

As Kizito ends with a flourish the women are hushed. They seem overawed at the idea of being put in charge of it themselves. After a short pause, one woman raises her hand.

'So we can tell our husbands to keep their hands off the money,' she asks.

'And no individual man can take over,' says another. 'Is that right?'

'That's right,' I say.

The women are nodding. Some are smiling and shaking their heads. And then an older woman at the back starts clapping. It's infectious. Soon they are all clapping, and some women at the front start cheering. The audacity of Mama Jayne's idea seems to delight them. They whoop, they sing, they hold hands. There's no doubt about it. They get it. They want to do it. We're winning.

It's the same at each of the boreholes. Ten boreholes, ten enthusiastic groups of women – first disbelieving ('Are we allowed to do this?'), then uncertain ('Are we able to do this?'), finally joyful ('Yes, we can!'). As we move on and leave them to organise the elections to the water pump committees, I can tell there's something happening here that has nothing to do with pumps or boreholes or sorting out the water supply. Setting the project up this way is empowering these women to take collective responsibility for both the pumps and the money. For many of them, though, this is the first time they've been given authority and put in charge. As Kizito and I ride off into the sunset, I just know they're going to make it work.

* * *

Within a few weeks, Joseph Wakesa has completed his task, I have parted with $50 000 and Siboti has ten newly-working boreholes. If each of these wells is serving a hundred families and there is an average of six people per family, that's 6000 lives that have been made easier already and potentially more productive too. You see people carrying the five-litre jerry cans to the boreholes to stock up on water. Some of them, even the little kids, might carry one of these cans a long way, but it's a start. People are excited and impressed. There's a momentum building up in support of the whole Siboti project. With the boreholes and the pumps, I have the early win that I needed.

It's still only a few months since that seminar in Florida that set my life off in this strange new direction. But it's all taking shape remarkably fast. I've found Siboti. I've got a plan that everyone has signed up to and a steering group of village elders that genuinely represents the community. I've got ten working boreholes as evidence of my ability to deliver what I promise. Most importantly, though, we are building a bond of trust that lays a real foundation for the big work ahead.

8

Education, education, education

'Education is the most powerful weapon which you can use to change the world.'

Nelson Mandela

Bungoma's Rickshaw Hotel is not the sort of place you'd choose for your honeymoon. Or for a weekend. Or even for your evening meal, if you could help it.

The dining room has scuffed and peeling walls, a makeshift reception desk in the corner and six battered tables. In the corner there is a big chest freezer, with a few frozen fish and a couple of packs of supermarket burgers, and a glass-fronted Coca-Cola fridge, full of double-size Cokes and Fantas and bottles of Tusker beer. A delicate aroma of chip fat and Calor gas wafts in from the grubby, blackened kitchen, glimpsed from the corridor as you make your way to the indescribably squalid bathroom. The Rickshaw is not for the fainthearted.

But it's the best Bungoma has to offer. Two new hotels are being built for business travellers, but they're not ready yet. And I can't wait. I can't carry on staying at Haven Kenya. It's out on the far side of Bungoma from Siboti and the road is just too pot-holed and treacherous to risk at night. To ride back safely before dark, I'd have to leave Siboti by 5 p.m., and that would take too much of a bite out of my working day. Like it or lump it, the Rickshaw Hotel is my new home. At least the mattress is clean, and they change the sheets twice a week. My room has a sofa, a coffee table and even a hot shower, power cuts permitting – all welcome luxuries after my mud hut at Haven Kenya. I negotiate a rate of $75 a week, excluding meals. Definitely excluding meals.

I'm lying in my room one night, watching the ceiling fan stir the humid air, and trying to work out what I can do to help improve access to schooling for the children of Siboti. In theory, free primary education has been available to all since 2003, but we now know that uniform and fees together come to about $50 per child. If the parents or guardians can't afford that, the child won't be going to school.

Here, the children who are least likely to get access to that vital $50 are the orphans. Thanks to HIV/AIDS, malaria, TB and various respiratory diseases, the area has a huge number of orphaned children. I've already met some of them, including the little girl who recited her moving poems at that very first public meeting. I can still remember the sadness and anger in that young poet's voice as she told her story of life without her mother, brought up by a distant uncle's reluctant wife, in a household where she has no rights and no one to stand up for her.

But this young girl did at least have school as part of her life. She had school friends, teachers who took an interest in her and, with education, some hope of a future. She had won a local poetry competition. What else might she be capable of winning? One thing is certain, though – if she had remained at home and not been to school, she would have been winning nothing.

When I think back on my own life, it's obvious that it would have been very different if I hadn't had the opportunities offered by Ireland's flexible and forgiving education system. After leaving school, I had spent three years treading water, going nowhere, frustrated, unfulfilled and lethargic. For me, the crucial turning point had come when I signed up for night school classes, three evenings a week, that helped me retake my school-leaving exams and get some decent grades. That was what had led to my degree course at Trinity College Dublin, and a good career, first in IT, then in project management and eventually in the rarefied world of international investment banking. There's no doubt that my path from Dublin to London and beyond – and now on to the remote reaches of Western Kenya – was opened up by that one decision to go back into education and try to make something of my life.

I was no orphan, of course. I had loving, conscientious parents who worked hard to provide everything I needed. And, like most children, I took their efforts for granted. When I was eight years old and told to bring money into school for a class project, my friend Martin 'Winker' Watson said he was scared to ask his parents for the cash.

'Money doesn't grow on trees,' he told me, gravely.

It was news to me. As far as I knew, if you needed something for school, you asked for it and you got it. You didn't ask for anything else, because it wasn't there, but for school there was never a problem getting the money. I hadn't realised it might be hard for my father to find it, but find it he always did.

I can't do anything to give the orphans of Siboti that kind of supportive family background. But education, even at the most basic level, will help ensure these orphans have some options in their lives.

The next day, Kizito and I hit the roads and laneways again, on our new blue motorcycles, to go round Siboti's nine primary schools. At each stop, we hear the same story. Every school tells us that more than 100 students have not returned for the new school year. Some pupils, but not many, will have moved away. Some will have switched schools, but, again, not many. Most of the missing children will have dropped out because of the school fees. When families with three or four children are hit by illness or failed crops, they often just run out of cash. So it's quite common for children who've had one or two years' schooling – especially the girls – to be pulled out of school. And once they've dropped out, they rarely go back.

On our way from one school to the next, we are flagged down by a group of men. I recognise them as village elders and the Chief. We stop, exchange greetings and talk.

'They're delighted to see you and like what we are doing,' Kizito translates for me, as I shake various hands.

The Chief steps forward, dressed as ever in khaki trousers and shirt.

'You're behind our community,' he says, in English. 'We are all so grateful and we thank you for your vision. You have a great vision for our people.'

The other men nod and gather round us in a respectful horseshoe.

'Thank you so much,' I tell him. 'We are very pleased that this project is welcome here.'

The Chief barely pauses before he is off on a monologue about my 'kind heart'.

'Mr Ken is going to save us from poverty,' he announces.

A couple of the men clap me on the shoulder and offer thanks again and again for 'your vision, your energy, your generosity'. It's too much. I am happy to plan, to chat and joke with them but this lavish praise makes me feel very uncomfortable.

Kizito shrugs, still smiling, and I'm reminded that his status is now higher because of his association with me. I don't want to be seen as the bringer of miracles, though. I can't wave a magic wand and transform this community.

'Actually what I really want to know is what they think about the school dropout problem,' I tell Kizito, keen to return to business.

'Can you ask them?'

I listen as he translates and the Chief listens carefully to the new question. The elders confer and then explain that there are any number of social reasons and family problems that prevent orphaned children going to school. The guardians are often biased against spending money on the girls, and the orphans are almost always last in the pecking order when it comes to school fees and first in line when it comes to working on the land. These children may well be the most vulnerable and the ones who are most in need of help to get into school, but actually getting them enrolled will be problematic. Even when they're going to school, there will always be a tendency for them to drop out again mid-year.

Their analysis is fascinating – these guys have their finger on the pulse of their community – and I don't interrupt. But the elders' conclusion is blunt. 'Steer clear of helping the kids who have never been to school,' says the Chief, 'and target the ones who are accustomed to being at school and have recently dropped out. Don't waste your money on children who will probably drop out again.'

I look round at the men. This is a very different world from the one I know. Poverty is endemic here. The elders are brutal in their judgements, but maybe they're right. In the final analysis, I am not a social worker, just a project manager aiming to get the most out of a limited budget.

Maybe getting some of the brightest and most promising of these reluctant dropouts back into the classroom would indeed provide the best return, in terms of educational outcomes. Forget the no-hopers – invest in the brightest – that's what these elders, these guardians of Siboti's future, recommend. It's harsh. If I had grown up here, what chance would I have had? I didn't excel until way after I had left school. What happens to the bright kids whose parents can't afford to send them to school in the first place, or to those late developers who would flourish with the right support? We complain about the lack of educational resources in the West, which can vary from region to region, but here....

I am torn. I'd like to help everyone, but with limited resources, who do you choose? At moments like this, I desperately want to believe that one day I might be able to influence and direct the use of far bigger resources. Perhaps that means getting involved in politics, or a large charitable foundation, or a multilateral institution. Perhaps my corporate career in finance, the long years of organising and running complex global projects and this Siboti experience will turn out to be a training, a preparation for a more senior, more challenging role in the world. But I know hard decisions would still have to be taken, just like today, so I turn back to the matter in hand.

'I think we need more information before we decide what to do,' I tell the Chief. He nods, and before he can send any more praise my way, Kizito and I say goodbye to these no-nonsense elders and ride on towards the next school, kicking up plumes of dust from the red clay road.

After dropping in on a couple more schools, and chatting to the teachers, we are seeing a clear pattern emerge. There are up to five times more children dropping out than we can hope to fund to return to school. A quarter of these children may be orphans – and that's still way more than we can afford to fund. Of these, some are children who have shown great promise. So, rather tragically, with such a huge pool of deserving cases to choose from, it is quite easy to identify the group to invest in – bright, orphaned recent school dropouts.

When we get back to base, Kizito and I come up with a name for this newest sub-project – 'Orphans Welcome Again'. He calls each of the head teachers and sets up appointments for us to make more formal visits to enlist their help.

The nine heads are all enthusiastic. They will each come up with a list of twenty-five orphans they know from previous years, the kids they believe are the ones who most need or deserve to get back into school. Some of the head teachers ask for a bit of flexibility to allow them to pick a small number of orphans who are less bright but have potential, and who really need to be at school because of abusive treatment at home.

'It's good to know that schools are taking an interest in the pupils' home life,' I say to Kizito as we leave the last school. 'What happens when children are being mistreated at home?'

He shrugs. 'People will know it,' is all he says.

A few days later, the lists are in. As I sit looking at the nine sheets, each with twenty-five names, I realise, not for the first time, how easy it is to underestimate the complexities and consequences of any action you take in Siboti. The orphans will need school uniforms, like all the other children, if they are not to stick out like a sore thumb. They'll need some of life's little luxuries, too – like shoes, for example. So the budget will cover footwear, too, but even providing a basic pair of plimsolls is not without drama.

One day, I'm with Kizito while he's measuring an orphan girl for a pair of shoes. She's been brought into our office by her grumpy old uncle, who's bringing her up after the death of her parents, and he has a face like thunder. He's muttering and chuntering under his breath.

'Shoes!' he's saying. 'I don't know. Children want everything these days. Shoes, indeed. We never had shoes. Never needed them. Kids today, they don't know they're born,' he grumbles in Swahili – or words to that effect.

It's rude to laugh, so I don't. Not, at least, until the uncle has stalked off with the orphan girl in tow. Just substitute the word 'iPhones' for 'shoes' and you've got a scene that could be played out in Dublin or Surrey or Long Island any day of the week.

In practice, it turns out that welcoming the orphans back is going to mean a lot of detailed logistics. You've got children of all shapes and sizes, male and female, and nine different uniforms to sort out. That's a lot of measuring and listing – a green jumper for that boy, medium trousers for this one, size four shoes for that girl and a small-size navy dress over there.

We arrange to get all the jumpers, at a good price, from a Kenyan knitting firm in Eldoret that rejoices in the name of Ken-Knit. I rejoice, too, as that's exactly what my sister always calls me, in her soft Dublin accent.

'Kennit, will I pick you up at the airport?' she'd say to me.

With the dresses for the girls, there's an opportunity to make the money work several times over within the local Siboti economy.

Each dress costs about $15, for the material and the labour. So I find a local tailor in Siboti and tell him I can give him an order for over a hundred school dresses, if he gives me a good price and agrees to use local women as seamstresses to do the sewing work. The tailor makes a profit and the piece-work money he pays out to the women boosts their family incomes, which will then be spent on buying food and other essentials from local stallholders in the market. The shillings go round and round and every dollar will be recycled several times and help several different traders in the local economy.

It takes a fair amount of effort all round, but within a few weeks we have two hundred and twenty-five children back in school and back on track for a better future.

The Chief is all smiles. He believes that schooling for the children of Siboti is the key to raising living standards throughout the community.

'You know, Mr Ken,' he tells me, 'you can give a man a million shillings, but unless you give him knowledge, he will soon have nothing.'

So I'm happy, and the Chief's happy, and the children are happy, too. But not everyone is quite as satisfied with the new arrangements. At the next *barassa* meeting, a few weeks later, I hear the first rumblings of dissent. There's an undercurrent of grumbling about how the beneficiaries of the Orphans Welcome Again programme were selected.

One or two of the elders are keen to take me aside and tell me that the lists of eligible orphans that the head teachers had given me may not be quite as sound as I'd assumed. Some children who had been nominated by the heads seem to have more parents than I'd have expected an orphan to have. There is a suspicion that some of the teachers may have been fiddling the lists to favour their own friends and relatives.

'You should have asked us,' these elders say. 'We know the people and their family circumstances. Some of these "orphans" you've helped back into school have a mother here in the village and a father who's away earning money in Nairobi. Next time, we'll help you put together a list of the real orphans.'

There's a language problem here, too, of which I had been completely unaware. Apparently the word 'orphan' is often used rather loosely to describe a child who has lost just one parent. If I want to direct my assistance towards the unfortunate children who have lost both parents, it seems I should use the more specific terms of 'double orphan' or 'full orphan' – not phrases I've ever come across before.

And there are some people in the community who are just bluntly jealous of the fact that money is being handed out and they are not getting any of it. One grim-faced couple feel particularly hard done by.

'Mr Ken,' the father complains. 'It's not fair. You're not being fair. Our children are orphans, too. Why don't you pay their school fees and give them uniforms?'

I don't want to get into an argument, but this kind of brass necking makes me cross. I turn away from the man. Next time, I'll wash my hands of the selection process and put it in the hands of the Chief and the elders, who know the ins and outs of each family's situation.

I'm pretty sure that some of them will be no more scrupulous about nominating the orphans than the head teachers – there will still be cousins and nephews who mysteriously appear on the lists, despite having a full set of parents – but perhaps it is impossible to completely avoid nepotism. At least this way I will be cementing my relationship with the community leaders, which will benefit the project as a whole.

In the end, knowing that some of the children are not wholly parentless doesn't worry me as much as I thought it would. Those who slipped through the net despite having one living parent are often likely to be little better off than the true orphans.

In fact, by any sane measure that I could come up with, virtually every child in Siboti would be a worthy recipient of the support offered by the scheme. When I stand back from the bickering about who should or should not have been on the orphans list, I realise that my stipulation that we should direct help towards the children with no parents at all is largely a matter of administrative and local political convenience. I decide it's simply not worth agonising over.

Instead of agonising, I recall the moment when I came across the statement by Edmund Burke, inscribed in stone in letters a foot high in the topiary garden of Cambridge University's Madingley Hall: 'Nobody could make a greater mistake than he who did nothing because he could do only a little.'

Looking from a Western perspective, it's all too easy to forget that writing wasn't invented to give us Shakespeare or Yeats or *Fifty Shades of Grey*, love letters and emails.

Knowledge is power. Being able to hold on to information, amend and update it in the light of experience and use it for your own purposes is one of the keys to controlling our destiny. It's an everyday miracle most of us probably take for granted. In Western Kenya, it can be the factor that shapes a family's life.

So, despite the so-minuscule-it-doesn't-even-register contribution that our Orphans Welcome Again scheme makes towards UN Millennium Development Goal No. 2 – universal access to primary education – we can do our little bit. For these expectant faces streaming into school, a little education has to be much better than no education at all.

'You can give a man a million shillings, but if you don't give him knowledge he will soon have nothing' the Chief said.

One million shillings? Well, I can't give the children that. But I can give a few of them the opportunity to learn to read, and with it, the chance to tap into the vast store of human knowledge that can help them for the rest of their lives.

9

The magnificent eight

'Only those who dare to fail greatly can ever achieve greatly'

Robert F. Kennedy

The overwhelmingly positive reaction at our first big community meeting, where I first told the people of Siboti why I had come and how I believed I could help them, is potentially a double-edged sword. The enthusiasm, the trust, the orphaned children and their poems, the readiness to believe that I had been sent to give them what they needed – it all adds up to a massive vote of confidence for the project. ('Are we going to let down God? No!') But it's also terrifying.

It gives me goose bumps just to think about the responsibility I've taken on. I have offered them hope and a vision of a better future, and they have signed up for that journey. I have privately set myself the task of tackling as many as possible of the UN's eight Millennium Development Goals for the 20 000 people of this remote rural Western Kenyan community. But how many of those Millennium Development Goals can I realistically target, even on this local level?

I should certainly be targeting Millennium Goal No. 1 – 'Eradicate extreme poverty and hunger'. OK, I may not eradicate it, but I can aim to alleviate it. The small print shows that the UN itself is also aiming to achieve significant alleviation by 2015, rather than complete eradication. The stated objective was to cut extreme poverty and hunger by half, within fifteen years. But supporting the people of Siboti to elevate themselves out of poverty and hunger will certainly be a big enough goal for me. If I can provide the impetus and energy, the training and the economic opportunities they need, they should be able to create new sources of income and begin the climb out of hand-to-mouth subsistence living. That would give them choices they've never had before, in terms of nutrition, healthcare, education, housing and security.

The UN's Millennium Goal No. 2 is to 'Achieve universal primary education'. I already know that although Kenya's government introduced free and compulsory primary school education for all in 2003 (and this had done a lot to raise the school attendance rate), the small supplementary fees charged by every school are often a hurdle that keeps children away. I can't tackle the whole issue of school dropouts, but we are already focusing on helping orphans back into school. That's a start.

Millennium Goal No. 3 – 'Promote gender equality and empower women' – is an area where I can aim to make some difference. I've gained some credibility among the women of Siboti as they start to benefit from the time savings that come from having the new water pumps. I've been thinking about how the ten women's groups that now own and manage the pumps provide a framework that can potentially be used in many other contexts. I am also interested in finding ways to get more girls into primary education.

Millennium Goal No. 4 ('Reduce child mortality rates', with a target of cutting deaths of under-fives by two-thirds) and Goal No. 5 ('Improve maternal health') will be harder to take on. Healthcare requires massive funding: that's just a fact. And the needs of the people of Siboti are huge. So what can I do with the limited budget I have?

Children are dying almost every day in this community of 20 000 – many of them from preventable health problems like malaria and diarrhoea. The impact on the families is devastating and so many of these deaths are avoidable. Diarrhoea? I mean, for God's sake. Clean water and cheap salt-and-sugar rehydration packs can cure that so easily. But parents in Siboti don't have the packs or, frequently, the clean water, and they often don't have the money to travel into town and pay a doctor. This is one area where it must be possible to make a big impact. No one dies of diarrhoea in Ireland, in Britain, or anywhere in the West, and no one should have to here. If we can bring in rehydration packs and use Haven Kenya's medical volunteers to teach the women's groups how to save dehydrated children's lives, I am sure we can cut the death toll from diarrhoea. That is doable.

The single greatest prevention technique to avoid deadly malaria among children in the developing world is simply to persuade them to sleep under a mosquito net. The UN and the big charities spotted this issue years ago and took action to do something about it. Millions of insecticide-treated mosquito nets were distributed in Africa, and the trucks came to Siboti, too, unloading bales of potentially life-saving netting. But, from what I can see, nobody seems to have responsibility for convincing people here to use the nets properly. People were told they should sleep under the nets, but they didn't do it. Adults didn't, because they believed an occasional dose of malaria was inevitable, a normal part of life. And most local people, living in mud huts with roofs of straw, didn't have beds. As a rule, they would sleep on a blanket on the floor, so there was nothing to attach a net to. And nobody got the mothers together in groups and explained to them that sleeping under these nets could actually save their children's lives.

Looking around me in Siboti now, I see mosquito nets being used as curtains. I see them being used to keep birds off crops. I've seen them being used as fishing nets. But I don't see them being used to protect people while they sleep.

Everywhere I look, it seems that the crucial final stage – dealing with the human factors – has fallen short. So maybe that is something I can tackle, working in partnership with Mama Jayne's Haven Kenya volunteers to educate mothers and persuade them that their children really would be safer sleeping under these nets.

The UN's global target was to slash maternity-related deaths by three-quarters, over the fifteen-year period. But here in Siboti, it is hard to know where to start. In this part of Kenya, traditional midwives, known as birth mothers, use folk techniques handed down from generation to generation, with little reference to modern medical practice. To be fair, the system mostly works pretty well, until there are complications. Whenever something goes wrong, though, the only hope is a hair-raising journey on the back of a motorbike to the hospital in Bungoma, where the long queues and unaffordable hospital fees mean few women end up getting the treatment they need. The result is often fatal for both mother and baby.

Might it help if I fund the purchase of an ambulance? It might, but who would run a community ambulance service, or maintain the vehicle and keep it on the road? And, anyway, the major challenge is not solely transport to hospital. It is the need for fewer serious emergencies in the first place, for medically trained people, regular check-ups and informed on-the-spot intervention, and there is little I can hope to do, with my limited resources, to change that. I have to be realistic.

Millennium Development Goal No. 6 – 'Combat HIV/AIDS, malaria and other diseases' – is different. The 'other diseases' that cause the most deaths round here are tuberculosis, pneumonia and respiratory diseases, often exacerbated by toxic fumes from lamps and cooking with charcoal inside people's homes. I do feel that I could do something to reduce lung disease, because just replacing those deadly paraffin lamps with cheap and practical solar-powered lighting would make a real difference – quite apart from reducing the danger of fires and the many horrible injuries inflicted by them. I could also arrange to educate people about the realities of malaria and HIV infection. I can't provide doctors and treatment centres, but I can probably partner with Haven Kenya to provide the education that will mean fewer people fall ill in the first place.

Malaria is tricky, though. There's a cultural dimension to it here. In Britain and Ireland, we tend to label every illness under the sun as flu. In Western Kenya, everything from a runny nose to a life-threatening sickness is usually put down to malaria.

'How are you, Kizito?'

'Thank you, Ken. I am fine. Just a little bit of malaria today, but my mama is making a big bowl of chicken soup, so I will soon be better.'

'Well, yes. Chicken soup does soothe just about every illness known to man, Kizito. I'm with you on that.'

I'm never going to get far in trying to address adult malaria in Siboti.

Kizito's mum's chicken soup might be just what I'd want if I was suffering from pneumonia or tuberculosis, the other major killers. But it won't cure them. Pneumonia needs antibiotics and TB needs multi-drug treatment over a period of weeks or months, so I'm not going to be in a position to do much about them. But maybe I can do something to reduce the local death toll from HIV/AIDS, where changing people's beliefs and behaviour can definitely save lives.

The myths that have grown up around HIV are a huge part of the problem. People in this part of Western Kenya generally think the infection can be transmitted by shaking hands with someone who has the disease. Worse, a widespread belief persists that AIDS can be cured by having sex with a virgin. This grotesque monster of all myths has led to the deaths of many young girls, despite government attempts at public health education. Mama Jayne's Haven Kenya charity has already developed a good HIV/AIDS education programme, so I reckon I should be able to organise regular meetings and events to spread the truth more widely within the community.

Even this is not going to be straightforward, though. I'm told we will only be able to talk to the women at these meetings. There won't be any men there.

'The men won't come, Ken,' Kizito explains. 'If they are seen at a meeting about AIDS, people will assume they're there because they are already infected and everyone will avoid them.'

'But we can explain, surely?'

'We can explain as much as we like, but I promise you there will not be any men at all at those meetings.'

If the men won't come to us, for fear of becoming social pariahs, we are going to have to find ways of getting out to them. We'll need to talk to them about HIV/AIDS at other gatherings that they are attending anyway. We'll explain the facts about AIDS at the big *barassa* meetings where we tell the community about our income generation projects. That way, people can hear the information they need to know, but there'll be no stigma attached.

As it turns out, the UN's target of arresting the spread and reducing the prevalence of HIV/AIDS will eventually prove to be one of the big Millennium Development Goal successes. At the turn of the twenty-first century, thirty million people in Africa were infected and one million a year were dying, while just ten thousand Africans were receiving treatment with the proper antiretroviral drugs. Now this deadly tide has finally turned, not least because of the major charitable foundations' successful efforts to negotiate affordable access to anti-retroviral drugs.

All I can really hope to do, in connection with the health-related Millennium Development Goals, is stick to some realistic aims, such as educating people about how to treat diarrhoea in babies, reduce the risk of malaria and HIV/AIDS, and spread awareness of nutrition-based life extension strategies for HIV sufferers.

I can contribute so little, compared with what's needed. So my plan has to be to help the people here earn enough money to access the healthcare and medications potentially available to them in Bungoma. That has to be my approach.

While the big players – the UN, the World Bank, governments around the world, Bill Clinton, Bill Gates, Bono and Geldof, Elton John and all the major institutions and charities – are busy pulling the big levers and getting the big stuff done in the field of healthcare, I will focus on the local goal of building incomes. If I can do that, I will be able to help the people of Siboti stretch upwards to reach the downward-stretching hands of the projects run by the big guys.

Millennium Development Goal No. 7 is about ensuring environmental sustainability. There are various aspects to this, shoved rather uncomfortably together in the original UN documents. As well as setting out to reverse the loss of forests and other environmental resources, this goal aims to halve the number of people without access to safe drinking water or proper sanitation and improve the lives of 100 million slum dwellers.

People in Western Kenya are well aware of both the positive environmental impact and the practical usefulness of trees. In 2004, the Nobel Peace Prize was awarded to Wangari Maathai, the Kenyan environmentalist who formed the Green Belt Movement, which oversaw the planting of 30 million trees in Kenya from 1977 onwards. Rural families have always planted trees on their land, partly for shade and partly to provide firewood for cooking. But some in Siboti are now also planting them as a future cash crop. Tightly spaced in a one-metre grid pattern, the tall, slender trees grow branches and leaves only at the very top of the trunk. Deflecting growth energy into forming branches lower down would leave a tree shorter than its neighbours and unable to get the natural light it needs, so every tree inside the grid has to shoot up, straight as an arrow, just to survive.

Within seven years, this will give these local farmers a lucrative cash crop – a batch of budding electricity poles ready for sale to the national power company, for use in the huge task of bringing electricity to homes across Western Kenya. My effort towards Millennium Development Goal No. 7 is going to be twofold – encouraging people to plant more trees and providing access to clean water through the new boreholes and water pumps.

The last Millennium Development Goal, No. 8, is always going to be well beyond anything I can influence. It is all about international action by governments to help the world's poor through initiatives such as creating a fairer trading system, increasing overseas aid budgets and easing the crushing burden of the developing world's debt. I am aware of some big achievements in this area, such as the 2005 Gleneagles G8 Summit agreement on debt relief that followed the 'Make Poverty History' campaign, but there's no way I'm going to be able to make any direct contribution to this Goal 8 through my efforts in Siboti.

So there it is. I've looked at each of the eight Millennium Development Goals and worked out where and how I can have an impact on the lives of the people of Siboti. I should be able to address six of the eight MDGs, at the local level, in ways that will bring direct benefits. Even on this small scale, the challenges will be enormous. But all projects are difficult. And navigating through project difficulties is what I'm supposed to be good at.

So the next step is going to be to go through all the proper disciplines of project planning, so familiar to me from the last twenty years of my professional life. All the essentials for a big, complex project must be in place. The fact that this is a pragmatic, informal effort, taking place in a very different environment from my usual haunts, does not remove the need for clear thinking and a methodical, realistic plan. I need to work out what the risks are, what needs to be tackled first and how the various initiatives are likely to interdepend on each other.

I've been through this project planning process so many times before that all these aspects feel second nature to me. But getting it right always takes a lot of thought and concentration, and I know that my dingy hotel room in Bungoma, with its unpredictable power blackouts and unreliable bathroom plumbing, is not the ideal place to be working on this.

So I decide to grab my notes and laptop and head back to Nairobi, where I can relax for a few days, with good food and a proper bed and shower, and get my head round the master plan. In time I will come to refer to this plan as my Elevation Method for the alleviation of extreme poverty in rural Western Kenya.

The overnight bus to Nairobi takes about nine hours and there are only a couple of stops, at Eldoret and Nakuru. I'm wide awake thinking about everything and jotting down odd notes to myself. We reach Eldoret, stop briefly and then resume our slow, relentless progress. The miles roll by, and everyone else on the bus seems to have fallen asleep. I stare out of the window, watching as the occasional roadside village or petrol station looms up and disappears away again into the darkness. The night goes on forever, but still I don't feel like sleeping.

So it comes as a shock to me when we lurch to a halt, I open my eyes to dazzling sunlight and I realise we have arrived. This is it. Nairobi. Time to get going. I reach up to the shelf above my head for my laptop. And it's gone.

Shit. It had to have been stolen at Nakuru – that second stop.

I was awake for the first stop, at Eldoret, and the laptop was definitely still there then. I must have fallen asleep before Nakuru and someone – another passenger, or maybe someone who had sneaked onto the bus during the ten-minute stop – has helped themselves to my computer.

It's only a $500 laptop, I know. But it contains all my information and planning and it really gets to me. Is that all I am here? A *mzungu* whose role is to be robbed for the benefit of some nasty little urban sneak thief? I know that this one criminal is not in any way representative. The people I've been meeting in Siboti have been warm, generous, hardworking and honest. They've appreciated my good intentions and made me welcome. But this feels like a slap in the face.

Maybe I should have forced myself to stay awake. Maybe I should have made sure I held on to the laptop as I slept. Maybe I'm just too naive, too trusting, too keen to believe the best of everybody. Maybe I've got lessons to learn, if I'm going to stick it out here and do what I've come to do.

I spend two hours with the bus company people. Some of them are sympathetic, but they don't inspire confidence. I stand in their offices under the railway arches, filling out forms and asking them to go through their records. Who got off the bus at Nakuru? They don't know. Long-distance bus passengers must give their names and produce ID. But the IDs are often fake and almost all the tickets are bought with cash. What can we do, Mr King? These things happen. They point me in the direction of the police station, and after an hour I realise I'm wasting my breath. It is just a form-filling exercise. All the police do is say they'll get back to me. They aren't even interested in details of what happened.

I give up, head to the InterContinental hotel, pay for an early check-in and take a shower. That feels better. When I emerge again, into the hot sunlight, the streets are jammed with rush-hour traffic, the pavements thronged with hurrying pedestrians. I make my way to a big store on one of the main shopping streets, Haile Selassie Avenue, and pay an extortionate price for a new laptop with the software I need.

I won't pretend I always back up everything I put on my computer, (after all, only Jesus saves) because I don't and I hadn't, and I deserve to feel a complete idiot.

For the next few hours, I'm rushing round Nairobi like a blue-arsed fly, in and out of shops and government offices. I've planned this as a short and strictly functional trip and the time lost because of the stolen computer means I'm way behind schedule. I need a couple of days clear to focus on writing the Siboti plan before it's back on the overnight special to Bungoma. I'll really miss seeing my brother Alan, who is swapping his posting in Kenya for a new role in London. It's a shame our paths haven't crossed for longer. Having one of my brothers nearby has made a big difference to me even though I have been so busy that we haven't seen much of each other. Alan is pragmatic, a realist, and sometimes a valuable curb on my more impulsive tendencies.

Nairobi is usually a welcome break from the realities and discomforts of life in Siboti. This time I've been going flat out and I'll be relieved to get back. As I'm packing my things and heading for the bus station, I know there's no chance I'll stay awake on the bus. I'm going to make damn sure the new laptop and the rest of my valuables are jammed down the side of my seat, next to my body, so no one can walk off with them. But I am so tired that a reasonably competent thief could probably steal the shirt off my back without waking me up.

'Lightning never strikes twice,' I tell myself. 'Or, at least, not within forty-eight hours.'

And anyway, I've got no option. I've got to get back and get the income-generating elements of the Siboti project off the ground.

10

First meeting

'Happiness requires something to do, something to love and something to hope for.'

Swahili proverb

I first see her at the bus stop at Nairobi. Medium height, slim build, well but casually dressed and with that indefinable self-assurance a lot of urban professional women have here. And very pretty. I wonder why she's going to Bungoma, but I know I'm dog-tired and slightly tipsy – not drunk, but relaxed enough to make a fool of myself – so I don't risk trying to satisfy my curiosity.

I squeeze down the narrow aisle and shuffle across into a window seat – remembering to stow my laptop away safely – and am ready to sleep the journey away. The next thing I know I'm being tapped – not hard, but repeatedly – on the head. The bus is full now and she, the smart urban professional, is sitting next to me, I have obviously gone to sleep on her shoulder.

'I'm not your pillow,' she says, smiling.

I check, but mercifully I haven't dribbled on her shoulder as well. 'I'm so sorry,' I add.

'No problem,' she says.

In straightening myself up, I manage to knock my heavy briefcase onto her foot.

'Sorry!' I say, trying to pick it up.

'A donkey always thanks you with a kick,' she says.

'Sorry? Oh, I see. A proverb?'

She nods.

'Nice one,' I say. Is she saying I am a donkey? Probably. But she is giving me the benefit of a wide, winning smile.

'Are you going all the way? To Bungoma?' I ask.

She nods again.

'Business or pleasure?'

'A bit of both,' she replies. 'You?'

'A bit of both,' I say.

She takes out her phone and starts checking her messages. Must keep the conversation going, I think. There's something about her. Smart, but warm, too. Or am I imagining the warm?

'Proverbs. Tell me some more.'

'Hmmmm?' she says, not looking up.

'I'm trying to learn about the culture here. Proverbs are good. The references people use – they teach you a lot about how they think. Tell me some more.'

She looks at me and turns off her phone, but keeps it in her hand.

'OK… let me think.'

The bus stops, a few people get off and an elderly couple, laden with bags and packages, stagger down the aisle and install themselves in the seats across from us.

'A heavy burden does not kill you the day you pick it up,' she says, finally.

'Nice,' I say, wondering if Siboti is the burden that will eventually kill me.

'He who cannot dance complains the floor is stony.'

'Ah, that's like "A bad workman always blames his tools". Got any more?'

I can't remember everything she says, but we talk a long time, comparing figures of speech. I've always been struck by how many English sayings are to do with being a maritime nation – things like being 'all at sea', or 'giving someone a wide berth' – but Kenya's are often to do with the land. 'Do not slaughter a calf before its mother's eyes', for example, or 'Just because he harmed your goat, do not go out and kill his bull'. I try to remember them, thinking I may get a chance to casually toss them into some of my conversations. As we grow more tired – and more relaxed with each other – the pauses in conversation grow longer and more comfortable.

'Having a good discussion is like having riches,' she says.

'Agreed,' I say, sleepily. 'Oh, is that...?'

'A proverb? Yes.'

Watching her reflection in the window allows me to scrutinise her for longer than would be polite directly. She really does have a beautiful face.

'Hearts do not meet one another like roads,' she says drowsily, her eyes shut now.

'A loved one has no pimples,' chips in the old lady across from us, smiling indulgently. She clearly thinks we are a couple. 'Talking to one another is loving one another.'

'Hmmm-hmmm,' says my companion.

Surely that's my cue. My unmistakeable cue. I lean slightly towards her lovely face. I will ask her if she'll have breakfast with me in Bungoma. I wonder, fleetingly, what it would be like to kiss her. Her eyes snap open.

'Never let a hyena know how well you can bite.' She smiles, turns away and goes to sleep.

I sneak another glance at her. She has great cheekbones.

* * *

When I wake up, the bus is trundling through the outskirts of Bungoma. She is already awake and checking Facebook.

'Good morning,' I say.

'Hmmm-hmmm,' she says, absorbed in her phone.

I wait until we have just stepped off the bus to ask: 'Where to now?'

'Siboti,' she says.

'Me too!' I say. 'Maybe we could share a taxi? I don't even know your name.' I hold out my hand. 'Ken. Ken King.'

It's as if I've just said my name's Vlad the Impaler, but not as funny. She shrinks back as if she's been stung.

'Oh. My. God. You're him, aren't you?'

'I don't think so,' I say. I can't imagine who she could have mistaken me for.

137

'Saint Ken!' she says.

'Saint Ken? No, I... But that's not...'

'I should have guessed... But you didn't seem... Goodbye!' she says abruptly, turning on her heel and striding off to where the taxis are waiting.

'Wait!' I hurry after her. 'What have I done?'

She carries on marching away.

'Stop! You can't just say that. What have I done?'

She stops and turns back to face me.

'What have you done?' she repeats, and throws her bag down. 'I'll tell you what you've done, because I've heard all about you.'

What has she heard? What is being said about me? I am intrigued, as much as anything. What can have made her so angry?

'You're going to end poverty, I hear.' She says it as though this would be some kind of crime. I stare at her.

'You're going to help the chicken farmers. You're going to finish the reservoir. You're going to get lighting for the polytechnic. You're going to save the orphans. You're going to inspire the young. You're going to sort out the water. Then I expect you're going to turn the water into wine and make the blind see and the lame walk.'

'Well, not quite. You make it all sound a bit ambitious –'

'Oh, do I?' she says, mock innocence barely concealing her fury – a fury which is still baffling to me.

'I don't say I'll necessarily be able to achieve everything I set out to do.'

'Mr King, Mr Ken King, let me ask you something. Do you think you are the first person to come to Africa full of talk and

138

promises? Do you think failing is the worst thing that can happen to you? You are wrong. Failing is the worst thing that can happen to *them*. You can always go home. They have to stay here. Just take my advice and go home now, and save everyone a deal of pain and disappointment. If you really care about these people, you will go home now.'

'Why? Why do you assume I'll fail?'

'Why do you assume you'll succeed where the UN hasn't? You're a banker! This is Africa – not a local branch of a bank. You are raising everyone's expectations and you will not be able to deliver. Do you not see that what you are doing is actually cruel? You are holding out hope! You have no idea what you're taking on. Your project is doomed and you, Mr Ken King, are either a crook or a fool.'

She picks up her bag and stomps off to the cab rank. I hurry after her.

'So,' I call out, 'I suppose sharing a taxi's out of the question?'

By way of an answer she gets into a cab and slams the door shut. I try to remember that sentence I love from Edmund Burke.

'The worst mistake a man can make is to do nothing, because he can only do a little!' I shout, but the quote is too long and the cab is too fast.

I'm shaken, actually. Stunned at her anger and sarcasm. It's the first time anyone in Kenya has accused me of having a messiah complex. I don't think anyone else here would be that rude to me. To them, I'm this hugely wealthy *mzungu* who seems to be on their side – putting in water wells, paying for orphans, buying motorbikes. Momentum investment I call it, and it seems to be working.

But of course, the things she said do resonate. What do I think I am doing? What makes me think I have the secret, that I'm the one person who can beat the odds and solve these people's problems? These are questions I've only asked myself. I didn't even raise them with Alan. Now they are out there, ringing in the air. Who else sees me like this? The elders? The local farmers in Siboti? Kizito? How many people actually think these things about me?

But just now there's a more immediate problem for me to solve.

What is her name, this cruel and clever woman, and how can I get to see her again?

11

Mobile clinic

'Health is the first wealth.'

Kenyan proverb

When I was trying to work out which of the UN's Millennium Development Goals I could begin to tackle in Siboti, I tried to be very realistic. Most of the UN's health-related Millennium Development Goals – things like reducing child mortality, improving maternal health and combating diseases such as HIV/AIDS and malaria – would clearly need the sort of resources and budgets that could only be brought to bear by government programmes or the big foundations or charities. But I was on the lookout for opportunities to make some impact locally.

Now I'm starting to think about the possibility of introducing some kind of mobile clinic that could give people in Siboti access to basic medical treatments and advice. I know that Haven Kenya's young volunteers from America already make regular visits to a number of neighbouring areas around Bungoma to provide this kind of service, dispensing antibiotics and other medicines and giving advice on health and nutrition. These volunteers – mainly trainee doctors from universities and hospitals in the American Midwest – bring supplies of medicines with them in their luggage (yes, it really is that basic) but there is never enough to go round. Twice a week, on Monday and Friday, they trek off in the battered Haven Kenya van, setting up temporary dispensaries in far-flung villages and settlements and treating as many people as they can before their stocks of medicine for the day run out. They'd like to do much more, they tell me, but the limited supply of drugs means that they can only run the mobile clinics two days a week.

This seems like a terrible waste of human resources. If the volunteers are there and keen to get out and treat people, maybe I can make it possible for them to extend their activities into Siboti. I need to talk to Mama Jayne and see if we can work out some way to make better use of their skills and enthusiasm.

Jayne is well aware that the idealistic students who come to Africa as charity volunteers – and who pay for the privilege, as well as giving up their time – want to do as much as possible to help the people of Western Kenya.

'It's just the medicines, Ken,' she says. 'They can only bring a certain amount with them from America, and it would soon run out if we tried to run the mobile clinics every day.'

'No, but wait.' I think I'm beginning to see how this might work. 'There must be suppliers I could go to – probably right here in Bungoma – who could sell us similar generic drugs and antibiotics. Drug costs are relatively low here, and we would certainly be able to negotiate discounts for quantity. If I got hold of the medicines, could we take the mobile clinic into Siboti, say, every Wednesday, and give the volunteers the chance to do a bit more, rather than just kicking their heels till Friday comes?'

'Yes!' cries Mama Jayne, clapping her hands. I knew she'd love it. It's exactly the sort of practical, down-to-earth idea that would appeal to her. But I don't know if she'd have the authority to give it the go-ahead.

'Would we need to get approval from anyone else?' I ask, tentatively.

'Oh no. Something like this would be my decision.... And if you can cover the cost of the fuel too, my decision is yes. Let's do it.'

When I make enquiries in Bungoma, I discover that the total price of each day's medical supplies for the mobile clinic is only going to be $150. So for about $700 a month all in, we will be able to bring these basic medical services to at least some of Siboti's people.

The mobile clinic will be able to help some of the children, pregnant mothers and old people who can't easily visit a doctor's surgery. Even if they can get there, they usually have to pay a fee of 150 shillings (about $2) to see a doctor, and pay for the prescribed medications – and that's enough to deter many impoverished families from seeking help. Our service will be free. I can't hope to provide comprehensive medical services for the whole population of Siboti, but the combination of informed diagnosis, advice and free antibiotics and other drugs should mean that many families will get some of the simple, basic healthcare they need.

When Mama Jayne and I talk to the volunteers about this, they are delighted. They're full of energy and eager to get stuck in, and they can't wait to get out there and take the mobile clinic service into Siboti. The one thing they are worried about, though, is whether we can get the word out and ensure that local people know when and where they will be turning up with the Haven Kenya van to hold their mobile surgeries.

'To be honest, we've sometimes been to places for the Monday and Friday clinics and found that no one was expecting us,' one bespectacled trainee doctor from Boise, Idaho, tells me. 'That just seems such a pity. And we don't like to say anything to Mama Jayne, as we don't want to criticise her. She's a great woman and she works her butt off to arrange these clinics, but some of her local organisers, the people she calls the mobilisers, don't do a good job when it comes to letting people know what's going on.'

When we start the Wednesday clinics in Siboti, I'm going to make damn sure we put the word around. We'll have posters on church notice-boards and stuck up on trees at crossroads, and Kizito and our own volunteer helpers will go round and tell people exactly where and when they can see the visiting doctors.

We're going to do a little to ease the health problems that haunt so many people in Siboti. We'll get some help to the children suffering from diarrhoea, infections and respiratory disease, and the students running the clinics will also be able to take the opportunity to give guidance on basic health and nutrition to pregnant mothers.

Most women who have babies in Siboti don't ever see a nurse or midwife at any stage of their pregnancy or labour, so this will be a chance to help more mothers The volunteers will also be able to talk to people about HIV/AIDS and explain how it is transmitted. Just being there, on the spot, will enable them to give out advice, as well as medicines – and this may be just as important as the prescriptions that are dispensed.

With Mama Jayne's backing, we get all the arrangements in place.

Two weeks later, I'm down at the Haven Kenya office early on the Wednesday morning to see the volunteer team off for their first mobile clinic in the Siboti area.

'Good luck. I hope it goes well,' I call, as the student doctors and nurses climb aboard the vehicle. The old Nissan van is crammed with boxes and bandages and packets of syringes. There are piles of leaflets about malaria and AIDS and the volunteers are squeezed in awkwardly wherever they can find a couple of inches of seat space.

'There's room for one more here,' shouts the trainee doctor with the thick glasses. 'You ought to come with us, Ken, so you can see the difference we're making.'

Kizito's already beginning to manoeuvre the old Nissan out of the courtyard when the penny drops. He's right. I should be there for this. I run alongside the van for a few yards, like a character in some old black and white movie, before Kizito glances across and sees me.

'You looking for a ride somewhere, boss?' he grins.

'Yep. I'm coming, too,' I shout, swinging myself up and clambering on board.

12

Chillies

'Agriculture is the foundation of civilisation and any stable
economy.'

Allan Savory, Zimbabwean environmentalist

I am sitting on the large orangey-red sofa in my hotel room in
Bungoma, trying to do some reading and trying to be philosophical
about the regular ten-minute power blackouts. There's a bottle of
decent South African Cabernet Sauvignon on the pine coffee table
in front of me, to help me put up with the power cuts. I pour myself
a glass and turn to the first page of my latest reading, and the room
goes black. OK. Par for the course. The light comes and the light
goes. I'll sit and think and the power will be back, sooner or later.

I'm going to need a glass or two to help me get through these
UN development progress reports. They're heavy-going, but they
provide a lot of facts that you don't see elsewhere. Every month, I
learn, roughly five million more humans join our planet than depart
this world. That means the number of people in the world increases
by 60 million – roughly the population of the UK – every single year.
So the UN's declared goal of cutting by half the proportion of people

suffering from extreme poverty and hunger is a moving target. And in Africa, where population growth is fastest, you need to run fast just to stand still.

The figures for Kenya show that each mother has, on average, 4.6 children. Boreholes, orphan scholarships, mobile clinics and a new classroom are all very nice. But they are handouts, and handouts are never going to be enough. If I'm going to help generate some real prosperity for this community, commercial enterprise will have to play the key central role.

That will involve both give and take. The farming families will need to be given new commercial opportunities, but they will have to embrace this chance to raise their income levels. What this area needs is some major commercial enterprise that brings in new money from the outside world. Ireland achieved the same sort of thing by attracting big technology and pharmaceutical companies that could create jobs and bring in new money through investment and export earnings. How can I get a miniature version of that going in Siboti, something that will pull in a sustainable flow of outside money?

I'm still sitting there in the dark, when the light suddenly dawns. It's bloody obvious, and I don't know why it hasn't struck me before. With Kenya's population growing by a million people a year, and Uganda, just forty kilometres away, growing even faster, there must be huge commercial potential for a new food production company, using crops grown by the local farmers right here in Western Kenya. Everybody needs food.

More mouths to feed, more customers being born all the time. That's the big opportunity. If I can help the people of Siboti get themselves organised to grow and sell basic foodstuffs, we can expand from there into food processing and production. There'll be some new jobs and the wider community can develop a growing income stream that doesn't depend on anyone's aid or charity. If we're really going to get Siboti out of extreme poverty and firmly set on a path towards rising living standards, this is how it has to work.

The cogs in the business part of my head start clunking and spinning. First, we need to grow a reliable crop, like sunflowers, perhaps. Then we need to add value by turning it into something people want to buy, like sunflower oil for cooking. Finally, we need to package it well, find the right markets and sell it as profitably as we can.

That's the strategy that can make the dream come true. I could start with the basics, signing up hundreds of smallholder farmers across Siboti to grow good, high-yield crops, with the seeds and fertiliser funded by microfinance loans. Later we can move into food processing and production, maybe starting with something easy like flour, progressing to bread and cakes and growing the core business as we move on to products that will generate bigger margins and more jobs. It's all about enlightened capitalism, I suppose, working for the people. But whatever you call it, it feels like a sensible path towards creating the prosperity that is needed here.

And as if to prove the point, right on cue, the lights suddenly come on again.

I'm too excited to sleep now. I'm up half the night, toasting this new insight and filling pages of my notebook with questions, diagrams and calculations. What should we grow? Where should we start? How can we get moving fast – this year – now?

One of the first things I want to do is get together again with Elizabeth Kwambai, the Kenyan government's agricultural adviser who was giving Siboti's self-help groups so much practical guidance on the ins and outs of chicken-keeping during my first exploratory visits to this region. She had impressed me then with her knowledge and enthusiasm, and I want to pick her brains now.

I dig out her number and call her first thing in the morning. The timing's good, and I arrange to see her at her home after work.

'Come over for tea,' she says. 'Stephen will keep the children out of our hair and we can have a chat about it.'

That evening, I'm weaving through the muddy, potholed, unlit streets on the outskirts of Bungoma, trying to find the house. When I get there, it's clear that Elizabeth and her husband take their family's security pretty seriously. Encircling walls and a forbidding metal gate shut out the world. It's not unusual for a professional person like Elizabeth to live in a detached house with a high perimeter and a locked gate, and it suddenly strikes me that I should be looking for a secure place to live myself. Apart from the one time my laptop was stolen, I've never thought of myself as a target before, and the thought isn't welcome.

'You know me, happy-go-lucky,' I said to Alan when I first arrived.

'Happy-go-lucky is great,' he replied, passing me another cold beer from the fridge. 'Just don't take unnecessary risks if you can avoid it.'

Elizabeth is tall, softly-spoken, with a natural air of authority, and she is very pregnant. I guess she is in her mid-thirties. She already juggles two children and a demanding job, but she's still keen to get involved with my project.

Inside her fortress there's a pleasant, brick-built family home, with electricity and an air of comfortable, no-nonsense domesticity. Stephen, an engineer, greets me warmly and takes the children off to do their homework while we get down to talking about my strategy for Siboti. I soon find out that even people in their enviable position have other income streams. Elizabeth and Stephen incubate and hatch eggs in a spare room under a heated lamp, have large wooden coops in their yard for growing chicks and supply chickens to local cafés and restaurants. It's all very well organised for a home-based business.

As we sip our tea and talk about what I'm trying to do, I'm struck again by her down-to-earth realism. Her advice is straightforward and sensible, refreshingly free from the management waffle I've met so often from advisers and strategists back home. She's not interested in hiding behind the contrived gobbledygook of 'leveraging stakeholder propositions' or 'aligning tactical processes with strategic platforms' that passes for thought in the corporate world. Instead, she's firing off simple, blunt recommendations about how to make my ideas work.

'You want to choose a crop some of them already know how to grow – and have made money from,' she suggests.

'Like what?' I ask.

'Like chilli peppers, maybe. They already grow some chilli in that area around Siboti. But the main market for chilli is four hundred kilometres away in Nairobi, so the local people don't have market contacts and they don't get good prices.'

I've already met one local guy, John Karanga, who buys most of the local chilli crop and takes it to Nairobi to sell. I liked him, but he's a small fish in a big pond when he gets the chillies to the markets in the city.

'John's a good guy,' says Elizabeth. 'But he can only buy small quantities of chilli, because he doesn't have a lot of capital. He cannot afford to fund the farmers to buy fertiliser and good-quality seeds, so he'll always be a small-time middleman with no control over quality.'

I'm smiling inside, as I can see where this is leading. A vision for the way ahead is beginning to crystallise, and it's so near I can almost touch it.

'So you're saying, that with a bigger capital base, we could scale it up and do chillies properly?'

'Yes. I don't see why not. I think you could mobilise a lot of farmers to grow for you.'

It sounds promising, but first I need to know whether there is a real demand for large quantities of chilli. I'll need to go to Nairobi and check out the markets. But Elizabeth is already looking further ahead.

'And when you've got chilli production running well, and you've got over the inevitable teething problems, you can move on to other products that may need more training and investment. If you can move on up the value chain into food production, you'll certainly be able to get higher margins.'

'Teething problems? Do you think I'll have many of those?' I ask.

Elizabeth looks me straight in the eye.

'Well, Ken, look at it this way. How easy do you think it's going to be to recruit large numbers of farmers, create a microcredit scheme to finance seeds, fertiliser and pesticides, train the growers in good horticulture and record-keeping, monitor how they plant, tend and harvest the crops, buy the chilli from them, grade it, pack it and transport it to Bungoma and then on to Nairobi, find sales outlets for it all, deliver the right quantities to the customers when they want them, deal with suppliers, farmers, employees, drivers, loaders, unloaders, cart-men and market traders, making sure you don't get cheated and nothing gets stolen, then pay everyone along the line and make sure you have a profit left at the end of it all…?'

She takes a breath, grins and pours me some more tea.

'If you're going to do all that, then, yes, Ken, I'd say you're definitely going to have teething problems.'

Ouch. I know she's probably right. And I know there'll be another complication, too, as I am going to have to keep the elders and the Chief onside while we work through these yet to-be-discovered problems. But I'm up for it, and Elizabeth agrees to get involved as my adviser and mentor. I'm going to need her.

We leave it there for now and Elizabeth turns her attention to preparing hearty helpings of chapatis and chicken stew, while I chat with Stephen and the children. By the time I say my goodbyes and clamber onto the motorbike to head back to my hotel, I'm full of admiration for these people. The children are bright, enthusiastic, confident and polite and the whole family seems to be the very model of decency, responsibility and good humour. If this is Kenya's future, it is very bright indeed.

Next morning, I snap into action. I call John Karanga and he's eager to meet me. He'll grab a *matatu* and come into town straightaway. Then he hesitates. Can I assist him with the 40 shilling fare?

This guy is the biggest chilli broker in the region and he's asking for his bus fare. I guess if you look after the pennies, the pounds will look after themselves, and it's less than $1 – but it's not what I was expecting. It doesn't cast him as a hotshot entrepreneur, to my mind.

'OK John,' I say, and we arrange where we'll meet.

My sense is that John is a penny pincher rather than genuinely broke. I find him at the roadside café where I take my morning coffee in the shade of a huge acacia tree. John orders a large Coke and fried eggs and chips, which he smothers with half a bottle of chilli sauce.

'I see you've got a taste for chilli, John. Is that just you, or does everybody here like chips with their chilli sauce?'

'Yes, yes, Mr Ken,' he says solemnly, ignoring my teasing. 'Most people take salt, but if chilli sauce is there, we'll take that.'

I jump straight to the point.

'So tell me, how much chilli do you sell in Nairobi each week?'

'Oh, 150 kilos, maybe 200.'

'And how do you get it to Nairobi?'

'Dennis and David help me put it in 40-kilo bags and we send it on the overnight bus. My friend collects it with a cart from the bus depot and takes it to the market.'

'With a donkey?'

John laughs.

'No, no. No donkey. He can't afford to feed a donkey. He pulls it himself. Cart-men don't have money, Mr Ken.'

'What's the demand like? If Siboti farmers grew a lot more chilli, could you still sell it in Nairobi?'

'Oh yes. No problem. The market will buy whatever I can offer.'

I'm not necessarily going to take his word for that. But at least he's optimistic, so I decide to show my hand.

I tell John that I might be interested in working with him in the chilli business. I'd like to go to Nairobi and see the buyers. Will he come with me? He agrees, and a few days later we take the nine-hour bus trip to Nairobi.

When we arrive, John goes off to stay with relatives and I check into the InterContinental Hotel. It's right in the centre of town, near the parliament buildings and Uhuru Park, and it is watched over night and day by a small army of huge, hunched and mournful grey birds, balanced on stilt-like legs in the high treetops. These are the marabou storks – prehistoric-looking scavengers with bald heads, beaks like swords and wings up to three metres wide from tip to tip. The storks are always there, but I have just a couple of days to enjoy a touch of unaccustomed luxury and I aim to make the most of it.

This is my chance to catch up on a few creature comforts and I'm looking forward to a cold gin and tonic, followed by a long, lazy half hour basking in the pleasure of a warm shower in a modern bathroom, uninterrupted by power blackouts. But I get a slight shock when I walk into the lift. There's this really scruffy, weary-looking white bloke in the mirror. It takes a split second to register that it is me. I stare back into the bloodshot eyes. I have the sense that I'm pivoting as a person, opening up emotionally to the universe around me. I'm working almost as hard as I did at the bank, but now I feel I'm having a real human impact and doing work that matters more. I wonder how much I've changed as a person and what my ex-colleagues or my ex-wife might think now of the guy in the mirror, before I push the uncomfortable thought away. I don't have any contact with my ex-wife anymore. This is my life now, my way, and I'm loving it.

An hour later and my body double is transformed: black shirt, black jeans, Prada loafers – I could be in London or Paris or New York, sitting down to a beef Wellington and a couple of glasses of Haut-Medoc, suddenly life doesn't feel so tough. It's a glimpse of my pre-Siboti existence, and it feels familiar and luxurious.

Next morning, I meet John and we set off bright and early for the Ngara market. We pass hundreds of busy, crowded stalls, crammed with new and second-hand clothes, pans and baskets, fruit and vegetables. John takes me to three family-owned stalls – each stallholder buys a bag of chilli from him every week. There are plenty of customers and trade is brisk, but this is a retail market for consumers, not a wholesale market selling to businesses. We might be able to shift another bag or two of chillies here, but this kind of market is not what we need. A place like this will never take the quantities we need to sell, and the whole plan will fail if we can't find big wholesale buyers.

Then John takes me to the huge central food market, Marikiti (the Swahili word is derived directly from the English 'market'). Known more formally as Wakulima Market, it's a huge place, bounded by brick walls and metal gates, with hundreds of businesses and thousands of dealers. In the streets around the market, cars jostle for road space with hundreds of handcarts, known as *mkokoteni*, piled high with produce packed in dirty, bulging sacks that look as if they are being used for the thousandth time. We file in through the tall gates and walk past separate sections for pineapples, for melons, for millet and cassava, for spices, groundnuts and everything under the sun. The fruit and vegetables are either in the back of trucks or stacked on lengths of sacking on the ground. Porters – the *carry-carry men* – hurry through the crowds with teetering sacks of onions or carrots stacked four high on their shoulders, and the whole place is abuzz with noise and activity.

We walk for what seems like miles, and suddenly we are in the chilli section. This is more like it. We find John's buyers and they are very positive indeed. Yes, they can take ten times as much as John sells. But at what price, I ask? Market price, they say – whatever that is at the time.

'The prevaoiling proice,' shouts one wise guy, trying to mock a posh English accent, but sounding more scouser than Etonian.

I get it. They say they'll buy, but they won't commit to any sort of long-term pricing deal. So it would be a risk. I'd be asking the smallholding farmers of Siboti to grow a lot more chilli, and while I could guarantee to buy it from them and sell it in bulk, I would not be able to guarantee the price I could give them. And I'd have to rely on the word of these traders to actually buy it. How long have they been trading?

'Oh, many years,' they tell me. 'Yes, yes. Many years.'

On examination, though, 'many years' turns out to be two years in one case and three years in another. Maybe that constitutes a track record round these parts, but it leaves me feeling exposed. Who knows whether the people I talk to today could be relied on to be here next week or next year? The last thing I can afford is to leave the Siboti farmers in the lurch.

John heads back to Bungoma on the overnight bus, and I decide to stay on for an extra day or two. I'm in no hurry to swap that comfortable InterContinental Hotel bed for the one in my room at the Rickshaw in Bungoma and, besides, I want to go and see my new friend Dipesh. On my first trips to Siboti, I used to hire cars in Nairobi from the local company that advertised itself as offering the most comprehensive insurance in Kenya. It was owned by an Indian family and the proprietor, Dipesh, was always friendly and keen to hear about my progress in Siboti. I'm getting to know my way around Nairobi, now, so I decide to stroll across town to say hello to Dipesh.

'Hey, Mr King. Great to see you.'

It's a heart-warming welcome and we're soon catching up on all the news and gossip. I tell Dipesh about my visit to Marikiti and he suddenly looks serious.

'You know, there was an Egyptian guy in here to rent a car last week and he was in the vegetable import/export business. Maybe you would like to talk to him?'

There are advantages to being in a place where data privacy is not taken too seriously. Unblushing, Dipesh gives me his customer's number and I make a call. To my delight, the guy is immediately interested and we arrange to get together. The InterContinental coffee area will do fine as my new Nairobi meeting room.

Vijay turns out to be an energetic international entrepreneur. He has spotted the opportunity to export fruit and vegetables from Kenya to the Middle East and he's set up a new company called Green Tulip to do just that. He assures me (don't they all?) there is a huge market for chilli in Saudi Arabia and Dubai and that I will be quite safe growing it in large quantities.

'They'll take whatever we can give them, Ken,' he says.

Vijay is a good contact. He wants to stay in touch and buy chilli from me in the future. But relying on overseas markets is always bound to be more complicated than just selling the chilli here, and I really do want to find established local businesses that will be strong prospective customers for Siboti's chilli crop. So I use a bit of imagination and look around online for some of the less obvious opportunities. Eventually, I stumble across a tea processing business that says it makes a special type of chilli masala tea which is a favourite with the Indian community in Nairobi. When I call these people, they are interested in seeing me about buying quantities of dried chilli. No one's promising anything, of course, but the range of possibilities is widening all the time.

Each time I've travelled into the city from the airport, I've noticed various companies along the way with names that indicate they are in the fruit and veg business – names like Evergreen, FreshPak, Makindu Growers and Vegpro. So I drop in to the rent-a-car office again to see if Dipesh can give me any more names. He doesn't know anyone at these places, he says. But wait. He has a golf buddy who runs an airline freight company. Maybe he deals with the veggie exporters. Dipesh calls Jonathan Ngiri, tells him I'm a marvellous chap who's trying to help Kenyans grow chilli for export and asks if he could see me and help me with my enquiries. He will. Can I come at 9 p.m.? I can. I walk back to the hotel. Rush hour traffic is bad on the roads, but on the pavements it is almost worse. This is one of the fastest-growing cities in Africa and it is teeming with pedestrians during the evening rush hour.

At 8.30 p.m., I ask the hotel to get me a taxi. The driver is James, a middle-aged chatterbox who, in time, becomes my regular driver in Nairobi and a good friend and ally. I arrive at the freight company and Jonathan suggests I walk round with him while he checks a cargo of ready-to-cook packaged vegetables that's flying to London tonight and will be on the supermarket shelves in the UK tomorrow. He shows me how he does it and I absolutely love it. This is real. I'm seeing the wheels in motion for the world's food supply chain. This is exactly the kind of stuff I will need to know if I'm ever going to help Siboti move up from simply growing crops to becoming a fully-fledged food production centre. I am starting to learn the food export business already and I'm giddy with excitement. Jonathan knows the general managers at every one of the major vegetable exporters, and he's perfectly happy to open his phone contact list for me to take all the names and numbers I want. Brilliant. Another key piece in place in the puzzle.

What a tremendous evening. What a great day all round.

James drives me back to the hotel but I'm too wound up to turn in just yet. The bar at the InterContinental is a place to meet interesting people, and before long I am chatting with a group of well-dressed girls who are enjoying a night out. By 2 a.m., I am dancing with them in some nightclub and having a whale of a time. I'm the only *mzungu* in a sea of locals, but I don't care. I am having great fun, and tomorrow I will be calling all the general managers in the vegetable export business to gauge their appetite for buying chilli. For a few hours now, though, I'm going to let my hair down.

Morning comes, as usual, far too soon. But vegetable exporters work Saturdays and the phone calls to them go well. By lunchtime, I've managed to get three of the general managers to agree to see me on Monday. This is great. There's no doubt now that the decision to stay on a couple of days longer in Nairobi was the right one.

On Monday morning, James rocks up to collect me in his spotless Toyota. At each company, the gate security man waves us into the compound without even a question. The first two general managers are interested in buying, in principle. But they have existing suppliers, so they will use me when they have gaps in supply or are facing extra demand. That's fair enough, and as much as I could reasonably expect.

With the last visit, though, I hit the jackpot. It's a big company, Makindu, and the general manager will commit to taking 300 kilos per week from us, week in and week out, once we are up and running and if the quality is good enough. That's a lot of chilli – and a lot of guaranteed turnover. With this big customer lined up, in addition to the Marikiti and Ngara buyers, I feel I have enough assured sales to go ahead and launch a serious chilli production business in Siboti.

I meet up for dinner with the girl I'd been dancing with on Friday night. We'd had a lot of fun larking about on the dance-floor. I tell her how pleased I am that the chilli production business fits so neatly into my overall plan for Siboti. She seems interested, so I carry on.

'I'm going to set up a new Siboti Foods business that will offer chilli-growing contracts to hundreds of smallholding farmers,' I explain over our starters. 'I'm excited.'

She pats her perfectly groomed hair. 'So how will this business of yours will work?' she asks.

During the main course I enlarge on how Siboti Foods will be the central business engine that brings outside money into Siboti by selling the chilli in Nairobi, setting in motion the economic multiplier effect within this close community. She nods at intervals, smiles, and glances over at our fellow diners while I run through my business plan. When I look down, I realise that she's practically polished off her plate, while I have barely touched my steak.

'I must be doing all the talking!' I say, and she laughs.

It won't feel like much at the beginning, I assure her over the dessert, but it will enable me to get the full production, transport and sales supply chain up and running, and position Siboti Foods to move on up into growing higher value products – things like baby corn, perhaps, or soya beans and asparagus. Then, in the next phase, we can possibly go into producing basic foodstuffs such as flour.

'All this stuff is so important to me,' I say, and pause to summon our waiter. 'Am I mad to think that I can make this work? What do you think?'

She smiles politely at me and says nothing.

My companion declines coffee – she has things to do tomorrow, she claims. Of course she does. I've been sitting here bleating on about stuff that's vital to me, and showing little interest in her. I suppose I thought she'd be interested in my groundbreaking project. But even if she wanted to listen to a monologue on the specialist subject of Ken King, I can't really expect a smart urban Nairobi girl to share my enthusiasm for a distant, poverty-stricken corner of Western Kenya. With her smartphone, her university degree and her high-end designer bag, she has more in common with her contemporaries in Milan or LA than she has with the people of Siboti. Or with me. I realise I'm in danger of becoming a one-track conversationalist at best and an obsession-driven evangelistic bore at worst.

When I return to the hotel to turn in for the night, my mate in the lift pauses to give me a long, appraising look. It's been a very long time since you've had a date, my doppelgänger notes. And you don't really know how to do it anymore. He advises me to switch off and enjoy one more night's sleep in a clean and comfortable bed before heading back to work in Siboti.

* * *

Sitting on the bus the next morning, I mull over how I should set up the new chilli business, bearing in mind that John Karanga already has an established business in that sector. I don't want to go into competition with John – better to have him inside the tent helping me. Eventually, I decide I'll try to buy John's business from him and use it as my starting point, if he is open to that, which I expect he will be. When I get back, I go looking for John and ask him if he'll be willing to let me go through his accounts so I can put a realistic value on the business. Silly question. John doesn't have any books.

Nobody keeps books around here. Why should they? They don't pay any tax, and they aren't really expected to. The rural people don't file tax returns – and, in return, they don't get to hold their politicians to account. It's like a tacit agreement between the ruling class and the rural poor. You get on with your lives in the countryside and we'll do our thing in Nairobi without any input from you, except for an occasional election.

The authorities don't seem to make much serious effort in Western Kenya to ensure that people in the countryside keep accounts and pay taxes. Even if they did, the money that came in would probably be less than the cost of collecting it. But this implicit trade-off – no taxation, in return for no accountability – creates a huge and potentially malevolent disconnect between the governors and the governed. I guess there's always a gap, in every country, between those in power and those at the bottom of the heap and I guess in time it will all change. But here today, the disconnect looks total.

So I sit down with John and we talk through the revenues and costs for each month of the two growing seasons each year. I do some basic corporate finance sums to calculate a rough value for the business, and, to be fair to him, add in a little bit extra in recognition of his dominant position and good reputation in the region. When I've finished, I put my offer to him, including the promise of a salaried job and a company motorbike, and he jumps at it. I have a big evangelist on my side now. Part of the deal is that John will do a major PR job for Siboti Foods, putting the word around and telling everyone that this is the future.

But we have no time to lose. It's March and already chilli planting time. We need to create a brand identity for the business and sign up the farmers who will grow the chillies for us. I go online and find a company in the UK that offers to create customised logo designs for about $150. I sit in my hotel room in Bungoma, night after night, while the designers send me version after version of the logo, gradually getting closer to the look I'm hoping for. After a week, we're there. We have the new logo and a brand identity that can carry us into the future. 'Siboti Foods: Be part of our success' is a rallying call that will soon be seen all over Siboti.

Meanwhile, Kizito is finding out what buildings are available for rent around Kimwanga Market. The market area is right on the boundary of the Siboti area – technically just outside it – but it's on the main road and at the bottom of the hill, so it's where we need to be.

He soon finds a building that would suit us very well, but the landlord believes the *mzungu* is the one who wants to rent it, so he quotes double the going rate. Kizito can't deny that I am behind it, but tells him I am no ordinary rip-him-off *mzungu*. I am here to help the community, he says, and the landlord shouldn't try to charge me any more than the normal rent.

We end up paying 25 per cent over the odds, but it's still only $20 a month. For that, we get a standalone two-room brick building, eleven metres by five, with strong metal doors front and back and a rear window with bars like a prison cell. Good security is important as we will need to store both equipment and chillies inside. The location is great, facing straight out onto the open space of Kimwanga Market and right by the main Bungoma to Malaba road, the main highway that runs from the Indian Ocean via Nairobi to the Ugandan border and on to connect with Rwanda, South Sudan and the Democratic Republic of the Congo.

The next thing we need is a team that can get out and recruit farmers to grow the chillies. Kizito and John are already on my payroll, but we'll need more people than that to get the business up and running. Two local men, Edwin Matua, the Chief's nephew, and Julius Wanyoni, have been around right from the beginning, helping out from time to time on an unpaid basis. Perhaps they have been hoping I'll employ them at some stage. Whatever their motives, though, they have certainly shown plenty of energy and enthusiasm. I find Edwin a lot more likeable than Julius, but I ignore my gut feeling on this occasion. I can certainly use both of them, so I offer them jobs. With a team of four employees, we are ready to go.

13

Branding

'A brand for a company is like a reputation for a person. You earn reputation by trying to do hard things well.'

Jeff Bezos, founder, chair and CEO of Amazon

We've got our team. Now we need to make sure we look like a team and that we have the basic equipment required for the first part of the project. John, Edwin and Julius will need to be able to get round to all the outlying farms, so we go into town and buy three more motorbikes, making sure that they are blue, to match mine and Kizito's.

There's a bit of brand-building going on here. We need some smart Siboti Foods shirts for the five of us and they'll be blue, too, with our new logo, created by the designer I discovered online. To get the shirts I want, I head for Bungoma's Shariff Centre, a noisy warren of tiny, crowded, windowless lock-up stores where you can buy almost anything, go online at an internet café, get a haircut or an illegal copy of your favourite DVD or find someone to repair your laptop. I'm in and out quite often, to go to the barber or my ambitious young friend Robert's computing shop, where I get my printing done. Robert is unusual, as he's an outsider who has come to Bungoma to make his fortune, attracted by the shabby little town's growth and the business opportunities it offers. He dreams of opening more shops, buying flats to rent out and becoming wealthy by being in the right place at the right time.

I've become a familiar figure around here – Siboti's mad *mzungu* – so I'm greeted with plenty of hellos and high fives as I walk through the busy rows of shops. The clothing stores are almost all run by Somali traders. I talk to one young shopkeeper who seems keen to win my custom, and we negotiate a good price for the ten shirts I want. They're a pleasant mid-blue and I'll want two large-sized shirts each for four of us, plus a couple of extra-large for Julius. I've already realised that Kenya's idea of medium is a bit on the small side – possibly reflecting the number of undernourished customers – so I'm buying shirts a size bigger than I'd get at home.

I nip into the internet café to download the logo design, get a full colour printout and take this with the new shirts to a nearby sign-painter who will hand-paint the logo across the back of each garment. He'll have them done within two days, by which time we'll be ready to start the process of signing up the farmers to grow the first chilli crop.

Back at Kimwanga Market, we get together in a small room behind John's hardware shop and draft the letter that will tell the community about our plan. We explain that we are recruiting farmers to grow chilli, that we will provide free training and lend them seeds and fertiliser, and that we will guarantee to buy their produce at the best price that is available in Nairobi – a price that will always be higher than the price the middlemen who visit their farms can offer. Loan repayments will be deducted from the money they get when they sell their chilli to us, so the farmers will not be required to put up any cash in advance. To get started, all they have to do is commit a quarter of an acre, or more, to growing chilli to sell to us, and have an ambition to establish a working relationship with Siboti Foods, which, in turn, is committed to helping create economic opportunities for them. Growing chilli will be the first step on a clearly defined path that should eventually enable each farmer to make an income of $1000 a year, more than double the UN's target.

There's a lot to do now, so the team agrees that we will have a regular 9 a.m. meeting every Monday, Wednesday and Friday to set the work agenda, keep track of progress and discuss any problems. It's what I used to call, back in the day, the Project Operating Rhythm.

I am determined that the little building we're renting will be a local landmark, a beacon of quality and aspiration, bright, light and clean – and that's going to require the co-operation of our landlord. I want the rough internal walls plastered and the whole building painted brilliant white. And we need a big Siboti Foods sign above this headquarters, so that everyone driving past on the main road, fifty metres away, across the market area, can see there's something new happening here in Siboti.

Our landlord knows the changes I want will enhance the value of his building, but he's not prepared to pay for the plastering and painting out of his own pocket. After a bit of haggling, we agree to split the refurb expenses 50/50, deducting his share from our rent, month by month, until we've recovered half the cost.

John and Edwin are sent off to the sign-maker in Bungoma to commission the Siboti Foods sign – shoulder-high and nearly three metres long – that will announce our presence to the world. The sign-maker finds a metal fabricator to do the structural work and a week later our sign arrives, looming huge on the back of a battered pick-up truck.

Back home, you'd need planning permission to put up a monster sign like this. Here you just need a ladder and a handful of massive six-inch bolts, driven straight into the wall above the doorway.

The team hoists the sign up and bolts it firmly in place, and we stand round admiring our handiwork. 'Siboti Foods: Be part of our success'. You can't miss the big, confident message. The huge letters, deep red and light green, stand out powerfully on the crisp, white background and the mean-looking red chilli that forms the first letter 'i' in the word 'Siboti' gives a strong hint of what we're about. With the sign in position, our modest building suddenly starts to look purposeful and quite imposing, like a proper business.

We're going to want to sort the chillies as they come in from the farmers, and that will need wire-topped grading tables where we can lay the chillies out and separate the large ones from the small and the green from the red. When a chilli first grows, it's green and plump. If you don't harvest it, though, it starts to lose moisture and turns red. As consumers, some people like red and some prefer green. But the farmers would always prefer to sell us chillies in the green state, as we pay by the kilo and the green ones are obviously heavier than the drier red chillies.

In line with my theory of making the most of the economic multiplier effect, I want to be sure that the job of making these customised grading tables goes to a local Siboti carpenter. That way, the money injected into the local economy will go round and round and bring benefits for many people.

John finds the right man for us and negotiates a price that seems reasonable to me, but Kizito insists that the quote is broken down in full and transparent detail. He demands to see itemised costs for the wood, the wire, even the nails, and a clear statement of the labour time and costs involved. I'm secretly rather pleased to see Kizito putting his foot down like this and imposing a rigorous financial discipline. He knows everyone supplying Siboti Foods is going to be tempted to offer us an inflated *mzungu* price, and he wants to make sure word gets around fast that that's not how it's going to be.

There's no great rush to get the grading tables in place. They won't actually be needed until the first crop is ready, three months from now. But it won't do any harm for people to see action occurring on several fronts. And if anything goes wrong and the tables are not right first time, we'll have a bit of leeway to get them modified.

We're almost ready to start recruiting the farmers now, but I want to be absolutely sure I have the full backing of the community leaders before I fire the starting gun. I call a special steering committee meeting, with the Chief, the two assistant chiefs, the forty-two village elders and the four Siboti Foods managers (Kizito, John, Julius and Edwin), to be held in the church hall beside St Peter's church, in the very centre of Siboti.

The architecture is almost medieval, with mud walls and unglazed windows made of bamboo-like sticks that don't quite fit in the uneven window apertures. The stools and benches are made of roughly carved wood and the only concession to modernity is the corrugated iron sheeting on the sloping roof.

I start by giving everybody a quick update on progress so far and introducing the four guys in the team. They are all fairly well known in the community and the elders are happy that these young men are working with me, pleased to see that local people are getting jobs with the Siboti project. Then I hand over to Kizito and he explains how we will go about recruiting the farmers.

'We are about to begin distributing the seeds, the fertiliser and the pesticides to the farmers who sign up with us,' he says, and there is a great hum of approval that radiates through the church hall and bounces off the roof, before the elders get to their feet and applaud us both.

I look round at their open faces and sense that they trust me now – I am no longer a *mzungu* come from outer space to experiment with their way of life. I am part of the fabric of Siboti. What would they think of my world, my one-man five-storey retreat in the heart of London? Most of these men have extensive families in tiny mud-walled houses. Despite our differences, they have placed their faith in me, and that is a great feeling – better than juggling projects for an international corporation. These are people who live off the land and take risks rarely. They can't afford to. But they have taken a chance on me.

'And what about the Siboti Foods office?' asks one man. 'It's not in Siboti, is it?'

The elders nod their agreement, and I mentally prepare my answer for Kizito to translate. These men may be poor on a global scale, but they cannot be hoodwinked. Elders are valued for their experience and their wisdom, and rightly so.

171

'Being at Kimwangam your office falls outside the official border of the Siboti administrative area,' follows up the Chief.

'Yes, yes,' the men say.

'We are not happy about that,' says the Chief.

I hold up my hands. 'This is for purely practical reasons,' I explain. 'Siboti is on a hill, right? If we set up in the centre of Siboti, in an effort to be fair to everyone, we would be halfway up that hill, and that would make life quite difficult for farmers who live below that point. Pushing bicycles laden with large bags of chillies up the hill to deliver their crops to us would be hard work. Far better that everyone should be able to balance the heavy bags on the bikes and freewheel them downhill to the office, with only the cash to carry when they cycle back up. It will also save us the costs of transporting the bulk chillies down the hill each evening, and those savings can go into providing the best possible price for the farmers.'

Some of the community leaders are nodding, others are shaking their heads, but they reluctantly accept the logic – all except one.

Unfortunately, that one is the Chief. He is not so easily convinced. As the pockets of conversation grow louder, the men turn to him. He raises his hand for silence, and everyone stops talking.

'Those nearest the honeypot get the most honey,' he says. How like the Chief to summarise the issue with a pithy proverb?

I am instantly reminded of the girl on the bus.

'The extra income available from jobs like grading and packing will probably go to residents of Kimwanga and not to the people of Siboti,' says the Chief. The elders again and clap.

I know he's doing what he has to, standing up for those who rely on him, being a strong leader.

'Please, everyone, take a seat again, and we will talk this through,' I say, and as Kitizo translates they settle back on the crude benches.

'I want you to know,' I say, addressing the Chief, 'that the Siboti project really is all about Siboti. The company is called Siboti Foods, the four workers employed are all from Siboti, and all the farmers we'll be offering contracts to live in Siboti. The boreholes we've repaired are in Siboti and the 225 orphans we've helped back into school are all from this area. So I promise you, that as far as is practical, any future jobs will be for residents of Siboti.'

'OK,' says the Chief, 'but what about Kimwanga? They will want something from you too.'

I pat my palms together in a gesture of supplication.

'You are right, Chief. I know that I will probably get a visit from Kimwanga's chief, sooner or later, asking me what I will do for his area. And I know I will have to be seen to be doing something for Kimwanga, too, though Siboti will always be my main focus. You must trust in me to do the right thing. Everything I do is to benefit Siboti.'

While I'm reassuring, persuading, cajoling – all the skills I've accrued over years in business – my mind goes back to that earlier incident, on my first trip to Bungoma, when I innocently started giving out sweets to a bunch of schoolchildren outside Mama Jayne's office and almost sparked a riot because there wasn't enough for every child. I still shudder when I remember the way the gate porter weighed in and started hitting the children with his whip. The last thing I want is to fuel grudges and jealousies because there aren't enough goodies to go round. Perhaps it's inevitable that if you help some people, their less fortunate neighbours will feel hard done by. It's not something I can control, but I do want to cause as little friction as possible.

Luckily, the Chief is a realistic man and he seems to take on-board my point. That's a relief. I know he'll reserve the right to tackle me about this again, if he doesn't like what he sees happening on the ground.

I tell the steering committee members about my quest to find buyers in Nairobi to take large quantities of chilli, and explain how they can play a part in helping to minimise the risks we face.

But, I say, if the farmers don't follow the advice they're given about planting and tending their crops, they won't have enough chillies to sell to Siboti Foods. If they don't harvest and deliver the chillies at the right time, or they don't pay back their loans for seed and fertiliser, the project will grind to a halt. The elders will have to use their influence to see that everyone plays by the rules.

In response, the elders seem very confident that everything will go to plan.

As the meeting runs into its third hour, the men continue to sit there patiently as if they have all the time in the world. My throat is parched from all the talking. I'm fully aware that I have to continually sell myself as well as the Siboti project.

'So. We'll organise and train the contracted farmers, dividing them up into twelve groups of neighbours, each with an elected captain,' I announce, taking a slug of water.

'The captain will be given a 200-shilling mobile phone top-up each month and will act as the group's point of contact with one of these four Siboti Foods managers. We'll organise regular visits from an agronomist, an expert in growing crops, who will arrange with the captain to meet the local growers at one of the farms. There will always be ready access to expert advice.'

As I start to go into detail like this, I can hear murmurs of approval. They like what they're hearing. They can see the level of planning and organisation that's gone into the project and they're as optimistic as I am that it can succeed.

'I think that's about it for now,' I tell the assembled elders, my voice getting hoarser by the minute.

'Unless there are any more questions?'

The group must communicate by osmosis, because they suddenly break into a torrent of enthusiastic applause. A combination of my ideas for a structured route out of extreme poverty, coupled with my raw determination and their intense hard work. This is why I came to Kenya, and it brings a gulp to my throat.

Now their doubts seem to have been dispelled, they're getting more involved with the idea, and the elders want to be identified with the project. They like the snazzy blue Siboti Foods shirts we're wearing and ask if they can have them, too.

'Of course, I'm very happy with that – after all, the more people there are wearing our logo, the higher our profile will be within the community.'

William, one of the two assistant chiefs, stands up. 'Only the Chief and the assistant chiefs should wear blue,' he states loudly, clearly keen to acknowledge the committee's hierarchy. 'The elders who make up the rest of the steering committee should have Siboti Foods shirts in another colour.'

I look round at the faces. Everyone still looks happy. That's fine with me. I know that my supplier in Bungoma has some smart light-green shirts, so we agree on a two-tier system – blue for the top three men and green for the elders. The elders would also like some 'minutes', top-up cards for their mobile phones, in case they need to get in touch with me or the Siboti Foods team. That's fair enough, too, and the costs involved are minimal. I take a snap decision to give each of them a 100-shilling top-up every month and they are all smiles as they get their phones out and punch in the contact numbers for me, Kizito and the other managers.

We're ending on a really positive note. The Chief is fully behind us now and he wraps up the meeting with a passionate call to arms and a prayer for the success of the project. He's some orator when he gets going, with the sort of powerful, inspirational conviction that makes you believe and want to change the world.

'I have a vision for a better life for all Siboti's people,' he announces, 'with everyone working together to make it come to pass.'

As the committee cheer him, he raises his hands in the air and his words rattle round the mud walls of the church hall. 'I have a dream,' he cries, and I wonder whether he knows he's quoting Martin Luther King. Maybe not, but he's speaking from the heart and people can feel the power of his vision. It's a good feeling to know we have a natural leader like that on our side.

Outside, everyone crowds around and we take group photos of the whole steering committee with my camera. There's an air of celebration, as if we've already achieved what we set out to do. That may be a bit premature, but the fact that the community leaders have given the chilli project their wholehearted blessing will surely help us with the whole community.

We've got the top people firmly on our side. Now we're relying on Siboti's farmers to grasp the opportunities and do their bit to help themselves.

14

Spreading the word

'Don't sell life insurance. Sell what life insurance can do.'

Ben Feldman, record-breaking salesman

We've set ourselves a target of signing up 400 smallholding farmers to work with us, right from the start. That might be a ridiculously optimistic figure, but there's no way of knowing what the take-up will be until we start inviting people to sign on the dotted line.

Back in my lair at the Rickshaw Hotel, I use the Siboti Foods logo to create some headed notepaper and I write up our message. It looks good, and I'm certain the deal we're offering will attract a lot of farmers, so I go back to the Shariff Centre the next day and get Robert to print off several hundred copies.

The key to reaching as many people as possible seems to be to make use of the fact that everyone around here goes to church on a Sunday. There are twenty-one churches in Siboti, so there is roughly one church for every thousand people. I remember reading somewhere that Dublin has fifty churches, but that's for well over a million people. If you want to talk to people in Siboti, just turn up at church on Sunday morning.

With the help of the team, I draw up a spreadsheet, listing all the churches and the names of the parish priests. Because all the churches begin their long services at roughly the same time, Kizito, John, Edwin and Julius will be able to get round two churches each on any Sunday, to talk at the beginning of one church service, and at the end of another. It's going to take us three weekends to cover the twenty-one churches, so we need to get going straightaway.

Once we've decided who will take responsibility for each church, we need to arrange an initial visit to talk to the priest and convince him to let us talk from the pulpit on Sunday.

The message must be consistent and persuasive, so we spend an hour or so working out just what the team members should emphasise to win from each parish priest the opportunity to address his congregation. Then we need to plan the actual speech from the pulpit. I take notes on the laptop as we piece together the points we want to make, and we end up with a crib-sheet that will make sure all the main issues are covered.

But it's not going to be easy for my four new recruits to stand up in front of hundreds of people and deliver a powerful and inspiring speech that will get farmers queuing up to sign contracts to grow chillies for us. They are not used to public speaking, and while John and Edwin are confident they can do it, the other two are not so sure. We do a dummy run and Kizito and Julius both giggle nervously when it is their turn to stand at the front and give an impassioned, informative speech about the history of the project and our plans for the future. They need to explain how we started with repairing boreholes, creating the women's groups and getting 225 orphans fitted out with uniforms and back into school, and how we are now turning to the serious business of helping the community make some real money through growing chillies as a cash crop.

We are guaranteeing that we will buy the chillies for more than any broker will offer, they'll say, because we are working in bulk and can get the best price available in Nairobi. The *mzungu*, i.e. me, has made many good contacts in the capital, and even overseas, that will make sure there are always buyers for Siboti's crop. Seeds, fertiliser and pesticides will be made available to every farmer, to be paid for later out of the profits from selling the chillies. No one's going to be cheated or short-changed, and we will be providing free training in commercial horticulture techniques and record-keeping for everyone who takes part. This is a great opportunity for every family in Siboti. The elders and the Chief fully support the project and this is your chance, now, to get involved, sign up for a contract with Siboti Foods and look to the future.

My thinking is that when and if I leave Siboti, I'll hand over the project along with any business contacts I've made. The concept of a franchisable method that can be repeated elsewhere in Africa is growing on me. Perhaps that's where I see my future now: in rural African countries, repeating the success of the Siboti project. Or perhaps I'm getting ahead of myself. It's just so inspiring watching my new employees hone their speaking skills. As we go over the material again and again, even Kizito and Julius relax and start to enjoy the challenge. After a couple of hours of gentle coaching and encouragement, all four are getting pretty slick, adding in their own personal touches and speaking with real power and purpose. We arrange to meet again the next day. This time they're going to imagine I'm a farmer sitting in the congregation waiting to be inspired.

I don't know how many hours' practice they put in overnight, but the next day you can see that each of them is pulling out all the stops to out-Obama the others. It works for me – and I can't believe it won't do the trick when they come to speak to the people in church.

The parish priests turn out to be easy to persuade. They want a better life here on earth for their people and they are all enthusiastic about what we're doing. With their help, we have the opportunity we need to get the message out.

For the next two Sundays, Kizito, John, Julius and Edwin speak at the beginning or at the end of church services and hand out leaflets to the worshippers. They tell people they can sign up at the new Siboti Foods office during the week. Or, better still, they say, call us on one of the numbers on the leaflet and we will come and see you, take a look round your farm, get to know you, explain how it all works and register you.

I go back to Robert's printing shop in the Shariff Centre in Bungoma and ask him to print off another 200 information sheets. This time we'll have the leaflets laminated and the guys will nail them to trees at road junctions and get people to put them up on market stalls, shops and schools and churches across the length and breadth of Siboti.

As the word spreads, you can feel the buzz building up. People round here have never seen anything like this before, and everyone is talking about it. Each of my team members keeps reporting back that he's sure he can beat his personal target of signing up 100 farmers. I like this buoyant optimism, but I'm refusing to get carried away until I see the results.

After two weeks, though, I can't doubt that we're onto a winner. We've already signed up 560 farmers, 160 more than our target. We're in some danger of being swamped, so we decide to call a halt and cancel the appointments to speak at the last five churches.

I haven't got a contingency plan for a runaway success like this and I'm a bit worried about how we'll cope with training so many farmers. There's also the extra credit risk that will come from advancing seeds, fertiliser and pesticides to 40 per cent more growers than I've budgeted for. But the biggest uncertainty of all is the risk of over-production of a single crop. We've got promises, but promises aren't cash. We don't really know for certain whether the buyers I've lined up will actually take everything we produce and give us good prices for it.

If we want to recruit more farmers in the future, we can always go back and talk to the congregations at the five Siboti churches where we have not done our presentation. There are also churches outside the official border of Siboti, such as the huge Catholic church in Kimwanga, just the other side of the main Bungoma to Malaba road, where the congregations include many Siboti residents. If everything goes well, we'll be signing up more growers after the first successful crop.

We spend the next week on our motorbikes, bumping up and down Siboti's hilly, rocky, potholed tracks, visiting hundreds of farms. I'd like to have had Elizabeth, the agricultural adviser, with me on these trips, but she's got her hands full with a new baby. For now, she suggests we get the technical support and advice we need from a talented young local agronomist called Thomas Wangera.

Thomas is tall, strong and well qualified, an imposing figure, really. But he doesn't strike me as a people person. He exudes an unfortunate air of arrogance, and I can see how he could rub people up the wrong way.

There's nothing wrong with his technical knowledge and he is brisk and efficient as he assesses the surprising variety of different soil types in different parts of Siboti. Some of the farmers are lucky enough to have wonderful red earth, rich, loamy and fertile soil. Other areas have a deep brown earth, while others have thin, pale, sandy soil that offers little in the way of nutrients. Thomas takes his samples and makes his notes with an air of slightly impatient efficiency. But it's obvious that he doesn't really fit in with the all-for-one, one-for-all team spirit that already exists within my little group of musketeers. They find him bossy and condescending and they tend to disappear as quickly as possible when he turns up at the office. If he's going to be as useful as I need him to be, I'm going to have to do a bit of personnel management.

I take Thomas out for a chicken dinner and a few beers. I want to find out more about him and make up my mind whether he can adapt to the situation and tone down this brusque manner he has. In my experience, people always have the potential to adapt the way they work with others, if they are motivated to make the necessary changes. I need to find out what Thomas wants in life and how he sees his career developing.

It's an interesting evening. Thomas is already working for himself as a freelance consultant and he's keen to grow his own advisory business. He's got the technical skills and background to make a success of it and he has the confidence and courage to go it alone. But when I ask him how he feels he comes across to other people, his reaction is prickly.

'People need to respect me, Ken,' he says. 'Sometimes they don't understand the expertise I have.'

Personally, I don't think anyone underestimates his impressive knowledge and qualifications. But I've seen his jaw jut and his chest swell as he says this. This young man has an ego the size of a house, and he needs to learn to listen to other people's needs if he's going to make the most of his professional skills. I ask him, gently, if he's open to hearing another point of view about the impression he creates. He hesitates for a moment, then invites me to go ahead, and I explain, as delicately as possible, that technical competence is not going to be the whole story if he wants to build a successful business. This big, proud, well-educated man needs to develop listening skills and empathy with his clients to go alongside his technical prowess. It's the next stage in his professional development, and it will help him win business and keep his clients coming back for more.

To my surprise, it turns out that what I'm telling him is something he already knows. He sees the problem, but he doesn't know what, if anything, he can do about it.

'Maybe it's just the way I am,' he says. 'What can I do?'

I explain that it's partly a matter of technique, of asking questions, listening carefully to the answers and letting people see that he's focused on solving their problems, rather than showing off his expertise. These are things that can be learned, and I offer to stay in regular touch with him and advise him over the next few months. This time there's no hesitation.

'I'd like that, Ken,' he says. 'You can be my mentor and I'll make sure your Siboti farmers get the best advice I can possibly give them.'

I'm already consciously mentoring my four team members, and, I suppose, I'm effectively trying to mentor the whole Siboti community of 20 000 people to elevate itself out of extreme poverty and achieve most of the UN's eight Millennium Development Goals. Teaching people how to organise themselves, make the most of the resources available to them, plan their activities and keep the necessary records (of acreage, soil type, planting date, planting volume, fertiliser and pesticide types, volumes and dates, irrigation method, watering dates) is beginning to look at least as important as finding markets for their produce.

With 560 farmers signed up, the next task is to buy the seeds and fertiliser they will need. Buying enough chilli seeds for 200 acres is going to be expensive, but we can't afford to risk getting low yields, so we choose Kenya Seed Company, a long-established firm with outlets all over the country, as our supplier. Other companies may be cheaper, but Kenya Seed has a reputation for high-quality seeds that will produce good and consistent harvests.

The other vital ingredient is fertiliser. Fertiliser is going to be far more expensive than the seeds, but it's a key element, especially in the sandy areas. After decades with no fertiliser and no proper system of crop rotation, the soil is weak. There is plenty of rain, but the soil is depleted. The best plan here would simply be to have root vegetables one year and an above-ground crop the next. Because of the huge variation in soils and depletion levels, different farms will be producing their crops at different times. This will actually work in our favour for now, though, as the harvest will be spread across several weeks, maybe even a couple of months. That will make it easier to shift large quantities of chilli in Nairobi without flooding the market and driving prices down.

I'm grateful to have Elizabeth back on the case part-time now. She, Thomas, John, Kizito, Edwin, Julius and I sit down together to work out how much of each type of fertiliser is required. The sums are startling. Altogether, we're looking at an investment of $25 000 for the first season. If the farmers don't do the watering and weeding properly, or if the seeds fail or the poorer soils are beyond redemption and the yield is low, a lot of that could be money down the drain. The biggest risk factor seems to be soil quality, so I ask Elizabeth to find me another agronomist, this time from outside the region, who can give me a second opinion on Siboti's soils.

The new expert is an older man, quiet and cautious and very different from Thomas. For the next two days, Edwin ferries him around to meet farmers, examine soils and collect samples. He won't make any snap judgements, he says, and he insists that the samples should be sent off to Nairobi for proper analysis in a soil laboratory. I wait on tenterhooks, knowing that bad news at this stage could throw a mighty spanner in the works.

The results of the soil analysis aren't great – but they're not disastrous, either. It should be OK to go ahead. I heave a sigh of relief and sit down to draft the standard two-page contract that will formalise the deal between Siboti Foods and each of our farmers. I'll want 1200 copies of this. Each of the growers will need to sign two copies, one to keep and one for our records, and I'll need some spare copies in reserve.

While I'm in Bungoma getting the contracts printed, I pick up all the bits and pieces we'll need for our basic record-keeping. I buy a big ledger for the central records, folders to keep the contracts in and smaller individual ledgers for each member of the team. We've divided Siboti up geographically, into four areas, and Kizito, John, Edwin and Julius will each take responsibility for a quarter of the farmers, 140 each. Without formal records, they wouldn't stand a chance of keeping track of what's going on, so I mark up each ledger with the columns and rows that need to be filled in and take the four of them through a quick crash course in the record-keeping we will need.

The next week, a truck pulls up outside the office with 160 20-kilo bags of potassium and nitrate fertiliser. It's a vast amount to unload – more than three tonnes – and we'll be getting the same again every second day for a fortnight. There's no chance of storing that much fertiliser in our little building, so we need to get the contracts signed and start getting the seeds and fertiliser out to the individual growers without delay.

Motorbikes are the ideal delivery vehicles for this sort of task on Siboti's narrow paths and tracks. With four sacks of fertiliser and four tins of chilli seeds balanced across the rear seat and luggage rack, held in place with elastic bungee cords, these basic but tough bikes can do a good job for us. Each of the team members puts on a fresh blue Siboti Foods shirt, stuffs a bundle of contract forms into his rucksack and wobbles off to get the necessary signatures from our registered farmers and hand over the first batches of seeds and fertiliser.

This is a landmark moment. The office is a hive of activity. Everybody wants to help us carry the sacks and load the motorbikes, and people can't believe the quantities of seeds and fertiliser we're giving out. Even the three-year-old urchins playing in the dust of the marketplace know something special is going on and there's a wonderful atmosphere of excitement and energy and hope.

It is less than a year since I first set foot in Kenya, hopeful, naive, well-intentioned and looking for my Millennium Village. And here we are now, with a proper functioning project going ahead at full speed. We've delivered the quick wins we needed to gain people's confidence. We've got a strong sponsor in the Chief, alongside the steering committee of 42 village elders and the project leadership team of myself and the four guys, supported by the agronomy experts.

Now we are moving into the main body of the project, the practical effort to create the education and economic stimulus that will raise this community out of extreme poverty and hunger. And I can feel the energy and drive of the entire community behind us, willing us on. I've never before felt the kick I'm getting today. I'm full of vitality and ideas, bursting with zest and creativity. Today I can walk on water, fight lions with one hand tied behind my back, clear tall buildings with a single bound.

I look out at the Malaba road, at the trucks lumbering by in the direction of the Ugandan border or racing back empty to pick up the next load, and I wonder where my own journey will lead me. I can't help feeling that I'm being helped, or looked after, in some way that I don't understand.

Ah, sod that. Get back to work, Ken. Are you going soft? You make your own success. You know that.

But these thoughts won't go away. Even the Blues Brothers were on a mission, right?

15

Thanksgiving

'So what do we do? Anything. Something. So long as we just
don't sit there. If we screw it up, start over. Try something
else. If we wait until we've satisfied all the uncertainties, it
may be too late.'

Lee Iacocca, US automobile executive

I've never really got Thanksgiving. To me, it just seems like a rehearsal
for Christmas – a time, as far as I can tell from the movies, when
families feel the irresistible need to be together, whether they like
each other or not. And, of course, it is a uniquely North American
thing: an annual commemoration of the first settlers safely gathering
in their first harvest.

The bunch of young American volunteers currently doing their stint
with Haven Kenya is determined to celebrate Thanksgiving in style.
At a time when I'm feeling a long way from home, I'm touched to be
invited to join them for their long weekend of holiday fun.

There is an Indian restaurant – more of a café, to be fair – in
Bungoma and the Americans have somehow persuaded the
staff there to get hold of a turkey and prepare it with all the

trimmings. Well, as many of the trimmings – and a few imaginative approximations – as could ever be procured in this part of the country. We wash this down with South African wine from a local supermarket and we're soon feeling pretty festive. During dessert, the games start.

'So, if they are going to make a movie about us, which Hollywood actors will play us?'

A great game, and I make a mental note to put it on my list of interview questions in the increasingly unlikely event that I ever return to corporate 'civilisation'. For now, though, it provides lots of opportunities to flatter and flirt, tease and torment, resulting in a good hour of howling laughter.

'OK, OK. Who's gonna play Lizzie?' someone shouts.

'Scarlett Johansson,' comes the reply.

I look at Lizzie. Nice kid, but a bit, well, squarer than Scarlett Johansson. Still, she's enjoying the moment.

'Ken next. Who's gonna play Ken?'

'Brad Pitt.'

'No. Way too young.'

'That's a bit unfair,' I point out. 'Brad Pitt's almost exactly my age!'

They holler. To these bright, energetic volunteers, anyone over thirty-five counts as ancient.

'George Clooney,' I suggest.

'Too handsome. Sorry, Ken.'

There's a pause.

'Morgan Freeman, yeah. That's the man. He's cool. He's wise. He's our Ken.'

Morgan Freeman? Fine actor, fine figure of a man. But not someone I've ever identified with. And besides, he's old enough to be my uncle. The comparison is absurdly inappropriate, so, of course, it sticks. For the rest of the holiday weekend, I answer to the name of Morgan. It kind of feels OK, too, after a while. I am sorry to let it go when this weekend is over.

It strikes me, as I'm chilling out at the restaurant with these young medics, how relaxed I'm feeling these days. Perhaps I'd forgotten how it felt to really relax. It's so very different from my life in London working for an international bank. Here I have no boss to satisfy, no all-night work sessions to prepare for 8 a.m. meetings. There is no stress to speak of. Yes, there's a huge workload, but no stress.

I glance at my reflection in the mirror opposite and take stock of my years. Those tired lines around my eyes seem to be less evident these days. Right now I live for today and trust in the future, not fear it.

While the Hollywood game continues to much laughter and another bottle of wine is opened, I nod at the man in the mirror and make a conscious decision to remember this moment. If you believe the future is going to be fine, there's very little that can touch you, I tell my reflection. My brain feels on fire with new ideas and angles for the project, possibly enhanced by the company and the evening, and I can't wait to talk it over with my mentors, Mama Jayne and Elizabeth. If the project works here, it could work in any number of rural African regions. Actually, I'd love to talk it all through with the girl on the bus. She was smart and feisty and the only person to have really challenged me since I arrived in Kenya. Another knotty problem: how will I find her?

In the morning, I shudder at the thought that we had travelled home over bad roads in four barely lit three-wheel *tuk-tuks*. We had been, potentially, one drunken truck driver (not as rare as you might think) away from being launched into oblivion. I give thanks.

My new American friends have invited me to join them on their weekend away trip. We are off on a jolly to Sipi Falls, a beauty spot in Uganda, and we're soon rolling off towards Bungoma on six *piki-pikis*. The main criterion when selecting one *piki-piki* from the fleets of motorbike taxis is not the state of the bike, but whether the driver is likely to give you a heart attack. An ability to assess whether a particular driver is likely to have a cheerful disregard for danger and an irrepressible need for speed or whether he might be open to a request to take it easy might indeed prove a matter of life or death. In Bungoma, we pick up a *matatu* (where you don't have the luxury of choosing your driver, but just sit tight and hope for the best) to take us to Malaba, the border town.

Everywhere I look these days I seem to see evidence of obvious impediments to economic well-being in Kenya – and how simply they could be remedied, given the will. Here, at the border, is a glaring example. We pass 200 trucks that have been waiting in line for two days to clear customs. They're all loaded with shipping containers full of goods imported through Mombasa, East Africa's main port. Uganda, Rwanda and Burundi (all three of them member countries of COMESA, an African free trade area) have no direct access to the sea. With only one road from Kenya, everything they import comes through this Malaba border point. And Malaba cannot cope.

The odd thing is, though, that the queue hardly ever varies in size. There is always a line of 200 trucks waiting to cross the border. It doesn't grow much day by day or week by week. So if some sort of SWAT team could be brought in, as a one-off, to clear the blockage, it should, in theory, stay cleared. More realistically perhaps, Kenya and Uganda could put on more staff and create some extra channels for vehicles to pass through. The economic payoffs for both countries would far outweigh the cost. But the most radical solution of all might be the one that was used to overcome a similar problem on the border of Lesotho, the landlocked country completely surrounded by South Africa. What happened there was that, eventually, tariffs and taxes were harmonised on both sides of the border. Suddenly, there were no payments to be collected, fewer searches were needed and smuggling stopped overnight. There's no incentive to smuggle whiskey, cigarettes or anything else across a border if the prices on both sides are the same.

If you want to get economic activity moving, surely you have to start with getting traded goods actually moving, instead of sitting. The delays and increased transport costs caused by the queues at Malaba must be having an impact on profits that could otherwise be ploughed back to help businesses invest and grow. The cost and inefficiency of border crossings makes trading in perishable goods out of the question and must put many Kenyan companies off doing cross-border business. All this deprives both economies of exports and the relief from poverty they could bring. Without the free flow of commerce across this border, export business cannot grow. It appears heartbreakingly simple and it seems as if all it needs is for the governments involved to make up their minds that it has to happen.

Crossing a border by car in Europe just doesn't compare with crossing an African border on foot. With a backpack and some local currency, we stride up to the border checkpoint. At the customs and visa office, my American friends each have to pay $50 to enter Uganda, while my Irish passport allows me in free. The Americans generously decree that I must stand everyone beers with the $50 I've saved.

We are in Uganda now. Money changers, hustling taxi drivers, tiny kids selling bottled water. Noise, dust, scorching sunshine. We negotiate with a mini-van driver with perfect English to be taken to Mbele, the next town. There are six of us, so we should just fit in. And we're off. But within a few minutes, he's stopped again.

He's picking up more people.

'Hey! There's no room. We've paid for this car. No room! No way!'

Suddenly the driver doesn't understand or speak any English at all. Rob, the most impetuous of our little crew, gets cross and starts berating the driver. But it's useless. We've got to shove over or shove off. We shove over and reach the town of Mbele.

Here we find another taxi. This time we're in luck. The car looks good and the driver is willing to take us all the way to Sipi Falls, a spectacular 300-foot waterfall on the edge of Mount Elgon National Park.

This man, apparently sane when we hire him, becomes a maniac as soon as he gets behind the wheel. By the time he's thrown the car round three or four hairpin bends, it becomes clear that one of the girls is genuinely scared she will never see her parents again. I make him stop the car and we get out and have words.

'Don't tell me how to do my job!' he bellows. 'I have to drive fast. I've got a living to make.'

'Don't kill us all, then, or you won't get paid.'

After a short altercation, an inducement of $20 to take his time calms the situation. I make it payable on arrival, though, just to be on the safe side.

Lacam Lodge is delightful. As we dine, the waterfall rumbles, unseen but powerful, in the background. I have never been one for bungee jumps, potholing, rock climbing and the like. But how times have changed – how Africa, rather, has changed me. Now I can't wait for the morning, for the chance to rope down a 300-foot drop in the spray of East Africa's largest waterfall.

Next morning, Edward and James, our locally-raised instructors for the descent, seem extremely knowledgeable about how we will drop down the cliff face, and claim to have done it hundreds of times and seen thousands of people safely down. But they don't seem to be bothered about things like safety helmets or gloves. Where we come from, an adventure like this might involve a health and safety assessment and signing away all your rights in the event of an accident. Here, the risk of being sued doesn't seem to be so important.

Standing at the top of the waterfall, I can't hear myself think. The roar is deafening. The instructors tie ropes around a rock and Edward hooks himself up, says he'll see us at the bottom, gives a wave and disappears over the edge.

'Who's first?' asks James.

'What about the instruction course?' I'm wondering.

'When you go over the edge, hold your left hand high on the upper rope. Hold your right hand beneath you. Then just move the rope in and out to let yourself down a few feet at a time.'

Is that it? What if it gets away and I start to slide down too fast? What happens then?

'Ah. There is a second rope, for safety. We won't let you slide too quickly. Believe me, we've done this thousands of times.'

'I'll be first,' Rob volunteers, full of confidence. He's an extreme sports nut and he's bursting to go.

I guess there's a medical reason I never wanted to do extreme sports. It's because I suffer from something we specialists call abject terror. But I decide to go next. No point in thinking about it too much.

I've just got to lower myself over the edge of a 300-foot cliff, attached to a rope that's tied around a rock, in a place that's hours from the nearest hospital, with no medical or safety equipment to hand. That's all. But it's all OK, because two African guys I've never met before say it'll be fine.

What the hell am I doing?

I've often told myself lately that I want to live every day feeling alive. But in order to feel alive I've got to actually be alive.

I can't do this. I won't do this. It's not that I am afraid. It's just that it's too dangerous. Actually, it is that I'm afraid. No, that's not it. I'm completely bloody terrified.

'Can somebody else go next? I'm not sure I'm going to do it.' I hear from a faint, weedy voice that surely can't be mine.

The next half hour expands and contracts with an intensity I haven't felt before. It feels as if my head is filling up with liquid or air and it's going to explode when the pressure gets too great. Everyone else seems a long way away. I watch them going over the top of the cliff, one by one. I can hear their voices and the roar of the waterfall, but everything is muffled. There's a giant bubble in my head, but I'm in the bubble too. And although outside everything is weird, inside it's becoming very clear.

The fear of going over that ledge is the fear of embracing the uncertainty. The desire to actually go over is my desire to embrace uncertainty. I have the desire, and I have the fear, too. This is where my life is now.

That all seems pretty obvious from here, looking back. But in that moment it feels more personal, more specific. Am I still the same corporate conformist I have been for the last twenty years? Am I just having a kind of adult gap year, all ready to bottle it and scoot off home the minute things get tough? Or will I be able to face up to my occasional mini-panics about selling up, leaving everything behind and going alone to work in Africa and overcome them? Do I have the grit, the defiance and the determination to live with a higher purpose? Do I, basically, have the balls?

My body seems to take the decision for me. I stand up and take a deep breath, bracing myself for action.

'Am I going to do this thing?' I ask myself silently.

I clench my fists. I'm almost there.

'Am I made of courage and determination or am I a regimented wimp?'

'You are the fucking *model* of determination.' I growl out aggressively, through gritted teeth.

I move towards the edge. It's a long way down. But then a rock track that Tony Robbins had pumped out a year ago comes screaming at me from inside the pressure bubble.

'IT'S... MY... LIFE...'

Oh, fuck, yeah. So it is. It's my life and I'm quite possibly about to end it in some African cliff madness. FUCK!

I laugh loudly, even demonically.

I hardly know if the voice in my head is mine or Jon Bon Jovi's.

Either way, though, it tells me what I need to hear.

Live your life with guts and determination. Live it with fun. Live it with passion. Live it today.

Quaking with fear, I stand at the top of the cliff and let first one foot, then the other, step over the edge into open space.

After fifty feet or so of inching down, clinging on to the rope for dear life, I stop and tell myself to man up. For the next two hundred feet I feel like the champ, flexing chest and biceps, pumping with adrenaline, pausing to let the waterfall spray hit me full in the face.

'IT'S... MY... LIFE...'

I'm thirty feet from the bottom when my grip momentarily slackens. The hard, waxy nylon rope slides quickly through my bare hands and no amount of clutching and grabbing will stop it. I come down fast, far too fast, and land with a thump that leaves me shaken and winded. Edward unhooks me.

'Whatever happened to "We'll let you down slowly"?' I ask.

He grins and says nothing.

I wipe the blood and shreds of skin from my torn palms. My hands are a mess, but I'm still in one piece.

I've jumped off into the void and survived.

Now I get it. For me, Thanksgiving has just taken on a whole new meaning.

16

Pawn takes rook

'The notion that aid can alleviate systemic poverty, and
has done so, is a myth. Millions in Africa are poorer today
because of aid; misery and poverty have not ended but
increased. Aid has been, and continues to be, an unmitigated
political, economic and humanitarian disaster for most parts
of the developing world.'

Dambisa Moyo, author of *Dead Aid*

As the Siboti Foods project starts to gather momentum, I'm inevitably
seeing less of Mama Jayne, whose office is about an hour away. She
is still one of the people I turn to first for advice, and the scheme
we cooked up together to extend the mobile clinic service into the
Siboti area is working well, but I'm no longer comparing notes with
her every day.

I have, though, found out a lot more about how Haven Kenya
works. And it's not altogether a pretty picture. Students from the
United States – mostly from Idaho, for some reason – come out to
Kenya for a three-week stint as volunteers. They genuinely want to
help people in Africa. And they certainly do.

Those who are business students hold workshops for entrepreneurs, to help them get a foothold on the economic ladder. The majority, the medical students (who have each raised funds at home to bring packs of medicines with them), travel around with the mobile clinic, dispensing care and health education and delivering information about HIV/AIDS. Some of them apparently get module points towards their degrees at home for doing it. Others just do it out of the kindness of their hearts, because they want to help people less fortunate than themselves.

This means, in reality, that the services Haven Kenya makes available to the community are actually provided by these volunteers. Haven Kenya's main task is to co-ordinate things, making sure both the givers and receivers of care and education are in the right place at the right time. That's something a born administrator like Mama Jayne could handle with her eyes closed.

But there's just one aspect of all this that doesn't seem right to me. The students pay quite a lot of money for the privilege of being here and doing their good works. They pay Haven Kenya handsomely for their bed and board – a wooden bunk in a mud hut, with sluice-down showers and very basic food – and it's obvious to me that someone is doing well, financially, out of this arrangement.

The volunteers know this is Africa, so they're expecting to rough it. But I'd have thought the least Haven Kenya could do was make sure they had a decent meal after a hard day's work. It's not like that. They get a meagre breakfast and lunch and a one-course dinner that's often the same nondescript bowl of overcooked pasta. Many of them dislike the food and slip away into Bungoma to make their own arrangements.

It seems to me that the volunteers are being squeezed for someone's profit. The guy who's ultimately in charge lives in a big house and is building another, and he drives a Toyota Land Cruiser. And I soon find out that some of the Haven Kenya staff are owed several months' back pay. Like the volunteers, they, too, are effectively working for nothing.

But the medics and business students are young and in Africa and they're determined to make the best of it and have a good time. One of the places they love to escape to for a weekend is the Kiboko Hotel in Kisumu, Kenya's second city, on Lake Victoria. They come back to Siboti full of it and looking well rested and well fed. I should go, they tell me. I need a regular break too, and they say the hotel is really something special. *Kiboko* is Swahili for 'hippopotamus' and the hippos come out of the water to lounge about on the hotel lawns every night. I'm convinced by the young volunteers' enthusiasm, so when I get a free weekend, I set off to unwind by the lake.

Three hours from Siboti, I find myself in another world, sitting on a terrace in shorts and a T-shirt, sipping a gin and tonic. There's nowhere in Bungoma you can get a gin and tonic. A cold beer, or maybe half a bottle of vodka, yes, but ice and a slice are unknown luxuries. I even find myself blessing the nice heavy tumbler it arrives in. This is more like it. I have a good dinner to look forward to, a real bath with unlimited supplies of hot water, and a proper big bed with clean white linen.

With nothing much on my mind but the prospect of dinner and bed, I sit watching the sun go down over the lake, savouring every minute, thinking how truly fabulous this is. Suddenly, though, something about a group of people at the other end of the terrace catches my attention.

They could be doctors, lawyers, maybe – young professionals, probably visiting Nairobi for the weekend. I don't know any of these people. But among them is… Yes, it's definitely the woman from the night bus, the smart, sassy girl who told me to stop trying to be Saint Ken and get out of Africa. I'm pretty sure she hasn't noticed me.

When the group has to pass me to go in to dinner, I turn towards her and say 'We meet again! How are you?' (Well, nothing ventured, nothing gained, fortune favours the brave, and so on.) But she completely blanks me and just walks on. Oh well, that's that, then. I'm not a quitter, but sometimes you have to cut your losses. Later, though, at dinner, I'm sure I catch her looking my way. So she did see me. What *is* it with her?

The next morning my whole body is on fire. Not sunburn: mosquito bites – hundreds of them. I count sixty bites on one leg alone. And they are itchy as hell. A kind of horror descends on me. Now I am going to get malaria and it serves me bloody well right. Yet straightaway Ken-the-hopeless-optimist is arguing his corner. Come on. Get real. I might as well have it now and get it over with, because I'm going to get malaria at some stage whatever I do.

The pros and cons of taking anti-malaria medications are widely discussed among the foreigners working in Kenya, and the prevailing wisdom is that it's better not to take them. Sure, if you're going for a holiday, do as the doctor says. It makes sense. But if you're going there regularly or staying for a long time, the cure can be worse than the disease. The anti-malarials can be harmful, as prolonged exposure can sometimes cause liver and possibly kidney damage. I reflect that these particular organs of mine are probably knackered anyway, due to previous lifestyle choices, so I don't want to muck about with that stuff unnecessarily. If you're in the cities a lot, it can be safer, especially if you avoid still water at dusk. Unless you're in a good air-conditioned hotel, you must sleep under a mosquito net, which is one custom I always observe quite religiously.

So now I'm at the Hotel Hippopotamus, believing that I've probably contracted malaria, and I sneeze once at breakfast, which proves conclusively that I am dying. I think I ought to find out where the nearest hospital is, just in case. But I don't sneeze again, so I don't. The girl from the bus makes a cool entrance wearing the same white linen trousers I remember from our first encounter. While she's choosing breakfast I curse my misfortune at the circumstances – me with a double pepperoni with extra chilli for a face. Great. But my bites seem to elicit the sympathy vote, at least – or maybe it's just sheer pity – and I get a smile – the big, winning one I fell for on the bus – as she crosses the room to join her group, which immediately cures the malaria. I decide to renew peace talks after breakfast, but she's gone by the time I've finished. Hey ho.

The immediate fear of death has subsided and soon I'm lying on a lounger in the sun beside the hotel pool. If you don't know East Africa, this may sound odd, but the climate – in Kenya, at least – is not what I'd expected. The weather is just glorious. It's not the kind of unbearably hot, searing sun that has to be avoided at all times. You don't have to wear a hat and cover yourself up every minute of the day. As far as the weather's concerned, it's more like holidaying in Spain.

Life is improving by the minute, with each chilled orange juice. And I've just seen another beautiful girl, a real stunner. What's more, I can't help noticing that she keeps looking over in my direction. I forget all about the girl from the bus.

Swimming Pool Girl is with a friend and what appears to be the friend's child. The looking over continues. She waves. I wave. I watch her diving into the pool – a creature of beauty. Eventually they leave. A few minutes later, a waiter brings me a piece of paper. It's her phone number. And she's called Lisha. This is rather amazing She would like to meet me, so I call her straightaway and we agree to have a drink that evening.

We meet up and go to a nightclub. She continues to be stunningly good-looking – and a thirsty drinker. I like her company and we're having a good time together, so eventually she asks me if I want to go on somewhere.

She's a singer, it seems. Would I like to come and hear her sing on stage? It's my weekend off and I'm ready for adventure. So we drive out of town. We drive and drive and I have no idea where we're going, no idea where I am. But I'm not worried. It's cool. This is living life. It might turn out disastrously, but for now it's just great.

Eventually we pull into what's almost a shanty town, way out in the sticks. But the venue has a bar and there's a live band. Lisha knows a lot of the customers and we join a group of about eight.

'Can we buy my friends drinks?' she asks

For a moment I become keenly aware that I'm the only European in the place, and again something tells me I should probably be worried. I'm used to being the only white face, but I'm usually somewhere where lots of people know me and could vouch for me – and, I now realise, keep a watchful eye out for me. Not only do I not have a clue where I am, but none of my friends knows I'm here. I've broken every personal safety rule in the book. But I'm loving it – chatting, laughing, having a real blast. It's after midnight by now, and people here have clearly been drinking for hours. I may be the only *mzungu* here, but no one's taking much notice of me.

The atmosphere definitely feels more edgy here than in Siboti or Bungoma. I always feel safe there. People wave at me. Kids follow me, smiling and calling out 'Mr Ken' or '*Mzungu Mzungu*'. Here it's, well, a bit more foreign.

'Ken?' Lisha prompts, slipping her arm through mine.

I look round at the bar. It's the kind of shabby place you'd find in a shanty town like Soweto. It's clearly prestigious for her to have me here. Why shouldn't I buy her friends a round of drinks?

'Of course,' I tell her.

Her friends clink my beer bottle and I enjoy watching Lisha flitting around the group, smiling and laughing. The alcohol is easing any sense of discomfort and I know my natural defences are down. Maybe I should feel more nervous than I am. If something happened and I was abducted from this bar, nobody would know where to begin looking for me.

Even as I'm sitting there, though, I know I'm intoxicated. But it's not the drink. It's the freedom.

The England I have recently left is a very different place from the England I arrived in twenty years before, and one of the big changes, to my mind, is that it has become a CCTV surveillance society, perhaps through necessity. So the idea of no one (including me) knowing where I am – the idea of my own anonymity – is a thrilling contrast to that Orwellian surveillance culture I left behind in London. And there is another factor. Just being away from corporate London, from the sense of living a controlled disciplined life, is exhilarating, liberating. I feel alive. Away from institutional goals and structures, I am taking risks, living a new life. I feel I've somehow graduated and renewed myself as a human being, as a man. The world feels very real and I am ready for anything – absolutely anything – to happen.

I learned a lot and changed a lot in that enlightening week I spent in Florida on the Tony Robbins course. It's no coincidence that within a few short months of Florida I had switched the direction of my life and arrived in Kenya to start what has become the Siboti project. I've reset my personal compass.

Part of this is to do with deciding to focus on making some contribution to the world. But the other part – exciting, unnerving and totally revitalising – is a conscious decision to embrace uncertainty.

You never really know in advance what embracing uncertainty will require you to do. All I know is that I'm having to teach myself to go against my natural instinct to play safe. I am going to take risks, welcome the unknown, live life more fully. I am going to live like there's no tomorrow. And if, one day, there really is no tomorrow, I'm going to go out knowing I've made the most of what I've had.

Lisha turns out to be a rotten singer, but it doesn't matter somehow. The conversation flows. There is a refreshing sense of living in the moment in that bar. People don't want to think about the future, probably because statistically the odds aren't great for them. Friday night in a shanty town bar is an opportunity to forget life's harsh realities. And I am paying for the drinks, so Lisha can sing what she likes and no one minds. I am subsidising the arts! Eventually we drive back – I'm not sure quite how, but I do remember the car sliding all over the gravel road. I'm not proud of that, now, of course, but at the time it is all part of the recklessness, the wild, untamed freedom of the night – a night I will remember for ever.

The next morning Lisha and I have both lost some of our lustre. A brief look in the bathroom mirror confirms that we've both developed what a friend of mine calls 'Monet faces' – good from a distance, but, up close, just a mass of blotches. I am tenderly nursing my gigantic hangover when there is a knock at the door. I'm hoping it's room service with a proper cup of tea and a blood transfusion. I couldn't be more surprised when it's the girl from the bus.

'A peace offering,' she says, with that smile, and offers me a tube of cream. 'It's good for the mosquitoes,' she says. 'I hear you are doing some good things. I was too hard on you.'

I feel unbelievably and irrationally grateful for this vote of confidence. I'm just about to ask her name when Lisha calls out, 'Ken?'

Talk about bad timing. The girl's face falls. Suddenly I feel like every exploitative *mzungu* there ever was, falling right into the stereotype. The girl just turns on her heel and goes.

'Wait,' I say, feeling that I can't let her go again.

But what for? Wait till I think of what to say next? Wait until I get this girl I hardly know and I'm never going to see again out of my room, so you and I can get to know each other? I feel sicker than ever.

* * *

On Monday morning, back in Siboti, my feet are firmly back on the ground. My head is clear; I've banished any thought of the girl from the bus – this really isn't the right time for a new relationship – and I am focused on what I have to do.

I keep thinking about my discovery that Haven Kenya's employees aren't getting their back pay, and my thoughts turn to Mama Jayne. She has seemed preoccupied and anxious lately, and I wonder whether she, too, is owed money. I find it hard to believe, though. It would be madness on the boss's part to risk losing her, as his whole operation – and probably his lifestyle – depends on her energy and organising skills. She is the one who mobilises the students, decides the destinations, arranges the schedules, publicises the clinics and workshops, organises the volunteers and takes care of a hundred other logistical details. But she's a proud woman. If she's got a problem, I doubt she would approach me about it. So I decide to approach her.

I find her hard at work in her office – which is a table, a chair and a rough wooden bench, upholstered with a bit of foam and lino tacked over it.

'Jayne. I want to ask you a question. Are you getting paid?'

She looks up, obviously surprised by the question. She hesitates for just a moment.

'Shut the door,' she says.

I close it and sit on the bench.

'So, are you being paid?

'Not really.'

'How much not really? For how long not really?'

'Four months,' she sighs.

'How are you living?'

'My husband works a piece of land. We manage.'

'But for how long?'

She sighs again. I'm pretty sure, at this precise moment, that she'd rather I just dropped the subject. But now I know my suspicions were right, I'm going to make sure we get this sorted out for her.

'What does your husband think about this?'

'He thinks, since I'm not getting paid here, I'd be better off helping him on the land.'

'Do you want to leave Haven Kenya?'

'No! Really. I love working here.'

'But you would be prepared to leave this job that you love?'

She thinks, briefly.

'Yes. I suppose so. If I don't get paid, I'd be prepared to leave.'

'You realise you're in a very powerful position, don't you?'

She looks at me as though she has no idea what I'm talking about.

'Listen. We're going to get you your money. You're essential to Haven Kenya. You do the jobs the boss doesn't want to do and probably couldn't do as well. And if you left, the students would turn up and find nothing was organised for them.'

Mama Jayne rearranges the pens on her desk and nods.

'I know this,' she says. 'I don't know how to challenge my boss. He would take it badly. That would not be good for me.'

'You hold all the cards,' I reassure her. 'The American volunteers would soon find they were paying good money just to waste their time, and word of this would quickly get back to their universities. The students would stop coming and your boss's revenue stream would just dry up. He simply can't do without you. Believe me, he needs you a lot more than you need him,' I tell her as she fiddles with the pens, an anxious look on her face.

'You've already told me you're prepared to leave if you don't get paid. That makes you an opponent with nothing to lose – and that's the kind of adversary no one wants. You have an ace up your sleeve. If you decide to quit, the boss will have absolutely no hold over you.'

She turns to me, uncertain.

'So, if I leave I win, and if I get paid I win?'

'Yes. And remember, he doesn't want you to leave. He needs you. And you may not want to go, but he knows you can.'

'So, how...?'

What follows amounts to an impromptu negotiation skills training course, with an audience of one. I tell Mama Jayne it is very important that she doesn't go in saying, 'I want my money or I'll leave.' That's her ace, her final trump card. But she mustn't play her ace, mustn't threaten to leave, unless she has to. She can probably win what she wants with a 5 or an 8 card.

'Make sure your boss doesn't lose face, and it'll be fine.'

'OK,' she says, her shoulders finally dropping. 'Tell me how.'

She should play this elegantly, starting off by flattering the boss. She needs to keep things cordial for the future. So she must begin by explaining that she admires him, loves working for him, and has come to him for some advice.

Her husband, she will say, is putting pressure on her to work on the farm with him, as she's not getting paid at Haven Kenya (a fact that just needs to be slipped in here, almost in passing). He's rented land and planted several acres of crops and stands to make a lot of money from it, but he needs her help. On the other hand, she feels loyal to Haven Kenya. She doesn't know what to do, so she's appealing to the great man for some guidance. How should she handle her dilemma? What would he advise?

We rehearse one or two ways the conversation might go, and Mama Jayne gradually comes to believe it will work. I tell her I've had many similar chats in the past, with very high stakes involved, and that the rules are always the same. Not only that, but she's a transparently honest, talented and hard-working woman who is entirely within her rights to press for the money she's already earned. Do it, Jayne. Just go in and get what you deserve.

I see her later that day, and she's smiling broadly.

'Did you get your money, Jayne?' I ask.

'Yes,' she laughs. 'I got it all. And I only had to play a 5.'

17

Re-inventing the wheel

'Water is the king of food.'

Kenyan proverb

Water is life. Fixing the ten water pumps in Siboti has helped maybe 5000 to 6000 people improve their lives. It's a big bonus for those who live near the boreholes. But that still leaves up to three-quarters of the population with no proper access to water, even for the basics – drinking, cooking and washing. These families are still relying on the women to go to the streams and waterholes every day and carry the water they need back in buckets and plastic jerrycans.

And anyway, it's not just about water for domestic use. If Siboti's farmers could get enough water to irrigate their smallholdings, that would change everything. At the moment, they get two crops a year, always assuming the rains come when they should. If they could water their plants properly, they could enjoy three growing seasons and sell the surplus to boost their incomes.

I'm on the motorbike one day, on my way back from the Shariff Centre, when I notice that a large shop, Bungoma Chemist, is demonstrating human-powered irrigation pumps. I pull up and take a look, and I can see the potential immediately. These machines are rugged, chunky, low-tech treadle pumps – like a StairMaster exercise machine – with a T-shaped handle and two big flat pedals. The pump is called the MoneyMaker and it's supplied by a non-profit organisation called KickStart, which developed it specifically to help subsistence farmers in Kenya get more out of their land and lift themselves out of poverty. As KickStart has refined its designs over twenty years, it has sold more than a quarter of a million of these simple, durable pumps, helping thousands of families across Africa make the crucial move up from subsistence farming to small-scale commercial agriculture.

I like the idea, and I like the look of the pumps. They are strong and simple, cleverly designed so that any parts that wear out can be replaced without the need for any tools or specialised expertise. There's a fat hose that can suck up the water from a river or pond, lifting it up to eight metres, and a narrower hose pipe that can lift it another sixteen metres and push the water 200 metres with enough pressure to power a sprinkler. In practice, that would mean that anyone within a couple of hundred metres of a stream or a waterhole ought to be able to irrigate all year round and possibly even get a third growing season. The pumps cost about $100 each, so it's a big investment, but KickStart's long experience shows that buyers usually recover the full cost within months. These pumps could have a huge impact on the productivity of farmers and the local economy.

When I talk to the people running the demonstration, it all sounds quite possible. They tell me KickStart's regional representative for

Western Kenya is a woman called Cecilia, and they're quite happy to give me her number. I call straightaway, and arrange to meet her for coffee.

'I know you've got arrangements with Bungoma Chemist and one or two other shops in town. Are they exclusive deals,' I ask, 'or could I become an agent, too?'

She laughs.

'There's no problem with that,' she says. 'If you just buy a couple of pumps, you can become an agent and we'll give you all the posters and brochures you need.'

The trouble with the shops, she tells me, is that they all have the same cashflow problems. They can't afford to have money tied up in stock, so they will only take one pump at a time. When they sell that, they'll wait a while to order another one, but it means that they often don't have a single pump in stock while they wait for the next delivery. That doesn't have to be a problem for us. I could fund the stocks and put my efforts into generating sales without needing to delay to pay for stock replacement.

I like KickStart's approach of producing affordable low-tech equipment and selling it to people who can use it to boost their income, rather than giving the pumps away. A handout is always a one-off, but this is the basis for a sustainable business, where KickStart's profit can be put into research and development to improve the product, make it more affordable and help more and more people out of poverty. There's a margin built into the price – a commission of about $20 a pump – that I estimate could pay proper wages for a team of demonstrators and sales people.

This is starting to make a lot of sense, and I'm impressed by Cecilia's energy and her competent, business-like approach. It turns out she's come to KickStart via a career in sales for big Western companies, including a stint as the regional head of sales for Coca-Cola. That's a big job, in a country where people love their sodas so much. She's just the sort of person I might need to employ in the future, so I make sure I keep her telephone number.

First, though, I need to talk to people in Siboti about these pumps, and have Cecilia present.

'If we set aside time at our monthly *barassa* meetings, could you bring your team along and do some demonstrations, so that people can see how the MoneyMaker pump could work for them?'

Cecilia's already way ahead of me.

'Certainly. No problem. And if I sign you up as an agent, you'll get to keep the commission on any sales we make. It's a win-win, isn't it?'

As I make my way back to the office, bumping and crunching through the ruts and potholes, my brain is humming. Using these pumps to irrigate crops every day is something that will take time and effort. But time and effort are plentiful in Siboti. What's missing is money. If a KickStart pump gives a family a way of turning time and effort into money, that's a really significant step forward. A third crop every year would change people's lives forever. There might even be the opportunity for them to grow some of the more drought-sensitive but higher-value fruits and vegetables that would be too risky without a guaranteed water supply.

And now I come to think of it, there could be even more interesting possibilities. Anyone who invested in a pump would have a valuable asset. Supposing a farmer watered his own plants every morning and hired the pump out to his neighbours in the afternoons, for a few shillings a time, so that they could keep their crops alive and increase their yield. The pump owner could become an entrepreneur, building up a little business on the side.

The KickStart pump obviously has huge potential for those people in Siboti who are lucky enough to live near a stream or a pond. But water is still going to be a major problem for all those families that don't live close to a year-round stream or one of the newly refurbished boreholes. What the Siboti project really needs is a way of helping these people, too, so that everyone in the community has the water they need for drinking, cooking, washing and irrigation of crops.

I don't have long to wait for the next idea, though. When I check my emails that evening, there is a note from a friend in South Africa. It's just the usual chit-chat. She's telling me about her work, her husband and the kids. But right at the end, in a PS, there's a link she thinks I might find interesting.

'Have you heard about the Hippo Roller?' she says. 'I like the idea of you hauling one of these cross-country.'

I click on the link and it's a breakthrough moment.

Never mind low-tech, this is the ultimate no-tech solution to the water problem. Maybe not a full solution, exactly, but a really useful component of one.

What I'm looking at is a photograph of a woman pushing a big blue plastic drum, like an oversized lawn roller. There's a U-shaped metal handle, a red plastic screw-on jar lid on one side of the drum and a lot of water inside – about twenty-five gallons, ten times as much as a normal bucket and five times as much as a jerrycan.

There are more pictures. Here are small children dunking their Hippos in a stream to fill up and racing them back to their village. There's an old lady, surely too frail to carry a bucket on her head, happily pulling her Hippo Roller behind her. There's even a photo of Nelson Mandela pushing a Hippo Roller and calling it an African invention that will 'change the lives of millions'.

The only problem is the cost. The Hippo Rollers are made in South Africa and they cost about $125 each. Plus, I have no idea what the freight charges would be to ship a container to Mombasa and then have the drums brought by truck all the way to Siboti, but I'm pretty sure they would be prohibitive. I need to talk to someone who knows, so I get straight on to Hippo Roller people in Johannesburg the next day.

Transport, it seems, is not the problem I thought it would be.

'We've done it before,' the man on the phone tells me. 'We've shipped to Ethiopia, to Tanzania. We've even had some go to the Congo.'

But the costs? How were the transport costs paid?

'Oh, the donors covered it,' he says, airily.

Apparently, charities have placed big bulk orders, bought container-loads at a time and shipped them up to give away in some of the most parched and godforsaken places on the planet, where they've transformed whole communities virtually overnight.

I can see it all makes sense, on one level. But there's still the usual underlying problem. What happens when the rollers wear out, after five years or so?

I've come to Kenya knowing I will have money behind me from the sale of my house in London. But the problems are so vast, the need so huge. In terms of handouts, anything I could fund would just be a drop in the ocean. It would vanish without trace and the waves would close over it. If I used all the money I had to buy a few thousand Hippo Rollers, I'd be helping roughly half the families in Siboti. But unless that help somehow enabled them to boost their earnings, it would not lead anywhere. Within a few years, I'd be gone, the rollers would have worn out and there'd be nothing left to show for it all.

OK. No Hippos from South Africa. So what's the alternative?

Easy. Of course. It's obvious. Get them made here. Not necessarily to that exact design – I don't want to run into any patent problems. But if I work out a design of my own, I must be able to get something similar manufactured here in Kenya. That'll cut out the transport costs and it could be cheaper, too.

Manufacturing water tanks is big business in Kenya, and there are lots of companies, mainly based in Nairobi, making plastic tanks of every shape and size. You see the trucks carrying big tanks to building sites everywhere you go. As Kenya's development accelerates and the country builds more schools, hospitals, offices and homes, the demand is enormous. So I am optimistic that I can find a company to make what I will need. I've started searching online and asking my contacts about possible suppliers, and I make up my mind that I will talk to some of the most promising companies when I'm on my next trip to the capital.

It's possible, too, that James, the taxi owner I met at the InterContinental Hotel who has become my regular Nairobi driver, will be able to offer some suggestions. He knows people who know people. There's always something rather random about any conversation with James. He talks nonstop, nineteen to the dozen, and you never quite know where it's all leading, but he's full of energy and stories, so a day in his cab is seldom dull. I'm looking forward to seeing him again and starting the search for a firm that can make water drums at a price Siboti's people can afford to pay.

When I arrive in Nairobi, with a bunch of photos of the Hippo Rollers and of similar designs, and armed with a list of plastics companies that I've identified online, James is more than happy to take me wherever I want to go. He knows Nairobi like the back of his hand and we find ourselves darting here and there all over the city, from tiny unmarked backstreets to the big, untidy industrial estates out near the airport. There seem to be any number of suppliers that are keen to win my order, from big companies like Roto Tank ('manufacturing tanks in seven African countries for more than twenty years') to the kind of small, hungry business with an office over a shop and a backyard factory that looks like it was set up the day before yesterday.

Everyone, of course, promises the earth and guarantees unbeatable quality and prices, and I am reminded, many times over, that a slick-looking website doesn't necessarily mean there's a lot to back it up. All these smaller suppliers seem to be Indian-owned family firms, run by groups of brothers dressed in the same 'business casual' uniform of neat plaid shirts, pleated chinos with turn-up trouser legs and wide brown belts. They're all eager to do a deal, but it soon becomes clear that I need to find a supplier that's already producing something similar to what I need. It's just not going to be economical for a company that usually deals in big thousand-gallon tanks to make the moulds and set up the production facilities needed for my twenty-five-gallon water drums.

Eventually, though, I find a firm that seems to be operating on the right sort of scale. James comes in and sits with us, drinking tea, while I show the proprietor, Ramesh, my photographs. He nods and pulls out some photographs of his own.

'We're already making something like this for one of our customers,' he says. 'You can see it's about the right size. But if your Siboti Wheel is going to be dragged over rough ground, we'd probably have to use heavy-gauge plastic. I think we could do that for you. How many would you want?'

That's a good question. The unit cost is obviously going to depend on how many I think I can sell in Siboti. I know I'll have to make an initial commitment to buy a good few – perhaps a hundred. So that's the minimum. But how many would I need altogether if the idea caught on? There are 20 000 people in Siboti – say, 4000 families. If it all goes well, I might be able to sell to a quarter of them.

'Well, I know it's not very precise, but somewhere between 100 and 1000,' I say.

He looks thoughtful.

'It's not really enough,' he says. 'I think the set-up costs would be too high. Unless there was some other way of getting a payback on the preparatory work and mould-making. Does this have to be exclusive to you? How would you feel about letting me produce more of them and selling them on myself, through my distributors?'

I haven't thought of that. But it's actually a great idea. This guy is a real entrepreneur and we're on the same wavelength. If my efforts have the side-effect of making these water drums available to Kenyans in other rural areas, that's all to the good. Fantastic, in fact.

'OK. That's fine by me. That's how we'll do it.'

We haggle a bit about the price and agree on a figure of just under $50 per drum. I can live with that. It's a lot less than the price of $125 plus transport that I'd have to pay to bring the original Hippos up from South Africa. There'll be the cost of the metal handles on top of that, but our home-grown hippos will still be much cheaper. I ask about the handles and Ramesh shakes his head.

'We only do plastics. You'd have to get those made yourself.'

I've almost forgotten James is there with us, sitting quietly in the background. I've never known him go for so long without saying anything.

'Don't worry, Mr Ken,' he chips in. 'I know someone. We can go and see him this afternoon. He will make you beautiful handles for your Siboti Wheel.'

James helps himself to another cup of tea while Ramesh and I work out the technical details. He'll make sure there's a good, heavy-duty bush-type bearing on each side of the drum that will hold the handle in place. We'll have the drums made in white plastic, with the words 'Siboti Wheel' embossed into the mould, and Ramesh suggests altering the design of the filler cap so that it's less likely to be damaged. He'll get to work right away to make a prototype and I'll be able to look at it in two weeks' time, when I have to be back in Nairobi again.

We've done well. We say our goodbyes and go back out to the car. We're about to drive off when James suddenly excuses himself and runs back into the office. A couple of minutes later, he reappears.

'OK,' he says. 'Let's go and see the man about the handles.'

'Are you all right, James?'

'Yeah. Sure.'

'What's up? Why did you have to go back inside? Did you have too many cups of tea?'

I like James. He's a chatterbox, and his heart is in the right place. But he's rubbish at deceiving people. I can see something's not quite right.

'James...?'

'Oh, I just wanted to have a word with them.'

'About what?'

He's reluctant.

'It's just... If you're going to order a hundred water drums, Mr Ken, he's going to give me something. Because I brought you here. I was telling him he ought to give me something for bringing you to him.'

I can't believe my ears. I'm paying James by the day, at over the going rate, to drive me around whenever I'm in Nairobi. He's making a good tick out of me. I'm happy with that, knowing I will always get first call on his time, but I'm not having him topping it up by extorting kickbacks from the people I do business with.

'Look, this is my money. If there's some discount or kickback or whatever you want to call it, that comes to me.'

He looks at me sheepishly.

'But I brought you here.'

'Come on, James. I hired you to bring me here. This guy's not even one of your contacts. You brought me here, in your car, because I'm paying you to be my driver.'

I should be used to this by now. It's the Kenyan thing, this culture of *kitu kodogo*. Backhanders are standard practice. And it's not just 'What's in it for me?' but 'What's in it for me *now*?' It's so frustrating. It's so short-term. James may have gotten himself a few extra shillings in his pocket now, but he risks alienating his most lucrative and regular customer – me.

Oh, listen to me. I sound like some pampered, self-righteous Westerner – and it's probably because I am. What do I know about scratching and scraping a living in a country where the short-term always wins because, if it doesn't, you may not get as far as next week?

'Oh, forget it. But please don't do that again. Let's go and find the handles man.'

I can tell James feels suitably chastened. You can tell by his incessant chattering as we drive back through town. Or maybe you can't, as he'd probably be chattering anyway. Either way, *kitu kodogo* is one of the real challenges for me here and I wonder if I'll ever grow to accept it without being driven mad with frustration.

When we come back a fortnight later, Ramesh has prepared his first prototype. He's come up against a couple of minor problems, so we discuss how to get round them and he agrees to have a second stab at it before my next trip to the capital. In the end, it takes four versions before we get it just right, but he's really involved with the concept now and he doesn't seem to mind.

I need to sort out this business of commission for James, though, so I spell it out to Ramesh, while James sits there squirming beside us.

'Look, I have to sell these things to as many people as possible, so the price has to be as low as we can make it. If there's any room for commissions, I need that money to come off the price. I know a lot of things in this country work via kickbacks, but I can't do things that way. I'm not blaming you. I'm not cross with James. But that's how we have to work.'

'OK, Mr Ken,' says Ramesh. 'Understood.'

The man James introduces me to, as a possible supplier of handles, has come up trumps. His name is Winchester and he's a welder, working in a ramshackle yard full of parts salvaged from crashed trucks. He's friendly, flexible and willing. He'll make a sample for us – not free, but for a very reasonable price – and we can try it out, tweak the design if necessary and make sure we're getting what we want.

After two or three visits, we get the design details right. Our water drums will have simple, strong, galvanised handles that will stand up to rough treatment and will not rust. Winchester wants me to commit to buying the full hundred from him, 'to make it worth my while', but he gives me a rock-bottom price of less than $10. James and I will take batches of them over to the plastics factory to get them fitted onto the drums and Ramesh will deliver them to Siboti as part of the deal, piggybacking them whenever the opportunity occurs on part-loaded trucks that are taking his big industrial water tanks to customers in Western Kenya.

18

Selling elevation

'Imagination is more important than knowledge. For knowledge is limited to all we now know and understand, while imagination embraces the entire world.'

Albert Einstein

The North London chatter has been swirling around my head for a couple of hours now, with talk of the housing market, a great Indian art dealer, children, nannies, private schools and tennis lessons. I glance at the guests lining each side of the long beautifully hand-carved table. While everyone looks like me – forties, well-travelled, pretty much in good shape – inside I feel like an alien. I try not to glance at my watch in front of my generous hosts, while I mentally pack my suitcase. At least I can start a new spreadsheet to work out the economics on my new irrigation tools while I'm on the plane to Nairobi.

'So what do you do now, Ken?' asks the wife of a top foreign exchange trader to my right. She's ultra-groomed from the top of her glowing head to her sparkling blue fingernails. 'Someone said you were doing farming in Africa.'

'Ken's got this chilli growing project in Kenya,' says the vivacious, petite hostess to her left.

The trader's wife's glass of bubbly pauses in mid-air. 'How interesting. Why Kenya?'

The comment coincides with a general lull and the other guests turn to me looking for a new conversational angle. I try to look genial.

'I'm not a farmer,' I tell the table. The chilli side is just one part of it. I've got a project to pilot, to try out, you know, a new method of alleviating extreme poverty in rural Kenya.'

'Gosh,' says a lawyer. 'So you must be involved with the NGOs out there.'

'Actually no,' I tell her. 'It's just me.'

'Like Bono but without the shades?' says the bald guy who keeps leaning forward and rubbing his head. He might as well have said, 'So you're a fucking do-gooder like Bono'.

I laugh along. 'Well no, I'm running this as a business model. A pilot scheme. If it works, I'll try it elsewhere.'

'Still, Africa's got so many problems. Some people might try to make an impact closer to home,' he says.

'And how long are you going to be there?' asks the television producer who's just signed some huge deal to create a mini-series for Sky TV.

The scrutiny is making me want to run for cover. 'Oh… two years, five years. I don't know. I'll just see, I suppose.'

'Living life without a plan. How wonderful,' says the deeply tanned wife of the bald guy, as the caterer brings in artfully decorated desserts on a tray.

The guests smile and conversation resumes and I polish off my wine. Nearly time for me to make my excuses and leave. Next time I'll change the subject. Last week in a Dublin pub I didn't get off so lightly.

'So do you believe in God?' asked my friend, over our pints.

After an hour of interested questions, building a deep understanding of my quest, this was an unexpected swerve.

I sipped my beer and wondered where this was going. I'd remember this Dublin pub, with its beautiful wood panelling and etched glass, when I am back in the dingy cafés of Bungoma.

'Ken?' he said. 'Are you there. I was saying…'

'Nah, the answer to that is no,' I said. 'Anyway, what's God got to do with chillies?'

My friend was smiling without a hint of humour, and I sensed that he'd been leading up to this moment.

'I mean, what possessed you to go to Kenya to be a bloody do-gooder?' He laughed at his own mini put-down.

'If there are so many ways you could lose piles of money on this, why are you out there doing all that for a bunch of Kenyans? Why aren't you doing something for the homeless here in Ireland? Just take a look around this city. They're the ones who really deserve any help you can give. All the money you've been spending over there, what's it all for?'

'Yes, but…'

'But what?' he said. 'You're probably a big fish in a tiny pond in this Siboti place. Do you get some kinda buzz from that Ken? Do you? You could make a big impact with that sort of money here, back home. You're free to go and do whatever you want. Why are you out there? You should look after your own first. Are you an Irishman or what?'

That wasn't my easiest hour and I think of his words on the flight to Kenya as I puzzle through my sums for the wheel and the pump. All I can do is resolve in future to keep quiet about what I'm doing. People back home generally think I'm mad or misguided. I wish I could explain to them why these two bits of kit thrill me to the core.

With the Siboti Wheel and the KickStart pump, I have the hardware I need to make a start on solving the water problem and enabling local farmers to get more out of their land. Those who live near the water just need the KickStart pump. If they live further away, they can use the Siboti Wheel to collect twenty-five gallons at a time. Back at the farm, they can take the handle off and stand the drum on its side, using it as the water source for the pump so that they can water their plants. I've done the sums. The extra income they can make from growing more will pay off the microfinance loans within a year. It really does add up. Now I must start thinking about how I am going to convince these low-income families to overcome their deep-seated fear of borrowing and make this investment in their future.

As well as the Siboti Wheel and the KickStart pumps, I want to introduce affordable solar home lighting kits so that people can have brighter lighting for comfort and to help school children do their homework and studies. Solar lighting would also eliminate those polluting paraffin lamps that cause so many serious burns and so many respiratory problems.

I'm going to need an organisation, a team that can get out and demonstrate the benefits and payoffs and persuade the farmers that this is the way forward. I need to be able to delegate this work to someone bright, organised and trustworthy who can help me build this into a profitable, self-sustaining business.

Finding someone with the right sales and management skills is not going to be easy, but my mind keeps going back to Cecilia, the KickStart representative. She knows the area and its problems, but she also has the kind of business background I need, from her time with Coca-Cola. Maybe I could sell her on the idea and get her to come and join me to run the new Siboti Elevation Products business I'm envisaging.

I've still got Cecilia's number, so I arrange to meet her again, over coffee in Bungoma. There's a café, a buzzy place and the biggest in the town, right next to the Shariff Centre, which is where I get my printing done and have my hair cut. It's where the bus pulls in from Nairobi. I spot Cecilia waiting for me at the café as I ride up on my motorbike and take off my helmet. She waves and her smile reveals an endearing gap in her front teeth. Like a lot of the women here she wears a straight wig made of horsehair over her natural razor-tight Afro hair.

We shake hands and I join her, pulling up one of the aluminium chairs. We order coffee – a sachet of Nescafé and hot water and she laughs when I insist on two sachets with mine. She has no real idea what's on my agenda, of course, but she listens patiently and with growing enthusiasm while I lay out my whole vision for the future of Siboti. With the pumps and the water drums to help with irrigation, the solar power units that I have in mind or cheap, safe, fume-free lighting and the Equity Bank microcredit loans I'm lining up to make these things accessible and affordable, I will soon have all the elements I want in place. Now I need to find the right people to work with, first in Siboti and then, if all goes well, in other parts of Western Kenya.

'How about you, Cecilia?' I ask. 'Would you come and help me make it happen?'

She strokes a minute crease out of her blouse and looks thoughtful. 'It all sounds great, Ken, but you couldn't afford me. I've been spoiled by Coca-Cola and then KickStart. I earn a very good salary. I love the idea of what you're doing, but I can't afford to take a salary cut. I think my salary level would not fit with your plans.'

'Try me.'

Cecilia tells me what she's being paid by KickStart and I wince. She's right. It's a lot of money. It will be a long time before Siboti Elevation Products can justify paying anyone that kind of salary, even if everything goes exactly to plan.

On the other hand, she'd be perfect. She's smart, practical, early thirties, and she speaks the local dialects. She's ambitious and proud of it, with a business degree and proper business experience under her belt. Culture matters, and she would understand about sales targets, keeping records, getting reports in and being held accountable for results. In many ways, Cecilia is a good example of a type, of Kenya's emerging managerial class. In Nairobi, there are probably hundreds like her. Out here in Bungoma and Siboti, not so many.

I can promise her lots of interesting managerial experience, coupled with a lot of autonomy and responsibility. I will teach her new financial and management skills and techniques. She'll have the chance to build, train and run her own sales team. She'll have a well-paid role she can really believe in – a mission, rather than just a job. As Siboti Elevation Products grows, she will grow with it.

'Ken, I understand all that,' she says. 'It's very attractive. And if I let you go on long enough, I know you'll talk me into doing it for less. But where would that leave us? It won't do either of us any good for me to join you and then start resenting the fact that I'm not getting what I feel I'm worth.'

I know she's right, unfortunately. Damn it. Even the fact that she's spotted that dilemma helps convince me she's the right person for the job.

It's not just the salary I have to worry about. There'll be wages for three or four sales people, the cost of buying and running a suitable pick-up truck, the need for extra office and storage accommodation. Getting Siboti Elevation Products up and running is going to make a big hole in my resources.

But without Cecilia, is this all going to happen? No.

With her? Well, it's got a fighting chance.

'Do it, Cecilia,' I say. 'I'll match what you're getting now, made up of a lower salary plus commission income that's guaranteed for the first six months. We'll start something really worthwhile. If it takes off, you could go on to make a lot of money in commissions.'

I think she's genuinely surprised to hear me say this. I know I am. But it's the right decision.

I suppose I've been thinking we need someone with Cecilia's attributes at half the price. When it comes to it, though, it's the attributes that are non-negotiable. The price will be what it has to be. The art of decision-making is really, in the end, the art of prioritisation.

Getting Cecilia's skills on board is more vital, at this stage, than getting the price down.

'OK. You've got me,' she says. 'When do we start?'

It takes a while to sort out her move from KickStart, but within a month or so we've done it, and acquired a battered but practical Toyota Hilux pick-up, a rugged four-door 4x4 workhorse with plenty of load space in the back to cart around the pumps and water drums. I get a local signwriter to paint the Siboti Elevation Products logo on the doors and we turn our attention to recruiting our sales team. We put up adverts on trees and signposts around the area and wait to see if we get many applications from people with sales experience.

I don't know what I'm expecting, but I'm certainly taken by surprise by the torrent of hopeful candidates. There are over 250 applicants. Every one of them claims to have sales experience, though Cecilia's interviews quickly establish that many have sold nothing more than a pile of tomatoes in Kimwanga Market. In the end, though, we find four educated, persuasive and ambitious youngsters – three girls and one guy – who seem to have the vitality and drive we need. It's clear that we're buying potential rather than well-honed selling skills, but Cecilia isn't worried about that.

'You should have seen some of the local distributors I worked with at Coca-Cola,' she chuckles. 'There was one guy who couldn't even write his name. I dropped in on him one evening and there were his kids, only about seven or eight years old, sitting there in their school uniforms, writing up the records and filling in the sales sheets for him. But he could talk the hind leg off a donkey, everybody liked him, and he sold truckloads of sodas for us. It's the same in all the rural areas. You learn to work with what you've got – and value it.'

I arrange to rent another small building, next door to the Siboti Foods HQ, as the Siboti Elevation Products office and storeroom. In the evenings, in Bungoma, Cecilia and I develop our sales plan and targets for the first three months. We'll hold regular team meetings every Monday morning to go through the plans for each week's demonstrations, visits and follow-up calls. Everything is in place.

Over the next month or so, I watch in awe as Cecilia gives these enthusiastic trainees a crash course in selling. First, she makes sure they know the products inside out. Then she explains to them how the sales funnel works – how you need to talk to a lot of people, collect names and qualify prospects to see if they really are potential buyers, filtering out the curious and the time-wasters, stage by stage, until you're finally left with the handful of people who are ready and able to buy. She teaches them how to set up product demonstrations and how to engage people in conversation about the pumps and the water drums. Using role play sessions, she shows them how to handle queries and objections and how to explain the finance arrangements to people who've never spent this much money on anything in their lives before.

'Our job is not to sell,' she tells them. 'Our job is to help people. If you have any doubt at all about whether you should be selling to a particular prospect, you've got to stop. The last thing we want is for any of our customers to feel we've sold them something that's not right for them. People have to know we're on their side.'

I also realise something more subtle is going on. Cecilia is not just teaching them to sell irrigation tools and solar lighting kits. By emphasising the agricultural training and the financial and business education on offer as well as the contract income from growing crops for Siboti Foods, she is training them to sell elevation itself.

The next Monday morning, I'm back in the office early, almost pawing the ground with excitement. When Cecilia and the sales team arrive, they spend an hour filling me in on their plans for the week and I make a few suggestions. But, frankly, there's not a lot I can add. She seems to have covered all the angles and I can see the team members are just busting to get out and strut their stuff. I help pile two pumps and a couple of Siboti Wheels into the back of the pick-up, roping them down securely, wish the youngsters luck and wave them off on their first sales mission.

Who knows what we're starting here? If Siboti Elevation Products does develop over the next few months into a sustainable, self-funding, modestly profitable, replicable business, this could be the start of something huge for the community, for Western Kenya for other parts of sub-Saharan Africa.

I watch the pick-up bounce and lurch its way towards the rough track that climbs Siboti Hill. For some reason it makes me feel wistful. As it disappears from view I try to unpick the sudden and unexpected shift in my mood.

Over a soda, perched on my parked motorbike outside our office, I realise that I may be staying here for the long term. When I left London I hadn't given it much thought, I was just going for however long it took. Now, when I go back to Ireland, everyone's married, and their kids are mostly already grown-up. My dad has made a new life for himself as a widower. Life is moving on. I'm here and I'm loving Siboti. What if this project works really well? What if Kenya becomes my home forever?

19

Borrowed sunshine

'Progress is impossible without change, and those who
cannot change their minds cannot change anything.'

George Bernard Shaw

Traditionally, people's homes here are lit by dangerous, unhealthy
and inefficient paraffin lamps. Better-off families use two or more
lamps. But even the very poorest – the families scraping by on less
than the UN's extreme poverty line of $1.25 a day – somehow
find enough money to buy the fuel they need for a lamp. I'd never
had to think about it before, but having light, so that your day
does not have to end as soon as the sun goes down, is a very basic
human need. One Florence Nightingale-style lamp for a whole
family isn't exactly luxury, but having no light at all would surely
be a pretty clear indicator of absolute bottom-of-the-barrel
poverty.

Kenya is a land of vivid contrasts. During the day, the light is dazzling,
raking down in solid bars of sunlight between the branches. At night,
it gets Guinness-black, with a thick, liquid darkness that rubs against
your eyeballs like velvet. So much light, and then so little.

It doesn't take a genius to work out that borrowed sunshine – solar power – is an asset that every person in Siboti could potentially enjoy. Even I can see that if I could find basic, affordable solar lighting kits, everyone, even the very poorest villagers, could have light that was brighter, safer, and maybe cheaper, too.

So I set out in Nairobi to track down the right sort of solar unit. And it doesn't take long to find what I'm looking for. Simple, basic, tough enough to cope with the wear and tear – these Australian-made solar kits are cheap, easy to install and come with a three-year guarantee. There is a neat little solar panel that's just the size of a sheet of A4 paper. This is wired up to a battery, about half as big as a car battery, which can power four bulbs for up to eight hours, each of them giving off a lot more light than the old paraffin lamps. With no fuel to pay for, families who had these solar units would no longer need to turn the light off at ten o'clock to keep their fuel costs down.

I grab a piece of paper and work out the sums, grinning as the figures fall blessedly into place. The solar kit costs $120, about a third of a typical household's annual income. Kerosene currently costs a family about $90 a year. It's clear that solar power would not only be safer but definitely cheaper in the long run. Unlike kerosene, it's sustainable and it's far better for people's health.

The logic is clear. The cost of the solar kit can be recovered within eighteen months, from not having to buy kerosene. And from month nineteen onwards the families will continue to have free light but no more repayments for the solar kit, giving them freedom they'd never had before to use the kerosene money to buy food, clothes or whatever they needed most. It will be a real upward step in their finances.

It is obvious to me that anyone who can afford a solar kit should buy one immediately. But that won't be possible in Siboti, as very few of these families have the cash they'd need. I have to find a way to get these units into the hands of the very poorest people, most of whom can no more put down the money to buy a solar lighting system than fly to the moon.

It's a financing problem, then, and after decades in banking, surely I should be able to solve that!

I need to find a local bank that's prepared to lend the cost of a fairly expensive solar unit, unsecured, to people who live on less than the UN's $1.25 a day.

'Well, would you?' my brother Alan asks, when I go to visit him in Nairobi just before he leaves.

'Would you lend to people with no money?' he says again.

'Yes,' I say. 'That's what microfinance is all about.'

'Hrrrrmph,' he says, and I can tell he thinks the sun has been getting to me. Alan's always behind me. Even if sometimes he might think privately that I am a bit bonkers, he never really says so.

A few weeks later, I've obtained some new senior contacts at Equity Bank. I'm in Nairobi, sitting in a plush meeting room on the top floor of the bank's new Head Office, talking to the senior managers from the credit and product development departments, and it's all smiles. For the first time in Africa, this is me in my natural habitat, and while there is something oddly nostalgic about being back in this environment, I'm aware of the glint in my eye and the primacy of the deal on the table.

Banker to banker, we talk it through.

'The new Siboti Solar Loan product that I want you to launch,' I explain, 'will have an eighteen-month term'.

It will put the solar lighting in the hands of the people who need it, end their dependence on the expensive and unhealthy paraffin lamps and save them money, making them more financially secure at the end of the loan period. That positions them for further credit products and a long term profitable relationship with the bank. It could be a big growth product that's highly profitable for the bank.

'It looks good,' says the head of product development, scrutinising the figures in the printed presentation that I have handed out.

'The solar product and the loan product that make it affordable are so desirable', why wouldn't all your rural customers want it?' I carry on. 'Once they are free of their repayment commitments after 18 months, and no longer have to buy kerosene either, that's a massive step forward financially for them.'

'Yes,' he says, leafing through some papers on the huge oval meeting room table. 'But we would want to send an education officer from the Equity Bank Foundation to that community to explain to people how it works. You know – explain their obligations. That would have to be a condition of the loan, for people to attend a financial education morning.'

'Great. No problem. Good idea,' I assure him.

This whole thing will even work financially for me. I have built a realistic margin into the selling price of the solar kits, so that selling them will cover the overheads of the business and pay for the sales staff. It should be financially self-sustaining from the start and won't need me to invest financially in it.

The credit manager turns to me.

'I can see the potential,' he says. 'But I think we will need to apply a higher interest rate than you have suggested and it will have a substantial risk-adjusted capital requirement.'

'No, no, no.' I tell them. 'Let me explain how your interest margin threshold is achieved. The headline interest rate is low because it is based on the nominal non-reducing balance, which means the APR is high, and the margin level is well ahead of your stated threshold. The structure and the numbers are shown on slide number eight.'

'On the capital side, I don't know the precise assumptions used in your internal models, but please let me explain some of the factors and considerations that can give you options on how to rate this credit product. I have put the details in the appendix.'

After some discussion, the credit manager nods and strokes his chin. He looks at his colleague from product development and says 'We should do this. I can sponsor it through the New Product Approval committee.'

Equity Bank is already the biggest microfinance provider in East Africa, and I walk out with a provisional agreement that the Siboti Solar Loan will be piloted in the Bungoma branch, starting almost immediately. As a final touch, I ask them to give me a dedicated loan officer to assess and approve the loans. They tell me to direct that request to the local branch of the bank in Bungoma, but they don't envisage a problem, in view of the high volume of applications we forecast.

This is wonderful. It all makes sense. And it is potentially scalable. If this takes hold in Siboti, we could potentially sell hundreds of solar units in Siboti, thousands in the Bungoma region, God knows how many elsewhere. The kits are great, the loans will work and the families at the bottom of the pile will benefit enormously. It's financially attractive to customers and won't require investment from me except for the early salary costs of Cecilia and the sales team she needs, a second-hand pick-up truck and some initial stock of the home solar lighting kits.

The new lighting systems are an instant hit with the end users. They love them. I give a handful of solar units away to community leaders – the Chief and a couple of the other local bigwigs – who proudly show them off at night to their neighbours and friends. People know I'm friendly with the Chief and it helps to convey to everyone else that the solar kit is a prestigious thing to own. When they see how the kits work in the evening, it's like watching a demonstration in a show home. It's a good tactical move – a little like the first time somebody in our street bought a colour TV and everyone crowded into their front room to watch the World Cup Final.

Soon the solar kits are the talk of the town and everyone wants one. There's only one problem. No one wants to pay for them.

People want the solar units, but they want to be given them for nothing. Cecilia and her team can explain about the finances till they are blue in the face. They can show how the price will be no more, even in the first eighteen months, than the cost of the fuel they would somehow have to buy anyway for the old paraffin lamps. There's no extra cost, and no risk at all. People's families will also be safer. Half the injuries to children that the local clinic has to deal with are burns caused by touching the hot oil lamps. When a home catches fire, it is usually because a lamp has been knocked over. The local children will be healthier, too, as the fumes from the kerosene lamps frequently lead to horrible respiratory problems. They can all see the benefits. But they still want them for free.

It takes me a long time to discover what's wrong with my great idea. I can't understand why people who are dead keen one day come back the next day and say no. But soon enough, Cecilia and I get it. The problem is the loan.

Even when the parents are convinced and eager to go ahead, their sons insist on vetoing the deal, because of the loan. The pressure from the younger generation, who have moved away from Siboti and are working in Nairobi or other big city, is immense. They are the ones who are blocking the kits. There are arguments within families, I hear, and even, in some cases, stand-up rows and threats of violence. The key point is this: for most of the families in Siboti, there is just one asset that stands between them and disaster. The small plot of land, just enough to grow maize and keep the family fed, is the only thing they own in the world. However much Cecilia tries to reassure them, they still believe that if something goes wrong and they have to default on the loan, the bank will take the land away. And that's not a chance the families of Siboti are prepared to take.

It is true that if restructuring of re-payments by the bank didn't resolve a customer's difficulties, the only thing the bank could go after would be their farms. But from what I've observed, in reality that's a miniscule or non-existent risk. All of the families can afford kerosene to light these little Florence Nightingale-style lights and the repayment for the loan is the equivalent of running one kerosene lamp. Even the most abjectly poor families will prioritise light.

But it doesn't matter how many times we reassure them that the bank would much prefer to reset the repayment obligations than attempt to repossess their land. There isn't a centralised land registry in Kenya anyway, and land ownership can only be proven by whoever has the physical title deeds. So it would be an almost impossible task for a bank to know who has the ownership and to gain the title deeds in order to possess rural family land. What if the deeds are lost, or disputed? When you don't have clear legal structures in place it's difficult to buy and sell property. If a father leaves land to four sons, does the family have four new title deeds drawn up? Often not, because there is no money to spend on legal fees. And then one dies and leaves it to his children and the ownership rights is only known by the families who occupy the land. Sometimes title deeds are forged. They are often photocopied so that side contracts can be signed to sell parcels of land. These photocopies, and the side agreements that go with them, are then passed down through inheritance. The next generation use them as the basis for further contracts. So in reality, the banks would have a very difficult time tracking ownership and repossessing parcels of land and it would cost more to try than the amount outstanding on these small loans.

But none of this reality seems to register with people. The fear of the banks' power is deep-rooted.

'You're not risking my inheritance for a couple of light bulbs,' the sons tell their parents. And that, in the end, is the clincher for most of them.

Even after giving demos, running stalls in the local markets and explaining every detail of the scheme to hundreds of enthusiastic villagers, we are still only able to sell a couple of dozen solar units. We've run into a big cultural barrier.

Everyone wants one. But everyone wants to be given one free. Cultural issues – always the hardest thing to fight. I'm getting my education, but I am paying for it in sheer frustration.

These poor people – unimaginably poor by any standards we are accustomed to – won't do it. To them, the stakes are so much higher. More than 12 million people in Kenya have never had any dealings with a bank. In Siboti, that would include at least 90 per cent of the population. How can I expect people who've never had any money to understand – and *believe* – that credit can actually help them?

'You want us to switch some of our land from growing maize to growing chillies,' the local farmers say to our team. 'But what if there's no market for chillies this year? What would happen about the loan for the solar power if we couldn't sell the chillies and we had no money?'

It isn't anything to do with chillies, we point out. One way or another, they will always find the money for the fuel to keep the lamp burning, somehow, *because they always have*. And all they need to do is use that money – that same fuel money – to make the payments on the loan.

'Think of the chilli project as entirely separate from the solar units,' we tell them.

No dice. They're not having it.

If the chilli crop fails, which is unlikely, I know that families might not be able to meet the school fees. But they would continue to grow maize which they would get milled into flour – for chapattis and pancakes and for ugali, the staple dish. Even porridge is made from corn flour. They might grow tomatoes and some families have banana trees, the piccolo bananas. They have a number of chickens. They grow cabbages and onions to sell, enough to generate a basic income. They produce enough for hand-to-mouth subsistence living – this hasn't changed in any meaningful way in centuries. The women might do some tailoring, young men might have a part-time job in a barber's or do bicycle repairs or a day's labour if someone is building a house. That might bring in 200 shillings a day (about $2.50). People make red bricks in a home-made kiln oven to make a few shillings. Some women would perhaps buy plastic basins from the market in town and try to sell those in the village, making 25c profit per basin – and that would fund a night's kerosene.

It's the same with the idea of investing in the irrigation products, the Siboti Wheel and the KickStart pump. Together, these can solve the irrigation problem at a stroke for many of the farms in the area, guaranteeing higher family incomes. But despite the hugely better yields growers will enjoy if they buy these products, they are reluctant to take the loans we have set up for them.

I can see it's going to take a lot of time, energy and effort to change the way these people think about borrowing to invest in their future.

So I find the names of the senior managers at the Equity Group Foundation, Equity Bank's charitable arm, and go to ask their advice. They agree to send their experts out to Western Kenya to talk to the people of Siboti about money and about banks. They will come to the villages and present the case to whoever will listen. They'll answer all the big questions for them. What is interest? How do loans work? And, critically, are their farms really at risk if repayments are missed? Rousseau said it more than 250 years ago: 'Money is the seed of money, and the first guinea is sometimes more difficult to acquire than the second million.' The Equity Bank Foundation's advisors will show Siboti's people how to use the system. How to get a start. How to get ahead. How to take the loans and make them work for them. It's a start but on its own it won't be enough.

We've come too far to give up now. There's a big cultural barrier to be overcome, but getting past it will open up so many new opportunities for the people of Siboti. This has to be fixable. I've got to figure out a strong and simple way to get us through this.

20

Keziah

'Kenyans must learn how to believe in themselves and
do away with this culture of dependency on donors for
everything.'

Mutahi Kagwe, Kenyan Minister for Information
and Communications 2006–7

After visiting the Equity Bank Foundation in Nairobi, I get back
on the bus for Bungoma, which is full.

I spy one seat halfway down and head for it. And there she is
again: Night Bus Girl. Her bag is on the empty seat. She looks at me,
sighs, glances around to check there isn't anywhere else for me to sit
and reluctantly moves her bag onto her lap. I sit down. I'm not going
to talk, I tell myself. I'm just going to shut up and chill out. Play it
cool. Just leave things well enough alone, Ken.

But I can't.

I find her so attractive, in so many ways.

'A flea can trouble a lion more than a lion can harm a flea,' I say.

'You're telling me,' she says, staring out of the window.

Soon enough though, the ice thaws and we start to talk. She's called Keziah Nyambane. And she's a lawyer. She works for one of the big legal firms in Nairobi, but does some *pro bono* work near Siboti, where she has family connections.

And, after making me work extremely hard, she appears to be prepared to give me another chance to prove my credentials as a decent guy. She does seem interested in what I've been doing. While the bus trundles towards Bungoma, I fill her in a bit on who I am and how I found Siboti, but I'm careful to avoid representing myself as a messianic figure sent to save the people of Africa. 'Saint Ken' had stung. She seems to get me, though, to understand where I'm coming from and to sympathise with my difficulties.

Unlike many of the people I deal with, she is familiar with both sides. She's cultured and very well-educated, but because she's from the region she's clear-eyed and commonsensical: she knows how people live and how they think. She's heard a lot about my project – not all of it completely accurate, but enough for her to have revised her view of me as a complete arse. I'm pretty confident she now thinks of me and my ideas as only half-arsed.

I start to tell her about the difficulties I'm having selling the idea of the solar lighting – how people resist them even though everything is telling them it's not just lengthening their day but cleaner, too, and not just cleaner but safer, and not just safer but cheaper…

'And Ken said: "Let there be light",' she says.

'Aw, c'mon,' I say. 'Take a day off and give me a break.'

'No, I get it,' she says. 'It seems a straightforward solution. But you can't get them to make the final leap.'

'Exactly. And I know I'm going to have my work cut out for me with the water carrier, too. Everything's such hard bloody work here.'

We get off at Bungoma and I'm determined not to let her get away this time.

'Why don't we get some breakfast?' I suggest. 'Then we could share a taxi – it'll be cheaper. You are going on towards Siboti?'

She nods.

Keziah rejects my proposal to eat at the café I usually use to have my breakfast Nescafe and omelette and takes me somewhere smaller and cleaner, where the food is much better and serves large glasses of freshly squeezed mango juice. How did I not know this place before now? I'm finding it a great relief to have someone new and professional to talk to, who seems to truly understand the problems and I am feeling very relaxed. Too relaxed, as it turns out.

'If it's not backhanders on a small scale, it's short-termism and a lack of thought for the future on a massive scale. It doesn't seem to be a culture that wants to help itself. Aid makes people accustomed to getting things for nothing. And yet what they get for nothing they don't value – hence mosquito nets for curtains, for fishing, for anything you can bloody name except keeping mosquitoes off...'

'I'm not sure that's exactly right,' Keziah frowns. But I'm on a roll, getting angry just thinking about my litany of complaints.

'And the short-termism, the inability to think further than the immediate moment, is like a handicap. The ignorance is almost wilful. No one will take a loan because –' and here I make the fatal mistake of imitating a whiny-voiced Kenyan – 'You are going to risk my birthright, father, on a new light bulb?' It's the sheer feckless bloody-minded short-termism that really gets me down. How can anyone help you, if you won't help yourself?'

I realise straightaway that I've gone too far. Keziah puts down her fork and sits back, the irises of her eyes seeming actually completely black, glittering in a baleful stare.

After a long time, she says: 'Combien de langues parles-tu?'

I'm baffled.

'What?'

'Wie viele Sprachen sprichst du?'

I'm catching up.

'Ah, getcha. You're –'

'Too slow,' she interrupts. 'Most of these people are fluent in three languages: English, Kiswahili, and Luhya or Bukusu. How many languages do you speak, Ken, with your degrees and your international career? Can you imagine how resourceful these people have to be just to put food on the table every day? Could you live the life they live?'

'No, I didn't mean…'

'It's not stupidity that makes their lives so difficult. It's the fact that every day is a struggle just to keep afloat. They can't afford to gamble with the only thing they own – their land. You can say their land is safe till you're blue in the face. But they won't dare to believe it, because that's the one mistake they can't afford to make – the one thing they can't afford to lose. Owning land is the only thing that means there's a future at all. Aid agencies, charities, they come and go. The only constant, the only thing that can be relied upon, is the land.'

'I take your point entirely. I'm sorry – I'm very tired and –'

'That's the first thing.' Oh fuck, she isn't even nearly finished with me. 'You're taking a cut, right? You aim to make a profit out of things like the solar lights, the water barrels?'

'There's a small built-in profit, yes,' I say. 'I can't give this stuff away. I need to pay wages and rents and reinvest to produce more.'

'So, you're taking a cut. You're not the UN. You're not Oxfam. You're Ken King, businessman. You're here to turn a few dollars.'

'Now stop right there,' I say. 'I didn't come here to make money. No way. But I believe I can use a commercial – capitalist, if you like – model to make an impact that's financially self-sustaining.'

'Yada, yada, yada,' says Keziah. 'Whatever. You're taking a cut of their money and they know that. Doesn't matter why. But it matters.'

I've never really thought about that until this moment…

'Thirdly – and this is just for the record – the mosquito nets are impregnated with a chemical that loses its effect after a couple of years. That means the nets are much less useful – against mosquitoes anyway. People recycle them, use them for other things. It's not stupidity. It's a common sense use of scarce resources. Anyway…' She stands up. She's going to walk out on me again and I can't really blame her. 'We'd better get going.'

I struggle to keep up with Keziah as she strides back to the taxi rank and hails a taxi. All the way back to Siboti we talk, and the more I listen to Keziah, the more I like her and the more I realise that it's because she is on a mission, too, that she is so critical of my methods. Quite simply, she cares deeply. Behind that beautiful face there's an equally beautiful mind. But there's nothing soft-centred about her.

Eventually we're back in Siboti. We've decided on a ceasefire and I've brought her to the office on the edge of Kimwanga Market, where Cecilia's team is demonstrating the Siboti Wheel to a group of the village elders, who are smartly dressed in their green Siboti shirts. It's a warm day and Kizito, Edwin, Julius and John have parked their blue motorbikes under the spreading acacia tree, which provides a lot of shade. That way they won't be boiling hot when they get back on them. The multi-coloured helmets that came with the bikes rest on the handlebars.

'Five times as much water as a jerrycan,' marvels Kizito, watching on, and trying to prompt the thoughts of the elders towards how the time could be used usefully on the farm.

'What on earth are the women round here going to do with all their spare time?'

'Give a man a fish and you feed him for a day,' someone begins.

'Buy him a fishing rod and you can get rid of him for a whole weekend,' adds Keziah, and all the guys laugh.

I catch her eye and she winks at me.

21

Getting better

'Education is learning what you didn't even know you didn't know.'

Daniel J Boorstin, historian

I can no longer recall with any clarity what I was expecting on the ground when I first arrived in Siboti. I think I'd imagined that subsistence farming for the rural poor would be a desperate struggle to scratch a living out of a barren, sun-parched and obviously hostile landscape. I do remember that my image of Africa involved drought and famine, stick-thin children with bloated bellies and hopeless staring eyes – one that was quickly revised when I found myself in a green and fertile place, surrounded by happy, noisy children and resilient, good-humoured people. I am still enchanted by both the people and the place and by the daily adventure of my life in Kenya, whether it's riding my motorbike through the mist rising from the baking tarmac after it's rained or visiting a farmer, stargazing in the glittering black night or making plans with the team.

The problems here, of course, are less enchanting – deadly diseases, sporadic access to water, and an almost total lack of employment options.

Offering opportunities to grow foodstuffs under contract is a first step for the farmers and for Siboti Foods to build the food production powerhouse that will eventually elevate the prosperity of the entire community. But we also need to unleash and channel the obvious entrepreneurial spirit, to help people create and grow sustainable micro businesses.

We need to explain how loans and interest work, and help people to avoid getting ripped off by the merciless local loan sharks who lend on a basis that's known as 'a shilling for a shilling'. It sounds harmless enough, but what this really means is that they are charging a swingeing interest rate of 100 per cent *a month*.

Borrow 1000 shillings at the beginning of the month and you will have to repay 2000 shillings 30 days later. Fail to clear the debt and you will owe the moneylender 4000 shillings a month later. Leave it another month and your 1000 shilling debt will have grown to 8000 shillings.

That's compound interest with a vengeance. And not being fully aware of how financial concepts like compound interest play out puts these people at a real disadvantage. A shilling for a shilling would be a pretty steep interest rate if it was applied on a yearly basis. Compounding monthly means it is almost guaranteed to drag families into deep trouble. No wonder credit has such a bad name among the rural poor. I've come to realise that this is a major source of the strong resistance to the credit schemes I've tried to establish to enable families to provide themselves with power and water.

I've also noticed the people who already run their own tiny businesses in Siboti are often not very good at knowing what loan finance is appropriate for. Edward Mungai, who runs a small local timber yard, wants to take out a loan to expand his stock. It's a good instinct, but he's not seeing the risk of being stuck with extra repayments to the bank and no extra income, if the new stock sits unsold. He needs to learn some basic business techniques. What can he do to increase the pace of shifting the current levels of stock? How can he advertise or build new sales channels? Could he get a preferential supply agreement for a building project or perhaps a tie-up with a builder?

Hellen Owiwo has a tailoring stall. She wants to borrow to stock more fabrics, arguing, reasonably, that 'bigger stalls make bigger money'. But she could be stuck with a loan for a lot of unsold stock unless she has plans to exploit it. Can she win a tailoring contract, perhaps to make uniforms for one of the many local security firms, or get a tie-up with a school to provide uniforms in bulk at a discounted price? A new sewing machine that can double the pace of output might be a better investment.

Lots of people want to buy lots of stock, driven by this belief that a bigger-looking business will mean bigger-looking profits. I have to explain many times that a loan for big levels stock will mean big levels of repayments. How can you get this stuff to walk out the door sold instead of sitting on the shelves?

Encouraging this kind of thinking has to become a vital part of any training programme. Equity Bank can give money advice – like advising businesses to keep their personal money separate from their income – and I can help increase business awareness.

When I ask David Kimisa, the tailor who made the uniforms for our Orphans Welcome Again scheme, how well known his tailoring business is, he admits that he doesn't really know many people, except those in the immediate rural locality. He hasn't capitalised in any way on having won that big contract from us. So together we design a business card for him, bearing the legend 'Top Quality School Uniforms at a Fair Price', with a picture of a sewing machine and his contact details. We knock out a couple of hundred business cards, using a small printer in my hotel room, sheets of white card and a pair of scissors. Over the next few days, he delivers these cards to local homes and wins himself orders for over twenty uniforms.

At the most fundamental level, people need guidance on how to decide what business to go into, taking advantage of whatever skills, assets and opportunities are available to them – whether that's having a motorbike or a sewing machine or being able to cut hair or mend bicycles.

They need to know how to record what's happening in the business and why they should keep business and personal money matters separate. They need to know how to get their pricing and stock levels right, how to recognise the trade-offs between volume and profit, how to advertise their goods and services and how to go about building a loyal customer base. Many aspects of this may seem self-evident to people brought up in Western capitalist societies. It's not so obvious, though, to many of the people here, where a necessarily self-sufficient culture is so absorbing and time-consuming that there is little evidence of lifting your head above the preoccupations of surviving the day.

Linking up with the Haven Kenya volunteers, it soon becomes part of my routine to spend a day or two a week spreading the entrepreneurial word. Kizito and I find ourselves travelling around and advising scores of businesses and hundreds of people on the viability of their ideas for breeding turkeys or ducks, setting up as a barber or starting a business making home-baked scones. Indeed, one of the earliest successes is a woman called Shani, who quickly becomes the Scones Queen of Siboti. Shani gets up way before dawn to bake delicious scones made of amaranth, a highly nutritious grain, in a mud oven behind her house – and she soon finds that she can sell every one she produces.

Tapping into the energy and ingenuity of these would-be entrepreneurs is a vital part of my overall plan for Siboti. It is one of the keys to helping these people lift themselves out of poverty – and it all depends on education.

I keep coming back to what Siboti's chief said to me: 'You can give a man a million shillings, but unless you give him knowledge, he will soon have nothing.'

From parallels in my own career, I feel the Chief was absolutely right. When I was twenty years old, sat over my study books one evening, one of my aunts, who had come with my grandmother to visit us, was intrigued as to what I was up to.

'What are you doing, Ken? Why are you re-sitting your school-leaving exams? You already have a good job as a clerk.'

To my surprise, my grandmother cut her off and flew to my defence.

'You leave that boy alone,' she snapped indignantly. 'He's bettering himself. That's what he's doing.'

Bettering himself? Yes. That had really struck a chord. She was right. I was literally trying to better myself. I was using education to lift myself into a future where I'd have more opportunities – a future where I could and would be a more valuable, successful and fulfilled person.

I find myself thinking about my grandmother's comment every now and then as the Siboti project develops – and especially when I come across a cheery little news story about a bunch of Kenyan grannies over in Kisumu who have organised classes for themselves and are getting together at night school to learn to read. They're bettering themselves. They know that once you've learned how to read, you can learn almost anything else by reading about it. They've found the key to unlock new possibilities in their lives.

Together, education and financing can change the future for both farmers and entrepreneurs in Siboti. Whatever interest rate the banks set for their loans – even if it's 20 or 25 per cent per annum – it will still give these new customers a much better option than the punitive 'shilling for a shilling' terms that are all they can get from local moneylenders.

I am busily nurturing the relationship with Equity Bank and I'm even applying for a licence to act in Siboti as a sub-branch of the bank, so that we'll be able to offer banking services to local people and businesses, like sub-post offices do in Ireland and England.

It'll be rather ironic if I've left my investment banking career in London behind to travel over 4000 miles to set up a sub-branch of a retail and microfinance bank in the Kenyan countryside. The difference is that it really means something here, now. I'm learning the sometimes painful lesson that strengths and weaknesses are amplified and magnified by living here. It's not just the Kisumu grannies who are bettering themselves every week. I am too. Perhaps you can hide in a business suit of a banker and the trapping of success in the West. Here, I'm a wildcard entrepreneur without a safety net. My thoughts and plans are coming together with my experience on the ground and I think I have a pretty good design now for the economic elevation of Siboti with Siboti Foods at the centre of a lot of new commercial activity. And, I'm learning in a much broader way just how different it is to run a project here compared to at an institution. Soft persuasion is the key lever to creating change in Siboti. I have no authority here – just a determination to build personal bonds so that I can influence and persuade the leaders and members of this community to trust me and my new methods.

When the first year's chilli crop is harvested, in spring 2010, a few of our farmers are unable, or unwilling, to pay back the loan.

'The agreement, and written contract, was that we would give them the seeds and the fertiliser they need, and they would return the costs of these to us with the revenue from their first chilli crop,' I remind Kizito in the office.

He nods, looking at the spreadsheet I have prepared. 'I expect they would pay if they had borrowed the money from the bank. Still, it's only about 10 per cent of the farmers. Ninety per cent have paid back the loan, Ken.'

'Yes,' I say, looking over his shoulder at the list of names. 'But it's not fair to the other farmers if I let them off, is it? Maybe we should make them pay.'

Kizito glances at me. 'How would you do that, Ken?'

I shrug. 'Tell them they'll be excluded from the scheme for next year?'

He thinks. 'The Chief will know what to do,' he says finally. 'The steering committee of village elders. They know our people. They know what works. I can set up a meeting with the Chief.'

'You're a good man, Kizito,' I say, so glad that I have people around me I can trust to advise me on the local mores.

'Will you set it up please?'

But late that afternoon, the Chief knocks on my door and asks if he can have a word. The three of us sit around the desk, and we each lift a large soda from the crate we keep in the corner.

The Chief has talked to the several members of the steering committee of elders and has a proposal. Some of the farmers haven't done so well with the first crop, and just haven't the money to repay the loans. The Chief feels this is not necessarily their fault, and as we talk I remember. There'd been some delays in getting the fertiliser and pesticides for the farms on sandy soil and also in providing the necessary training.

'You must let these men off their debt, Mr Ken,' says the Chief. 'Show them they can trust you. If you do that, the men will work hard next year. They are good farmers, you know.'

I nod, drumming my fingers on the printed spreadsheet in front of me. I want to show willing If I force them to pay back the loan, perhaps they could not then afford school fees or food. How would that generate goodwill in the community?

However, if you let people off their loans they may default again. It's what bankers call a moral hazard. This could be a ticking time bomb. On the other hand, these are desperately poor farmers, not avaricious banks.

'OK,' I say, swigging my soda and wishing I could let go of the uneasy feeling between my shoulder blades. 'I suppose it is only 10 per cent'. I will write off this debt and let them take new loans to join us again for the second crop. If these farmers had owed this money to the bank instead of me, you know the bank would have done all it could to restructure the missing payments. But I will let them off if that will include them in the push to escape poverty and will build goodwill for the project.'

The Chief rubs his chest and nods his approval. What concerns him is that his flock are safe.

'You're a great man, Mr Ken,' he says.

As Kizito shows out the Chief, discussing me approvingly in Swahili, I hope I've made the right choice. I don't want to alienate the local farmers so early into my second year in Siboti, but equally the kind of flexibility I've just shown could create expectations and future problems that we really don't want to promote. I have a strange feeling about what I have just agreed to.

22

What a wonderful world this could be

'A man may die, nations may rise and fall, but an idea lives on.'

President John F Kennedy

It is a bright morning. I've come in to work early and I'm in the office, reviewing and forecasting our costs and revenues. It's market day and I can hear hundreds of people coming and going, laughing and shouting, buying and selling. Today, it seems as if half the population of Siboti is at the Kimwanga Market, and everyone seems to be happy and excited, bustling about and full of the joys of spring.

It's too good to miss, so I park the paperwork for a few minutes and step outside into the sunshine, into the noise and colour and the dazzling, shimmering light. I remember Bob Geldof rejecting the idea of Africa as the Dark Continent.

'This is not a dark continent,' he said. 'Look around. This is the luminous continent.'

It is indeed luminous today, and full of colour and contrast, too. The women are wearing bright patterned frocks, tall headdresses, sparkling oversized earrings. They're selling battered-looking but tasty tomatoes spread out on sheets on the ground, charcoal-cooked tilapia fish from Lake Victoria, second-hand shoes and clothes and enormous stacks of plastic basins – large ones, small ones, round ones, square ones, orange and blue, green and purple, yellow and red. Some of the sellers have piles of second-hand clothes, pre-worn shoes and Wayne Rooney shirts in the team strip that Manchester United wore five seasons ago.

Tiny children, some as young as two years old, surge backwards and forwards or hide behind the blue-painted corrugated iron of the little barber's shop. '*Kinyozi* All Styles' it says, above the door. There's only one style here, though, the classic Number One. All the men choose the Number One haircut, shaved close to the skin with electric clippers run from an old car battery. Why wouldn't you? Haircuts cost money and it takes a lot longer for a Number One to grow out.

There's no marketplace as such, just a strip of scrubby land set back from the main road, where Siboti meets the neighbouring district of Kimwanga. A major highway, the lifeline for trade across East Africa, runs past our front door. Huge trucks grind slowly from left to right, groaning under the weight of forty-foot shipping containers. We see the same trucks on their way home, too, bucketing along, empty and rattling, making their way back for the next load. The Chinese are building a new railway that will eventually run from Mombasa to Kigali, the Rwandan capital, and take a lot of this traffic off the roads. But it's a 1500-kilometre building project, involving funding and co-operation from at least three governments, and that could take half a lifetime.

Today, the market is teeming with life. There's a delicate scent of lime in the air, from the little green leaves scattered on the ground. As my eyes get used to the light, I see a knot of enthusiastic people gathered round one of the stalls on the far side of the market and I go across to see what the excitement is about. It's only as I get nearer that I realise what's going on. It's my own Siboti Elevation Products team running live demonstrations, proudly showing off our solar panels, the Siboti Wheels and the rugged, pedal-powered irrigation pumps that can give these smallholders and subsistence farmers a higher yield by daily watering and the huge bonus of a third crop every year.

I didn't know that was happening today. Our team has just got on and organised the stall and the demos. And they're doing it really well, too, following a proper sales procedure, just like Cecilia trained them to – capturing leads, filling in forms and taking down interested people's details, qualifying prospects to rule out the obvious tyre-kickers and timewasters. It's slick and professional and they're obviously getting through to people. I'm watching my plans being translated into reality before my very eyes.

The people of Siboti are educating each other in the ways of elevating their families economic well-being.

'Good morning, Mr Ken,' somebody calls as he walks by.

'Good morning.'

Good? It's *fantastic*.

It's not just a good morning, it's a wonderful, wonderful day. This is a day I've been waiting for since I came to Siboti. I've had some great days in my life, but this is something special. This is something money can't buy. My Elevation Method has all been thought through and structured in the background, but here, today, in the foreground of real life, I'm seeing the first proof that what I'm trying to do in Western Kenya really can work.

Today we've reached the point where I no longer have to drive everything myself. It feels like a milestone moment. We've got a team and we've got momentum. We're setting out to help people change their lives for the better, and the changes are beginning to happen. We have what you might call an integrated poverty alleviation business.

The Siboti office I work in has already become the hub of a bigger operation. I've rented a few of the neighbouring buildings as they've become available, so we have the infrastructure we need. There's a training room, a room for the fifteen trainee field officers whom we've taken on, the Elevation Products building, the chilli weighing and buying room, the chilli sorting and packing room and a finance office. And I've bought a piece of land beside us where I hope to build our future food processing and packaging facility. It's turning into the Siboti Centre that I've envisaged, a hive of economic activity that can be the catalyst to lift the whole community out of the current level of extreme poverty.

We've got a party coming up at the weekend, on Sunday, the Farmer of the Year awards, to honour the top performers from our first year. After what I've seen today, I'm really looking forward to that and hoping for a good turnout. I've promised there'll be free cakes and plenty of sodas, and there'll be dignitaries like the bishop and the district officer, as well as the Chief and his assistant chiefs.

We're going to give out certificates to all the successful growers and trophies for the top three people in the Farmer of the Year category.

It can be hard to motivate people to attend any sort of meeting here – and even harder to get them to turn up on time. If you say a *barassa* is due to start at 11 a.m., you can expect people to start trickling in at around 11.30. It'll be 12.30 before you've got enough of a crowd to get the meeting going. So with the bigwigs arriving at the scheduled time of 1 p.m., I'm worried that they'll be standing around talking to themselves.

When Sunday comes, though, there are whole families streaming in from all directions an hour before kick-off. Maybe it's the lure of the sodas. Maybe it's the fact that we've announced it as a party, rather than a business meeting. Whatever the reason, we've certainly got an audience. By one o'clock, the place is heaving, with several hundred people waiting expectantly for the show to begin.

We've worked with 560 smallholding farmers in the first year. We've got certificates for the best hundred performers and trophies for the top three, but there is one shining star today. His name is David Waswa, and he's just done everything right. He's the model farmer, careful about his planting, meticulous in his watering and weeding, keen to learn about business and money from the financial education experts we've brought in and enthusiastic about taking the advice of the agronomists we hire to lend their expertise.

He's used the fertiliser we recommended and paid off the start-up loan we provided. He's getting one of our solar lighting kits and he's already bought one of our KickStart irrigation pumps and put it to good use, boosting his income to over $500 for the year. What's more – in a very heartening and untraditional way – he's done it all in a really close working partnership with his wife.

When he wins the Farmer of the Year award and is presented with his trophy by the Chief, everybody's clapping and cheering and stamping. But David Waswa is up there on the stage, beckoning to his wife to come up and share the glory.

'Come on up. It's your trophy, too,' he shouts.

It's a beautiful moment, the young couple standing there, side by side, holding hands and flushed with pride, receiving the applause of the whole community. As I survey the scene I realise this is my private moment too. It beats the buzz of a thousand banking bonuses. If I hadn't come to Siboti, this wouldn't be happening. It may be my ego talking, but it still feels immensely gratifying. Maybe I'll be able to realise my dream to design and prove a structured, step-wise, integrated approach by which extreme poverty can be beaten. If my Elevation Method really does work, I could spend my life at it. A deeply worthwhile and gratifying life. The thought is intensely moving. It's a genuinely life-affirming moment, and I feel radiant with hope.

The farmer who's won the runner-up's trophy is still standing at the back of the platform and he obviously feels he's missed a trick. So he calls his wife up onto the stage to stand beside him, too. Not to be outdone, the third trophy winner decides he should call his wife up as well. And the Chief himself, who has been presented with his own special award for leading and supporting the project, decides he should follow suit. His two wives are both there, one of them over by the left side of the stage, one off to the right, and he's frantically waving both arms, beckoning both of them to come up and join him. When they get there, he stands between them, holding an arm aloft on each side, as if they're two boxers who have both won the same fight. The audience hollers and claps. Suddenly, teamwork and family values are the order of the day. It's a heart-warming sight, though I don't think it would have occurred to anyone to think like that until David Waswa – model farmer, model husband, model family man – showed them the way.

'Congratulations, Ken.'

That voice. I turn and it's Keziah. She's here, the golden girl on my golden day. I can't quite believe it.

'Not like you to be lost for words,' she says and kisses me on the cheek. 'Well done. I've got to hand it to you. This is great.'

This is a bit weird. We've been exchanging emails – unashamedly slightly flirty on my part, inscrutable on hers – but we haven't seen each other for a while. That we're both busy has been the official reason. But it's unexpected to see her here, unexpectedly fantastic. The party's breaking up and people are moving past us, saying goodbye to me and talking loudly. I don't want her to slip away.

'David Waswa and all the high achievers get extra opportunities and extra privileges now,' I start babbling. 'We'll work with them closely this year to get up to silver status – that's when they reached an income of $750 from us in a single year. And then it's onward the next year to gold status, when they hit the magic $1000 a year. That's double the UN's target of getting people above the $1.25 a day threshold. There's lots more detail, of course, but when you put it all together, it adds up to what I call the Elevation Method.'

'What?'

I realise she can't hear a thing over the noise from the crowd.

Somehow or other I manage to get Keziah to agree to have dinner with me back in Bungoma. She agrees, provided it's not at my hotel, and we wind up in the same restaurant she took me to before. She's interested in hearing about the project and how we've got to what she saw today and I'm interested, of course, in talking about it.

There've been plenty of moments since I arrived in Siboti when I've wondered if my plans can really succeed. But this has been one fantastic week. Seeing my team hard at work giving their demonstrations in the market the other day, and today seeing the huge, enthusiastic crowd at the awards ceremony, it feels as though we can't fail. And if we can succeed here…

Why not other communities in Western Kenya? Why not the whole of Kenya – and Tanzania, Uganda and the rest of East Africa, too? Why not the rest of Africa? Why not Latin America and the poorest parts of Southeast Asia? It won't work everywhere. I know that. There are certain conditions that need to be met. It could only succeed in places where there's reasonably fertile soil, a decent amount of rainfall, potential borehole access to clean water, a large degree of stability and security and ready access to roads and markets. But given those few basics, it's got to be replicable. Once the Siboti Foods project is well established, with loans being repaid and farmers making enough extra money to look after their families and gradually expand their operations to grow high-value crops and supply my planned food production facility, it won't need constant top-ups from me or anybody else. It should be economically sustainable, a private enterprise answer to the problem of rural extreme poverty.

I'm starting to think big now. We're not giving the solar lighting kits and water drums and irrigation pumps away. We're selling them at prices that can easily and quickly be covered by the extra money they generate for the farmers. But there's also a small margin built in for me. What if – while I am helping these people boost their incomes and climb out of poverty – there was still scope for me to make a modest profit of, say, $10 per household per year?

I pull a piece of paper out of my pocket and do the sums.

'Ken.'

Just a minute. The census says there are 4.3 million people in Western Kenya – maybe a million homes, with three-quarters of them in the rural areas. If I could recruit just 10 per cent of those 750 000 households, that would be 75 000 families. At $10 per family, that would bring in $750 000 a year.

'Ken!'

That would give me a good income and provide a revenue stream that could be used to plough into the next project, and the next, and the next, the ripples widening across the face of Africa and the world. It's a dream that knows no limits. I would be able to stay doing this for the rest of my life. As it scaled up, it could be huge – a benign capitalist response to extreme poverty, with a self-sustaining momentum that could change the world.

The paper is snatched out of my hand.

'Hey!' I protest.

'That's enough! You need to think about something else for a bit.'

But she's not cross – Keziah is laughing at me.

'Lighten up! You've done a good job. Now chill out!'

We end up having the best evening I've had for a long time. She puts her fingers in her ears and sings quite loudly every time I talk about my project until I stop, which is helpful, and I find out a lot more about her. ('You'll discover,' she advises, 'that you can hear a lot better when you're not talking.') I learn, for example, that her guilty pleasures include long hot baths and supporting Chelsea Football Club. Both disconcerting thoughts.

We drink and laugh and tell stories and, finally, oh bliss, she lets me kiss her. And then she lets me kiss her again. I mention in a roundabout way that I don't suppose she would consider coming to my hotel room.

'Ken, even *you* don't want to go to your hotel room, because it's a dump,' she replies, and I have to admit she's right.

'Well, maybe another time, then,' I say. 'So where would you really like to go?'

She thinks, a faraway look in her eye.

'London,' she says. 'I've been to Switzerland, but I haven't been anywhere else in Europe. I'd love to see London. When can we go?'

23

USAID

'In terms of competitiveness in the new global environment, Kenya will have absolutely no choice but to tackle the most important constraint to its development: it has been corruption.'

Obiageli Ezekwesili, former VP of the World Bank's Africa division

We are well into the second year of the project and I've been away in Dublin for two weeks – a welcome break from the challenges of my life in Kenya. It's always great to stay at my father's house and spend time with him and see my siblings and their families. This time I don't say as much about what I'm trying to do in Kenya, except to say my chilli project's going quite well. I get the feeling that people think I'm a bit off the wall. There is an element of me that doesn't want to risk a backlash so I don't give much in the way of updates anymore. That way you can't be analysed or criticised. It's easier to quip, to say something funny, and move on, to talk about old times or current affairs.

Arriving back in Kenya, there's always a special thrill as I arrive back and walk the last few yards up to the collection of stark little buildings that started as the buying station for chillies and has grown to what we have today – the Siboti Centre. Now it includes the *pièce de résistance*, the building where we will house our new agency branch of Equity Bank, when my licence application gets through all the approval stages. Together they will be the engine for raising the income of our contracted farmers, while the adjoining land I am have bought will be the site for the powerhouse food production facility.

I reach the front door and step into the operational headquarters. There is no welcoming committee, but I wasn't expecting one.

The front half of the little office is empty today. I unlock the door into the secure finance office that I share with Kizito at the back of the building. It's cramped, airless, with a small, barred window looking out onto the scrubland behind. There is one large desk and a chair on either side. At the desk sits Kizito, bowed over a pile of papers and obviously under pressure.

He jumps up and smiles as I come in. There's no doubt he's pleased to see me, as I am to see him.

'Oh Ken, welcome, welcome. It's very good you came back. I have been waiting for you.'

'It's good to be back, Kizito.' But there's something wrong. The desk is covered in official-looking paperwork I don't recognise – blank forms in one pile, another pile of forms covered in figures and names written in Kizito's careful, painstaking handwriting. 'What's going on?'

'It's good Ken, very good. I have much to inform you. Things have been happening.'

'I can see that. What are all these forms?'

Across the top of each form I can see the word USAID. That's the US government's Agency for International Development. But we don't have any arrangement with them, so why is Kizito filling in these forms? I pick one up. Kizito has filled in the name of one of our Siboti farmers, followed by details of what he is growing, the yield from his land and even the price he has been paid for his crop.

Kizito's discomfort is unmistakable.

'It's USAID, Mr Ken. I have to get all these forms filled by five o'clock, before the man comes back.'

'Wait. Stop. What's this all about, Kizito? We're trying to be a commercial business here. We're not going to give away confidential information about everything we're setting up here. Why are you doing this?'

It turns out that the local representative of USAID, a Kenyan called John Wangui, was driving back to Bungoma last week and had been surprised to see the big Siboti Foods signs above our suite of buildings. He'd stopped and come in to talk to Kizito, who'd explained a bit about what we were doing and said that I would be back within the next few days.

'No time for that,' Wangui had said, handing over a sheaf of USAID forms. 'We can give you money for projects like this, but I'll need these forms ready by five o'clock. Just fill them in. Your Mr Ken King won't mind if it means we can give you US government money.'

I'm not impressed with Wangui's approach, which sounds unlikely to be the official process. I don't approve of Kizito being pressured to drop everything and fill in a mass of paperwork to meet an obviously arbitrary deadline. Above all, I'm damned if I'm going to allow all the details of our business and our partners to be handed over to USAID or anyone else. But Wangui might be useful.

More funding might mean we can do more, more quickly. I need to find out how we can make the most of this and potentially tap into a share of the millions of dollars the US is putting into development projects in Kenya.

This is not the right way to go about it, though. I don't want to do this at the local level, and I'm already a bit wary of John Wangui. I'd like to talk to the people who are really in charge.

'No way, Kizito,' I say. 'We can't release data just like that. Raw data can be interpreted in any number of ways. You can stop filling in those forms. I'll meet with this guy and find out more, OK?'

Kizito hands over the sheaf of papers. I notice his forehead is shining. 'Thanks, Ken.'

I take a seat and flick through the documents. I learnt during my banking career that data can easily be given the wrong context. It's best to understand the questions before you give out any answers.

A week later I'm at the USAID office in Nairobi, face to face with a quiet, thoughtful charming Englishman. I like Nigel Harrogate instantly. He is an appealing combination – both idealist and realist, and a man who knows how the system works. He explains that I could potentially be given hundreds of thousands of dollars, as long as I match it dollar for dollar, for an approved project. But the money would always have to be tied to the eligible items – the seeds, tools, fertilisers that have met the criteria laid down by Washington DC for improving farming methods in Kenya.

Fascinating stuff. Then it's my turn to explain to Nigel what I've been trying to do in Siboti. He listens, thinks, and delivers his verdict.

'Come back tomorrow afternoon and meet my team. Tell them your story. Your customised step-by-step method for raising families out of extreme poverty that's based around high-yielding commercial horticulture – that is something we can support. We should be able to hammer out a deal.'

It seems too good to be true. But Siboti's taught me to accentuate the positive, so I go to bed a very happy – or at least very hopeful – man, and the next afternoon I present myself again at Nigel's office. He does the introductions and then leaves. And then the hard sell starts. And not by me. The four officials he has introduced start trying to persuade me that we should become OFSP producers.

'OFSP?' I ask. 'What is that?'

'Orange flesh sweet potatoes.'

'Like, yams, right?'

Yes, like yams. Right.

In the next fifteen minutes I learn that OFSPs don't need much in the way of pesticides, or even much weeding. They're very nutritious and can be dried and ground up to make flour. They've done the research. There's a market and they're looking for partners to grow them. And they will supply the vines.

'Vines?'

'Yes. You can't grow OFSP from seed. You need to plant the vine cuttings. When the plant is established, it'll just keep on producing, year after year.'

In fairness, the USAID team's enthusiasm is infectious. They claim OFSP is a major crop in neighbouring countries like Uganda and Tanzania, so there's good reason to think it'll work in Kenya. But it won't work for me. I'm based in Siboti, otherwise known as the middle of nowhere. We chose chillies as our primary product at least partly because they are light in weight.

'Hold on, guys. Think of the challenges we would have with transporting tons of yams from the farms. They're bloody heavy, right, and bulky, too. For it to make any sense, we'd have to produce huge volumes, and we'd need to pay to cart them off to Nairobi in big trucks. Siboti could never be price competitive if I have to cover the huge cost of transporting that kind of weight.'

They look disappointed. And I'm disappointed too. But although I duck out of the OFSP dream, for now – and their other idea, a passion-fruit project that they are also promoting – I feel there must be an angle where we can come together. We agree to go away and think.

* * *

A few weeks later, I'm back in Nairobi, presenting my pitch to Nigel and his funding committee. I have a way to avoid the transport logistics problem. I propose that we train a selection of our top farmers to grow OFSP vines next season. We can arrange for other Siboti farmers to be buyers of those vines, using microfinance loans that we will arrange for them. These buyers will grow the potatoes the following season. That will give me two seasons to build a small flour-milling and packing facility and to get supply arrangements sorted out with the local supermarkets. It could be the first step towards our vision of a food production business that engages and elevates every Siboti farmer who wants to put the work in and be part of our success.

I've done my homework and produced the figures and projections that will make a clear case for USAID support for this project. USAID will fund the training, the vines themselves, a demonstration plot and lots more beside. I'll continue to fund and retain control over the other elements of the broader Siboti project – things like the existing chilli project, the solar power initiative, the mobile health clinics and the sales team for the irrigation products – and I'll arrange the microfinance loans for the sweet potato vines project, because USAID is strictly concerned with the horticulture side of things. But they are definitely looking to be as helpful as they possibly can be.

By the time we've finished working on the outline, a few weeks later, USAID and I have agreed a framework that will commit the agency to putting in the mighty sum of $300 000 for us to take our next steps towards positioning Siboti's farmers to become suppliers to a food company.

The money, if the project is formally and officially approved, will not come without strings, of course. Visibility and transparency are key elements in this kind of arrangement. 'Monitoring and evaluation' is a big deal in the world of international development aid and I will have to provide highly detailed monthly M&E reports, so that the agency can track the spending and account for it to the American taxpayer. But that's certainly a price worth paying. The next step will be a detailed due diligence process that will be co-ordinated by the local USAID office in Bungoma and run by the brusque and assertive Mr John Wangui – he of the urgent forms that appeared during my last absence.

My initial reservations about the USAID man on the ground in Bungoma soon turn out to be well founded. I know I will have to build a working relationship with him, so I start off by meeting him for a coffee to understand what details he will need. To give him his due, he's been reasonably helpful ahead of my meetings with Nigel Harrogate, telling me a bit about how to make my application for funding line up with USAID's expectations. He has helped me shape my detailed financial proposal – suggesting what I can request with confidence and indicating the areas of expenditure that are outside the scope of possible funding – and this has been constructive and valuable input.

Now I feel that I need to get to know him better if we are going to work well together. But I quickly realise we are never going to be friends in any meaningful way. I don't like the way he double-parks his big USAID jeep awkwardly and prominently outside bars, as if to make sure everyone knows that he, an important man, is around. And though he's swinging his dick around town, playing the big man, he expects me to pay for his beer in return for guidance about how to make progress with the application.

Still, I need to get on with him. As we chat more informally, I mention how fed up I am with staying in the lousy hotel in Bungoma and that I would prefer to get an apartment or house if I could find a good place to rent. I've been on the lookout, but I haven't found anything remotely suitable. I don't think it's picky to want to live somewhere secure. Part of the dark side of trying to get things done here is the thieving. Everything gets stolen. The doors get stolen from outhouse toilets. If you try to help by putting in miles of piping to bring water to where it's needed, there's the constant worry that you'll look round one day and it will all be gone. It's not a problem that's unique to Kenya, but there's a lot of it about. Whatever factors can prompt people to steal for a living, rather than work, in Ireland or Britain, the people here often have an altogether more compelling motive: survival. If I lived my life right on the edge of starvation, worried about even scraping together enough to feed my family, I guess my view of property rights might be different. But it's still a pain.

Since the project began to pick up pace, I've been taking large amounts of money out of the bank regularly, and I've had no real fear of being robbed. Maybe I haven't really been aware of the risks. I remember Alan warning me not to carry much cash around, that I could be a target for criminals. I've never felt threatened in Siboti or Bungoma, but it would be sensible to live somewhere safe.

It's not just safety, though. I'm used to Western standards of building construction – a decent kitchen, a reliable water supply – rather than lumpy plastering and doors that don't quite close. The trouble is, most rental properties in Siboti are low quality and offer neither.

'I'm just moving apartments myself,' Wangui tells me. 'I know what's available. I can find a good place for you.'

Well, that seems promising. I'm sure he's got his ear to the ground and knows much more local information than me. If he can line me up with something suitable, it'll save me a lot of hassle trying to find somewhere. I decide to take him up on the offer.

'I do have one little problem, though,' he says, looking me straight in the eye. 'There will be a slight overlap for a month, where I'll have to be paying for both my old flat and the new one. Could you assist me with 10 000 shillings for the deposit and 10 000 shillings for the first month's rent, Ken?'

Ah, no. This isn't right. I have an application for 300 000 US Dollars waiting for approval in Nairobi and he's the local USAID representative whose support I need. What am I going to do? If I say no, there's every chance he'll raise some query or other and the $300 000 could be kicked into touch. Am I going to jeopardise all that by refusing?

I feel there's no option but to lend him the money. There's no way around this. I might get it back, or I might not. But I'm not going to risk screwing up an application for $300 000 for the sake of the equivalent of $250, right?

I smile, through gritted teeth, buy him another Tusker and tell him to meet me tomorrow afternoon to get the money. We chat for another ten minutes and part on good terms.

When I see Wangui again, he's full of enthusiasm. He tells me about a newly built block of appartments in an ideal location for me. I know the building he is talking about and it does look like a good secure place. But I need to fly to Dublin for a family event and have no time to view it. He offers to put down the deposit, if I give him the money, of course, to secure one of them for me. I am a bit suspicious, but the thought of coming back to one of these new apartments, rather than the awful hotel in Bungoma, is enticement enough. Wangui tells me that only one apartment is still available and he can get it for me if we are quick. I decide to take a chance on him.

'Could you do that for me then, John?' I ask.

'No problem, Ken. No problem at all. I can do this for you.'

'So how will it work?'

'You'll need to pay the deposit, of course, plus a month's rent, so that would be 20 000 shillings altogether. That'll secure the place for you, and I can get it done while you're away.'

Despite my distaste for the man and my dislike at having been asked for a loan a few days earlier, I do have to build a working relationship with him. If he can sort out accommodation for me, that's a problem solved. I'll go with it.

I give him the necessary 20 000 shillings and leave for Nairobi that evening on the dreaded night shuttle.

When I get back to Bungoma a week later, though, there's been a hitch.

In the end, it turns out that someone else got the last of the apartments.

'OK,' I say to myself, 'these things happen. I'll have my money back and we'll start looking again'.

But apparently there have been some awkward problems affecting the Wangui family. He's had to use the money to deal with the emergency, and it will be a week or two before he can return the cash to me. Warning lights are now flashing in my head. This has the potential to go badly wrong.

Sure enough, when I meet him again a few days later he has bad news for me.

'Your application, Ken. There are quite a few questions, you know? I am doing my best, but it's not easy. I hope you're going to be very grateful if I can get this big, big application through for you.'

While everything else could just about have been explained away, it's now clear that I am about to be shaken down for a bribe.

I'm realistic enough to recognise that I'm often going to have to pay more for everything and that I'll often have to pay people to help me. I'm a Westerner, rich in Kenyan terms. I don't like the assumption, however, that I'm a walking wallet that's open for every passer-by to dip into. And I don't like being put over a barrel. I have an elephantine memory for this kind of thing, and I'm not going to forget this in a hurry.

But there's not going to be much chance to forget. Wangui is moving in fast now. He'll have to go to Nairobi to sort it out. He'll have to stay overnight, have a meal or two while he's there. And restaurants in Nairobi aren't cheap by Bungoma standards.

'My allowances aren't… You know, they aren't very good. Hardly enough to cover the trip. I wonder, perhaps, if you could assist me?'

So that's it. He's really broken cover. He wants a bribe now and he's looking forward to a long and profitable relationship. The bastard.

He's risking his job, of course. If I mention any of this to Nigel Harrogate or anyone at USAID in Nairobi, this chiselling little chancer will be toast. No doubt he'll be suspended while a full investigation is carried out. It will be his word against mine and when all the facts are heard they'll have to get rid of him. They'd be bound to freeze my application, however, while they investigated my allegations. And it's so close to being approved. I don't want it put on hold now, so I have to make a decision.

'Right. What do you need, John?'

'Well, I'll need 3000 shillings – or, no, 5000 shillings.'

He's unreal. He knows I know the bus fare is only 1000. The grubby little B&B where he'd be staying will be about another thousand. He's looking for 3000 shillings as spending money to have a great time wining and dining and letting loose in the nightclubs, and he can't even be bothered to make up some decent story to cover his greed.

'I'll get you, you little bastard,' I think, handing him the cash. 'I'll have you. When that $300 000 goes through, I'll be on your back for this.'

After a couple more weeks of tweaking, the contracts are signed. Having access to that sort of additional funding feels fantastic. But so too does the feeling that USAID actually believes in my method. I give myself a metaphorical pat on the back. I dreamed up the whole Elevation Method based on giving people the training and access to the microfinance that lets them participate in the income opportunities I have devised. I mean, what the hell do I know about Africa, really? Very little. But I do think that people in any walk of life want to better themselves if they have the opportunities. That's the simple idea at the core of the Elevation Method, and now USAID is backing it. That feels un-fucking-believable! Yippee!

Days later I find out the shameless Wangui has been nibbling away at Kizito, my right-hand man, who handles all the money, probably the most honest and dedicated person I've met in all my time in Kenya. He's asked Kizito for a loan of 5000 shillings. Kizito said he didn't have that kind of cash, and that he certainly couldn't give it to him out of the company's money. If Wangui wanted a loan from Siboti Foods, he said, he would have to talk to me about it. Oddly enough, though, John never mentions the matter to me.

I could put up with Wangui getting all he could from the *mzungu*, but the idea of him leaning on young Kizito… It's just bloody wrong.

In the end, though, it's all handled very nicely. Nigel Harrogate is a class act, and he shows it again in this tricky situation. I go to Nairobi and we meet for lunch. I inform Nigel there's something very sensitive we need to talk about, and we agree that we will have twenty minutes of straight talking.

I spell it all out to him. The way Wangui is trying to line his pockets on the back of his position with USAID. The way he's taking loans from me and not paying them back. The way he's tried to put the screws on Kizito. I tell Harrogate everything and he listens gravely and quietly.

'I'm really glad you talked to me, Ken,' he says. 'This is the sort of thing that no one in my position ever wants to hear…'

What a disappointment. I'm going to get the official see-no-evil-hear-no-evil line.

'…and you're right, we can't tolerate that shite. Excuse my French. The problem with corruption is that once people taste it, there's no end to it. The greed can't be satisfied. They never say: "Ah, that was great. I've had a bit of easy money and I'll use that wisely and go back to my normal life." They always want more and more. They can't stop. It's an insatiable human appetite, I'm afraid.'

I'm impressed. And I watch, over the next few weeks, as he deftly and subtly makes it all happen. Harrogate is an Englishman in Kenya, working for an operational partner company of the American agency USAID. He has to navigate the politics and procedures of the institution he is representing, take account of the values and assumptions of the people he's working with and get the results he and they expect. He does it brilliantly, and I learn a lot from watching the way he handles the situation.

Recognising that it's all about the art of the possible, Nigel Harrogate reports our conversation to his superiors, with my agreement, and gets a formal investigation underway. I am interviewed by phone from this HQ, overseas. He makes sure Wangui knows he's being watched. Apart from that, he appears to be recommending no action.

But Harrogate is one smooth, sophisticated operator. An exemplary official. He knows there'll be all sorts of hassles if Wangui is fired. And the guy is getting near the end of his renewable two-year contract. So USAID just lets the contract run down. Wangui behaves well in the meantime, probably because he thinks he's got away with a warning. But when renewal time comes around, there are several strong candidates for the job of Bungoma representative and Mr John Wangui is not the chosen one.

I like that. It is pragmatic and purposeful. It seems to me a good example of how institutions do what they have to do and behave like institutions must behave. Institutions like USAID shouldn't act like hard-nosed commercial businesses. They shouldn't throw their weight around inappropriately. But, when they have good governance combined with pragmatism, an experienced professional like Nigel Harrogate can navigate the institution and make it come to the right decisions and do the right things.

But I still feel slightly compromised, and definitely a bit of a fool.

24

The price of safety

'At his best, man is the noblest of all animals; separated from law and justice, he is the worst.'

Aristotle

There's a long tradition in England of nicking the lead off church roofs. They do that here, too. But the difference is that people here love their churches with an intensity of passion you don't find in home counties suburbia. If it happens here and someone is identified as the thief, there is likely to be a more summary kind of justice than we are used to.

I've heard talk of two horrible cases of vigilantism recently. A sixty-five-year-old man suspected of stealing cattle has been doused with kerosene and set alight, and a supposed sneak thief has been thrown into a pit latrine and left to die a peculiarly horrible death. People often seem to take the law into their own hands here. When matters are reported to the police and suspects are arrested, you don't get a lot of community service orders or suspended sentences handed out in Western Kenya. Custodial sentences seem to be common if you're found guilty by a judge. If the legal system is brutal, why wouldn't the people follow suit?

There is another way. Instead of approaching the police, people often ask the Chief to arbitrate. He will try to reach a consensus and make the accused atone. Domestic issues, interfamily disputes and conflicts between neighbours over land are often dealt with by the Chief. The success of such a system is dependent on the objectivity of one individual. This is often a better and more effective alternative than the police and the court system.

At the Rickshaw Hotel yesterday, I needed to pop out to have some lunch.

I lock the door behind me, leaving a mass of papers spread out across the floor and my laptop open on the coffee table, and go five minutes down the road to the café that sells fresh orange juice and tasty omelettes, albeit cooked with way too much vegetable oil. (Only in Bungoma, I thought, could you get fat by eating omelettes.) Half an hour later I am back, only to find that my laptop has disappeared. The bedroom door is still locked and there was no sign of anyone coming in through the window, but the computer is gone.

It can only have been the staff, or someone getting in with the assistance of a member of staff, so I hurry downstairs to report the theft to Doris, the manager. Only the hotel staff have keys to the room, but Doris refuses to interview them to let me put questions to her handful of on-duty staff and insists I go to the police station to report it. It might have been one of the other guests, she claims, and apparently there was one man who had checked out during the time I was having my lunch. She has a copy of his ID card, she says, from when he checked in, and she'll give the police his details if I want to go and report it. So I go to the station, take an hour to get it logged in a huge ledger at the front desk and then another hour later, a police Land Rover arrives at the hotel with four heavily armed cops. They are officious, asking me about the laptop and studying the guest register, but ignoring the obvious need to question the staff or search the small hotel for the laptop.

'The man who checked out, he's our chief suspect,' the senior officer pronounces. 'But this ID number is probably a fake.'

'So what are you going to do? Aren't you going to interview the people here?' I ask.

'I can follow up the ID number with the identity card office in Nairobi,' he says, ignoring my question. 'But that will take time and resources. Would you like to assist with the costs to make sure we can get it done quickly?'

I am used to this by now. For me, it isn't actually a question of whether I want to pay the police to do the job they should be doing anyway, or whether I want to give this officer money to follow up the ID, but that we both know that the accomplice, and possibly the thief and the laptop, are right here in this building now. So NO, I don't want to 'assist' you!

I had an incident report number that I could use to claim on my insurance, but it was clear I wasn't going to see my laptop again. And it was equally clear that no one except me was particularly bothered about the incident.

The theft of my laptop and the police's attitude towards my loss has got me thinking seriously about my own safety, living here in Bungoma. I think of Alan's warnings and of Elizabeth's fortress. I am becoming increasingly aware that I must be a target. I'm usually the only European out and about in Bungoma and people must know I have money. They see me spending on equipment, materials and wages for the Siboti project. They see that I am living long-term in a hotel when whole families are making do in one-room mud huts.

I must stick out like a sore thumb, and I'm starting to realise I may need some serious protection if anything goes wrong. And it's not just me. It follows that my staff in Siboti must be at risk, too. They're handling large amounts of cash, by local standards, carrying valuable items like solar kits and irrigation pumps, and riding around on motorcycles and mountain bikes. Anyone could knock them over the head and rob them. Plus, we have thousands of dollars' worth of equipment, pesticides and fertiliser in our storeroom. We have the place well locked-up, but what will I do if our buildings are broken into and all our gear is stolen? I realise I need to secure a level of protection so that I, and those under my umbrella, feel protected.

We could easily be attracting the wrong sort of attention. For safety's sake, I need to get a clear message out to potential thieves and troublemakers that our staff, offices and equipment are not to be interfered with in any way. And that is going to cost money.

Realistically, there is only one way to do this, I reason to myself. I must make more of an effort to build a relationship with the top man at the local police headquarters. If anything bad happens, I need the police chief to be willing to do whatever it takes to get me out of trouble. He's got to be seen as my friend – and to know I'll have to make it worth his while to help me if I ever need to call on him. He needs to know me, and he needs to like me, and he needs to get what he wants out of me. If I or my staff are attacked or robbed or run off the road on our motorbikes, I need to have that guy's number in my phone. I need to be able to call up the man in charge and get whatever's necessary from the police. It's simple, and horribly necessary.

I need to be untouchable. I need all the local thugs, criminals and opportunists to know that I'm a good friend of the police chief and that they dare not mess with me, or the staff, or our equipment. It all feels a bit surreal, a bit like *The Godfather*.

I've already met Protus, the police inspector, and I've seen enough to know that he is a cold-blooded thug. He's young, in his thirties, clever and educated. He's got a degree and he's rising fast in the police force. But he's already casually mentioned to me, in the course of our very first conversation, about the unfortunate necessity of beating his wife, every now and again, just to remind her who's the boss. On the rare occasions when he takes off his Ray-Bans, the eyes that look out at you are disconcerting – cold, calculating and brutal.

Methodically, I decide to set about building a closer and more public relationship with this odious man. One morning I pay a courtesy call on him in his office. As I am shown in, his narrowed eyes follow me. I tell him I'm grateful for all the security we enjoy in Siboti and ask if he'd like to have a drink one evening. Suddenly, he is all benevolence.

'Sure, we should have a drink some time', he says, standing to shake my hand. 'That would be my pleasure.'

The next day, my phone rings. It's the police inspector. I have a hundred things to do, but this may have to take priority.

'I'm in town,' he says. 'Where are you?'

He's in some dismal bar in Kalamisi. If I push it a bit, I can be there in half an hour. What a godforsaken dump that place is, though. There are rocks in the middle of the road, litter everywhere, and menacing-looking drunks sitting in the shade outside run-down bars. This is café culture – Dodge City style. But for Protus, the police inspector, the man at the top of the heap, it is a little fiefdom.

I'm troubled by the realisation that his world is my world now. Since being in Kenya I've already seen enough corruption to make me hate it with a passion. But supping with the devil – in this case, Protus – is the price of safety, for myself and for those I'm employing.

When I walk in, I can see the inspector is dying of thirst. I get the drinks, a beer for me and a vodka and Coke for my mean-eyed friend. A vodka, in this context, means half a bottle of the clear spirit. When I get my second cold Tusker, he is already ready for another half bottle of vodka. But he has enough mixer left over – no need to get him another one of those, he says.

We chat. I'm cautious. I know what I want and I'm not going to blow it. There's bound to be an etiquette, so there'll be no talk of money at first. He tells me about his day so far. It's been busy, and he's just got back from a lynching.

'Someone has been robbing homes in a far-flung part of this district,' he explains. The community had decided to take matters into its own hands. A group of about thirty local men confronted the burglar. When he ran, they chased him, caught him and beat him.

'We were called to sort out the mess and pick up the body. He was a well-known criminal', Protus tells me, his dead eyes flashing.

'He'd robbed a lot of places. He'd been warned a lot of times and, well, you know, people just lost patience with him.'

'What happens now?' I ask. 'How will you find out who killed him?'

He finishes his glass and looks at me with withering scorn. It's not a problem that's been worrying him.

'Ha. Mr Ken King, what can you do? There were thirty of them. How can we ever know who struck the fatal blow? It was a mob, and you can't prosecute a mob.'

So nothing's going to happen.

'And anyway,' he adds, 'he was a well-known burglar.'

After a couple of hours of conversation about Protus – his family, his background, his ambitions – we start to wind up the conversation. I can sense what's coming next.

'Yes,' says Protus, answering a question I haven't asked, 'I'll have to get something to eat. And I don't have money.'

Well, that's not a problem. I have a few notes in my pocket, maybe thirty dollars. That'll pay for his evening.

'Here,' I say, pressing the notes into his hand. 'Enjoy your evening.'

'Thank you my friend,' says Protus, and shakes both my hands.

We part on the best of terms, with, I hope, the beginnings of a friendship that will provide the security I need for myself and my staff.

The next time the inspector is thirsty and I get the call, I'm there again, as fast as the motor bike will carry me. I get him his vodka and we sit down and talk about Protus again. After an hour telling me about his life, his triumphs and his problems, he pauses to take a breather. His bloodshot eyes look me over appraisingly. You rarely see Westerners in this town and in this bar I stand out, as I do in Siboti.

'You should have a gun,' he says, 'for your protection.'

Wow. Now I'm really in his world.

'You really think so?' I ask.

'Every big man here needs a gun. You need to carry a .22 pistol. The permit won't be a problem. I can sign the papers. I can get the gun for you and make sure the permit is approved. No problem. No problem for you, Mr Ken King.'

Ah. I get it now. My getting a gun involves him doing me a small service. A service I will, of course, appreciate and pay for.

I don't like the idea of having a gun. The real protection, the real insurance policy for me, is not the gun but the relationship with this uniformed gangster. I have no doubt about the significance of that. If I'd shot someone and needed to get out of the country fast, he'd see I was all right. As long as I paid up the right amount of money, it would just be a case of 'Oh, that guy pulled a gun on him and he shot him in self-defence.' Now he is my friend – and I am in his, too, I suppose – I could probably shoot anyone who took it into their head to attack me, as long as I was prepared to pay off the inspector.

'So, Mr Ken King. I get you a gun, yes?'

I take a long look at the police inspector's reptilian expression. You don't say no to a man like him.

'I'll have a think about it and get back to you. Thanks for the offer.'

He nods, eyeing the bottom of his now empty glass.

'You are welcome, Mr Ken King.'

If I ever get a gun he would probably extort more and more money out of me. And if I ever used it, well, let's say that would be a red-letter day for him.

Within a few weeks, Wednesday afternoon drinking sessions with Protus have become a regular event. At my suggestion, we meet in Bungoma, too, sometimes, so that people there see us out and about together. Sometimes he's been drinking vodka for a couple of hours by the time we meet. That's when I get the evil eyes. It's proving quite expensive, but now I feel absolutely protected from broader harm. And as my managers know I am friends with the inspector, they feel protected, too. They know that no harm will come to them from bullies or thugs, despite their regular incomes and relative affluence. I hear from Edwin and Kizito that everyone around Siboti Foods feels really happy about the level of security we enjoy. And, of course, we are also safe from being broken into and having our goods and equipment stolen.

My relationship with this man is pragmatic, born of necessity on my side and greed on his. It's something less than friendship, and something more than trade. At times, he even shows a fleeting interest in the Siboti project itself. He won't let sentiment get in the way of business, but I realise he's getting to like my company. I flatter him, listen to his woes, buy him drinks. What's not to like?

'Siboti feels secure with you in charge,' I tell him. 'That's good leadership.'

He grunts and I try to pretend that I'm not being a prize sycophant. It's a small price.

'I don't get paid enough,' he informs me. 'My bosses do not appreciate what I do, how hard I work. The community needs me, the police station needs me. I am always in demand.'

'You have many challenges,' I agree, and his glass bashes against mine.

I remember a wealthy stockbroker telling me once that the rich always want to buy themselves out of the state system. They pay for private health treatment, private education, private members clubs and maybe even private security, and they like to think they don't depend on the state at all.

'But you try getting your own private water and electricity supplies, your own sewage disposal and rubbish collection, your own fire brigade, your own police and justice system,' said my stockbroker friend. 'It doesn't matter how rich you are, you just can't do it. Services like that are almost invisible until something goes wrong, but they are a huge part of what living in a mature, developed nation means, even for billionaires.'

Just now, I'm getting a glimpse of what privatised justice looks like. It's ugly. But for me and those around me, it's the price of safety. And I've got no option. I have to pay it.

25

Hong Kong

'Ninety per cent of selling is conviction and ten per cent is persuasion.'

Shiv Khera

Some bloody do-gooder – someone like me, I suppose – has started a chilli pepper-growing project with the local people in the Maasai Mara national park area of Kenya. The Maasai are an ancient and proud warrior race, and I met some of them in Tanzania. As far as I could see, they were almost exclusively interested in cattle. That's how they measure their wealth and status. So can it be true? Are the Maasai suddenly emerging in competition with us as producers of chilli peppers?

If it's them, they certainly seem to be good at it. Too good, actually. It seems their chilli project has produced such vast quantities that it's flooded the market in Nairobi and made the price collapse. Last year it was 32 shillings. Now it's dropped to 24 shillings. I'll have to subsidise part of that drop by paying the full transport and wages costs myself. In order to minimise the impact to the farmers so early in the project, I'll eat the losses on this crop and hope the price will soon recover. It means that all my financial calculations and projections for Siboti are blown out the window. At that price, any hope of reaching profitability so that Siboti Foods can start to pay back my working capital loans goes up in smoke.

The chilli project is in deep financial trouble. I knew anything to do with growing fresh produce was always going to be risky. I'm used to managing risk. But how do you manage a risk like a 25 per cent price drop that wipes out any hope of breaking even? How can a young business survive something like that?

The only answer, of course, is to inject more capital to tide us over. The USAID money is earmarked for the new OFSP project, and anyway that funding approval process has proved more lengthily than expected, with its pile of administrative demands, and Wangui's unwillingness to do anything until his palm is greased. I am going to have to put up more of my money to keep everything afloat. My house sale in London has now gone through so I have more cash behind me. I've already invested a massive chunk of that capital into Siboti. I'd long harboured the hope that one day Siboti would be able to sell into the export market, but now it looks like we are going to have to go into exporting in a hurry, now, to get higher prices. I discover that there's a big export business based in Eldoret – called, rather engagingly, Canken – that sends huge quantities of vegetables out to Dubai every week, so I arrange a visit to see Canken.

On the way to the company's base at Eldoret Airport, I see women at the roadside selling potatoes. They're rather elegantly arranged, stacked up on little metal buckets, like a starchy version of the Ferrero Rocher chocolates in the adverts. And behind them, the other side of the perimeter fence, there's a jumbo jet taking on pallet-loads of Kenyan vegetables to be airlifted to Europe or the Middle East or wherever. The contrast is dramatic – mediaeval one side of the wire, twenty-first century the other. It's suddenly crystal-clear which side of the fence Siboti Foods needs to be on.

I've thought about it before, and once I've seen the Canken operation running out of Eldoret Airport it becomes an absolute imperative: we need to go international to shift the chillies.

So how do you find overseas buyers for a product like chillies? How do you find international buyers for anything? The manager at Canken tells me the company finds its customers at Fruit Logistica, the annual fruit and vegetable trade fair expo in Berlin. But that's in February. Damn! It's late August now and I need to sell the chillies now, not next year.

There is another expo in Hong Kong, though, for the Asian fruit and veg market, and that's in early September. I download the blurb and it looks promising. There'll be exhibitors from all over the world, it seems, including America, Australia, New Zealand and Europe, as well as many Asian and Middle Eastern exhibitors. Fantastic! I'll sign up for a stand, book a flight and take the chance to see Hong Kong again.

Fuck, fuckety fuck. September. It's the same date I've promised to take Keziah to London. I've been seeing her regularly for a few months, sometimes in Bungoma but often, when I get a break, in Nairobi. She is right behind the chilli project now and offers a wonderful counterbalance to my often uninformed enthusiasm. We have become very close. As with my new life in Siboti, though, I'm thinking on my feet, living in the moment, rather than planning to far ahead.

After a few minutes' thought, I reason that Keziah and London will be around for a while but that the trade fair is a one-off opportunity I can't afford to miss. I pick up the phone and prepare to open delicate negotiations.

'...so I thought we'd do London and then go to Hong Kong on the way back.'

'On the way back?' Keziah asks. 'What kind of map is that you've got?'

'Come on,' I say. 'You'll love it.'

'What's going on, Ken? What's in Hong Kong?'

So I have to be straight with her, of course.

'You want me to come and hang around while you're at a trade fair?'

'Not hang around. You could help me. On the stand. You'd be great.'

'You want me to come and help on a stand at a trade fair?'

Why does she manage to make everything sound so... true? I decide to play my trump card. I'll appeal to her altruism.

'Kezzy. Think about it. It's for my project. Think of all those orphans. Those little ones need your help. Those little children need you to come to Hong Kong with me.'

'I'll think about it,' she says, carefully.

The next day, the call comes and she's in. I'm delighted. And I can't help reckoning that Keziah's magnetism will probably double the number of people who come by our stand.

* * *

We spend a week in London and I see it all anew, through Keziah's eyes. She may have studied in Switzerland for two years, but this is all new to her. So I give her the works. We have lunch at The Ivy and tea at The Ritz. We go round the Globe and up the Gherkin. And we see all the sights: the Tower of London, Buckingham Palace, Stamford Bridge. It's a joyful time.

Keziah's in love with London and I think I'm in falling in love with her. That's good enough for me, for now. I don't want to scare her off by being too full-on (it has been known), so I'm concentrating on just being in the moment. I'm better at embracing uncertainty now. In fact, I'm so good at being in the moment that I manage to overlook the fact that we're shortly going to be on a stand at a major international exhibition, trying to convince people to commit to big contracts to buy our chillies – and I have forgotten to bring any of our produce with me. It's an oversight. Maybe I'm distracted by Keziah.

Actually, I have one chilli that I carry around as a kind of talisman. One little red chilli. It's not exactly going to fill a stand.

I dash round the supermarkets. They've got plenty – fat, green Padrón chillies, long, thin Cayenne chillies, cherry-like habaneros and plump green jalapeños, orange Cheyennes and Hungarian blacks. What they haven't got is anything I could pass off as ours. I hit the greengrocers and the markets, pulling out my increasingly battered little Siboti sample and comparing it, side by side, with what's available.

I'm getting some funny looks, but that's the least of my problems.

This is getting silly. It can't be true that a huge cosmopolitan city like London is devoid of the right kind of chillies, just when I desperately need them.

On the Sunday morning, a few hours before our early evening flight, inspiration strikes. Keziah and I jump in the car and drive to Southall, a district in West London with a large Indian community. And lo, we find a shop that has some very Siboti-like chillies that will do just fine. Great. I'll take them.

'Have you got any more?' I ask the shopkeeper, looking at the small handful I've plucked from his display.

'No, but I think Daud, round the corner, may have some.'

Daud has a few, but he puts me on to Sachin, a few doors down, who has more, and he points me in the direction of Jasbir, further up the road. I'm getting there. By the time we're finished, we have gone from shop to shop, the length and breadth of Southall, cleaning the place out. We take all the reds we can find, and a few handfuls of greens as well. There'll be a chilli shortage locally for weeks to come, but that's not my problem. I still have nowhere near as many chillies as I'd like, but at least we've got something to show on our exhibition stand.

I rush back and hurl some clothes – and the precious chillies – into a suitcase, along with our Siboti project posters. After thirteen hours in the air, we arrive in Hong Kong, touching down gently at the ultra-modern Chek Lap Kok airport.

The doors open and the climate hits you full on. It's not so much the heat. It's more the thick, damp air, nuzzling at your face like an invisible and insistently friendly Labrador. 'Humid' just doesn't do it justice. Whenever you step outside, whether it's nine o'clock in the morning or half-past midnight, it hits you the same way.

The show starts on Wednesday, so we swing into action on Tuesday to set up the stand. It's soon clear that we are the little guys. Some of these exhibition booths are gigantic. Lots of Dutch companies have taken a stall together, and organised it with meeting tables, display areas, coffee machines and reception desks at either end. We look around at our little booth, three metres by three. We put up our eight A2-sized posters that tell the Siboti story, describe our product and explain the sort of supply relationship we are seeking.

It looks a bit weak, to put it mildly. A company on the next door stand is selling shallots. That's it… Shallots. Just shallots. And what have they got for their 3x3 booth? Wall-to-wall high-gloss posters of shallots, a huge glass container with thousands of shallots, flyers that wax lyrical about shallots, catalogues describing the company and its shallots, an enormous plasma TV screen showing workers and machines efficiently grading and packing shallots, and six guys and girls who look as if they've all just graduated from shallot university. It's all under the beady eye of a woman whose look says 'You will buy shallots, and you will do it now or I will not be responsible for the consequences.' No one's going to mess with the Lady of Shallots.

How can we match this firepower? What have we got on our stand? Eight A2 posters and the few kilos of red and green chillies that fitted into my suitcase. Oh fuck. We'd better be on top form tomorrow. The old blarney will need a bit of polishing up. We're going to have to rely on Irish charm and Kenyan brains and beauty, and some good old-fashioned determination.

The Star Ferry from the island to the Kowloon peninsula is a must-do on any trip to Hong Kong, particularly at night when the skyline is ablaze with neon on both sides of the harbour. In the Temple Street night market, on the Kowloon side, Keziah bargains for a couple of wicker baskets, one for the dried red chillies, one for the fresh green ones. The baskets look a bit African, maybe. And a red tablecloth for the table that comes with the booth. It'll look better than a blank table for the baskets of chillies, apparently. We haggle energetically for several minutes and save ourselves about a dollar. Then we go for dinner and gird our loins, ready to play David tomorrow in a room full of Goliaths.

Day One, 5 p.m. The day will soon wind down and we have had, in round numbers, precisely zero visitors to our booth. Some people pass by and pick up a chilli, sniff it and leave. They won't talk. One guy took a bite out of one of them. He must be on fire. Serves him right. With just an hour left to run on the first day, we've done nothing.

We need a plan. We need to get out there and take control. Sitting around is getting us nowhere. We go through the show catalogue, looking at the company names and the countries they come from, highlighting everyone who is listed as an importer. They are our targets, so let's go out and get them.

We home in on our first target, just across from us. They're Koreans, and it's quickly clear that they are not interested in buying anything. In fact, they are trying to sell to us. Guess their catalogue entry – 'importer' – isn't so accurate, then. Lesson learned. First question each time has to be 'Hi, do you import?' Next up, Malaysia. Yep. All the Malaysian companies exhibiting do imports, but only fruit. Damn. Thailand. 'Hi, do you import vegetables?' Nope. Six o'clock already and the show finishes. That's OK. We've got the hang of it now. Roll on tomorrow, when we'll go for the big one: China.

Day Two starts with an action plan. We make a list of all the Chinese companies at the show, and their locations in the hall. We set out for China, striding confidently across the floor towards the Middle Kingdom. Two hours later, we have spoken to every one of them. There may be 1.3 billion people in China, but it seems they are pretty self-sufficient in the chilli department. At 3 p.m. I write a quick summary of where we've got to. It doesn't take long and it doesn't cover much of the page. We can't begin to compete with domestic producers in China because we have the extra cost of international shipping.

For India, the sale price of chillies per kilo is 30 rupees. We need more than that just to cover our freight costs. For Korea and Indonesia, all the exhibitors are exporters, not importers, and they don't seem able or willing to tell us about any importers we could contact. Turkey – same thing. Australia has lots of rules and restrictions on the import of fresh produce, often tied in with reciprocal trade agreements. A quick look at the internet reveals that Kenya is not on the approved list as a source of chilli peppers for Australia. New Zealand has some similar restrictions, but even without checking the web, New Zealand just seems too far away to export to.

I already know that exporting by air to the UK, and hence, I guess, the rest of Europe, will not be viable, as the airfreight charges are more than the ultimate sale price of the chillies. Maybe shipping to the UK and Europe by refrigerated container could be possible.

But nobody else is doing it for chillies – and that's a bit suspicious. Either I have stumbled on a market gap and am an unknowing entrepreneurial pioneer, or, more likely, I am just not fully informed of the challenges involved in sending chillies by sea. Kenya is just south of Somalia, so maybe Somali chilli pirates are the problem, as Keziah suggests.

Damn it, where the hell are we going to sell these chillies? I think about that Nairobi exporter who bought some small consignments of John's Siboti chillies before John sold his business to me. What countries could his exporter have sold them to? It can only have been the Middle East, as the distance and the freight costs would be much lower, and Kenya could maybe compete on price. Have we come all this way to Hong Kong just to find out we're at the wrong trade fair?

We need to be at a trade fair in the Middle East, if one exists. That looks like our only chance. Let's just hope that if we go there we don't find reasons why that won't work too. We can't sell at a decent price to domestic buyers in Kenya, because of the Maasai – or someone – flooding the market, and now things are not looking good internationally either.

As I survey this gloomy summary, my heart sinks with an almost audible thud. I need Siboti Foods to become a sustainable, profitable business if it is going to be the economic engine for poverty alleviation in Siboti. But if I can't make Siboti Foods sustainably profitable, the Siboti project might have to become a part-time passion, while I try to earn a living elsewhere. And how easy will that be? Since I've been away following the global financial crisis, banking has downscaled and jobs are in shorter supply. I've been out of the loop for a few years now and I love the freedom of roaming around Siboti on my motorbike. Returning to an office environment, even if I could, might be a challenge.

How will I feel if the Siboti project isn't the success I want it to be, and the people of Siboti need it to be? What if my customised Siboti project methodology turns out to be no more than a single-donor charity – only as good as the cash I can pour in? That would be failure. That would not be achieving the Millennium Development Goals, or creating a model that could be replicated elsewhere. I need this to succeed. For all of us, I really need this to succeed.

At that moment, with timing that would not be out of place in a Hollywood movie, a German guy and a Thai girl stop by the stall. They import to Germany from Thailand, by air, and they want to find a source of chillies to match the seasonal gaps in Thailand's production.

'By air?' I ask.

'Sure. Why not?'

'Because the airfreight charges are so high.'

'Our customers in Germany know the prices. We import all the fresh produce from Thailand by air. Then we send it by truck across Germany and Europe, even to the UK.'

Is this guy bullshitting me? The sums don't add up. I know it costs £1.70 to airlift a kilo of chillies from Nairobi to London, and they sell at London markets for £1.40. To get around that, the London wholesalers import from Holland in summer and from North African Morocco and Egypt in winter, and avoid or minimise the onerous airfreight costs.

Wholesalers and supermarkets don't import chillies from West Africa or the even more distant East Africa, because of the extra miles and extra airfreight costs. But these two people seem genuine. They get into a deep and serious conversation with us about different types of international food standard certification, what volumes we could provide, what months of the year we produce, what arrangements we have for freight, price expectations, and so on. The German gives me his business card, and says to contact him as soon as we have achieved our international food certification, as he is definitely interested in taking an initial shipment of chillies. This is starting to sound promising.

Next up, two guys from Spain stop by. They import fresh red chillies to Spain from Uganda. Their supply is inconsistent and they are looking for additional sources.

While I am swapping contact details with the Spanish guys, I hear that Keziah has caught a live one. In fact, her catch is in charge of sourcing fresh produce for 400 supermarkets in Asia, part of the Carrefour chain, one of the world's largest food retailers.

Carrefour Asia imports fresh produce into Dubai and bundles various products for transfer to Asian countries, including Indonesia, Thailand, Singapore, Malaysia and Taiwan. We talk about price, about quality, about volumes, about transportation and shipping, about maintaining an unbroken cold-chain (a temperature-controlled supply chain) from our fields to their refrigerated warehouses in Dubai. This lady is serious. She will send us information on the processes her suppliers have to follow. I will price up the shipping and send her an all-in quote. If the price is good, she is confident an order will follow. One twenty-foot container to start. That's 7000 kilos. To start! And she is in charge of *all* fresh produce sourcing. If we can land this order and do a good job with it, surely we have an opportunity to supply other products to Carrefour next year. This could be massive. Things are definitely looking up.

Six p.m. comes, and we're starting to pack up when Esther arrives. Esther is a Kenyan bundle of joy. She wanders up to the booth, says she looked at our stall earlier today, and was inspired by the story of the Siboti project. Ah, the A2 posters. Not entirely useless then. Even those posters are adding to our feel-good factor now. Esther runs the sales operation for a large Kenyan exporter of fresh vegetables and she's at the show to see her customers and find new ones.

Esther exports several types of vegetables to Sweden, mainland Europe and the UK. She has a customer in the United States who asked her last week to supply a twenty-foot container of dried long slim chilli peppers, but she couldn't find enough dried chillies. She had heard about the Maasai project, but they are supplying only fresh green chillies, not dried.

'We can supply you, Esther,' I yelp. She agrees to contact her buyer to see if the order is still unfilled and open. I tell Esther my price target, which is right in line with what she expects to pay. If the order is still open, we'll do a deal. Wow. We may have just sold the next two months' worth of chilli peppers.

Esther tells me the problems she's been having getting reliable large-scale high-quality supplies of fresh produce to meet the orders from her overseas buyers.

'That's fine. Mobilising the community to do large-scale agricultural production is what we do best, Esther.'

'I can see that. Would you be interested in entering into a contract for a regular supply of chilli peppers to us, on a large scale?'

Would I what? Would I ever? I work hard at keeping a suitably calm and professional exterior, while I actually want to jump up and down and hug her. Holy shit! This Siboti thing is going to work! Zip-a-dee-doo-dah, zip-a-dee-ay, my, oh my, what a wonderful day!

'Well, Esther, I have plans for a one hundred per cent increase in production next year, in order to include more of the community of Siboti. We want to grow other varieties of chillies – and aubergines, sugar-snap peas, French beans, mangetout, baby corns, courgettes, garlic, ginger and herbs like mint, rosemary and coriander. Are you interested in contracting us for any of these?'

Esther smiles, a great, beaming smile. 'You must have done your homework, Ken, because these are all products that grow well in the western region of Kenya. Let's send our agronomist team out to see you when we both get back, and we can decide what products you can do for us.'

Esther leaves. We will meet again tomorrow and talk some more.

Keziah radiates an elegant, demure happiness. Three hours ago, we were dead in the water. Now it looks like we have potential orders for the rest of this year, and a possible contract for next year. I skip around the booth like a kid with a new bike on Christmas morning, trying not to scream out loud for joy. We need a serious discussion about what this all means, so we head off to Aqua Spirit, rated one of the world's top one hundred bars, looking out from the thirtieth floor with a spectacular view of Hong Kong harbour and the nightly light show. I knew it's notoriously difficult to get a window table at that restaurant on a Friday night, but somebody or something is shining on us and we get the best table in the place. I struggle all evening to contain a grin that feels wider than my face, while we drink champagne and dance the night away.

After the next and final day of the show, with several more contacts in the bag, it's easy to dream of an end to poverty in Siboti and maybe also of many more Siboti-type projects for hundreds of thousands of people. The Siboti model will work. It will be replicable. A successful export business awaits me, giving me the chance to make a living exporting the produce while ensuring the farmers get the best prices. And I'll be able to stay on, initiating and running Millennium Development Goal projects, long term. We are done in Hong Kong. What a trip.

With our optimism sky high, we take a high-speed hydrofoil trip across the Zhujiang River estuary to Macau, the Vegas of the East, to spend our Saturday night in one of the huge and glittering casinos. Crazy place, full of crazy people. Maybe we are doing such important work that the gods will reward us with a win on the tables. No such luck, as it turns out. But that's OK. I'm beginning to feel the bigger gamble might come off.

26

Ambush

'I'm not upset that you lied to me; I'm upset that from now on I can't believe you.'

Friedrich Nietzsche

The trip to Hong Kong with Keziah has been pure magic. Even so, I'm still dying to get back to Siboti. That's how big a draw the place is for me now. The momentum I've seen building up over the last few months is making me feel more sure than ever that I'm doing the right thing here – for the people of Siboti, and for myself, as well. This is, I'm convinced now, my new purpose in life: to find my own unique way of solving extreme poverty under certain conditions. If I can succeed here, I will be truly fulfilled. I can't wait to get stuck in and push on with all the plans that have been taking shape in my head, and I can feel my pulse racing as the mini-bus rattles along the road from Eldoret towards Bungoma.

It's a beautiful day. The sun is hot and the local children are laughing and shouting as I park my motorbike in the market square in front of the office, dancing around me like a swarm of friendly bees.

'Mr King! Mr King! What did you bring? Mr King! Mr King! What did you bring?'

They know there's a good chance I'll have some sweets in my bag when I come back from a trip. This time, though, they're out of luck.

And so, it seems, am I. As I walk across to our little row of low buildings, I can see the whole place is locked up. That's not right. Where is everybody? I walk back and sit on the motorbike while I call Kizito. As soon as I hear his voice, I know something's wrong. He sounds frightened.

'Oh Ken,' he says. 'Thank God you're back. You have to go to a meeting. The elders and the high-achiever farmers want to see you. There's been trouble.'

'Trouble? What sort of trouble?'

'There's been a riot.'

I'm baffled.

'What do you mean, a riot?'

I've never heard Kizito sound so agitated and overwhelmed. I suspect he'll feel that whatever's gone wrong while he's been left in charge is his fault, but he's the most conscientious and reliable man this side of Lake Victoria. Whatever the trouble is, it won't be because of anything he's done.

'Where are you?'

'I'm in hiding, Ken. At my sister's house in town, in Bungoma.'

Hiding? What the…?

'OK. Look, I'll meet you at the coffee place in half an hour. OK?'

'Yes, very OK. I'll see you there.'

Thirty minutes later, sitting in the shade of the big acacia tree outside the café, Kizito explains what has happened. He's pale and anxious, and his voice is trembling.

'The farmers. They came to the office yesterday and there was a riot. They were angry. They think we're cheating them.'

I can't believe my ears.

'But we're not here to cheat anyone, Kizito. The farmers know that. I'm here to help them grow good crops and get good prices and make their lives better. Why on earth do they think we're cheating them?'

'That's just it, Ken. The price has gone down. It's not 24 shillings a kilo any more. We can only get 16 shillings for the chillies now. But they don't believe what we say.'

Kizito fills me in on the previous day's events. The morning had started quietly, he says, and there were twenty or thirty farmers waiting outside the office. As usual, they had each filled one or two sacks with chillies, slung them over a bicycle and wheeled them down to Siboti Foods.

Now they were waiting patiently to check in with Julius, hand over their chillies for grading and weighing and get their money from Kizito. (This was the second chilli crop for most of them and they knew the routine by now.) After a while, though, they realised they'd been waiting a long time and they started to get a bit restless.

So they were in no mood to take it quietly when Julius stepped outside the building, called for hush and announced, bluntly, that the price of chillies had fallen by 8 shillings a kilo and they'd only get 16, rather than 24.

For poor farmers with large families who had been waiting weeks to get the money from the crops they'd been tending, this was the worst possible news.

'You're cheating us,' someone shouted from the back. 'I've got two sacks here, at least 50 kilos. I want 24 shillings a kilo. I want my 1200 shillings for my chillies.'

The situation was not helped by the fact that Julius wasn't popular with the farmers, any more than he was with the casual workers we employed to sort and grade the chillies. They thought he was rude and condescending, and while everyone knew he was studying to become a pastor, they saw him as sanctimonious, rather than saintly.

Within seconds, rumours were spreading that Julius was collecting 24 shillings a kilo from the buyers, giving the farmers a measly 16 shillings and pocketing the rest for himself. They thought he was cheating both them and me. And they weren't going to stand for it.

I stop Kizito in his tracks.

'Well, has the price we're getting really dropped 8 shillings in a matter of days? That's a hell of a fall.'

'Yes. It has. We didn't know what to do. We couldn't contact you and we knew we couldn't give the farmers more than we were being paid…'

'Hold on, Kizito.'

He pauses in mid-flow, rubbing his fingers together. I notice the vein on his forehead is prominent today.

'Why didn't you call me? My phone works fine. It was on all the time.'

Kizito's eyes slide away from mine and examine the marks on the table. We're in the shade but still I sense he is holding something back.

'Maybe the signal is not there. I couldn't get through,' he says.

I sit back in my chair and realise how much I need a coffee, even in this heat. It's not uncommon for people to tell you what they think you want to hear, for fear of otherwise giving offence. That can happen in any culture, but it's often frustrating. For some reason, Kizito didn't try to contact me, but he won't come clean. Maybe he didn't want to bother me, or he thought it inappropriate to call me while I was in Hong Kong. Whatever the reason, now he's trying to save face. It doesn't change the problem.

'OK, Kizito. Do we know why the price went down?'

'The buyers were just saying "It's 16 shillings, now – take it or leave it." It was like they didn't need our chillies. So I only got 16 shillings a kilo. I think maybe the market is flooded again.'

'Hmmm. So what happened next?'

'Well, we're all outside, with Julius at the front, and suddenly there's a lot of shouting and pushing and someone tries to punch at Julius. And he's pushing them away and the crowd's jostling forward and our people just bolt inside and lock the door. And the crowd's banging on the metal door and it's all looking very nasty.'

'And where are you while this is going on?'

'I'm not proud of myself, Ken. I just grabbed my motorbike and got out of there. I came into town and I haven't been back. They know I handle the money and I don't want to be lynched by an angry mob.'

I look at Kizito and he stares back at me. I've never seen him like this before. His fear is tangible.

'Surely not, Kizito. These men know you. They deal with you every week. They know and respect you. There's no way they would do this.'

He just shrugs, his shoulders hunched, and in that moment he looks surprisingly frail.

'Kizito?' I touch his arm and he almost jumps. 'You look like you need to eat something.'

I look around the café. No one pays us any attention. Many peaceful meetings have been spent here under the spreading shade of this acacia tree. I find it almost impossible to believe that the farmers we deal with every week could have tried to hurt a man they know well from within their own community. But looking at Kizito, I can see how wound up he is. He feels threatened. In that moment I realise how easily the mood can change in a community where the stakes are so high, where life is focused on survival. These are local people who know where he lives. It's a truly sobering thought. I sit forward.

'So what happened then?'

'You know William, Julius's uncle, the assistant chief?'

Yes. I know William. He's a big, leering lump of a man, with white socks, ridiculously pointy black shoes, a lot of airs and graces and no principles at all. He won't lift a finger to help me or his people without a *kitu kidogo* to grease his palm. William is trouble, and I always try to steer clear. I recoil at the sound of his name.

'Well, William is the saviour of that situation,' Kizito says, smiling for the first time. 'William turns up and he calms everything down and asks the farmers what the problem is. And they say: "It's Julius.

The way he treats us. And now he's stealing our money." And William says: "No, no, no. You're wrong. He's a good man. He's studying to be a pastor." And someone shouts, "He's not a pastor, he's a cheat and a thief." But anyway, William has the authority of an assistant chief and he gets it under control. The farmers gradually drift away, grumbling and looking back over their shoulders. They're still angry, though, and now the elders and the high-achieving farmers want you to go for a meeting with them.'

I fan myself and think. I'll have to deal with Julius later. For now, the main priority is to talk to the elders and the most successful of the farmers – the ones that have already earned their high-achiever certificates – to reassure them and hear what they've got to say. Our meeting is going to take place at the house of one of the elders, but I'm not sure, at this stage, how many of us are supposed to be involved and how many of them will be there. Edwin knows the place, so he leads the way up there, up Siboti Hill. The elder's house is like a smaller version of the Chief's, made of mud, with a corrugated tin roof, sofas around three walls and a huge coffee table that leaves hardly any floor space. As my eyes adjust to the gloom, I see there are at least a dozen people already inside, waiting for me.

I'm expecting complaints about Julius and questions about the 8 shilling drop in the price paid for the chillies. But they have something else they want to tell me, and they come out with it before I've even sat down.

'Mr Ken,' the elder says. 'The problem is John.'

John? This is John Karanga, who joined Siboti Foods when I bought his one-man chilli business. But surely the problem is Julius?

'The problem is John, Mr Ken. John is the reason why the price you are being offered for our chillies has fallen so low.'

I don't get it. How can John, who is working as our sales manager, be responsible for chilli prices falling over a cliff?

'You are too trusting, Mr Ken. John is still running his own business. He has his own business, in competition with you. He is buying chillies up near the Ugandan border, at Malaba, and he's sold so many in Nairobi he's flooded the market.'

That's disturbingly plausible, I quickly reflect. He knows the market and he has the contacts. But would he do that now, when he's working full-time for us?

'You shouldn't be employing John, Mr Ken. You must dismiss him.'

'But there's no proof that that's what he's doing. I will talk to John, but I can't fire him without any proof.'

'We'll get you all the proof you want,' the farmers say. 'Come with us to Malaba. We'll show you where he stores the chillies, at the house of the Indian lady, Mrs Peeka. Come with us and you can catch him red-handed.'

So we end the meeting and I agree to go with a few of the farmers the next day. We'll go to Malaba and they'll help me find Mrs Peeka. If there's any evidence of John running his own chilli-trading business, competing with Siboti Foods while he's employed by us, I will have to take decisive action.

As I make my way back to Bungoma this evening, I can't help seeing the silver lining in all this. The elders and the high-achieving farmers clearly accept that I'm on their side and that Siboti Foods is not cheating them. They didn't bring in the Chief, or either of the assistant chiefs, for this meeting. They wanted to talk to me first about what was going on, without involving the authorities. They obviously trust me, even against one of their own. There's a serious problem, but they are relying on me to get to the bottom of it. We're in this together.

The next day, we turn up in Malaba. Eventually, we find Mrs Peeka's house. But she doesn't know John Karanga.

'I don't know him. I've never heard of him,' she says.

'She does. She does,' the farmers shout. 'He gets all the chillies delivered here and she stores them until it's time to ship them off to the buyers.'

'I'm sorry. I can't help you,' the old lady says politely. 'I will get in touch with you if I hear anything about this John Kamanga, or whatever his name is.'

I have no idea whether Mrs Peeka is lying or not. But there are tell-tale chilli stalks and yellow seeds scattered on the ground and the farmers seem very sure she's involved in John's secret side-line. Looking at her calm, almost serene face, I really can't read what's going on behind her eyes. But there's no proof of John's involvement here. If I'm going to get at the truth, I need to talk to him.

There aren't many HR specialists out here in rural Kenya, and the finer points of disciplinary procedure are not generally recognised. But he's earned the right to give his side of the story and explain what is happening. So I call him in for a formal meeting.

'John, there have been serious allegations about you and I want to hear your comments. People seem to have a certain set of beliefs about what you are doing, and I want to get your view on why they might believe these things.'

He sits there opposite me, wearing his anorak, as always, and listens carefully until I've finished.

'No, Mr Ken. I don't do this. I don't trade in chillies anymore, except for Siboti Foods. And I don't have any business in Malaba.'

He seems cool and unruffled. Firm, but not defensive or defiant. If I'm going to find out what lies behind the problems, I need to shake him out of his composure.

'John, who's Mrs Peeka?'

'I don't know a Mrs Peeka. I've never heard of anyone called Peeka.'

'Is that your company phone? Can I have it a minute, please, John?'

He shrugs and hands over the mobile phone.

I flick through the contacts list. I look under 'P'. And there's her name – Peeka.

I go back through the undeleted text messages.

'There's a message here from Mrs Peeka. It says "Confirm 24 for kg." But you say you don't know her. Are you lying to me, John?'

'No, Mr Ken.'

'John, I'm going to give you one more chance. I want you to tell me the truth, and if it turns out you've been cheating me and trading behind my back, we'll have to decide then how we're going to handle it.'

He's still pretty cool. I hold the silence for a few seconds, hoping the pressure will get to him. But he doesn't flinch. I have to turn up the gas.

'On the other hand, if you tell me you haven't been cheating and I find out that you have, I will have to make it a very serious thing. It's important. It affects hundreds, maybe thousands, of people in this community. You know I have a lot of contacts around here now, that I know the police. I can get things done, you know.'

This is horrible. I'm starting to sound like some mafia don. I'm embarrassed to hear myself making thinly veiled threats like this. But I'm still hoping, against the evidence of that text message, that there's some innocent explanation. Come on, John. Help me. I don't want to have to behave like this.

'Look, John. Let me ask you one more time. I encourage you to tell me the truth, and then we'll deal with it. Whatever it is, you and I will work it out together. You've helped me build this business. You've played a big part in getting us going. You were great when you were going out meeting all the farmers and talking to church congregations. We've been a good team, and I enjoy working with you. But I need the truth.'

I sense I will have to make it easier for him to come clean.

'If you've been going up against me in the market, we won't be able to continue working together, but we'll find a way to handle our parting, with some delay so you have no dishonour in the eyes of the community. But if you've been working against me and you lie to me as well, then it's going to be very serious. So, John, please tell me the truth. Are you running a chilli business in Malaba?'

'No, sir.'

'OK. So how do you explain this message on your phone?'

'I can't explain it.'

He knows. He knows there's no possible innocent explanation. He knows I know. Why doesn't he come out with his hands up?

'Right, John. I'll leave you to think about what needs to happen next. We're done for today. I'll come back to you.'

* * *

Over the next few days, nothing changes. John won't offer an explanation. He simply says that he's done nothing wrong and that the farmers are all against him, for reasons he can't explain. Despite the damning evidence of Mrs Peeka's text message, he won't budge. As usual, the only person I can confide in is my trusty right-hand man.

'What on earth can I do about John?' I mutter. 'He's put in a lot of good work for us, particularly back in the early days, and I don't want to sack him. But we do need to get to the bottom of this.'

'Have you talked to the Chief?' says Kizito.

Brilliant. Of course. That's how offences and disputes are dealt with in this community. So I call the Chief, explain that I have a very delicate matter to discuss with him and respond immediately to his invitation to come up to his house and talk about it.

The next day the Chief calls John and me and several of the elders together and holds his own investigation. It's not exactly a court hearing – more like those parliamentary committee sessions where people are grilled about what they've done and why. It's tense and thorough, though, and, as the evidence emerges, it's absolutely clear that John has been trading in chillies through his contacts in Malaba.

So I'm genuinely shocked when the Chief announces that he cannot come to a decision on the matter. It's an open and shut case. Why can't he see the truth when it's staring him in the face?

I soon realise that he simply does not want to take a decision. For whatever reason, he's going to sit on the fence. For me, that looks like weakness. How can you exercise the authority of a chief if you can't face taking the occasional decision that someone or other won't like?

As the little blue motorbike carries me back down Siboti's switchback hillsides, I realise I'm going to have to live with the situation unresolved. Having turned John's case over to the Chief, expecting a guilty judgement that everyone would have to accept, I can hardly now decide unilaterally that he is guilty and dismiss him. But there are two things that are incontrovertibly true. One is that the farmers are now suspicious of John, and that reflects badly on my whole operation. The other is that he has caused a massive disruption to the smooth running of the business. On these grounds, I issue him with a formal disciplinary warning and explain to him that if he's responsible for any further damage to our reputation or disruption of our business, he will be fired. John still denies that he has ever been involved in the chilli market in Malaba, but he does, at least, give me a solemn undertaking that he never will be. And there we leave it. There's not a lot more I can do.

When I tell the elders and the high-achiever farmers how things have turned out, they aren't happy. There's a lot of grumbling at first, as they are absolutely certain that it was John who caused the chilli price to crash. In the end, though, they accept the realities of the situation, as I have had to do, and we part on good terms.

As it turns out, John and I manage to get back to quite a reasonable working relationship over the next few months, though I can never quite trust him again. He goes about his work with his anorak and his usual dogged persistence and he's a useful member of the team. In fact, on a day-to-day basis, it's Julius who's giving me the biggest problems.

We employ up to twenty people at the busiest times to help with sorting and grading the chillies. We pay them 250 shillings a day, about $3. It's not a fortune, but it's far more than the going rate for a day's low level manual work – and there are always plenty of people keen to do the job. But Julius's aggressive, condescending style upsets the workers. He's supposed to be organising them, teaching them to work to our methods and checking that everyone is doing what needs to be done. Instead, he seems bent on intimidating them.

The first time I see this for myself, I'm appalled. Julius hasn't noticed me come in and he is shouting and browbeating the women and youngsters who are doing the cleaning and grading, in a really unpleasant way. I can't have that. I can see, at a glance, that there are whole chillies and smaller bits (which we can sell to my contact in Nairobi who grinds them up to flavour his masala tea) lying around on the floor under the grading tables. The smaller bits are supposed to be thrown into the big basins I have bought, but it's clear that they are just being thrown down on the floor, to be swept up later, along with who-knows-what dust and dirt. That's no way to handle foodstuffs. I already know that if we are ever going to get into the food production business, we will need to get formal certifications. But even now, selling fresh produce within Kenya, we have to have higher standards than this. Julius is operations manager and he shouldn't be letting this happen.

I call Julius into the office.

'You can't treat people like that. What do you think you're doing?'

'Well, they are not doing their work.'

'What about when you're not doing your work? I've come in here and found you reading your bible when you should be supervising the sorting. And what about when you let people throw chillies on the floor instead of using the basins? You're supposed to be running this place. But you scream and bluster and insult our staff.'

'Yes, Mr Ken.'

'What do you mean: "Yes, Mr Ken"? No, Julius. I've had to talk to you several times about things you aren't doing right, but I don't get aggressive and condescending and insulting towards you, do I?'

'No, sir.'

'So why do you do it to these people? And why are they throwing chillies and bits of chillies on the floor?'

'It's just easier.'

'What? You mean it's easier to throw them on the floor than to throw them into the basins? You know what our procedures are. It's your job to make sure everyone sticks to the rules. Julius, it's not good enough. You have to do better, and you must stop bullying the people who work here. I'm going to have to give you a written warning. If this sort of thing happens again, you will be dismissed.'

I walk outside into the sunshine and watch a group of tiny children playing with an old tyre. What is happening here? In Siboti Foods I have four managers and two of them are on written warnings. I can't understand their attitude. John and Julius both have good jobs with proper contracts, very good pay packets by local standards, the use of their motorbikes and the high status that comes with being involved with the Siboti Foods project. They are the envy of half the adults in the region. If I had to replace them, I'd be besieged with candidates for the jobs. Why don't they make the most of this opportunity?

'How can they be so short-sighted?' I say out loud. I want to be fair, give them a chance. The first port of call shouldn't be to fire someone, especially if you have already invested in their training. Better if I can just turn things around, somehow.

The toddlers with the tyre have spotted me now and they drift over, noisily and happily.

I smile at them while cursing this culture of short-termism – for that's part of the problem as I see it. Here in Siboti, where life expectancy is markedly less than in the West, it's all about getting through that day, that week, that year. It's the legacy of famines, of poor healthcare, of malaria, of high infant mortality. You might be dead next year, so live for today. I think this has informed this general outlook of short-termism – because life isn't likely to be long. When you think you have less time to play with, how does it shape your outlook? It's highly frustrating for me, with my medium and long-term plans for local economic growth. Winning hearts and minds is all about changing cultural mind-sets.

'Mr King, Mr King,' the children chant, 'What did you bring?'

Today they're lucky. I share out the two packets of sweets I have in my bag and they dance away in delight.

I don't know. There's so much that's joyful here, and so much that's incomprehensible. My confidence in the chance of success here goes up and down like a yo-yo. So many signs of progress, so many setbacks on the way. Am I ever going to be able to complete what I came here to do?

27

Not–so-civil servants

'Leadership is a privilege to better the lives of others. It is not an opportunity to satisfy personal greed.'

Mwai Kibaki, president of Kenya 2002–13

Keziah is constantly in my thoughts and I want to see her. We agree to meet at a Lebanese restaurant, one of Nairobi's best. I have been there before and loved the food, and it had a pleasant bar as well. She is running late so I'm having a quiet drink, reading and thinking about life, Siboti and everything.

Seated at the bar, I become immediately aware of two stunning, Beyoncé-like girls around the corner of the bar with a very loud, very heavy, older, drunk guy in a suit. He doesn't look like fun company. One of the girls keeps glancing over in my direction and catching my eye. The man looks around, then ignores me and turns back to talk to the girls. I go back to daydreaming about the project and what needs to be done next until, a couple of minutes later, she looks over at me again and smiles.

Suddenly, the big, drunk guy looks at me a second time and beckons me over. Who me? Yes, his hand says. It would be rude to blank him so I take my drink and approach them.

'Can I help you?' he says.

'I'm fine, sir. How are you?'

The man gives me a long, stony look. 'It's not good to be looking at other men's wives,' he says slowly, slurringly.

It is clear that neither of these girls is his wife, but I'm not going to argue.

'That is very....' he pauses... 'dangerous.'

'Ah, I'm sorry. I really wasn't looking at anybody.' I'm not always a diplomat, but this seems the right time and place to take a conciliatory line.

'You've been looking at my wife,' he goes on. 'Do you know who I am? I am a government minister. *A government minister*. If you look at my wife just one more time, I am going to have you killed.'

For a second, I wonder whether government ministers are allowed to do things like that. Surely, if they had people killed, even they would get into real trouble afterwards.

Ah, afterwards. There's the rub. But he has no case for accusing me of anything provocative. The girl was looking over at me, and I did nothing at all, except, perhaps, smile back.

I've never been threatened with death before, and I need the right response. It comes to me in an instant.

'I was just leaving,' I say.

I step outside, and there is his black Mercedes in the car park. GK registration – Government of Kenya. Burly, dark-clad chauffeur sprawled in the driving seat.

I spot Keziah at the gate. She's talking to a tall, man, well dressed in dark suit and white open-neck shirt, who, even at a distance, exudes authority. They shake hands and his driver closes the door to his blue Mercedes.

'And who was that?' I ask, as we embrace.

'The ex-chief of police. He's being investigated by the International Criminal Court in The Hague about the burning of the church in Eldoret after the election', she whispers in my ear, and pulls back. 'And how are you?' she says, looking me over.

'All the better for seeing you. Best if we go somewhere else though, there's a guy inside who doesn't like me much.'

She nods, taking in the other Merc with the moody driver, and I'm glad I don't have to give a longer explanation. Keziah's street-smart and she knows a lot of people.

It's a damn fine restaurant, and one I would love to revisit so she can taste the excellent food. But we won't be going back. It's just not worth the risk.

* * *

I've been trying for months to get a work permit. There is always some kind of hitch, and apparently only one person who can deal with my case – this slip of a girl. As a result, I have become a regular visitor to the crowded immigration and registration office, Nyayo House, a skyscraper in Nairobi near the InterContinental hotel. You wait to be served while the grumpy civil servants move around on the powerful side of the counter at a snail's pace.

'Can you tell me what's happening with my application please?' I ask a woman in a cardigan, holding a sheaf of files.

She finds my details.

'The person you need is out of the office today,' she says. 'Come back next week.'

'She wasn't here last time I visited either. Can someone else deal with my case please? I just want to know when I will receive my work permit.'

The woman looks at my notes and shakes her head.

'No, only my colleague can help you. Next week,' she says.

Another week passes. This time I spot my contact as soon as I join the queue – oh joy – but when she finally beckons me over, it's not good news.

'Your application has gone to another department for processing,' she says, shuffling a pile of papers on the counter.

I try not to sigh.

'You didn't tell me it would be delayed when I came in last month,' I remind her. 'Is there a problem?'

The woman looks up at me with slightly puzzled eyebrows.

'There are a lot of high-priority applications going through our system,' she says, 'and you will have to be patient. Come back and see me in one week and I should have news then, Mr King.'

Next Monday morning, I join the long queue of applicants who wait at the counter. I spot her mooching around the office on her phone. She is petite, with a head of very straight, shiny jet-black shoulder-length hair. Will she come to the counter? She does. As soon as I am standing in front of her, my ticket to official status in Kenya, I find my heart is going like the clappers.

'Name please sir?' she says, as if she has never seen me before.

'Kenneth King.' I try to smile at her, but it doesn't come naturally today. Some inner divining rod is tingling.

'I've been coming to see you for four months now. I was told last week to come back today. Could you check if my work permit is ready for collection please.'

She nods, her chin ever so slightly jutting at me. I sense what's coming and I'm ready for it.

'I'm told there is a slight technical problem with your application, Mr King,' she says smoothly. 'There are so many very high priority cases going through our department. We need many colleagues to get your application moving along so that it goes through the system. I do my best for you, but my job is very difficult.'

'I see,' I say. 'So how do I get on to this high priority list? What do you advise?'

I'm used to this now. If you want to get anything done in this country, it seems, you need to dance to the tune of *kitu kidogo*, especially if you're a *mzungu*.

'Yes, very difficult for me,' she continues, examining her long nails. She returns my gaze, and something tells me this girl is older than her face suggests.

'Mr King, there are a lot of people involved in putting your application through and I'll have to talk to every one of them. In order to get their attention, I need to give them all a little something.'

'Right,' I say. 'How much will that be then?'

She purses her lips and consults her list once again.

'I hope you understand that this department is overwhelmed with applications like yours and there are so many colleagues involved. I have been working very hard to process yours and have looked at everything that needs to happen. I think we can get your application moving through the system today for 50 000 shillings.'

'Sorry?' I am sure I've misheard her.

'50 000 shillings,' she repeats.

A king's ransom in Kenya – several month's salary.

I put my hands on the counter and try to quell my mixed feelings.

'What? You want how much? Just to process my visa?'

'Yes,' she says, without a flicker of shame. 'There are a lot of people in the chain and so many applications. There is nothing else I can do to make your application happen.'

'I don't believe you!' I say, my voice rising. 'I don't believe the reason for the delay is because there are so many people and so many applications in the chain.'

Conversations dwindle in the crowded room as people waiting in the long queue hush and listen to this fascinating exchange at the counter, but this woman is unmoved.

'Do you wish me to process this, or not?' she asks enquiringly, tapping her pile of paper.

My heart is a powerful drum beating out a warning. Something tells me I'm heading for an impasse. I need the work permit in order to settle in Kenya, but she – not the system – has created this delay. Let's make the *mzungu* wait a bit. Let's make him so desperate for his work permit that he is literally prepared to pay any outrageous bribe to get what he needs. It's that fact, more than any other, that is preventing me from submitting to this. This young woman has forced me to come backwards and forwards to Nairobi on the overnight bus – travelling hundreds of kilometres every time – so that she can generate a need in me that will only be fulfilled by paying her off. The audacity of it almost takes my breath away, especially as I am not here trying to get rich off the back of poor Kenyans. I'm sinking my money into the place. I'm not an oil baron drilling for profits or a property magnate or the head of a multinational company. And she's not even embarrassed. It's take it or leave it. Yes, I may be wealthy by Kenyan standards, but the way the whole system operates by bribes is beginning to rile me to the core. A *mzungu* has money. If I help him, why shouldn't he want to help me back? You have to grease palms to get anything done. That I have learned to live with, but this woman has just taken bribery and corruption to another level.

All I can do is stare at her with incredulity. What she is demanding is non-negotiable, and so far out of the park from what might be acceptable. It's way more than I would be willing to slip her. I don't even have that much in my pocket. If I pay it, I'm a mug. Am I going to allow myself to be taken so blatantly for a ride like this? I know there are underlying reasons for this demand and it's probably just part of the culture, rather than a sign that she is a civil servant who's gone especially rogue. She may be depending entirely on bribes to keep herself, her children, maybe even her parents and family. But surely this is no way to run a country. She's a civil servant!

This nation seems to me to be working against itself. So many people here seem to be trying to line their own pockets. I do wonder why I don't just look after number 1, too. I could be off in New York, working in a very decent position and earning good money instead of being here. I love New York. I love the energy. I love the food. And I have some very good friends there.

Then it hits me, like a ton of bricks. Six hundred dollars! Six hundred fucking dollars being demanded from me by some junior civil servant just to do her job.

She might as well be blatant about it. She could just as easily have said:

'Give me 600 dollars and I will allow you the proper legal status to stay in my country and help my fellow Kenyans. Give me 600 dollars and I will allow you to provide us with access to clean water, education for orphans, mobile clinics, affordable irrigation. Give me....'

Why the fuck should I give this civil servant 600 dollars of my hard-earned money, just for her to undo a block she has invented out of thin air on my application for a work permit?

I am incensed. Absolutely livid. I want to scream. Why the hell should I pay you 600 dollars? She's created the situation. She's contrived it. But it also means that I now have a clear-cut choice facing me. I can stand firm on a matter of principle and go away without the permit I need or I can grit my teeth, pay up and keep moving forward with what I came to this country for. What should I do?

'Yes I do want you to process it. But no, I don't want to pay you a 50 000-shilling bribe,' I snap at her, finally. And in that moment I know the battle is lost.

To her credit, she doesn't flinch.

'That's what it costs,' she says, cool as you like.

'For god's sake! I'm running a water project in western Kenya, and now you want me to give you 50 000 shillings so I can do this work for your countrymen. If all you want to do is exploit my good intentions, why should I spend my life, my energy, my money, on helping you people?' I burst out, with such force that she takes a step back from her papers on the counter, looking really surprised.

Then I realise that I'm actually screaming at her. I must sound like a madman. Trouble is, I can't stop.

'If you won't help your own country, why the fuck should I?'

I throw a pile of paperwork in the air – hers, mine, I don't care anymore – and leave before she can summon the security guards.

In the foyer, I call the elevator and I'm shaking by the time it arrives. If only Alan hadn't left Nairobi – but if he was here, what would he say?

My brother would be very clear, I think.

'You're trying to help Kenyans to beat extreme poverty and the civil service wants to screw money out of you to allow you to do it? Forget the corrupt civil service. Don't waste your money' he would probably say.

Sensible and tempting as that would be, it's not a solution that would get me what I need for the project. This woman is part of a culture that accepts bribery, and that is not the Siboti farmers' fault. They shouldn't have to lose out on account of this.

Alone in the lift, I am aware of a heaving, shuddering rasping sound. It is me. I think I'm hyperventilating. Something has finally snapped in me. Living in Kenya is becoming too much. Corruption may exist in every society, but you can't easily bribe police officers in the UK and Ireland. Our civil servants are bound by laws. If an individual employee tried to do this in Dublin, surely her colleagues would blow the whistle? The scale of it is breathtaking. How do NGOs here deal with this kind of behaviour, I wonder? On the face of it, they don't pay bribes. But how do they get anything done?

It's a bloody shame. An absolute total frustrating bloody shame.

When I reach the lobby, the city world of Nairobi is bustling in front of me, I try to get a grip. Stepping out of the building and into the city, I remember to look up at the sky and roll out my usual comforting mantras to soften the blow. Tomorrow's another day. I'll come up with a solution, I always do, I tell myself, as I notice that people are gathering on the pavements and cheering.

A crowd is snaking along the road in front of me. They are shouting and waving banners. Ah, the referendum. I'd almost forgotten. It's mainly young men, chanting and swaggering across the width of the road, their arms aloft. Nairobi is yes vote territory. What I'm witnessing, I realise, is a huge political rally for the yes vote that is needed to usher in Kenya's proposed new constitution.

It's a jubilant display of strength for the new constitution. Watching the crowd move I have a real sense of a country on the march, and yet the heavies lining the route signify menace to me. Will there be a new dawn for Kenya after the vote? No one wants a return to the violence of barely three years ago, when the country erupted into chaos and murderous violence following President Kibaki's election.

I take a step back and pull my baseball cap over my eyes. It's hard to believe that such terrible things can happen, when you're standing in the middle of a modernising city like Nairobi, before a country can slip back into normality again. There are barely any Westerners here, and looking around at the families and business people thronging the route, I feel alone. Who would have my back if the rally decided to take a dislike to me? This is a place where people live closer to chaos, where your fortunes can pivot at the ballot box.

Mob violence is often random, but sometimes they target individuals. There was the episode when Kizito felt so threatened that he stayed away at his sister's place in case the farmers knocked on his door. I'm plying Protus with alcohol and flattery and whatever else he demands to buy myself and my employees an air of protection. I've been advised by the same inspector of police to carry a gun. A government minster threatens to have me killed. Mob violence is rife in the town of Bungoma where I make my home. To me, this place is starting to feel ominous, sinister and dangerous.

'Ken, this is Africa,' my friend in Johannesburg tells me on the phone, back in my hotel room. 'Don't you know that phrase? This is Africa. Either you go with it or you go mad.'

I thank my friend and hang up. I'm sitting on the bed in my hotel room in a fluffy white bathrobe. I've taken a long hot shower and I look around the room. I've got every comfort I could want here, but I can't enjoy it. I realise with a kind of dark, seeping dread that, for the first time ever, I am not looking forward to going back to Siboti.

If they won't give me that essential work permit, how many more signals do I need that I don't belong here? Needed, maybe, but an unwelcome outsider.

28

Grit in the gearbox

'Love all, trust a few, do wrong to none.'

All's Well That Ends Well by William Shakespeare

Keziah waits at a big café terrace that's filled with oversized sofas and comfortable leather chairs. This place is a magnet for similarly oversized fifty-something Somali businessmen, dressed in ill-fitting double-breasted suits. I am told that business with neighbouring Somalia is run from this place. Nairobi's high-end house prices have been rocketing and Somali cash buyers are reputed to be part of the market's upward surge. The café also attracts a young sharply dressed business crowd who come for the great coffee and salad wraps, and it feels safe.

Keziah is wearing large black Dior sunglasses and is immersed in her iPhone. I'm struck again by how beautiful she is. As I approach, she looks at me over her glasses, as if reading my mood.

'What was the excuse this time?' she says.

I pull up a chair and look at the menu.

'She tried to sting me for 50 000 shillings.'

Keziah gives a bemused chuckle.

'She's been playing you for months. Ken, it's not right, but remember, this is Africa. I'm surprised by the scale of it, though. If I were you I would try to find someone else in her office to deal with your case.'

'Hold on.' She thumbs through the extensive contacts list on her phone. 'There's an outside chance I can find someone to help you.'

I look up gratefully.

'That'd be great, Kezzy. I don't know how to handle these people. I don't want to pay her – we're talking 600 dollars. That's a lot of money for a junior clerk to fix a problem she invented.'

I tell her about my outburst at Nyayo House.

What was it Keziah said when we first met? *You have no idea what you're taking on. Your project is doomed and you are either a crook or a fool.*

'Do you still think I'm a bad guy?' I ask. 'Or maybe just stupid?'

She pats my arm and laughs, shaking her head.

'Neither. You are my wonderful endeavourist. What is it you Irish say, Ken, God loves a trier? Well, that's you all over.'

By the time the bus has arrived to ferry me the four hundred kilometres back to Siboti, Keziah has chased away my bad mood and I've parked the work permit problem. I'm going to try view that civil servant incident as just a logistical blip. With Keziah's help. I'll hope to make a different, perhaps more senior contact and see if I can get it sorted out.

* * *

At least some things I've attempted in Siboti are actually, definitely, measurably getting better – or I'm getting better at them.

In the second year of the Orphans Welcome Again project, we have exactly the same backstage mutterings and the same suggestions that the wrong children are getting the benefit of the project's patronage as we'd had initially, even though (or perhaps because) the elders had more of a say in who was really an 'orphan'. Nepotism and cronyism are habits that die hard and it's only when we are running the scheme for the third year that I find a system that seems to work. The key seems to be transparency – an open, public system of applications for the 225 places that are available.

We put up notices in all the churches and schools and once the applications and nominations are in, I sit down at a *barassa* with the assistant chiefs and a large crowd of local people and we go through them, more than 800 applications, one by one.

'Is this child a full orphan, with no parents to look after her?'

'Yes.'

'Has she been going to school here and had to drop out?'

'Yes.'

'Does she live in Siboti?'

The prospect of an absolutely free education and free school uniforms is quite enough incentive to persuade outsiders to come in and try their luck. As someone explains it to me, 'It doesn't matter what the rules say. If you apply, you might get lucky. If you don't apply, you've got no chance.'

It's a long process, but the fact that anyone with something to say can pipe up and make an objection means that there is some serious vetting going on. Gradually, we whittle down the 800 candidates to an agreed list of 225 orphans and honour is satisfied. At last, third time lucky, I have a cohort of unquestionably deserving orphan children.

Over three years, we end up funding 675 years of schooling for the most underprivileged children in Siboti, helping prepare them for a better life in the future. At about $50 a year per child, for the school fees and the basic uniforms, it has cost about $35 000 – the price of a second-hand Porsche and probably 675 times more valuable to the world's future.

* * *

The chillies are coming in and being weighed, sorted and bagged up in big 50-kilo sacks. Towards the end of the day, our people drape the sacks across the pillion seats of several *piki-piki* motorbike taxis and watch them chug slowly off to Bungoma, to link up with the evening bus. The sacks are loaded onto the bus, the driver is slipped a *kitu kidogo* to make sure the goods arrive safely, and they go off to Nairobi, where our man with the handcart meets the bus and collects the chillies. The moment when the convoy of bikes sets off is the highlight of our routine. On a good day, when there are eight full sacks to go, we are shipping out about 400 kilos of chillies. That's a lot of revenue. We're getting somewhere.

In order to export to Europe and other major overseas markets, we are going to need to achieve the international 'Good Agricultural Practices' certification. To get certified, we will have to go through a whole process of preparation to be audited by inspectors. We'll need to define our operating procedures, produce manuals and train our staff to abide by them. Our people will need to wear hairnets, coats and disposable gloves.

They will have to wear masks, too, partly for reasons of hygiene and partly because capsaicin, the natural chemical that makes chillies hot, is a powerful irritant and should not be breathed in for several hours a day. Capsaicin, after all, is the active ingredient in the pepper sprays used by riot police in many countries.

So I make the investment and buy the lot – hairnets, green coats, hundreds of pairs of plastic gloves and plenty of lightweight masks, like the ones people in Tokyo wear when out in public. I spend evening after evening writing policies and procedures and day after day working with the managers to train our workers. When it comes to applying for certification, I want us to get it right first time. There's a certain amount of amusement, in some quarters, at this imposition of elevated developed world standards on a place where even survival is a messy and unpredictable business. But there's no room for irony here. We have to do it, if we want the crucial food safety certificates.

At first, everything seems to be going well. But one morning I arrive unexpectedly at the little cluster of huts that look out over Kimwanga market, and the place looks like a food inspector's worst nightmare. Nobody is wearing gloves. People haven't put their coats and masks on. There are chillies all over the floor. And Julius? Julius is sitting in the corner, in his green coat, studying his Bible. He stands up quickly when he spots me by the door and tries to look busy.

'Why aren't people wearing their gloves?' I ask, and the snarl in my voice must be evident, because he turns and snaps at the nearest sorter.

'You! Hey, you! Why aren't you wearing your gloves?'

The youngster, the son of one of the elders, looks terrified, and his expression triggers a wave of resentment in me. What was the point of the written warning I gave to Julius? This isn't making an effort. What does he think he's playing at? Or is it me that's stupid? What I am missing here?

'Julius!'

Now everyone jumps, and I realise how close he is to a public loss of face. That won't do. Much as I want to, I cannot scream at this employee.

'Come in my office, please.'

I open the door for him and he slopes inside, carrying his bible. Taking the opportunity to shuffle some notes on my desk, I try to remember to breath. Shouting at Julius won't help, but I'm a millimetre away from losing it. I'm still smarting over the work permit. The bible-reading wasn't a one-off – perhaps Julius picks it up because he needs some moral support during his working day. Or maybe Julius just thinks I am a soft fool?

He waits, expressionless, while I pull up my chair and lean my elbows on the desk. Outside the others have fallen silent, obviously not wanting to miss any drama if voices are raised again.

'You cannot verbally attack that young worker, Julius,' I say, and I'm relieved to have regained control of my voice. 'This is *your* team to manage. *You* are responsible. You can't go shouting at them because I've come in and asked about the gloves. We've had this before – many times. You must make sure they follow the rules, all the time, whether I'm here or not. That's your job. If they're not wearing their gloves and masks, that's as much your fault as theirs.'

He picks up his Bible from my desk, glancing at it as if to call God's thunderbolts down upon my head.

'And what are you doing with that here, during work time? You know you are here to work, not to study.'

I pray that Julius will tell me that this was a one-off and he won't do it again.

'I'm preparing for my pastoring,' he says, and strokes the Bible. 'I have to read my Bible when I need to read it.'

'But this is work time.'

Julius doesn't reply. He was one of the first to join me on this journey to bring change to Siboti, to lift people out of extreme poverty. He gave me every indication that he understood the project when I interviewed him for the job. How can he now care so little about doing his part to help achieve that goal? I feel myself lapsing back into banking culture, calling in a badly performing employee for a disciplinary.

'Look, Julius. It's godly to work. It's not godly to sit there and not do your work, with nobody wearing their masks and gloves.'

He says nothing, and sits there looking sheepish and resentful. I realise my fingers are twitching. There is that dark flash of irrational fury again that I felt in the work permit office, and I'm surprised at the strength of emotion I feel towards Julius. I feel personally shafted. I've noticed that I'm becoming increasingly short-tempered. I'm reacting to challenging situations in a more volatile way. Are these the first signs of losing it? My tolerance is evaporating, but you have to stay easy-going in a place like Siboti. When you lose your sense of humour, your sense of proportion, well…

It slowly dawns on me that this is it. I feel so let down and so unable to rely on Julius to do his job that I may actually have to sack him. I know in my heart that I want to fire him, that I've wanted to drop him from the team for months. But this is a different world from the one I'm used to. These people live closer to the edge, closer to disaster. Even so, I dread the fallout of firing an employee. I sense it will leave a stain, somehow. But how many of these body blows can the project, can I, take?

As he's already on a warning, I'd be entitled to do it now, on the grounds that he's been reading when he should be working and that he is completely failing to enforce our hygiene and health and safety procedures. It's all covered in his contract. I make up my mind what needs to happen.

'I'm giving you a second formal warning now, Julius. One more mess like this and you're out.'

He looks at me, and I can see the surprise and the anger in his eyes. Has he got the message?
Within a few days, though, the whole scene repeats itself. I drop in at Siboti Foods to find Julius poring over his Bible, chillies all over the floor and not a mask or glove in sight.

This time I am outright furious. I am really going to do it this time.

'Julius, you're dismissed,' I tell him in my office, before my anger has had a chance to subside. After all, what is the point of a discussion? Julius knows what is required of him at Siboti Foods and I've given him three chances.

'You've had your warnings. You've had your chances to change your behaviour. You're fired.'

He glares sullenly at me but says nothing. I make him wait while I write out a formal letter of dismissal ('Subsequent to your previous verbal and written warnings…') and hand it to him.

'Now, where's your phone? I want your phone.'

'Oh, I forgot it. It's at home.'

But you remembered to bring your Bible, didn't you? Keep it together, Ken, I remind myself.

'I want your phone. I want the logbook for the motorbike and I want your two Siboti Foods uniform shirts. You can go home now and get them, please.'

Julius stands without another word. His disdain for me is undeniable. I watch him slink out of the office.

We all make mistakes. But in letting Julius ride off just now, I've just made is a big one, a schoolboy error of the first degree. From our front porch, I see Julius riding off on the motorbike, still trying to puzzle him out. Why does he insist on screwing up in his job? Have I been unreasonable? What is going on in Julius's life to make him so resistant to common sense? As it turns out, I will never find out, because I will never see him in Siboti again.

I call his number over and over again and later in the day he finally picks up the phone. Is he bringing everything in, as instructed?

'Oh, I'm too stressed. I can't come back. I'll come back tomorrow.'

'But Julius…'

He cuts me off.

Tomorrow comes and Julius doesn't return. He refuses to respond to my voicemail messages. After a couple more days, it's beyond all doubt that Julius is not coming back. The mobile phone and the logbook and the uniforms and most importantly, the motorbike, appear to have left the building with him. He's stolen the lot.

This realisation sets off a chain reaction in me: a little flame that triggers a line of gunpowder. All along, I've been willing the project to work. But after the elation of the awards party, every week seems to bring a new setback. I've been weathering setbacks well, but my skin is feeling thinner these days. I've been feeling increasingly vulnerable and, if I'm honest, isolated. If I let Julius steal from the project, who will attack us next? I'm being taken for a mug. So what am I going to do about it?

The next day I call Protus.

I've been nurturing my relationship with this unlovely man for several months and now I need his help. I want my motorbike back, whatever it costs me. I've been feeding the beast that is Protus for months, and now it's payback time. If I don't stand my ground, opportunists like Julius will make mincemeat of Siboti Foods.

The inspector of police sounds pleased to hear from me.

'How nice to hear your voice, Mr Ken King,' he drawls. 'Is there perhaps something I can do for you?'

I tell Protus that I have fired my employee, after due warnings, and that he seems to have stolen the company's motorbike. Warming to my task, and using the right technical terms, I explain that Julius is a lazy, hypocritical bastard, that he treats the staff like shit, that I've had any number of complaints about him and that now he's nicked the bike and I want it back.

Protus is a man of action, when it suits him. He sends a couple of his men to visit Julius and get the bike, but they come back empty-handed.

'The problem, Mr Ken King,' says Protus, 'is that you gave him the motorbike. He says you gave it to him for all the work he did.'

'I bloody didn't. He got a salary for that, and a good one, too.'

'He says you gave him the bike as a thank-you for all the work he'd done before, before he was on the payroll, when he was helping you out of the goodness of his heart.'

'That's a lie,' I splutter. 'The bike comes with the job. You can ask the other managers. They'll tell you. The motorbikes all belong to Siboti Foods.'

Protus sends one of his underlings to take statements from me and the managers. As Kizito, Edwin and John are all happy to confirm, the bikes had only ever been put in the individuals' names because, back then, right at the start, Siboti Foods hadn't yet been set up.

'And if Mr King wanted you to transfer the bikes into Siboti Foods' name, would you have a problem with that?' asks the young policeman.

'No. Of course not,' they all say. 'They belong to the business.'

That's good. The young cop will report back. Protus will go to Julius's house and arrest him and I'll have my motorbike.

My phone rings. It's Protus.

'This may not be straightforward, Mr Ken King,' he says. 'I'll need to take four men with me, in case the criminal tries to resist arrest. Can you give me something for each of the men? And we'll need to rent motorbikes for them. That'll be, let's say, 2000 shillings altogether.'

I'm outraged by the man's effrontery. That's a word I've never used in my life, and I think I must have been saving it up for this situation. He's the top cop. A crime's been committed. He knows who did it and where the stolen property is. It's his job to make the arrest and get the bike. Why should I have to pay him to do his job?

Steady, Ken. This isn't about the rights and wrongs. It's about getting the motorbike back. So I send an M-Pesa payment of 2000 shillings to his mobile phone and Protus checks he's received it and goes off to make the arrangements.

The next morning, I get a phone call. Guess who?

'He wasn't there. We went last night, but he wasn't at his house. We'll go again tonight, very late, and surprise him. We'll need to pay for the men and the bikes again, of course…'

Of course.

That's another 2000 shillings.

Of course.

After three nights of this and 6000 shillings, they still haven't got Julius. But Protus has a plan. When I meet up with him, he explains how it will work. Julius, the trainee pastor, will be going to church on Sunday. He won't miss that. He will have to come home for his good clothes. The police will swoop on his house before church and get him and the bike.

I can guess what's coming next.

'2000?' I say.

'Ah no, Mr King. Sunday is extra. Give me 3000 and we'll get him on Sunday.'

So that's 9000 shillings it has cost me so far, and the motorbike only cost 85 000 brand new. I pay up and wait to hear from Protus.

On Sunday morning, I get the call.

'We've got him. He's in the cells. And we've got the motorcycle.'

I hurry over to the police station and they show me the bike. It has been trashed. Someone's taken a hammer to it. The lights have been smashed, the petrol tank has been battered, the brake cables have been cut and the front forks have been wrenched out of shape. If Julius isn't allowed to keep the bike, I can't have it back either. He's got his revenge in first.

We drag it round the corner to a motorcycle repair shop and leave the mechanic to survey the damage and work out a quote for the repairs. He knows what he's looking for, so he's obviously come across this kind of thing before. After a while, he gives us his verdict.

'It'll be 25 000 shillings to put it all right,' he tells us. 'Whoever did that made a good job of it. He's even poured sand in the gearbox.'

I ask to see Julius in his cell. He's sitting there, in the half-darkness, looking very small. He's been roughed up and his face is swollen and bruised. I'm shocked to see him in such a state and feel pretty terrible. I should never have got Protus involved. And yet, what choices did I have? Who do you turn to when somebody steals your property, the police or the local vigilante? And what do you do when there's nothing to distinguish between the two?

'Who did this to you?'

Julius only glowers at me. It's beyond obvious, his eyes seem to say. Don't you know anything, you foolish *mzungu*?

'Look, I'm sorry this has happened to you,' I tell him slowly. 'I'm not going to take this any further. I'm going to get them to let you go, as long as you pay for the bike to be repaired. You'll still have to pay for that.'

'But I didn't do it, Mr Ken. The police must have damaged the bike.'

For a moment I wonder if he is right, but I also know that Julius will lie his way out of any difficulty.

'Don't make it worse, Julius. Don't lie to me again. The police won't release you until you pay up. If you don't, you'll end up in front of the judge and he'll probably send you to prison. What'll that do for your future in the church?'

He just stares at the floor, and for a moment he looks so pitiful that I wish I could take it all back. If only I'd listened to my gut before I gave him the job. Something was tapping me on the shoulder telling me not to, and I didn't listen.

Feeling like a prize bully myself, I leave Julius to think about it, and go to see Protus in his office. He's enjoying this, and he's doing very well out of it. I'm beginning to see why a career in the police has such attractions. It's a great life for the up-and-coming entrepreneur, and you get to throw your weight around as well.

'He has some bruises on his face,' I say. 'Did your men have to do that to him?'

The police inspector shrugs, uninterested. 'Self-defence, Mr Ken. He tried to fight my men, and he needed to be restrained. We're not letting him out on bail until he pays a 20 000 shillings fine. He can rot in there,' Protus tells me, and he stands to shake my hand, our brief meeting already over. 'I'll have to put one of the men on guard overnight, though, Mr King, so I'll need another 500 from you. The guard will have to have a meal.'

I nod with the sinking feeling I get whenever I'm around Protus and reach for my wallet.

The next morning, nothing has changed. Julius is stubbornly refusing to co-operate. Looks like I'm going to have to press criminal charges if I want my bike back. Still, it's an open-and-shut case and there's only one possible result. The law will take its course. But not, naturally, without a little help from Protus. I'm beginning to realise that the police chief regards the law as his own private property, to be exploited in whatever ingenious ways he can come up with. Last December, I bought a bottle of whiskey for the main man and Kizito took it up to Protus. When Protus saw the whiskey, he said, 'But it's the season of festivities – what am I supposed to eat?' so I had to buy some food as well and send that over too.

Protus stretches and cracks his fingers.

'We're preparing the case now, Mr Ken King,' he tells me, laying a heavy hand on my shoulder.

'But you know, there's so much work putting the evidence together. Lots of work. The paperwork we have to go through. Unbelievable. Then we'll need to make sure we get the right judge, and that he comes to the right conclusion.'

I'm getting the hang of this now. It stinks.

'OK, Protus, how much will that cost you' I ask, allowing a semblance that none of the costs are his own.

'Oh, don't worry. The judge will be someone we know. If not, we'll get it moved to a different court. We'll need to pay something small – not so much, you know, just to make sure everything's fine.'

'What does "make sure everything's fine" mean?' I blurt out. 'That guy stole my motorbike and deliberately wrecked it, and you're saying I need to pay people off to make sure the case goes my way.'

Protus looks at me pityingly, like someone explaining the world to a very small child.

'This is Kalamisi, Mr Ken King. We do things our way here.'

So that's the deal. I'm the *mzungu*, the European cash machine. What is the point in anybody helping me and not asking for something? Why wouldn't you? There is money to be made from me. Let's be reasonable about it. Ask those locals out there on the streets of Bungoma. Here I am, a wealthy man, drinking with the inspector of police. Why wouldn't I pay up for a good service? Surely I can afford it. And from the other perspective, whether I'm a judge or a policeman, I'm helping a *mzungu*. Why wouldn't he help me back?

'OK, Protus, overall then, what is needed?'

'Oh, if we give the judge 5000 to start with, that will be fine. Yes, 5000 is very fine for him. And we'll need something for the clerk, too, to make sure the case comes up quickly.'

I tell Protus I'll need to go to the bank, and walk out, suppressing the urge to scream. The street is busy with people, just getting on with their lives. There's a grubby little café further down the street and I sit down outside, wishing for oblivion.

The whole morning has been deeply depressing. Julius is a bully and a hypocrite, but I'm shocked that the police have beaten him up, just for the sake of it. It won't do me any good if he's sent off to some filthy local jail for a few months. What kind of Faustian deal have I struck? My ally in all this, the police inspector, ought to be put away for twice as long. I need to keep him on my side, for safety's sake, but that doesn't mean he isn't a cruel, thieving bastard.

The more I think about my situation, the more it gets me down. This place is crushing me. I've got four managers at Siboti Foods. Julius is in the cells and John's probably been cheating me by running his competing business on Siboti Foods' time, and is now on a final warning. Kizito and Edwin are the only Siboti Foods managers I can trust – as Edwin is hardly more than an enthusiastic, promising, early-twenties management trainee. If I didn't have Kizito, who looks after every penny, I think I'd go mad.

Perhaps I'm going mad anyway. Besides Kizito and Edwin, the only people I can rely on to act with honesty and integrity are Mama Jayne, Cecilia, who is running Siboti Elevation Products, and Elizabeth, the government's agricultural adviser. The Chief means well, but he ducked the issue when he refused to judge that John had been double-crossing us by dealing in chillies on the side. And everyone else seems entirely driven by this terrible what's-in-it-for-me-today culture. Except Keziah, of course. She's got integrity in spades, she's sharp as a knife and I know she cares about me. But whether she thinks I've got the stamina to make a success of the Siboti project is something I still don't know for sure.

The practical difficulties of organising large-scale chilli production and lining up buyers are things I can probably cope with, but the corruption and cheating and the short-term view of life are getting me down like they've never done before.

I've had two laptops stolen, one from my room, almost certainly by the hotel staff. I can't get a work permit because I have refused to pay the 50 000 shilling bribe that the official in Nairobi demanded from me. And without a work permit number, I can't register the Siboti Foods business. I keep thinking about whether Protus is right that I need to carry a gun because I am not safe here and I am stuck in a loop of having effectively to pay this corrupt police inspector every time I want anything done. I've threatened one of my own managers with the sack, with a sense of menace that I only partly veiled, and now, today, I've sat in a cell with another manager, after he was beaten up on my account. What the hell have I got myself into here? This isn't what my efforts in Siboti, to help people move towards the Millennium Development Goals, was meant to be about.

'What the hell have I got myself into,' I hear myself say again, this time aloud, and a couple of passing women shoot me a wary look.

Ever since I was robbed in the hotel I've felt unsettled. I sense that I'm getting near the end of my tether. I'm hardly sleeping at night and now I'm talking to myself on the street. What next?

29

How I became a bastard (again)

'There is a humanitarian impulse that one aspires to and
there are days when one doesn't do it very well.'

Ralph Fiennes, actor and Unicef ambassador

Back at Siboti Foods I find Edwin preparing to set off on his
motorbike, presumably to do a recce around our chilli farms, leaving
me in the office to get on with the paperwork. All the figures are
now in from the farmers regarding our second crop, and I'm keen
to see how they compare with our first harvest. Edwin has been
responsible for collecting the raw data from the farmers who have
not yet delivered what we expected from them. I intend to convert it
into a spreadsheet to analyse what this data is telling me.

'So how do you think we did this time, Edwin?' I ask as he fires
up the engine. His back is to me and I have to ask the question a
second time to get his attention. I want to find out how much better
he thinks we have done. This harvest should be better than the last.

Early on in the Siboti project, we'd experimented with growing
sunflowers. The results had been disastrous, but I'd taken this on

the chin as part of our learning curve. It was clearly not because of anything the farmers had done wrong. The poor-quality seeds we'd been given by our partner, a sunflower oil company, meant that no amount of loving care and attention could guarantee a decent harvest. Maybe we could go back and try sunflowers again at some point in the future. But I have other options I'd like to try out, too, once the core Siboti Foods business is running smoothly.

I keep coming back to the idea that we could create a high-value, high-margin branded product that would stand out on the shelves and command a premium price in European supermarkets. Edamame beans might be the answer. If we could grow top-quality edamame beans in Siboti, shelling and packaging them ourselves, we'd have something we could really build into a sought-after brand. I'm sure I could persuade a PR firm in the UK or Ireland to put together a publicity campaign for us on a pro bono basis – emphasising how buying our delicious edamame was changing lives in Kenya – and we'd work with the corporate social responsibility teams in the big food companies and the supermarkets to promote the product and make it something shoppers asked for by name in high-end shops like Waitrose or Whole Foods and order in restaurants. That would have real potential, and it would be a lot more profitable for Siboti's farmers.

'Ah yes Mr Ken,' says Edwin, and he turns off the engine and pulls the key from the bike. There is something about his demeanour that puts my antennae on the alert. He looks flattened.

'What's up?'

He takes off his bright patterned helmet and his eyes meet mine.

'I think the second crop will give disappointing results,' he says.

'Oh?' I beckon him through to the office with a sinking heart. 'You better come back in and tell me all about it.'

When we are sitting either side of the office desk, Edwin puts his signature red baseball cap back on.

'Shoot,' I say. 'Is there some kind of blight?'

Edwin shakes his head.

'It's the farmers,' he begins. 'It's the loans. Because the price of chillies has fallen, some of the growers say they can't pay us for the seeds, fertiliser and pesticides we lent them.'

I feel like growling.

'There's always going to be a reason not to pay. Last year it was the delay in getting the fertiliser and pesticides to the farms with sandy soil and the training they needed. That was only 10 per cent who said they couldn't pay.'

'That dip in the price was only temporary' I sigh, 'plus we cushioned most of it for them. Who is refusing to deliver their chilli and pay off their loans Edwin?'

He lets out a long breath.

'The same 10 per cent of farmers say they can't pay back the loan this year.'

My forehead feels hot, and I fumble in the corner cupboard for a bottle of water, tearing at the plastic wrapping.

'I see. So it's the same farmers?'

'This year, there are more of them. More of less the same 10 per cent who didn't pay back the loan last time, and another 30 per cent of the farmers, Mr Ken.'

'Forty per cent of our growers are going to default on the loan?'

I grip the table, reminded of the advice I've been given by a friend. *Remember, this is Africa. Either you go with it, or you go mad.*

Edwin keeps on nodding. He waits for me to recover from this new blow. I scribble 40% onto a piece of paper on the desk and try to keep a calm head to understand this newest, most troubling problem. Only when I have something measured to say, do I resume the conversation.

Back in the beginning, when we signed up 560 growers to produce chillies for us, I was happy to personally offer Siboti's farmers the seeds, fertiliser and pesticides they needed to get going, under a contract that said they would pay for them out of the proceeds of the first crop. The farmers were resistant to bank loans, so it seemed easier to offer the horticultural loans from my own funds. After the first crop there were several outstanding successes, including David Waswa, who won our first Farmer of the Year award. Altogether, nearly a hundred of these pioneers produced large and profitable crops, achieving incomes they had never enjoyed before and easily paying off the loans. Others weren't so lucky, for whatever reason – sandy soil, lack of training, poor methods, whatever it was – and after being lobbied by the Chief I had let them off their unpaid loans, so that we would start with a clean slate for Season Two.

'So let's get this clear in our minds, Edwin. The same farmers who I let off after the first crop have also failed to produce a second crop. How? They've had all this help – seed, fertiliser, pesticide and your training. It doesn't make sense. Why would they do that? And why are an extra 30 per cent going to default this year? What is going on?'

Edwin points to the information sheets he has put on the desk in front of me.

'But look, Mr Ken. Sixty per cent of the farmers have kept to our agreement. Sixty per cent of the farmers have grown chillies and been a success.'

I rub my nose where my glasses have been resting and try to keep up.

'Do you know which farmers can really afford to repay us?'

Edwin shrugs.

'How can I tell? The farmers will all give a reason why they can't afford to repay the loan.'

'But they have a signed written agreement with us,' I say, more loudly than I intend. 'We loaned them the seed, the fertiliser, the pesticide, so they could produce great chillies and maximise their income. It wasn't a gift!'

I get up and pace around the office, looking out of the door at the market. All of life is there. People are swapping stories while they make deals and sell produce, as they have done for hundreds of years. Why is my elevation method not working? It is designed to give these farmers a medium and long-term improvement in their incomes and lives. I have given the farmers a carrot, but some of them have resisted and decided to renege on our deal. Do I now pick up a stick to force them to repay the loans?

I have no way of judging who really can't repay us and who just prefers not to. But now I face a serious problem, I realise. If I forgive the outstanding loans a second time, it will be grossly unfair on those growers who have repaid their loans for both the first and the second crops. Going into the third year, what incentive would there be for any of the farmers to pay up, if they knew I had let the non-payers off two years in a row?

For now, though, I still don't know why the second chilli harvest has fallen so far short of the volumes we were expecting. We'll soon be ready to get going on the third season's crop and I still need to know what went wrong this time, so that we can correct any logistical mistakes. A sizeable chunk of Siboti's farmers are in the project, 20 to 25 per cent. Was this poor second harvest the result of bad seeds, bad training or just bad farming? Or is there something else going on that I don't know about?

Edwin is my ear to the ground. But he has little idea why the chilli crop was so far below our predictions, and he offers to spend the next couple of days going round the outlying farms, talking to people and trying to get to the bottom of the mystery. I feel he should know more than this, but he doesn't.

'There has to be a reason, Mr Ken,' he says, before setting out on his bike. 'There are over a hundred farmers who've delivered no chillies at all for the second crop. Let me see what I can find out.'

I'm still mulling this over the following day when my thoughts are interrupted by a call from Edwin.

'Mr Ken, I think I know what's been happening. And you're not going to like it.'

'What do you mean? What's been going on?'

There is a long pause, and when Edwin speaks again his voice is quiet.

'Honestly, Mr Ken, I don't want to tell you over the phone. I'll come straight back and we can talk about it properly.'

Half an hour later, Edwin comes into the office, looking more agitated than I have ever seen him. He's a slightly built man who favours a red baseball cap – I can always identify my field manager from a distance. Today the peak of his cap is angled downwards, indicating that his head is bowed.

'Well?' I ask.

He rubs his knees and glances at me quickly from under his cap. The look in his dark-brown eyes concerns me.

'The reason some of the farmers produced no crops at all is simple.'

'Go on.'

'Those farmers didn't plant the seed. They just took the seed and the fertiliser we'd advanced to them and sold it. There were dealers hanging around, offering them cash on the nail, and some of them took the money.'

He shrugs, and his shoulders seem to sag with the gesture.

I curse inwardly. That's really taking short-termism to the limit.

'They signed a written contract with Siboti Foods to accept the seeds, fertiliser and training. They agreed to grow chillies, on the basis that they would repay the cost of the seeds and fertiliser when their crops were harvested.'

I hammer my desk with each point, and Edwin flinches.

'They agreed to deliver their chillies to us, and we agreed to make sure they get the best possible price.'

The baseball cap nods at the floor.

'It's a two-way deal that's all about putting them on the road to a better life. But these farmers – a minority of the growers we've signed up, but a big minority – aren't sticking to their side of the contract. As far as they are concerned, the tins of seed and sacks of fertiliser are a freebie, a one-off gift from the gods, something to be turned into cash at the earliest opportunity. Is that what you're saying?'

'Yes Mr Ken.'

'Help me understand this. These guys sold the stuff without ever planting it?'

Edwin nods.

'They then took the pesticides from us and sold that too?'

'I am saying that, yes Mr Ken.'

I think of the fifteen field officers we employed at the outset of the second year's season, whizzing around Siboti on their bright-green mountain bikes, to monitor the farmers and the crops. The mountain bikes weren't robust enough for the rough terrain and their maintenance was quite high, but the young trainees themselves seemed to make up for any shortfall in their equipment with their sheer enthusiasm. I knew it wasn't always easy for them to tell a farmer how to plant, but that was part of their job. Why on earth didn't they notice that some of the farmers hadn't been planting the seeds we gave them as a loan?

'You're telling me your field officers who are supposed to be monitoring this growing and planting have missed this the entire season?' I challenge him. 'How can that be? *How can that be?*'

The baseball cap gets even lower.

'I don't know Mr Ken but I think it's happened. We did miss it.'

I can see from the expression on his face that he knows he's really screwed up. Now I regret giving Edwin and those field officers too much free rein to let them oversee the planting their way. That was a bad judgement on my part. I should have monitored Edwin much more closely. I gave him too much freedom to manage the field work, and he wasn't ready for it. So, although it's very different to the circumstances surrounding Julius and John, Edwin is now the third manager I cannot rely on. Who's left? Only Kizito in Siboti Foods and Cecilia in our Elevation Products unit.

And what do the farmers who've sold their seed do when that cash runs out? They will still be in the same situation, reliant on a poor market for their other crops. This is my *bête noire*, this kind of thinking. What is the point of trying to make a difference here if farmers think the project is just a hand-out? Or worse, perhaps they think I'm too stupid to notice that I'm being ripped off and too soft to respond to that in any material way.

This is all beginning to sound like those half-remembered bible stories about buried talents, with maybe a bit of Cain and Abel thrown in. I can't remember the details of those biblical tales, but I know that they often concerned people who failed to stick to the terms of a deal. These farmers who have ignored their contractual commitments are left with future prospects that are no better than those they had in the past.

'Hold on a minute,' I say, as a lifeline suddenly presents itself. 'You said *some* of the farmers. How many of the farmers actually sold the seed and the fertiliser?'

'I'd say maybe 30' he says.

'Oh. OK, That's less than 5 per cent', I say slowly, and hope flares.

'So…what about the others? You said 40 per cent will default on the loan. What about the other 35 per cent? Why can't they repay the loan?'

Edwin just looks at me and says nothing. Does he think I'm telepathic? Despite all my years dealing with strategies and goals and anticipating people's motives and the ways they act in the workplace, it takes several moments for me to work it out.

I like to think I'm an optimist. But it seems I really am a fool. The farmers who will default on the loans – whether they sold the seeds and fertiliser or whether they used them to grow the chillies – are banking on me forgiving the loans *again*. They don't intend to repay the money for the second crop, because I let 10 per cent off the first time.

'So 40 per cent of the farmers will not, for one reason or another, repay the loan. But what about the chillies the 35 per cent have grown?'

He nods. 'There's another reason for this problem,' says Edwin, breaking into my thoughts.

I look up at him, and his eyes shift back to the floor.

'Go on.'

'Maybe I should show you,' he says, as if the weight of any more challenging news might just boomerang back at him.

'I will take you to meet this man, and he can tell you himself.'

We beckon to Kizito and get on our motorbikes and chug up hill and down dale to one of the farms in a distant part of Siboti.

As we get there, I can see strong, well-tended chilli plants on either side of the track. We stop for a minute and the three of us walk into the field and go over to the nearest plants. There are no chillies on the bushes. The crop has already been harvested.

'This is one of the farmers who will default, yes?'

Edwin nods.

'So what are we looking for?' I ask him. 'This guy's obviously grown a good crop. Looks like a success story to me.'

'No, Mr Ken,' says Edwin, shaking his head. 'Kizito and I have already checked the records. This man has not delivered any chillies to us.'

I'm not usually all that slow on the uptake. But I do perhaps have a blind spot (or a deaf spot) today when it comes to things I don't want to hear.

'You mean he's harvested his chillies but not brought them in yet?'

Edwin looks sorry for me.

'No, Mr Ken. They're gone. He's sold his crop to someone else. And he's not the only one. I think maybe quarter of our farmers have sold their chillies to brokers. Brokers aren't authorised by anyone, they just turn up at your door and offer you money for your crops. That's what this farmer has done. He has sold his crop to a broker.'

I look round the harvested field and try to rationalise what I'm hearing. *About a quarter of our farmers.* I don't say a word. I'm thinking numbers.

So this is the upshot.

Five per cent of the farmers sold the seeds and the fertiliser and the pesticide.

Of the remaining 95 per cent of the farmers, something like 25 to 35 per cent have sold the chillies to someone other than Siboti Foods.

This means that 60 per cent of our growers have observed our contract and have paid back our loans and sold us their chilli crop. But why haven't the others? We have provided them with excellent support and financial incentives to lift themselves out of poverty. Why have a sizeable minority of the farmers chosen to defy the terms of our contract and sell their chilli stock to someone else?

We get back on the motorbikes and ride onwards till we get to the farmer's house. The man is outside the front door, busy stacking bundles of firewood. As we pull up and he sees who it is, he looks as if he's going to make a run for it and disappear into the undergrowth.

'Hey' I shout. 'I need to talk to you.'

The farmer puts the wood down and waits for us with a resigned expression.

'What's going on here?' I ask, as I take off my helmet. 'Where are your chillies?'

The man looks older than I'd first thought. A lifetime of grafting in his field has aged him. He stares at us blankly.

'Tell Mr Ken what you've done with the chillies you've grown,' says Edwin, in the local dialect.

Still nothing.

'Have you sold the chillies you grew for Siboti Foods to someone else?' asks Kizito, translating for me.

The man looks wretched.

'Friday was too late,' he says, and glances quickly at me. 'I needed money on Tuesday.'

'Friday?' I say, and then I remember. We arranged a special collection on Fridays for the farmers in this particular area, to save them the trouble of bringing their chillies all the way over to our office. If the man had waited till Friday, we'd have collected his crop and paid him the full 24 shillings a kilo we had promised him.

But it turns out that some enterprising broker had heard that the farmers up here were producing a good harvest and had gone round many of the farms on Tuesday, dangling cash under the farmers' noses and buying up as much of our chilli crop as he could.

'You signed a contract with Siboti Foods,' I tell the man. 'You've used the seeds, fertiliser and pesticides we provided, taken advantage of our training and advice, grown a fine crop and then sold it to some jackal middleman. How could you do that? We had an agreement. Doesn't that mean anything to you?'

There is a brief exchange between him and Kizito in the local dialect. The farmer looks shamefaced, but doesn't say a word. Then a thought strikes me.

'Did he offer you much more than 24 shillings? Was that it? How much did you get for your chillies?'

Kizito translates for me.

'He got 17.'

'17 shillings? You took 17 shillings a kilo from a broker on Tuesday, when you were guaranteed 24 shillings from us if you'd just waited until Friday?'

The man shrugs a yes, as if he wants to shrink into himself, and he looks at the ground.

'But why?' I ask him.

He says nothing.

'You could have made 7 shillings more a kilo if you'd waited till Friday.'

Kizito fires off a volley in translation and the man nods. Did he owe a moneylender or did his wife need a doctor? What kind of money pressures were so great that he couldn't wait three more days for his extra shillings? Why can't he tell me? Or perhaps it's nothing to do with timing. In this world, people live in the short-term. Did he think Siboti Foods wouldn't pay him?

'Ask him why, Kizito.'

My right-hand man and the farmer continue a dialogue, but he doesn't seem prepared to justify his decision in any convincing way.

'He says he just needed the money, Mr Ken,' says Edwin.

If this guy had stuck to our arrangement, he could have got 40 per cent more for his crop. He'd have an extra few hundred shillings in his hand and he'd be all set to plant a third crop as part of the Siboti Foods project and continue taking his first steps out of poverty. The thought riles me. But he's forced my hand and I need to take firm action.

I take a few steps and try to get some perspective, but I'm just seething. Life in Siboti has thrown up one provocation after the next. My blue sky outlook is crumbling.

It's very important that I send out the right signals. The growers need to know that the project can't tolerate this kind of behaviour. There has to be a sanction, a sign that we are prepared to discipline anyone who steps that far beyond the basic rules of fairness. I'm going to need the stick as well as the carrot.

While the farmer and Kizito continue their heated discussion, I walk on and survey my options. For someone who has spent years swimming with the sharks, I feel uncomfortably out of my depth in this rural backwater. Was it my fault for not monitoring the growing process properly? Why have some farmers embraced the project and followed all the rules, while others are trying to screw us? Overall, I'm conscious that some seed of destruction was sown when I let the first 10 per cent of defaulting farmers off after the first crop.

I realise I am grinding my teeth. Part of me wants to make this man pay a price. I look around the farm wildly, trying to find the right solution. There's the farm, the field, the road ahead of me. A short, sharp shock, that's what's needed, a signal to other farmers that our goodwill, and our contracts, cannot be so blatantly abused. My eyes settle on the borehole just beyond the farm. This man is lucky – he lives near one of the boreholes we lovingly restored. He's been offered a better income through Siboti Foods. And look how he repays us! I march back to the man.

'Does your family get water from that borehole over there?' I ask the farmer, pointing.

He nods.

'Right. You're banned. You're banned for a month. You can fetch your own bloody water from some stream for the next few weeks, see how you like that. That's what was happening before I mended the bloody boreholes. If you break your contract so blatantly, you can't expect to get the benefits. See how you like it.' Kizito translates immediately.

Edwin nods his acceptance of my verdict. He pokes the earth with his toe and says nothing. The farmer just stares at me, curiosity in his brown eyes. He's bemused rather than angry. I suppose he knows that I am this big noise, this important *mzungu* around Siboti – what was it my friend called me back in Dublin – a big fish in this little pond? For a moment I do feel like some medieval lord of the manor, a man who can impose his mind however he pleases.

The words are hardly out of my mouth before I sense I may have just made another monumental mistake. I may have had the boreholes re-drilled and equipped with new pumps at my own expense, for the benefit of the whole community, but I don't actually have the authority to impose a ban on this man's family using the pump. The punishment will affect his whole family, including his children. And, of course, it's usually the women who collect the water. His wife and kids are the ones who will have to trudge miles to the stream, which will impact on their time and perhaps on the children's homework or studies.

But on the other hand I need to see through my decision. I can't be seen as a pushover or the Siboti project will never work. He has to be seen to be paying *some* price for such blatant disregard for his contract.

I leave Kizito and Edwin standing around with the farmer and set off on my motorbike, driving faster than usual. I halt and wait for Edwin and Kizito to catch up, and have an idea.

'Kizito, in your phone do you have the numbers of the women who run the local borehole?' He does. He makes four calls to arrange an immediate meeting with the elected officers of the women's committee – the chairwoman, the vice-chair, the treasurer and the pump attendant. We go back on the motorbikes to visit them. I reluctantly tell them I'm banning the farmer.

'And you need to do this ban?' says the chairwoman.

I nod grimly, noting the lack of enthusiasm on the women's faces.

'Otherwise the whole project could fail,' I assure them.

I can see the women don't like the idea of having to police this family's use of water for the next month. They seem to accept that I have the right to impose the one-month ban, but they aren't happy about the situation. After all, the women know how much effort it takes to collect water from the well.

I try to soften my stance to get them to co-operate more willingly.

'Look, it's only for four weeks,' I say. 'I need your help. The whole Siboti project depends on everyone doing his part. I do my part, don't I?'

I see them exchange worried glances.

'OK, Mr Ken. We understand.'

There's no great enthusiasm for the task, but I know they'll do it. The signal has been sent. Word will soon spread across Siboti. People will get the message that I'm prepared to enforce the necessary discipline for the good of the project as a whole. Other farmers will think twice now before they sell their chillies to anyone else. That's what I tell myself over and over, as I ride into Bungoma. How can we plan our expansion and commit ourselves to export deals and a future food production business if we don't know how many of our growers will be there to deliver on the external contracts we enter into?

30

The end

'When, in the end, the day came on which I was going away,
I learned the strange learning that things can happen which
we ourselves cannot possibly imagine, either beforehand, or
at the time when they are taking place, or afterwards when
we look back on them.'

Karen Blixen *Out of Africa*

Next morning, I call Mama Jayne and ask her if I can come out to
see her.

'Of course my friend. You are always most welcome'.

When I arrive she gives me a big hug that feels maternal and
soothing.

Taking a seat on the bench in her office, I know I have a friend
who will understand me without judgement, who will understand
the problems I am struggling to handle.

'Everything is crumbling Mama Jayne', I begin. 'I've made so
many mistakes.'

'Tell me, my friend' she invites. So I update her on the recent
developments.

'So, in summary, I screwed up on the monitoring of the farmers and I should have insisted that they borrow from the bank, not me. If I had persuaded them to accept the bank's microfinance scheme, they wouldn't have defaulted on those horticulture loans.

'But Ken the farmers wouldn't have borrowed money from the bank. You know that. So you took the only path you could.'

'Yeah I suppose so. But I definitely shouldn't have let the Chief talk me into letting the farmers off their loans after the first season. I should have carried those forward into the second year. Now more farmers than ever are not repaying their loans – 40 per cent of them. I can't enforce the loan repayments. If I let 40 per cent off this time, how will the 60 per cent who do repay take the news? What is their incentive to repay next year? The loan scheme is falling apart, Mama Jayne.'

I feel a mixture of frustration, sadness and pent-up anxiety as the words spill out.

'You see if I stop the microcredit loan scheme, there will be no high-quality seeds next season, no fertilisers, no commercial horticulture, no Siboti Foods, no engine for bringing new external money into the area.

The logic is crushing and the implications are devastating.

That means no increased incomes for the families to fund irrigation or a third season each year, no health or education benefits from replacing paraffin lamps with home solar lighting kits. In short, without the loans there is no Siboti project.

'I understand Ken. You have brought a great vision for our people, but they are not ready.'

I hope she is right. That would leave my conscience a bit lighter. I hate the idea that I've raised their hopes and not achieved the vision.

My black mood isn't helped that night by the Wild West atmosphere in Bungoma's main street. The town is beginning to feel sinister and out of control, or maybe I've just spent more time there in bars with Protus recently and those dark encounters have coloured my view. Either way, there has been another horrible public lynching recently. Four alleged thugs, including a woman accused of being 'the gang's cook', have been stoned to death by an angry crowd. The general attitude in town seems to be one of approval – 'The police aren't going to do anything so people are doing it themselves' – and no one has been prosecuted. There has always been a slightly chaotic feel to Bungoma, but this vigilante justice is the dark side of frontier town life. Maybe there is an undercurrent of violence in this place that I'm only just becoming aware of. Maybe I'm just too naïve for my own good. I've been riding around Siboti and Bungoma on my motorbike for a couple of years with no real concerns for my personal safety. Perhaps I've been oblivious to the reality of a country where there is no state welfare system and most people live from one week to the next, one day to the next. The newspaper talks about the death as if this improvised mob justice is only right, and I've noticed that some politicians have been actively encouraging their constituents to take the law into their own hands. I know, from my own dealings with Protus, how greedy, cynical and corrupt the police can be, but I never expected to see this kind of murderous brutality accepted as normal in the area where for almost three years I have overwhelmingly felt the warmth and welcome of the people

As I sit in a local restaurant, staring at my evening meal – the usual tough-textured tilapia from Lake Victoria, teamed with a glum knot of soggy, reheated chips – the night feels airless and oppressive. The day's events have been a painful reminder that my quixotic efforts to help Siboti's people work their way out of extreme poverty face massive cultural barriers as well as all the physical and practical problems. If people are going to sell their seeds without even planting them or flog off their chilli crops at knockdown prices because they can't wait three extra days to get 40 per cent more money from us, what chance do I have of creating any economic improvement here?

Working in banks, I have puzzled over figures all my professional life. They are strangely reassuring in a time of crisis. Now I tot up what I've spent on this venture in Siboti, and I realise I've put in three years and almost half a million dollars from my house sale money. That has paid for me, my travels, and trying to get this poverty alleviation project off the ground, and I'm beginning to wonder what there is to show for it. I hope I can make money again. If I pull out of Kenya and go home, I'll hope to get back on my feet again within a few years. But that would be a defeat. It would mean that I had given up on these people I've come to know and care about. My legacy would be a schoolroom, ten working boreholes, a core group of high-achieving farmers with improved horticultural skills that should mean they are better equipped to face the future, some pockets of improved commercial skill and a few hundred orphans who have been getting the education that would otherwise have been denied them. Apart from that, there would be a handful of KickStart irrigation pumps, some Siboti Wheel water drums and a few dozen solar lighting kits within the community. That doesn't seem like much of a result.

Shoving the leathery tilapia around the plate, I watch a group of kids kicking a football around the dusty street and try to think clearly. People have to work in their own self-interest, otherwise I can't help them. A major problem is the culture of very short-term gain, which works against their own long-term interests. I've been in denial for months, I reflect.

Going back further, I start taking apart my personality and look for the answers there.

Headlong. It's a word that friends say characterises me. I make decisions in a moment. I can be dynamic but impulsive. Without knowing anyone in international aid and barely a soul in Africa, I rushed headlong into a crazy scheme in a place I'd never been, determined to create my very own millennium village, with insufficient research but with bags of misguided optimism that I could achieve results. I've been foolhardy and ignored all the signals. I've fundamentally misunderstood the complexity of this place, and I've been naive to think that trying to lead a community through a structured integrated method to beat extreme poverty was enough. Naive to think that an outsider could influence a community to adopt his way of thinking. Naive to believe that I can fix extreme poverty where others have not.

'It's not your role,' I say aloud.

If enough people here don't want to adopt my scheme, it can't work. I'm not going to force the issue. I'm not a dictator.

Or am I?

It's been a long day. I nudge the cold food around my plate, but I'm not hungry. I swig down the bottle of Tusker and order another.

It's not just that my dream for Siboti is fast becoming a nightmare that's upsetting me. The question that's really bothering me now is not 'What have I got myself into?' but 'Who have I become?'

I know that this whole enterprise will fail if we don't have some basic rules of engagement. But I didn't come here to ban people's children from getting water from the local well. Who the hell am I to tell that farmer's family they can't have 'my' water for a month? Have I set myself up as some little tin god, a wealthy, patronising neo-colonialist who's only prepared to help if everything is done my way? The road to hell is paved with good intentions. During the last three years I have thrown everything I have at this project, but in the process have I turned into some kind of monster? I feel sick to my stomach, and it's nothing to do with the tilapia.

* * *

'It's beaten me, Kezzy. The sheer practical difficulties of getting any bloody thing done here – I feel I can't do this anymore. I can't make it work.'

The usual street scenes carry on around us – kids flocking around their mothers on their way to the market, groups of men resting in the shade – as I look at Keziah, sipping her sparkling water, and surveying me. One of my hands is quivering ever so slightly. She doesn't say anything, just sighs and pulls up her shades. She's got to be thinking that she predicted all this.

'Kezzy. Say something. Please.'

'You know what I said when I first met you on the bus.'

'That I'd fail and just leave, disappointing everybody?'

She lays her hand on the table and I admire her long fingers, her rings.

'I've come to admire you very much Ken, you know that. It's bigger than you. The challenges here are bigger than anyone. This is a deep-rooted culture and people live hand to mouth for much of their lives. No one can change the way so many people think overnight. You've had some great successes here – don't you see that?'

I look at her and nod, and I can see tears in her eyes. She's already talking in the past tense. Her sadness is infectious.

'To be honest, I never thought you'd get this far,' she says.

She nods.

'Maybe I thought you would persuade them. Ken, you've tried. But it's killing you. You need to go home. You can always come back next year.'

I can hear a crack in her voice. If I leave Siboti, it won't just be the end of the project, but the end of us, too.

'Maybe you could c….' I begin.

She reaches over and puts her finger to my lips.

'Don't', she whispers. 'You have to go. And I have to stay.'

She clasps my hands tightly. Our arms shudder with the struggle to contain a tsunami of sadness and emotion.

31

Escort

'Ever tried. Ever failed. No matter. Try again. Fail again. Fail better.'

Samuel Beckett

I sit in my hotel room and type up twenty-eight glowing references for my twenty-eight staff, whom I need to make redundant. Losing a job is tough in the UK and Ireland, but here there is no social welfare benefit system. Apart from John, they are all young and unmarried, but they are also breadwinners, with extended families reliant on them. I feel a real sense of responsibility for the loss of their essential income.

It would be great if I could hand over Siboti Foods lock, stock and barrel, as a profitable business, and say to Kizito and Cecilia: 'Here it is. Why don't you run it and keep the money yourselves?' But the truth is that I've been having to dip into my own pocket every single month and stump up whatever's needed to keep it going. The businesses aren't yet generating enough money to cover their costs. So I can't pass it on to some local entrepreneur because it needs continual subsidies.

Inspiration strikes later that day. I'll just give it all away. I'll find a local charity to take over the Siboti project and give it all the buildings and assets. Maybe a Kenyan charity can make the project work? Instead of the Irish rat who promised the earth and then let people down, maybe I can get out as the decent guy who came in, set everything in motion and then handed it all over to the locals. I can leave, if not as a hero, then at least not as the villain either.

It doesn't actually take very long to find a suitable charity. It's called CREADIS, which stands for something ridiculously high-flown like Community Research in Environment and Development Initiatives. Or maybe it's Can't Really Envisage Anyone Doing It Successfully. Elizabeth is on the charity's board and she knows all about the problems I've had with the loans. But it has the advantage of being locally based, in Bungoma, rather than in Nairobi, and the woman who runs it is full of energy and good ideas. Elizabeth will help CREADIS push it all forward, she says.

To be honest, I've heard this sort of talk before. I'd like to believe it will all happen. CREADIS promises the sun, the moon and the stars, but then so does everybody. But at least CREADIS claims to have some funding lined up from several major donors. And it will provide me with a fig leaf to cover my embarrassment as I make my exit.

* * *

Mama Jayne is the first person I say goodbye to. I go to see her at her office. This is where I started out in 2008. It feels like a lifetime ago.

'Ken,' she says, holding my hands, 'you mustn't feel bad about going. You have fantastic vision, a good heart. It's a great shame.'

'Yes.'

We hug and I can feel her smile branding my shoulder. People like Mama Jayne are built of steel, I think. They weather the good and the bad. They are the rocks of any society.

I wish I could have done more,' I say, as I take my leave.

'But now you must go home,' she says. 'You must see your people. They miss you.'

My people. I think of my dad and my sister and my brothers and their families.

'People here will understand,' says Mama Jayne. 'They know you have your people too.'

I wave and slip the motorbike into gear, feeling more of a traitor by the second. As I drive through Bungoma, I think of all the staff I've employed. How will they react? So many of their families are dependent on their income from Siboti Foods. The thought makes me feel deeply sombre. What have I really achieved other than elevating people's expectations, only to dash them?

As I drive on, I make out a roadblock ahead of me. I slow down as I approach the men and the piece of rope they have stretched across the dusty road. It's not unusual on this busy track that runs across the northern border of Siboti, unfortunately. Some guys take it into their heads that they will put up a blockade on a popular route and charge people to go through it. If the police can flag you down and charge you for nothing, why shouldn't they?

'Good morning,' I say, as I slow down, pushing up my visor. You can almost see them rubbing their hands as they calculate what outrageous sum I might be made to cough up.

'We are supervising some work on the road today,' a beefy guy in sunglasses announces. 'It will be a thousand shillings for you to have a special pass to go through.'

'Really?' I say. 'The police inspector is the only one I know who can authorise a block on this road.'

'You have to pay us,' says another, his foot wedged under my front tyre. They quickly gather round me.

Quickly I flip open my mobile and show the nearest the contact details for Protus.

'Look here. If this isn't authorised by Protus, I'll be on my way. We are good friends. You want me to call him?'

'You'll call Mr Protus?' says the guy at the tyre.

'No no,' says the biggest one, 'You do not need to do that.'

They part like the Red Sea and wave me through. I pull down my visor and prepare to ride off. It seems, with this corrupt police inspector, it's not a wise move to challenge me if I am his friend. A corrupt bully's associate. Is that what I set out and succeeded to become?

But still, I reflect, that was a bit of a relief. What could have happened back there if I hadn't had Protus on my side? Those guys could have taken my wallet and my motorbike and I would have been helpless. And untraceable. That's a worryingly scary thought. In this moment, the reality of the personal risks I've been running for three years smacks me between the eyes.

I'm beginning to think that things could get tricky for me when I do the staff lay-offs, from the personal safety point of view, even with the extra month's salary each employee is getting to soften the blow.

If I tell twenty-eight people they haven't a job anymore, will they think: 'Oh well, he tried, and it was good while it lasted'? Or will they think: 'That's my income gone, and it's all his fault'? I need to face up to the fact that some of them might bear a grievance against me. Somebody's relative might want to take it out on me. I could be in danger. It's probably an unworthy suspicion, but I can't afford to take a chance.

Since Alan left Nairobi, I've missed having my brother around to bounce ideas off. My other brother, Norman, is an experienced police personal protection officer in Ireland, driving the government's justice minister and carrying a gun every day of his working life. It is so reassuring to hear his voice and draw on his advice right now. I tell him that my sense of well-being has deserted me. I feel more than a little frightened.

'Can you hire some personal protection?' he says, after I've outlined the situation. 'Look, I'll take a week off. I'll come down right away and we can assess the risks and sort out some support. I'll help you.'

'That sounds really great, Norm. I need to lay off the majority of the staff and transfer the rest to CREADIS, and I'll fund them for a few months while they sort out long-term finance from one of their donors. It'll make all the difference if you're here while I'm doing that.'

'But what about the next forty-eight hours. Can you lie low somewhere?' asks Norman.

I catch sight of myself in the mirror on the wall and think about all the things I still need to do. I'll have meetings with all my staff, hand out the redundancy letters and deal with any fallout. I need to get rid of the land I've bought up around the market, where our buildings are. This was going to be the site for the future food processing, production and packaging facilities. The last thing I want is to turn up in Kenya at some future date and find I'm liable for a heap of unpaid property taxes and renewals payments, and maybe some fines on top.

'Ken?'

'Sorry. Yes. I'm listening.'

'I asked about now. What about the local criminals? Are you safe enough until I arrive? Realistically, are you a target?

'I don't know. Should be OK, I think.

'I'll travel to Nairobi and meet you at the airport.'

The acute anxiety and tension I've been feeling begins to ease off with the knowledge my brother will soon be here.

Within two days, Norman arrives in Nairobi, and the next day we travel to Siboti. His presence changes my perspective on the next few days. We discuss the options and he suggests that while it might be expensive to get the protection we want through Protus, at least it will be solid and dependable.

We find Protus in his usual haunt, in the middle of the afternoon, drunk and irritable. I tell him I need some help from him, and that I have a *kitu kidogo* – a little something – for him. It's a bottle of whiskey Norm has brought for him.

He takes off his imitation Ray-Bans and looks at me with disdain, and I can see the depths of darkness behind his eyes.

'Why is it always something small?' he leers. 'Why can't it be something big?'

Does he already know it's crunch time? Does he know that I can't afford not to buy his support this time round, whatever it's going to cost me? He is the only man with the authoritative force I can hire to guarantee safety. If I don't get his co-operation, I could be in trouble.

'I'd like to be escorted everywhere I go for three days,' I explain, in as light a tone as I can manage, 'if you can spare the men to do it.'

Not a flicker. I can't read his reaction at all, other than the dollar signs flashing in his eyes.

He nods.

'I want two armed guards with me night and day. I want them standing outside my office when I lay off these people. When I travel anywhere, I want them on motorbikes beside me.'

'It's maybe not so "*kidogo*",' he says.

'How much would it take?'

'I need 10 000 to organise it,' he says, 'and 40 000 more when it's finished, to pay the men.'

He nods again. There's a pause, and I keep a poker face. Can he smell my anxiety? Is he about to up the price?

'All right, Mr Ken King,' he says. 'I will arrange it. But now I'm thirsty. I'd like a vodka and Coke.'

The barman brings the half bottle of Smirnoff and a large Coca-Cola and I pay up and we leave Protus to slake his thirst.

'You probably got off lightly there, Ken', says Norman, as we turn the corner of the street. He must like you. After all, you had nowhere else to go if you think he's got the only posse in town worth having.'

Over the next few days Norm mucks in and helps me organise the sale of motorbikes, and all the bits of wrap up I need to do.

He's around when I have the awkward conversations with my employees.

The face-to-face meetings with my staff are emotionally gruelling, especially when I have to inform Kizito. But people seem to accept this new turn of events with a sense of resigned fatalism, as if they expected it all along. No one accuses me of betrayal or of letting their families down. I try to engage them, but they have little to say – perhaps they feel that any objections may prove counterproductive – and their silence bothers me.

Kizito has been so loyal, hardworking and completely honest, and I would dearly love to be able to offer him something better than my thanks and an envelope with money inside. But he seems almost philosophical. He's probably got used to life treating him badly, and he doesn't seem to hold me responsible for what's happened.

'The farmers should have paid back the loans,' he says, without any real trace of bitterness.

Kizito has been my trusted colleague, adviser and friend and he's worked tirelessly to hold the project together. We shake hands and I assure him that CREADIS will pay his salary for at least three months.

'Thank you for all you have done Kizito. You have been my top man. I hope we will always be friends.'

I glance outside where his motorbike waits, gleaming. He keeps it clean and shining every day.

'I want you to keep that bike.'

Finally, Kizito smiles. 'Thank you for everything I have learned. I have learned so much. We tried to make the project work, Ken. We tried hard.'

It's time to break the news to the whole community. We hold a big meeting in a field with lots of acacia trees for shade and benches from the nearby church. Everyone is there, including the board members of CREADIS, the Chief, the two assistant chiefs, Kizito, Edwin and John, my brother Norm, the farmers, their wives and children. I have the outline of a credible story to tell the people of Siboti, without having to embarrass anybody by talking about why the project has failed.

'I have personal commitments back home,' I announce. 'I may not be here, but I will be watching what happens and giving CREADIS my support. I want to thank everybody for making me so welcome.'

The women and children clap, followed by everyone else, and I'm deeply touched that the atmosphere is so charged with goodwill. Despite the problem with the loans, I feel like a defector. Maybe my elevation method was before its time. Maybe it was destined to fail.

'Everybody here thanks you for everything you have done for Siboti and its people,' says the Chief.

David Waswa, our Farmer of the Year, is in the crowd. His wife, Maureen, stands and claps loudly. When it has died down, I add my thanks.

'I'll be keeping an eye on the project,' I assure them, and wipe my forehead. 'I promise I'll be back soon to see you all again.'

In the end no one gives me any trouble, but it still feels better to have Norman and the two policemen around.

Suddenly, it's all over and Norm and I can be on our way. I pay the two policemen, handing them a sealed envelope to give to Protus, and we quietly leave Siboti by taxi, heading for Bungoma.

I have a heightened awareness of what could happen to me now, pulling out of Siboti like this, and I don't like the thought that someone might get it into their head to follow me, so I want to break the trail. In Bungoma, I get the driver to drop us off and we walk a few hundred yards through a side street before we spot an out-of-town taxi and hire the driver to take us to Kisumu, on Lake Victoria, about two hours away.

We spurn the Kiboko Hotel and its hippos and spend the night at the Imperial, with a decent steak and a bottle of South African wine. I'm quiet over dinner, very aware of how safety-conscious I am these days. When you lose your blind faith that everything's going to be all right, the world can seem a tough and dangerous place. Today, Kenyan society feels like a complex puzzle, whose winners understand, better than I, the rules of how it works, and how to triumph. But I guess life itself is also an imperfect project that we don't always understand or win at.

I miss the gung-ho Ken who thought nothing of hiring a car and driving across Kenya alone. That was three long years ago.

We catch an internal flight from Kisumu to Nairobi the next morning, but even now, I can't quite relax. It feels like I'm running away from my responsibilities. In a sense, it *is* running away.

In Nairobi, we stay at the familiar InterContinental, waiting for our flight home. I have no idea what I will do next. What will it be like in London without a home, without a job? Twenty-five years after leaving Ireland, I'm going back to London to start all over again.

I'm still tense, eager now to get the flight, when a call comes through as we sit in the twin bedroom.

Norman watches my face change. First surprise, then disbelief, then some kind of delight. When the call is over, I flip shut the phone and put it on the table next to my coffee.

'That was one of my old bosses. He's got a new job and he's asked if I'm interested in working as a consultant to help him', I say. 'It's an opening to get started again Norm. Offered today of all days? Why? And why today? Can you believe it?'

Norman grins. 'You tried to do good for people here Bruv. Always remember, what goes around comes around.'

I think about it for a moment, looking out the window at the view of Nairobi. I have been very happy and felt real affection for people in this country.

'I guess Africa was my salvation from London, but now London is going to be my salvation from Africa. Something like that.'

My brother jumps out of his chair, animatedly.

'I think a beer by the pool is in order'.

As we sit looking across the sun-dappled water, he clinks my bottle with his.

'Ah now, Ken,' he says, 'You have to put it behind you. You did everything you could'.

A few hours later, it's the voice from the cockpit that re-connects me to the world I know. The accent is smooth, comforting, reassuring.

'Good afternoon, ladies and gentlemen, and welcome aboard this British Airways flight to London Heathrow.'

That's it. I feel closer to home. No longer away.

'Alan helped get you into this place but I had to come to get you out', laughs Norm. 'Will we take Da out tomorrow evening when we get back to Dublin? He would like that.'

'I would like that too.'